AF753324

COMPUTER SCIENCE, TECHNOLOGY AND APPLICATIONS

AN EXPRESSIVE CONVERSATIONAL-BEHAVIOR GENERATION MODEL FOR ADVANCED INTERACTION WITHIN MULTIMODAL USER INTERFACES

COMPUTER SCIENCE, TECHNOLOGY AND APPLICATIONS

Additional books in this series can be found on Nova's website under the Series tab.

Additional e-books in this series can be found on Nova's website under the e-book tab.

COMPUTER SCIENCE, TECHNOLOGY AND APPLICATIONS

AN EXPRESSIVE CONVERSATIONAL-BEHAVIOR GENERATION MODEL FOR ADVANCED INTERACTION WITHIN MULTIMODAL USER INTERFACES

MATEJ ROJC
AND
IZIDOR MLAKAR

nova publishers
New York

Copyright © 2016 by Nova Science Publishers, Inc.

All rights reserved. No part of this book may be reproduced, stored in a retrieval system or transmitted in any form or by any means: electronic, electrostatic, magnetic, tape, mechanical photocopying, recording or otherwise without the written permission of the Publisher.

We have partnered with Copyright Clearance Center to make it easy for you to obtain permissions to reuse content from this publication. Simply navigate to this publication's page on Nova's website and locate the "Get Permission" button below the title description. This button is linked directly to the title's permission page on copyright.com. Alternatively, you can visit copyright.com and search by title, ISBN, or ISSN.

For further questions about using the service on copyright.com, please contact:
Copyright Clearance Center
Phone: +1-(978) 750-8400 Fax: +1-(978) 750-4470 E-mail: info@copyright.com.

NOTICE TO THE READER

The Publisher has taken reasonable care in the preparation of this book, but makes no expressed or implied warranty of any kind and assumes no responsibility for any errors or omissions. No liability is assumed for incidental or consequential damages in connection with or arising out of information contained in this book. The Publisher shall not be liable for any special, consequential, or exemplary damages resulting, in whole or in part, from the readers' use of, or reliance upon, this material. Any parts of this book based on government reports are so indicated and copyright is claimed for those parts to the extent applicable to compilations of such works.

Independent verification should be sought for any data, advice or recommendations contained in this book. In addition, no responsibility is assumed by the publisher for any injury and/or damage to persons or property arising from any methods, products, instructions, ideas or otherwise contained in this publication.

This publication is designed to provide accurate and authoritative information with regard to the subject matter covered herein. It is sold with the clear understanding that the Publisher is not engaged in rendering legal or any other professional services. If legal or any other expert assistance is required, the services of a competent person should be sought. FROM A DECLARATION OF PARTICIPANTS JOINTLY ADOPTED BY A COMMITTEE OF THE AMERICAN BAR ASSOCIATION AND A COMMITTEE OF PUBLISHERS.

Additional color graphics may be available in the e-book version of this book.

Library of Congress Cataloging-in-Publication Data
Names: Rojc, Matej, editor. | Mlakar, Izidor, editor.
Title: An expressive conversational-behavior generation model for advanced
interaction within multimodal user interfaces / editors, Matej Rojc (Associate professor, Faculty of Electrical Engineering and Computer Science, University of Maribor, Slovenia) and
Izidor Mlakar (researcher, Panevropa d.o.o., Maribor, Slovenia).
Description: Hauppauge, New York : Nova Science Publishers Inc., [2015] |
Includes index.
Identifiers: LCCN 2015040894 (print) | LCCN 2015045776 (ebook) | ISBN
9781634829557 (hardcover) | ISBN 9781634840842 ()
Subjects: LCSH: Multimodal user interfaces (Computer systems)
Classification: LCC QA76.9.U83 E97 2015 (print) | LCC QA76.9.U83 (ebook) |
DDC 005.4/37--dc23
LC record available at http://lccn.loc.gov/2015040894

Published by Nova Science Publishers, Inc. † New York

CONTENTS

PREFACE

The book addresses issues and algorithms for the planning, generation, and realization of co-verbal behavior on general unannotated text. The generated co-verbal behavior is completely aligned and synchronized with the synthesized speech signal. The represented, highly flexible and efficient system is capable of reproducing human-like co-verbal behavior represented by movements of body parts. The movement is synchronized with the meaning of verbal content and prosody of the accompanying synthesized speech through the exploitation of the semiotic grammar and co-verbal behavior lexicon. The co-verbal behavior represents that movement of body parts (such as hands, arms, fingers, head, and lips) which is synchronized with verbal information in both meaning and form. This type of human-like behavior can be used in multimodal user interfaces in order to arouse emotion and affect in users.

There are several systems that incorporate embodied conversational agents for the visualization of conversation in the form of co-verbal gestures. Most of them have their origin in the SAIBA framework. The correlation of verbal and co-verbal behavior, which such systems feature, mostly relies on semantic and/or syntactic rules and sub-domains. Such systems and platforms may also perform behavior planning from the perspective of functional intent. However, often the platforms realize the pre-planned behavior that is described by some procedure. As such, most ECA-based systems reflect or integrate the generation of co-verbal behavior by following these three levels in the SAIBA framework: *intent planning*, *behavior planning*, and *behavior realization* level. Each individual level is realized through the proprietary or ad hoc software components and transferred to the next level via variations of XML-based markup scripts, such as: FML, BML, MURML, EMBRScript, APML and others. Further, the first level of SAIBA's architecture and variations thereof is *intent planning*, in general realized by rules and grammars that have their basis in the multimodal annotation of face-to-face dialogues (e.g., laboratory set-ups, interviews, talk shows, cartoons etc.). The *behavior planning* level then exploits lexical affiliation and complex synchronization points, originating from both semantics and prosody. Finally, the third stage of SAIBA's architecture represents the behavior realization and visualization on an ECA. The markup scripts describe the behavior as a procedure of complex synchronization points, which co-align speech and gestures in the temporal domain. The system for realization (animation) then decouples these points, and visualizes them as an animation that is synchronized with speech and which incorporates the movements of the individual articulated body parts of an agent.

The key problems in the process of generating co-verbal behavior, especially when general and unannotated text is used, arise mostly in the *intent planning* and *behavior planning* levels. Namely, the co-verbal behavior does not comply with some underlying uniform grammar. Furthermore, gestures in spontaneous dialogues are rarely deliberate, done for a purpose. Nevertheless, gestures are non-accidental and not just simple visual supplements of verbal content but rather actual components of speech. As such, therefore, no finite set of rules for deterministic planning can be defined, nor is there a definite (1-to-1) correlation between verbal and co-verbal behavior. In the context of co-verbal behavior, humans have tendencies to use similar behavior along with certain expressions, words, and actions, while participating in face-to-face communication. Several studies and annotations support this statement by showing the existence of a high semantic and functional correlation between verbal and co-verbal behavior, along with some degree of prosodic coherence. Another issue in *intent planning* and *behavior planning* levels is the enormousness of semantic space in which gestures must be related with different intents and interpretations of verbal content. As a result, the *intent planning* and *behavior planning* are often divided into sub-problems. In the *intent planning* level, concepts such as communicative functions (*feed-back* and *turn-taking*) and syntactic analysis are taken into account. The *behavior planning* level incorporates speech prosody and domain-restricted semantic grammars (e.g., gesticon), or the limited semiotic classes generated through parameterization of the semantic space and subspaces (e.g., generation of iconic outlines, generation of deictic signals). These approaches define smaller and more manageable sub-sets, in which the specific semantic/syntactic and prosodic relationships can be established between the co-verbal and verbal behavior.

The main focus of this book is the design and development of more advanced natural interaction between a man and a machine. In order to achieve this, we represent a novel conversational-behavior generation model, which takes care of the correlation and synchronization of text and synthesized speech accompanied by co-verbal gestures. Furthermore, we propose the interpretation of co-verbal gestures through contextual linking between independent motor skills (shapes, movements, and poses that a conversational agent can display), and the intent (context) of their use, instead of semantic/syntactic mapping. The intent of the spoken content is classified into semiotic classes and sub-classes through linguistic analysis and classification of input text, mediated by language-dependent semiotic grammar. In addition to the research regarding the synchronization of speech and gestures, we also represent a novel annotation scheme named EVA-Script. The annotation scheme includes an analysis of the correlation between speech and gestures on a context-dependent functional level, as well as an analysis of the internal dynamics and shapes of gestures at a context-independent, descriptive level. By using this scheme, we have annotated a corpus of spontaneous communicative behavior, named EVA Corpus. The data extracted from the annotation is then used to design and populate the semiotic grammar, the repertoire of motor skills, and the co-verbal behavior lexicon.

The idea behind the presented expressive conversational behavior generation model, known as the EVA expressive model for generating the co-verbal behavior (or EVA-model), is to convert any text (phrase/sentence/statement) into a communicative act – that is, into a more human-like exchange of information – and convey it through highly synchronized verbal and non-verbal communication channels. Such interaction favorably affects both the cognitive process of thc listener (the person you address), as well as the cognitive processes of the speaker. Furthermore, the information presented in the form of synchronous multimodal signals, where the co-verbal behavior is properly intertwined with the verbal one, is not only more understandable, but establishes social relationships among interlocutors. Therefore, in order to achieve an acceptable level of naturalness, a consistent relationship between verbal and co-verbal behavior must be established. Such a relationship must reflect the intent of the information presented, as well as the interlocutors' abilities to understand the physical realization of it. The main problems that the model deals with are, therefore, cognitive and pragmatic in nature, since in the communication between people the co-verbal behavior does not follow the same rules as language does. Further, the represented shapes and their propagation throughout the dialogue are not subordinated to some well-defined grammatical rules. In addition, general unannotated text does not contain a lot of context in terms of the intent/meaning identification, nor does it contain any deterministic markers. Such input, therefore, does not allow for direct and deterministic conclusions about the shapes of gestures to be used, and about their propagation or synchronization with the verbal parts. The EVA-model, therefore, covers a wide variety of concepts that include: analysis of multimodal corpora of conversational behavior, context-independent prediction of shapes, and movements (the motor skills), design of semiotic grammar and context-dependent co-verbal behavior lexicon (gesticon), algorithms for generating the co-verbal behavior, space- and time-efficient architectures for the integration of linguistically dependent and independent sources, and a framework for the realization of the co-verbal behavior, which also includes the design of procedural description language, named EVA-Script. Further, the EVA expressive model for generating the co-verbal behavior is modular, and can be used for different purposes and in different domains.

Further, the algorithm for the generation of co-verbal behavior is decoupled into two stages. The first stage resolves the problem of behavior formulation (the intent and behavior planning), while the second stage resolves the problem of behavior realization (animation). The first stage, therefore, incorporates: a) identification of the semiotic intent by considering the linguistic features of the unannotated text; and b) the selection of gesture primes depending on the semiotic nuclei, and their synchronization with synthesized speech based on prosody (e.g., by considering the phoneme durations, accented syllables etc.). The tasks of the first stage are based on efficient tuple structures, heterogeneous relation graphs, finite-state machines, and CART trees. The output of this stage is then a hierarchically-based procedural description of the co-verbal behavior, the so-called EVA-event written in EVA-Script notation. The second stage of the algorithm then represents the conversion of procedural descriptions into a series of coherent animations of individual parts of the articulated embodied conversational agent. In this regard a realization framework, named EVA-framework, has been developed and is presented in the book. It supports the realization of procedural animation, descriptions and plans, multi-part volumetric and mesh-based models, and key animation concepts such as: skeletal animation, forward and inverse kinematics, blend shapes, and the animation of predefined (pre-recorded) animated segments.

The discussed EVA-model has the ability to re-use shapes and movements maintained within the co-verbal behavior lexicon. Namely, this lexicon contains a rich, context-independent repository of motor skills, which is based on the analysis and annotation of spontaneous dialogue. The context of use and the verbal context are then introduced via semiotic classes that depend on the morphology. This allows for the conversational agent to express a wide range of communicative concepts, such as: diversity, motivation, relevance, relation to theme, etc., and to incorporate emotional states and emotions, both simple and complex, into ECA co-verbal behavior. Since EVA-model can formulate various forms of co-verbal behavior with respect to general unannotated text, and since it can adjust the co-verbal behavior to different contexts, the use of an ECA can be flexibly extended to a variety of HMI concepts, ranging from virtual web readers to story tellers, intelligent virtual sellers, IPTV managers, virtual companions, listeners, therapists, etc.

To sum up, in the context of EVA-model and the generation of co-verbal behavior in general this book exposes the following research and technological issues:

a) Definition and design of annotation scheme for the analysis and classification of the co-verbal behavior. The scheme combines the concepts of functional and descriptive annotation schemes and allows: identification of the functional characteristics of verbal behavior; identification of the intent of linguistic expressions; description of individual configurations, shapes and poses in high resolution as abstract concepts, or in the form of detailed 3D configuration of movement controllers.
b) Definition and design of a multimodal corpus, named EVA Corpus, which contains natural spontaneous dialogue between at least three active interlocutors (both male and female speakers). The corpus is based on an entertainment talk show. The interaction takes place in a relaxed environment and contains a great deal of indicators of spontaneity, such as the unsupervised exchange of speakers, takeovers, overlapping speech, dialect etc. The corpus, together with EVA-Script, serves as the basis for building language-dependent and independent resources (semiotic grammar and repository of motor skills).
c) Definition, design and implementation of language-independent resources, which are used in the algorithms for generating the co-verbal behavior. The main language independent resource is the repository of motor skill, maintained as part of the co-verbal behavior lexicon. This repository maintains its functional and contextual independence from speech or dialogue itself. As such, the repository maintains three concepts: pose, shape, and movement. The pose and shape constitute a functional and time-independent physical appearance. The movement is then represented as a sequential concatenation of shapes/poses over a spatial trajectory. Movement is time-independent; however, by itself (without any context) it does not add relevant meaning to the conversation. On the other hand, a gesture is understood as co-verbal movement; a movement which is a result of semiotic intents and prosodic features of speech.
d) Definition, design, and implementation of language-dependent resources, such as gesticon (is maintained within the co-verbal behavior lexicon), and semiotic grammar. The gesticon maintains gestures and is based on morpho-syntactic features and serves as a contextual link between intent and co-verbal behavior. Gestures are actually sequences of shapes, poses, and movements with a given context or with specific semiotic intent. The semiotic grammar represents a set of morphological rules, which can be used for the definition of several intents in the text. These intents can be identified by using semiotic classification.
e) Definition and design of algorithm for generating and modeling the co-verbal behavior that can be used on arbitrary, unannotated text, by exploiting its morpho-syntactic and prosodic features, and using the semiotic grammar and co-verbal behavior lexicon. The algorithm is designed as a common processing deque based on

finite-state machines, HRG structures, suitability functions, CART trees and resources (features) shared between core text-to-speech synthesis and co-verbal behavior generator modules. All knowledge is stored in common HRG structure.

f) Design and implementation of complex deque architecture (and mechanism). This architecture integrates TTS modules and co-verbal behavior generator modules into an efficient engine in a highly modular way that is based on common HRG structure. This structure keeps linguistic and co-verbal information and consists of linear and tree-based relational structures. In this way, the key features can be complex, properly related, and easily accessed.
g) Definition, design, and implementation of web-oriented architecture with integrated system for the co-verbal behavior generation, named the MWP platform. The architecture is based on a distributive and modular service environment, which is underlined by the DATA system. The presented system can be flexibly used in any ECA-based Web and non-Web environments.

The content of this book is structured as follows. The *first chapter* reviews the baselines of interpersonal exchange of information performed in the form of interaction of interlocutors (*face-to-face communication*). First, we focus on theoretical frameworks and studies of co-verbal behavior in face-to-face communication that represent a well-defined theoretical background for the correlation between verbal and non-verbal elements. The frameworks and studies also identify the used communication mechanisms, which originate from the human needs that are reflected throughout the exchange of information. These mechanisms are further categorized as part of the need to manage communication (Interactive Communication Management, ICM) and as part of the need to manage own formulation and presentation of the content (Own Communication Management, OCM). This chapter also discusses the aspects of existing embodied conversational agent engines and underlying conversational models. It identifies existing studies and solutions presented as a paradigm of planning, formation, realization, and presentation of social behavior in different user interfaces (different contexts and domains of application). A brief review of existing applications is followed by a presentation of the key approaches used for generating co-verbal behavior and its realization through various conversational agents.

The *second chapter* is dedicated to the representation of an innovative architecture through which the proposed algorithm for generating and modeling the co-verbal behavior is realized. This chapter also proposes key data structures, modules, and concepts of the architecture and describes how resources can be integrated into a common engine (consisting of speech synthesizer's modules and co-verbal behavior generator modules) in a modular, and time- and memory-efficient manner. By intertwining the processes of the speech synthesizer with the processes of the co-verbal behavior generator, we enable the use of a common relational structure which extends the structure of the input sentence by integrating the results of the individual phases performed by either of the modules. The architecture ultimately generates a description of co-verbal behavior concurrently with the synthesized speech.

The *third chapter* then presents different aspects of multimodal annotation in detail. Multimodal annotations represent a starting point in which theories and approaches to the planning and realization of natural, human-like co-verbal behavior can be formulated. Namely, the multimodal annotation of corpora captures and allows for detailed analysis of that cognitive mechanism which is activated in the phase of the formulation of speech. By using these mechanisms, humans plan and design the verbal and co-verbal behavior and synchronize them into an inherent flow of information exchange. The first part of the chapter identifies established theories and annotation schemes, while the second part presents a novel annotation scheme based on EVA-scheme notation and the coupling of functional (function-oriented, context-dependent) analysis with descriptive (form-oriented, context-independent motor skills) analysis of spontaneous multimodal behavior. This EVA-scheme annotation scheme captures different communicative concepts (at different levels), as well as co-verbal shapes and movement (trajectories), both in high resolution.

The fourth chapter continues with the presentation of how human-like behavior can be transferred into the virtual environment of ECAs. The chapter discusses a novel formal markup language, named EVA-Script, by representing its formal syntax in detail. EVA-Script markup language is used in various segments of the EVA-model. Namely, it is used to build the content-independent repository of motor skills, and it also represents the form in which behavior generator outputs the generated co-verbal behavior (behavior procedure). The EVA-Script was designed with a presumption in mind that co-verbal behavior may be decoupled into a series of co-verbal events. Each such co-verbal event then contains the procedural description of co-verbal behavior as well as the speech source and all necessary temporal synchronization points. In this way, the co-verbal event is directly understood by the virtual agent EVA and can therefore be animated into a co-verbal visualization of thought, idea or statement. The co-articulation, emotions and gestures are within EVA-event interpreted as separate entities, which are visualized concurrently, but in line with the provided temporal synchronization. Such an event, therefore, integrates important concepts in communication, such as delays, abrupt finishes, interruptions, etc.

The fifth chapter represents the concept of a context-independent repository of motor skills (shapes, poses and movements). In this chapter we describe how EVA-Script and EVA-annotation concepts are used in order to design the basic and complex motor skills of an embodied conversational agent. The motor skills are represented as templates as structured in the EVA-script, and support modeling through different dimensions of expressivity (e.g., power, time, repetitiveness, etc.). Each template contains the bone configuration of the body parts, the trajectory of movement over which one pose is transformed into another when hand/head gestures are described. At the end of this chapter, the co-articulation through visemes and shaping of the vocal tract as a whole is discussed. The represented co-articulation technique is used in the EVA lip-sync process.

The *sixth chapter* addresses the context-dependent level in EVA-model. It identifies and describes the semiotic grammar and formulation of the co-verbal behavior lexicon (gesticon) in detail. The semiotic grammar and gesticon are built based on the results of the functional annotation of EVA Corpus. The semiotic grammar represents a formal grammar (language-dependent rules) based on morpho-syntactic features. By using this grammar, various interpretations of intent may be identified in general and unannotated input text. In the next step the identified intents are minimized by considering predicted prosodic features. Further, the gesticon establishes a correlation between speech and co-verbal forms (shape, pose and movement) based on semiotic intent and in semiotic space. In general, co-verbal forms do not carry any meaning when used in isolation; however, when used together with verbal behavior (and in proper context), the co-verbal forms become meaningful additions to speech and are named as gestures.

The *seventh chapter* represents the core of the proposed EVA-model; namely, the algorithm that can be used to plan and generate co-verbal behavior automatically, and can be well synchronized with the synthesized speech. The idea behind the algorithm is to transform the text into a communicative act (or series of acts). The baseline of the algorithm is derived from the following statements: '*gestures have no definite grammar under which they are formed,*' '*gestures are complements to speech, however components rather than integral part of speech,*' and '*unannotated statement bares no wider context regarding its intent or the ideas it is representing.*' In light of this, we first define the mechanism and procedures through which possible interpretations of intent can be indicated. Nevertheless, in each statement several semiotic intents may be identified. Furthermore, the identified intents may overlap and consequently introduce inconsistencies and ambiguities into the understanding of the statement. The second phase of the algorithm, therefore, implements procedures which resolve these inconsistencies and ambiguities. The output is a definite classification of ideas and intents, which will be represented in the co-verbal behavior. The third phase of the algorithm introduces prosodic features into behavior planning and generation. This phase structures the co-verbal visualization of ideas in the form of movement phases. In general, the stroke-phase of each gesture should, in its form, interpret that word (or phrase) which carries most meaning. The temporal correlation of the stroke phase (stroke and post-stroke-hold) should be in line with the prosodically articulated segments of speech. The fourth phase of the algorithm then classifies the final forms of visualized co-verbal behavior and the trajectories over which the gesture propagates through its shapes. This phase of the algorithm takes into account the following features: base structure of gesture (movement phases), semiotic classification, and morpho-syntactic and orthographic nature of meaningful (content) words. The chapter, therefore, defines the algorithm for the automatic design and generation of meaningfully and prosodically synchronized co-verbal behavior, and is concluded with the description of the last phase, which transforms the predicted co-verbal behavior into EVA-event.

The *eighth chapter* is devoted to the representation of EVA-framework, which is used to realize and visualize (animate) the co-verbal behavior, as generated by the EVA-model on an embodied conversational agent. Within this chapter we describe the concept of multi-part, mesh–based, and articulated conversational agents, and the procedures for the realization of EVA-events. The framework also supports the generation of subconscious behavior, e.g., spontaneous eye-blinks.

The *ninth chapter* identifies and describes a platform, named MWP, which is used for the flexible integration of EVA-model and EVA engine into general multimodal user interfaces. The text-to-speech synthesis and synthesis and visualization of co-verbal behavior are from the context of the system resources regarded as highly challenging. Further, this chapter also represents a novel architecture through which EVA-model and EVA engine are integrated with a distributed system, named DATA. We also demonstrate how an ECA may be integrated into the domain of web interfaces. Such integration needs EVA-plugin and a multi-threaded web-based core, which converges web and non-web technologies into a modular mesh network. The chapter is concluded with several real-life scenarios of ECA integration and use of MWP, such as multimodal web news reader, web-based machine translation, multimodal smart IPTV system, etc. The last part of the chapter also represents how the co-verbal behavior for ECA may also be transferred to artificial bodies (e.g., robots).

Finally, the *tenth chapter* defines and describes the experimental environment and perceptual experiments through which the various possibilities of generation, synthesis and realization of the co-verbal behavior can be performed, tested, and evaluated; e.g., firstly, the synthesis of facial expressions and emotions is presented. These experiments involve the synthesis of basic emotions (and transitions between them), which originates from Ekman's definition of the six biologically induced emotions (joy, sadness, fear, anger, disgust and surprise). These emotions may be further modeled by considering the intensity, when secondary emotions, such as terror, serenity, grief, etc., can be synthesized. The secondary emotions are complex and originate from psychological and sociological nature rather than human biology. Another category of complex emotions is based on the blending of basic emotions. These experiments are based on Plutchik's wheel of emotions, which illustrates various relationships among the emotions. By blending (mixing) the basic emotions, we can create secondary and tertiary feelings such as love, anxiety, aggressiveness, contempt, etc. The last category of complex emotions incorporates a synthesis of facial expressions which are the results of the concealment of one emotion with another. *Ambivalent feelings* are generated when humans do not wish to express their true (primary) emotion or attitude and overlap it with another emotion. By using the mechanism of ambivalence, we are able to synthesize feelings, such as sarcasm, masked fear, malevolence, masked satisfaction, etc. The experiments representing expressivity are followed by experiments of visual synthesis of co-verbal behavior as generated by the proposed EVA-model. Through the last set of perceptual experiments, we discuss the inner mechanism of the algorithm in detail. The chapter is concluded with the presentation of a subjective evaluation of the proposed model and implemented in the form of the quality assessment over the Likert scale.

Matej Rojc
Faculty of Electrical Engineering and Computer Science, University of Maribor
Smetanova ulica 17, 2000 Maribor, SLOVENIA
Telephone: +386 2 220 7223, FAX: +386 2 220 7272
matej.rojc@um.si
PhD in electrical engineering, Associate Professor

Izidor Mlakar
AI Solutions d.o.o., Ob ribniku 24, 2000 Maribor, SLOVENIA
izidor@panevropa.com
PhD in electrical engineering, Researcher

Chapter 1

AN EXPRESSIVE MODEL FOR THE GENERATION OF CO-VERBAL BEHAVIOR

INTRODUCTION

The perception and understanding of information (meaning) conveyed is closely interlinked with visual cues and visual non-verbal elements that speakers are generating throughout human-human dialogues. For instance, Cassel and Stone (1999), Pelachaud and Poggi (2002), Diesbach and Midgley (2008) and DeCarlo et al. (2004) have shown the significance of co-verbal behavior within interpersonal communication, which primarily consists of facial expressions, emotions, expressions and hand gesticulation. The visual cues generated in parallel with speech mainly complement and clarify the meaning of spoken content. Furthermore, the physical manifestation of synthetic co-verbal behavior also enables machines (or user-interfaces) to respond in a way that inspires social attitude and effect. Among the major benefits of social enactment in HMI are efficiency and viability, as well as a higher degree of persuasion and, in general, more constructive behavior from users. As a result of the integration of co-verbal behavior into user interfaces, the possibility of unacceptable or incorrect user-responses declines and the feedback provided by the machine is rarely ignored or concealed. By integrating co-verbal cues the human-machine interaction becomes clearer; the machine gains the ability to engage itself in communication in a more active, affective way, as an equivalent interlocutor.

The understanding of how different interlocutors integrate information about their emotional state or attitude toward a certain theme (through facial gesticulations and hand and body gestures) represents the basic knowledge (grammar) necessary for the development and design of advanced multimodal interfaces. The detailed analysis of verbal interaction through the annotation of co-verbal cues within face-to-face dialogues has been a favored research method. Namely, it allows for the highly complex mechanisms of human-human interaction to be revealed, further investigated and properly interpreted (Cassell et al., 2001, Cereković 2014, Lee & Marsella, 2006, Heylen et al., 2008, Viljhalmsson et al., 2007, Heloir & Kipp, 2009, Allwood, 2013, Krauss et al., 2011, Kendon, 1973, Goodwin, 1991). In particular, the interactive mechanisms are mostly interpreted semantically and prosodically, through the correlation between words (e.g., words, word-phrases, and/or corresponding prosodic features) and hand gestures/facial expressions (Rowbotham et al. 2014, Dick et al. 2014,

Krivokapić 2014). The more advanced studies also investigate the articulation of gestures/emotions/gaze through the intent that drives the articulation of co-verbal cues (e.g., turn-taking, the completion of topic, highlighting the importance of parts of content, concepts of dishonesty and lying) rather than relying solely on semantic interpretation (Holler et al. 2015, McNeill et al. 2015). The research on co-verbal behavior is, in general, carried out mostly on monologues (Redcay & Carlson 2015, Bick 2014) and interviews (Caridakis et al. 2013, Jong et al. 2014) and with a specific focus on the behavior of an individual person (Jokinen & Pelachaud, 2013, Martin et al., 2006). Further studies incorporate corpora in the form of theatrical plays and/or other types of “artificial” dialogues in which the behavior is performed (played-out) according to some pre-defined scenario (Bilakhia et al. 2015, Oertel et al. 2013, Sun et al. 2011).

Despite it already being a well-researched area, there are still open issues, especially regarding the functionality of generated co-verbal behavior and the understanding of the complex mechanisms that drive the co-verbal interaction and correlate it with speech. Namely, gestures (hand, head, gaze and facial expressions) represent the major sources of discourse cohesion (McNeill et al. 2015). However, they are unwitting and generated as movements orchestrated also by significances other than pragmatic actions, and driven by intent rather than some specific goal. Gestures represent non-goal-directed actions generated non-accidentally. As co-verbal behavior, these gestures are not just simple visual supplements (decorations, “add-ons”) of verbal content, but rather actual components of speech. Namely, spaces in which gestures appear are not filled at random. In some cases, for example, pointing at something or outlining a spatial component and position may carry semantic significance, but often the significance is something other than space. In face-to-face communication co-verbal behavior may carry semantic significance; however, more often it provides additional information on an idea, as well as the attitude and emotions of the interlocutors. Through the visualized co-verbal features each interlocutor can gain information such as:

1. The identity of the other interlocutors (especially speakers): the biological definition of the speaker (e.g., gender, age etc.), the psychological definition (e.g., speaker’s personality, such as restrained, or opened), and the socio-cultural definition (e.g., ethnic characteristics, social class, education, the role in activity).
2. Psycho-physical states of the other interlocutors: e.g., fatigue, illness, proper physical fitness, etc.
3. Emotional states and attitudes of the other interlocutors: expression of attitude (and emotion) toward the theme or idea, toward the co-speakers (and other participants), toward the situation and state of discourse, etc.
4. Illustration of facts and ideas: e.g., by outlining the idea when proper words cannot be found, obtaining extra time for proper formulation of an idea or the response, etc.

Gestures occur in different types of face-to-face dialogues such as conversations, route directions, narrations, and lectures. Gestures synchronized with speech (co-verbal behavior, co-verbal gestures) are by far the most frequent kind. In its everyday occurrence (with the exception of pre-prepared speeches and acting) the co-verbal behavior is spontaneous (unwitting). The form and existence of the co-verbal behavior is orchestrated by speaker-created significances and induces imagery in listeners (McNeill et al. 2015). Co-verbal behavior also carries discourse information. As such, the communicative functions (Allwood,

2010, 2013, Allwood & Ahlsén, 2009) may represent the most suitable used theory, through which the complexity of the correlation between verbal and non-verbal behavior can be interpreted. Namely, the co-verbal behavior can be decomposed based on its functional and non-functional role in the communication and identified by its intent rather than its goal, as suggested by Kendon (2004). Based on its intent, the co-verbal behavior can then be classified as part of:

1. *Interactive Communication Management (ICM),* which mostly concerns the handling of interaction between interlocutors engaged in the dialogue. It involves turn-taking mechanism, feedback processing and generation of feedback, and sequencing.
2. *Own Communication Management (OCM),* which is the basis of communication and interaction. It concerns the inner mechanism used for generating and representing information in face-to-face dialogues. It describes how the interlocutor continuously manages the planning, execution, and representation of co-verbal behavior throughout the interaction (while having the role of the speaker).

Following the theory of the communicative functions (Allwood, 2010, 2013), the existence of one part of co-verbal behavior may be explained through OCM mechanisms. Such spontaneous behavior occurs when speakers need to obtain extra time for the formulation of the response, when speakers unwittingly express concentration or other difficulties in the proper formulation of verbal content (e.g., finding the right words), or when the need to change already acknowledged facts, ideas or even a previous statement is expressed. The ICM mechanisms then explain the existence of the remaining part of co-verbal behavior, which is mostly related to the functional part of discourse. By incorporating co-verbal behavior underlaid with ICM, the interlocutors try to induce order into generally chaotic and unordered exchange opinions and ideas, which interaction without ICM certainly is. Namely, the ICM incorporates a mechanism like turn-taking (Herrera et al., 2009, Grothendiecka et al., 2011), which tries to ensure that one voice at any one time gives information. Furthermore, the ICM incorporates feedback (Kopp et al., 2008, Bevacqua, 2013), as well as other mechanisms, through which listeners may respond to the perceived information (Wredea et al., 2010). Through feedback, interlocutors not only express agreement or disagreement, but are also able to indicate the state of their attention, e.g., understanding of the idea, the need for repetition or the need for further clarification.

The co-verbal behavior (which in a broader sense encompasses all types of gestures), synchronized with speech, although unwitting, does not occur accidentally. It primarily serves to emphasize the perception and the importance of the information. In some cases it may even substitute or change the meaning of what was told or what was meant to be told. Furthermore, the co-verbal behavior accommodates the natural flow of exchanging ideas/thoughts and induces order into interaction. At the same time, speech synchronized gestures also maintain high interactivity and dynamics in face-to-face dialogues, which involve the use of verbal information as well as additional non-linguistic elements (signals), such as: prosody, hand and head gestures, body poses, eye movement (gaze), and facial expressions (facial gesticulation). When these signals are used in proper context, and when they are truly a part of speech, e.g., well synchronized with speech, they can lead to the formulation of attitude as well as a socially/emotionally founded flow of information. Such a flow not only improves the perception and understanding of interaction, but also properly guides the course of the dialogue in an organized manner, and thereby accelerates problem solving, as well as resolving communicative conflicts.

In face-to-face dialogues the formulation and use of co-verbal behavior is natural, mostly unwitting, and quite spontaneous. The non-linguistic signals occur concurrently with speech, prior to speech or (shortly) after speech. In some cases, the non-linguistic signals may even completely or partially substitute words/word-phrases. In HMI, however, the non-verbal signals are still quite synthetic and are yet to be integrated in a full scale. Throughout this book we are mainly interested in those gestures that are driven by OCM mechanisms. Such gestures temporarily occur concurrently with speech (representing emphasis, outline, or some other non-spatial significance) or shortly before speech, and may still represent links between information fragments, preparation time, expression of concern and/or failure to interpret.

EMBODIED CONVERSATIONAL AGENTS AND MANAGEMENT OF INTERACTION

Embodied conversational agents (ECAs) play a crucial role in mimicking the natural flow of communication in HMI interfaces. They may enhance the effectiveness of the delivery of information, as well as introducing more natural, human-like aspects while interacting with a machine. Namely, the interaction in the form of "message ping-pong" represents an insufficient model of communication (Kopp, 2010). It cannot account for the dynamics of the face-to-face conversation the interlocutors are often engaged in, such as mimicry (Chartrand & Bargh, 1999) and linguistic alignment (Pickering & Garrod, 2004). In most multimodal applications and HMI interfaces, however, ECAs are, where they exist, often still simple objects. They are capable of using a rather limited collection of non-linguistic signals at best (e.g., some facial expressions, emotions, a limited collection of hand gesticulations, gaze, etc.) as well as rather limited synchronization mechanism. In most cases the generated behavior is more in line with Kendon's (2008) term of accompaniments rather than integral parts of speech (Allwood 2013, McNeill et al., 2015).

The researchers in the area of HMI (human-machine interface), which incorporates communicative solutions grounded on ECA technology, are mainly focused on the realization of individual types and semantically/prosodically founded contexts of co-verbal behavior. The deployed or theorized solutions rely mostly on the pre-defined lexicons and animations that correlate co-verbal behavior with speech through prosody, semantic correlation and some rule-based models (Cassell et al., 2000, Kipp et al., 2007a, Robertson et al., 2015, Pelachaud, 2015, Cafaro et al., 2014). Further solutions incorporate prosody, extracted via speech recognition, as main features orchestrating the co-verbal behavior (Bozkurt et al., 2015, Fernández-Baena et al., 2014, Zorić & Pandžić, 2006, Zorić et al. 2011, Ngo & Bui, 2015). The focus of ECAs, however, is shifting toward correlating speech and co-verbal behavior through affectiveness, e.g., prosodic and emotional features detected in speech (Ngo & Bui, 2015, Bozkurt et al., 2015) and through non-linguistic mechanisms as observed directly in face-to-face conversations, such as:

1. *feedback*, given by the listener during the communicative dialogue,
2. *reactive behavior*, the ability of realizing the unplanned and dynamic responses to a given situation,
3. *turn-taking/turn-giving*, understanding the role and mechanism behind the exchange of speaker roles, etc.,
4. *representing spatially significant behavior,* semantically defined outlines and pointing gestures.

In general, therefore, most ECAs nowadays incorporate some sort of non-linguistic signals limited to contextually narrow sets of static and pre-defined movements generated according to a scenario, set of rules or prosody. In order to mimic the natural interaction as observed between humans, researchers rely on annotated data and video annotation schemas used to observe face-to-face dialogues in detail and for the analysis of co-verbal behavior generated during conversation. Based on the theory of the communicative functions and the abstract interaction model (as proposed in Allwood, 2010, 2013), the face-to-face dialogue (human communication) is formulated through the main message (verbal part) and its representation in the form of co-verbal behavior driven by ICM and OCM mechanisms. The abstract interaction model is outlined in Figure 1.

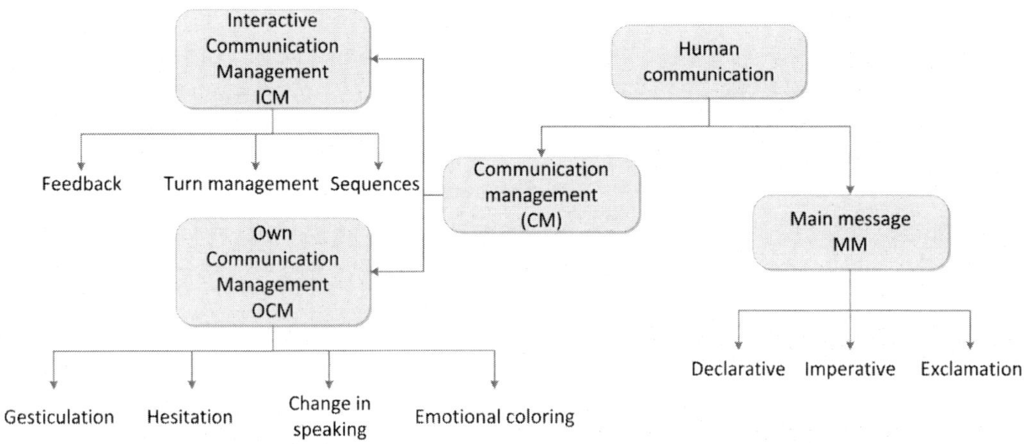

Figure 1. The abstract interaction model.

The interlocutor must, in order to communicate, participate in a number of interaction processes. These processes provide the means for the successful correlation of verbal and non-verbal channels through which goals of communication are to be achieved. As outlined in Figure 1, humans have evolved the *communication management* (CM) as part of tackling non-verbal signals (co-verbal behavior) during communication. Among more important CM mechanisms are the aforementioned ICM and OCM. The main message (MM) in Figure 1 represents the reason why an interlocutor contributed to communication and also the verbal component of communication. The MM contains *communicative acts* (e.g., statements, questions and requests), *referential content* (e.g., factual content providing further emphasis), and *expressed attitudes* (e.g., affective-epistemic aspects) that are to be shared among interlocutors. Features of the social identity, however, (e.g., personality) are more complex and can be integrated into any aspect of MM and even CM.

ICM mostly concerns the handling of interaction between interlocutors engaged in the dialogue, and it implements processes such as: *turn management* (e.g., exchange of speakers), *feedback* (e.g., indicating agreement/understanding), and *sequencing* (e.g., opening or closing an activity). OCM is the basis of the representation of information in face-to-face interaction. It mostly concerns the inner mechanism used for generating and representing content. OCM implements mechanisms such as: *choice* (e.g., choosing words, choice of modality), *change* (e.g., changing what was said/gestured, negation of previous ideas), *hesitation* (e.g., hesitation words, or prolonged duration of syllables, or hesitation gestures), which allows speakers to change statements, search for words, or plan further steps in their presentation, and *planning* (e.g., as a function of choice used for the construction of effective exchange of information).

Own Communication Management - OCM

OCM is, from the perspective of the discussed expressive model for the generation of co-verbal behavior, mainly focused on those processes that manage how the speaker complements the verbal aspects of information with gestures (different body movements, expressions and poses). Namely, speakers try to reach the goals of communication as effectively as possible through co-verbal behavior. During communication they also form their own communicative styles through which they can be identified. The more important OCM processes are: hesitation, planning, self-repair, choice, and change. During conversation speakers typically tend to use choice and change more often. The “choice” mechanisms allow the speaker to “insert” appropriate time intervals used for pre- and post-processing of the information. “Choice” ensures that formulation and representation of content and expressions are continuous throughout the delivery of the message. Furthermore, the mechanism “choice” allows the speaker to change/adapt already generated content and expressions. When co-verbal behavior is analyzed through OCM only movement carried out within specific word/prosodic phrases (or discourse units) is retained as relevant.

By using OCM theory and the temporal position of movement in regard to the underlying word/prosodic phrase (or discourse unit), one can determine what function such a movement represents in conversation (e.g., identify and classify movement as co-verbal behavior). McNeill in his study (in accordance with the hypothesis about a common point "growth" - common growth point hypothesis) argues that the top of iconic gestures coincides with the emphasis on the word that this gesture tries to describe (McNeill, 2000, 2005b).

In view of the expressive characteristics of conversation of the OCM units, combining both verbal and co-verbal behavior generated during the delivery of information can be classified as outlined in Figure 2 (Allwood, 2013, Allwood & Ahlsén, 2009). Figure 2 presents the classification of OCM units according to the expressive characteristics of face-to-face dialogue. The first level divides the OCM units into so-called simple OCM units that have one expressive characteristic (simple characteristic), and into complex OCM units that concurrently combine more expressive characteristics (combined characteristics). Furthermore, the so-called simple OCM units are classified into basic OCM expressions, and into other OCM units that are affected by the basic OCM operations. The difference between these two types of simple OCM units is based on the fact that basic OCM units define their meaning according to the OCM function, while the second type of OCM unit can have any meaning, whereas the OCM function is obtained by considering the OCM operation. The

OCM units with combined expressive characteristics represent those types of OCM units which are influenced by the composition of basic OCM expressions and operations, as can be seen in Figure 2.

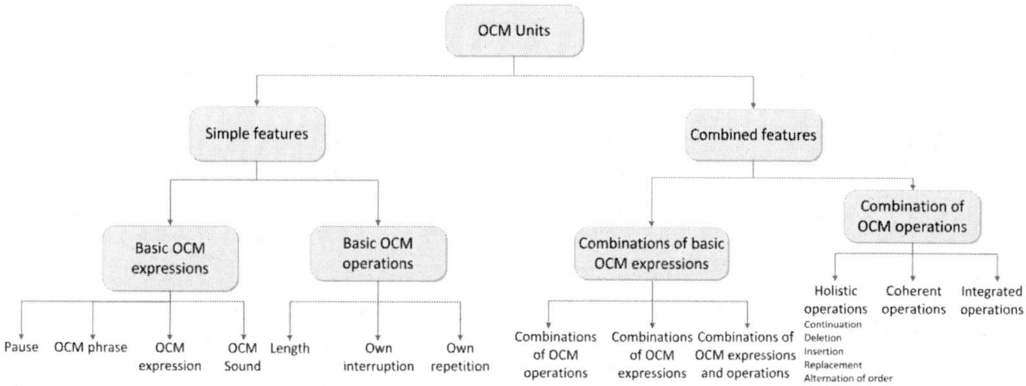

Figure 2. The abstract model of the mechanism of own communication management (OCM).

INTERACTIVE COMMUNICATION MANAGEMENT - ICM

ICM is focused primarily on those processes that are used during the interactive dialogue between at least two people, such as: *turn-taking* (exchange of roles speaker/listener), and providing *feedback*. Therefore, ICM mechanisms represent a way to keep a natural dialogue flow and appropriate form of information channels with the co-speaker (by which the information is exchanged). *Feedback* is defined as a linguistic mechanism that allows speakers to exchange information through the four basic communicative functions. These functions are necessary to provide the appropriate level of direct interaction (face-to-face) and are identified as follows:

1. *Contact*: whether the co-speaker is prepared and able to continue the interaction.
2. *Perception*: whether the co-speaker is capable to receive the message.
3. *Understanding*: whether the co-speaker is capable and able to understand the message.
4. *Reactions*: whether the co-speaker is able to respond to the message (he receives or rejects the message).

These basic functions of linguistic *feedback* are derived from the four basic requirements in human communication. The first one says that for communication the existence of at least two agents that are capable of performing it is required. The second one states that the agent that is receiving a message must also be able to perceive visual cues (co-verbal behavior/gesticulation), or other channels through which the information is conveyed. The third one then states that the agent that receives the information must be able to understand the co-verbal behavior/gesticulation, or any other cues received through other channels through which the information is conveyed. At the same time it is also important that the recipient can receive and understand the non-verbal cues that additionally outline the verbal information (e.g., accents, gesticulation, etc.). The last requirement says that the recipient of information has to be able to produce several co-verbal responses which are different for different aspects of the received message. It is also necessary that the sender of the original messages understands these indications (feedback) and if necessary acts on them.

Applications of Conversational Models and Agents

Conversational agents and underlying conversational models are becoming much more than just visual decorative supplements in which human-like articulated bodies are creating movement. The agents are also much more than just virtual interfaces in which proactivity is reflected through animation techniques, enabling the generation of credible and almost lively movement of articulated body parts. Key directions of conversational agents and underlying conversational models are social behavior and affect, realized through the careful planning, formation, and realization (animation) of co-verbal behavior synchronized with verbal content to an almost human-like extent. The generated behavior reflects similar characteristics to those that can be found in the interaction between people and may incorporate context and emotion, as well as personality. Specifically, the interaction between humans does not involve only statements (and expressions) about the individual tasks. It incorporates processes through which the goals of speakers and the common goals of all interlocutors are achieved.

Often, interaction among humans also involves conversation that does not add any new concepts, or does not directly affect the course of the dialogue; this is so-called small talk (Bickmore & Cassell, 2005). For instance, real estate agents use small talk to obtain information about the stereotypical characteristics of their clients. An example of reasoning processes used in order to extract the relevant information from small talk in this case is: "It is likely that people who drive minivans have children. Therefore, they are probably interested in larger homes that are located in the neighborhoods with good schools." Salesmen who, through small talk, raise the level of intimacy in their relationship with the customers are also a good example of the exploitation of irrelevant conversation (Bickmore & Cassell, 2005). The demand for conversational agents and conversational behavior models that can not only guide or direct the user, but also communicate with users in some sort of social dialogue, is increasing in, for instance, online stores, software applications, computer games, websites with services etc. (Chattaraman et al., 2012). For example, Swedish commercial enterprise Ikea has integrated in its website a virtual assistant, named Anna, which wears the uniform of the company and answers questions about Ikea products and services (Allwood & Ahlsén, 2009b). Similarly, the company Alaska Airlines on its website hosts a virtual assistant named Jenn. Different forms of virtual humans are also being used as building receptionists (Rist et al., 2013), as pedagogical agents (Veletsianos & Russell, 2014), in online stores and other online applications (Mimoun & Poncin, 2015, Verhagen et al., 2014).

Co-verbal behavior therefore plays a particularly important role in social dialogue as well as the perception and acceptance of user interfaces. Namely, important business decisions and meetings are usually executed through direct contact (dialogue) rather than via the telephone, or other means of electronic communication. This intuition has also been confirmed by several empirical studies. Chattaraman et al. (2012) state six key reasons and issues in the adaptation and use of the Internet for web stores; the *risk* (spent time/user friendliness regarding navigation and purchasing steps, the financial/security risks, the actual product characteristics), *trust* (credibility, liking), *social support, user familiarity, user experience* (the lack of satisfaction during shopping, the lack of personal contact), and the difficulties encountered when searching products. The study presented by Chattaraman et al. (2012) also shows that the presence of so-called social strategies has the potential to reduce the importance of specific issues and can positively influence the decision about using web services. Furthermore, the study also shows that even the use of quite simple conversational agents has the potential to (at least partially) substitute the real salesman. Most existing web stores and websites with web services integrate quite simple conversational agents (chat bots), whereby the user's input is processed in a rather limited and controlled way. One example is project AiA (Andre et al., 1999) (Adaptive Communication Assistant for effective Infobahn Access). This system integrates a virtual traveler agent whose task is to collect, to structure, and to present the information about the touristic destination, which depends on the user's profile.

Similarly, Fabri et al. (2007) introduced the concept, named asymmetrical interaction, in the form of a virtual postman, whereby two users meet in the virtual world. The conversational agent is in this case capable of expressing six different emotions (human-like natural facial expressions), through which the users can express their attitude toward some theme. Such a relatively simple concept of a conversational agent, who is actually not supported by a co-verbal model, can already greatly help in the participation of users and can improve the user experience.

Rigas and Gazepidis (2007) present the conversational agent that is able to visually present three pre-prepared descriptions of products. The agent is able to realize during communication manually defined metaphors according to a pre-defined behavior plan. Although the agent does not contain any advanced co-verbal model and for each product description a specific animation graph has to be prepared, it has been shown that the multimodal presentation of products is more effective and more persuasive in comparison to textual descriptions. The metaphors that the conversational agent expresses during communication actually help in decision making and the actual purchase.

More complex conversational agents are able to carry out the communication with the user by using several co-verbal models. These models are based on the domain and intended use, communication functions, communication goals and ideas. In this way they are able to present some information by using speech that is accompanied by synchronized co-verbal movements and gestures. Nunamaker et al. (2011) presented an automated information kiosk, whereby the used conversational agent interviews the users. The agent, with the help of the psycho-sociological system, also recognizes in their responses the changes regarding arousal, the changes regarding behavior, and the changes in cognitive effort. The primary purpose of these conversational agents is not direct interaction, but to learn more about the psychology of human behavior during interaction. However, in order to achieve the goals and to create different relationships in human co-speakers, Nunamaker et al. (2011) used different techniques for modeling interaction in the form of multimodal messages and recommendations, co-verbal states and poses, emotions, etc. Similarly, Stocky and Cassell (2002) presented an automated information kiosk, named MACK. This kiosk integrates the conversational agent, who can answer questions about the research groups, projects, and about employees in the MIT Media Laboratory (MIT Media Lab). At the same time the conversational agent also provides instructions on how to access the individual locations of people/groups. During communication MACK "talks" with the users, and uses gestures and indicators presented on the map that is placed between the user and the kiosk. In order for MACK to be able to plan and to generate the verbal and co-verbal behavior (in the form of speech and gestures), the system implements the conversational model. This model makes decisions on when and how to distribute (to structure) the information presentation through different modalities; for example, when only speech should be used, or when only gestures should be used, and when both speech and gesture should be simultaneously used. At the same time, the system makes decisions as to which type of gesture should be used (iconic, metaphoric, deictic etc.), and how to synchronize gestures with the corresponding speech segments.

In another study (Baldassarri et al., 2008) the conversational agent MAXINE has been presented, which can be used for the multimodal presentation of information in several domains. The agents based on MAXINE, for example, have already been used as virtual presenters in PowerPoint presentations. Even users without any specific knowledge about computer graphics or programming are able to create 3D presentations of information that is extracted from the content in PowerPoint slides. The MAXINE conversational agents have also been integrated into smart environments, where they have been used as advanced communication interfaces for managing and controlling the environment. In addition to the presenter and controller, the MAXINE agent can also personalize the virtual teacher, and is able to simplify and to improve the present concepts of teaching in the field of computer graphics. The conversational agents in smart environments, e-health, and e-learning services, represent the largest potential for the conversational agents' technology, the co-verbal models, and dialogue managers.

The conversational agents are, due to their articulated and human-like representation, not only able to communicate with the users (e.g., realizing the conversation), but are able to establish (more or less) intimate social relations. These conversational agents are usually regarded as companions. A good example of companions are those social agents who provide social support to older people, when their independence becomes more limited, or in the case of the illness or death of a close relative (Ring et al., 2013). Loneliness and social isolation is also a major problem for the elderly population. The use of conversational agents can, according to the results of psycho-sociological studies presented by Ring et al. (2013), proactively motivate older people to interact with the agents. Namely, the agent is able, as a proactive entity, for example, to directly provide companionship, to provide some kind of social support (e.g., small talk) (Bickmore & Cassell, 1999), or to manage different social activities that are carried out during interaction with the older person (e.g., solving crossword puzzles and other games, as well as designing and modeling activities (Baylor, 2009). The agent can also help to establish and to maintain social contact between older people and their relatives. Further, the conversational agent can recommend and manage several services in electronic communications (e.g., coordination of online contacts and conversation; help in reading and writing online messages, e-mails, etc.), which are in general, particularly for older people, often too complex and difficult to understand. Moreover, the conversational agents can also carry out different concepts of the so-called conversational therapy, which may include the active listening methods (Klein et al., 2002), the cognitive behavioral therapy (Colby, 1995), the psychology of positive interventions (Tugade & Fredrickson, 2004), etc. By using all these methods and therapies, the agent can directly impact on the well-being of the older people, including depression and mood disorders. Ring et al. (2013) designed the proactive and passive conversational agent, which is used as a companion for older people. Its aim is to reduce the impact of loneliness and social isolation in older people through the proactive and passive roles in social interaction that include co-verbal behavior in the form of hand gestures, head movements (nodding), speech, and facial expressions.

In addition to typical social companions, the conversational agents may play a key role in maintaining and improving the health status of people. For example, health coaching presents a technique of intervention behavior that can assist participants in helping to determine a medical diagnosis and in achieving those behavior changes that relate to their lifestyles. The trainers in the health coaching practice are able, through active involvement and personal counseling, to represent a proactive role regarding the support and the persuasion of patients in achieving their self-imposed goals. In another study (Ruiz et al., 2012) the concept of medical conversational agents is introduced. These agents can be used to perform techniques of proactive health coaching. The presented approach is based on the concept of pedagogical conversational agents (e.g., in Gulz et al., 2011, Hoque et al., 2013), and theories regarding cognitive social learning (Baylor, 2009). Since the conversational agents increasingly look like humans, the speaking entity (with accompanied co-verbal behavior) can much better establish a social relationship with the participant (or patient), who will then not only be more willing to cooperate, but will also be more motivated in achieving the self-imposed goals. The conversational agents, in comparison with e.g., brochures, catalogs, or static images, raise the preparedness level of patients' collaboration, and their motivation in performing long-term activities that can enhance their lifestyles.

The conversational agents and conversational models represent a multi-disciplinary conversational paradigm, and their use is virtually unlimited. The conversational agents can be included, for example, in several websites and in other user interfaces, from acting simply as virtual assistants in helping with browsing and navigating through the content, to more complex virtual 3D information presenters.

More complex concepts of conversational agents, including conversational models and different dialogue managers, can also perform symmetrical interaction through which they can achieve both their own and common communicative goals, and are able to represent different communicative concepts. The complex conversational agents and models can be used in various domains, from social companions for elderly people, assistants, companions in IPTV systems, and in other digital environments (Rojc et al., 2013), to virtual teachers and health promoters. In the following subsection, those conversational models and conversational agents will be presented, based on the communication theories and interpersonal dialogue, and are most relevant for the proposed expressive model of the co-verbal behavior presented in the book. Their main common point is: how to plan, synchronize and present the so-called co-verbal behavior for a given context (for a given annotated/general text in a given domain), which includes internally and externally synchronized verbal and co-verbal elements, and that can be integrated into multi-modal interfaces in order to support social interaction between a man and a machine.

The Types of Co-Verbal Models

The spoken language (as used, for example, in communicative dialogue) is in general a complex multi-modal process, whereby people use several communication channels and provide information by using complex verbal and co-verbal elements (cues). The listeners receive those communicative elements and convert the received information into a message. Further, in human-human dialogue verbal (speech) and co-verbal (gestures) elements are inseparably connected and planned in such a way that they reflect or highlight the most important idea in the message. In order that such behavior can be transferred on the system or machine, and in order to use it for achieving more natural interaction in multimodal human-machine interfaces (HMI), the researchers from several research areas (psychology, sociology, computer science, medicine, etc.), are studying and developing the so-called conversational models (non-verbal generators), which are based on the data-driven, linguistic, and prosodic features of the accompanying speech, semantics, and annotation of the communicative dialogue.

Data-driven conversational models are based on the capturing of movement and the composition of verbal and co-verbal elements in the form of the co-articulation process (Stone et al., 2004, Busso et al., 2007, Mariooryad & Busso, 2012). For example, Stone and his colleagues presented a method for the simultaneous use of pre-recorded speech and recorded body movements that are used for the generation of animated conversation. The concept that they propose is based on the following processes: pre-preparing the content (content authoring), preparing data, planning the behavior and animation (generation and animation). The basic idea of their concept is based on the understanding and on the fusion of the captured natural verbal and co-verbal units into multimodal sequences. As the authors (Stone et al., 2004) emphasize, however, the main problem of their system represents the possible variability and generality. In order to achieve acceptable variability, they have suggested using splicing and warping methods on the captured gestures in video. Data-driven conversational models establish a relationship between speech and gestures (especially facial expressions) through complex mechanisms that combine verbal and visual (co-verbal) utterances, based on the acoustic information in speech (Mariooryad & Busso, 2012). Yeiha and his colleagues (Yehia et al., 2000) have proposed a linear regression method, which is used to make conclusions about the shape and the trajectory of head movements, from the fundamental frequency contour (F0 contour). Also, Rao and colleagues (Rao et al., 1998) proposed the use of Gaussian mixture models (GMM), but they do not take into account the already established temporal correlation of the audio-visual information.

Similarly, in another study (Zoric et al., 2011) the co-verbal model based on the synchronization of facial expressions (including lip synchronization) and prosodic features of the speech signal is presented. This model includes head movements (nodding and swinging), eyebrow movements, eye-blinking, eye tracking (gaze), expression of emotions, and lip synchronization. The mapping between the speech signal characteristics and co-verbal behavior is defined using HMM models. Specifically, they trained five continuous HMM models (for the left and the right parts of the face). Further, they classified winks, eyebrow movements, and head movements in the interval that contains four frames of speech. The acoustic features that are calculated on each frame include the fundamental frequency (F0), root-mean square amplitude (RMS), and acceleration values. They perform the recognition of the segmentation of those speech segments that most reliably reflect various facial expressions.

In another study (Chiu & Marsella, 2011), the authors generalize the model for the synchronization of co-verbal behavior based on the speech signal characteristics, from facial expressions to co-verbal behavior, that are formed by the arms and the whole body. In the extended model they propose the generator design used for the co-verbal animation that is based on a hierarchical factored conditional restricted Boltzmann machine (HFCRBM). The model recognizes those feature vectors (including accents, intensity, prosody, etc.) that describe human gesticulation, and binds them with its own gesticulation space (captured and analyzed recordings of conversation). The prosodic characteristics of the speech signal are used for the selection of the appropriate segments of the movement, and for the control and management of the transitions between individual movements. The main disadvantage of data-driven co-verbal models results from the concepts of general use and diversity. The data-driven co-verbal models otherwise can produce a very good time synchronization, dynamism, and kinematic coherence between verbal and co-verbal elements. Nevertheless, the diversity of co-verbal elements and the diversity in using gestures depend mainly on the dimension and the diversity in the captured video recordings (Kipp et al., 2007a).

In order to achieve a higher diversity and more generalized interpretation of the synchronization of verbal and co-verbal elements, the *co-verbal models*, based on a higher analysis level and on the formulation of speech and gesture synchronization, have been designed. These systems are based on a set of rules and machine learning strategies, based on multi-disciplinary analysis and annotation of interaction between people (human-human dialogues). In another study (Bergmann & Kopp, 2010) the co-verbal model for creating iconic gestures, based on a sketch model, has been presented. This model can be used to build specifications of iconic gestures and co-articulation (the synchronization of verbal and co-verbal behavior elements). Neff et al. (2008) proposed a similar concept that is used in the system to mimic the communication style of the human speaker, as realized on general input text. Further, the Nonverbal Action Generator (NOVA) system, described by Neff et al. (2008), can recreate the co-verbal behavior that is specific for some observed human speaker, by using statistical models, a static semantic set of gestures, and the procedural animation. The NOVA system approach for creating a natural behavior is based on rules that have been defined based on the multimodal corpus. Like the majority of similar systems, the NOVA system is also constructed on the basis that the use and the form of co-verbal elements (gestures) primarily depend on the idea that the speaker/listener wants to communicate. Specifically, the prosodic relationship between the speech signal and the co-verbal gestures can be established through the correlation of acoustic features and gesticulation units (or movement phases) (McNeill, 2005a). The methods that are based on the creation and synchronization of the co-verbal behavior by using linguistic features (e.g., semantics, syntax etc.) result from the following hypothesis: speech and gesture have a common source, named also the *growth-point* (McNeill, 2005a), or *idea* (Kendon, 1980). In the case of people, the common *growth-point* for speech and co-verbal elements is obvious. It is reflected in the hierarchical structure of speech, and co-verbal behavior (Kopp & Wachsmuth, 2004). The co-verbal elements or gestures, based on this hypothesis, are usually fused in semantic lexicons (gesticons) that bind the semantics of word phrases and the co-verbal elements. The gesticons in general represent the co-verbal linguistic and audio-visual features that are common to the observed realistic speakers and to the forms that are fused with the given set of linguistic and audio-visual features. In another study (Kopp & Wachsmuth, 2004) the incremental co-verbal behavior model is presented. This model combines the synthesis of multimodal elements, including speech, gestures and facial expressions. The incremental model is able to convert the verbal and co-verbal elements, as specified in the XML description, into continuous sequences that include natural co-articulation. The framework BEAT/Spark presented by Cassell et al. (2001) can consider general (unannotated) input text. By using a set of rules, as defined from annotations of the multimodal corpus, the system is able to specify the intent for the input text, and also to specify and synchronize the co-verbal behavior. The algorithms in the BEAT framework perform on the general text input the syntactical analysis, and analyze the text input into themes, rhymes, objects, and actions. For the text input a tree-based structure is then created, whereby each leaf in the tree stores information about the sentence, rhymes/themes, objects, and actions. By using a manually defined set of rules, semantic correlation of words, gestures, and linguistic elements that are fused together in a semantic knowledge base, the BEAT algorithms select and temporarily synchronize the appropriate co-verbal elements.

The non-verbal behavior generator (NVBG) presented by Lee and Marsella (2006) is another system for generating co-verbal behavior that is similar to the BEAT framework. As in the case of the BEAT framework, in this system the semantic-syntactic rules are also based on the analysis regarding the communicative intent, the emotional state, and the dialogue. The NVBG combines these rules and the input context specified in form of function mark-up language (FML) (Heylen et al., 2008) in order to select those gestures, from the semantic repertoire, which vest correspond to the input text.

The output is written in BML procedural description (Vilhalmsson et al., 2007). Also, the NUMACK generator presented by Kopp et al. (2007) is based on the semantic lexicalization of co-verbal gestures in the form of 'words.' and on the direct integration of decision-making algorithms, for natural language generation. The NUMACK generator embeds the so-called micro-planner (SPUD) that does not use a static set of pre-defined gestures. Namely, the system integrates in the SPUD planner the gesticulation dictionary fully dynamically. The gestures and speech are then bound using a pre-defined set of grammatical rules.

The Methods and Frameworks for the Realization of Co-Verbal Behavior

Most systems for the planning and generating of co-verbal behavior using conversational models describe the co-verbal behavior in some procedural language, such as BML (Vilhjalmsson et al., 2007), FML (Heylen et al., 2008), MURML (Kransted et al., 2002), EMBRScript (Heloir & Kipp, 2009), and APML (DeCarolis et al., 2004). In this way the behavior can be presented through the animated visualization of various body movements that are performed on a conversational agent's virtual body. The methods and frameworks for the realization of co-verbal behavior thus make it possible to convert the XML behavior procedural specification into animated movements, and to perform it on the conversational agent. Some well-known frameworks are *ACE* (The Articulated Communicator Engine) (Kopp et al., 2003), *SAIBA framework* (Jeremy et al., 2011), and *SmartBody* (Thiebaux et al., 2008). The SAIBA represents a framework and general architecture for the generation of multimodal behavior using conversational agents. The whole process from text to behavior is divided into the following three phases: *intent planning*, *behavior planning*, and *behavior realization*. The *intent planning* and *behavior planning* are performed in those systems used for designing and generating the co-verbal behavior, and the *behavior realization* is performed in agent frameworks that are able to interpret and realize XML behavior descriptions as animation. Often the methods and frameworks used for the co-verbal behavior realization are based on (or originate from) the SAIBA architecture.

The *SmartBody* (Thiebaux et al., 2008) represents a modular and open source framework for animating co-verbal behavior on conversational agents, where specifications must be described in BML. For the interpretation of BML events this framework implements so-called movement controllers, which can be mutually hierarchically linked in real time, and used for the generation of continuous co-verbal behavior. Individual movement controllers implement various animation techniques, such as *key frame interpolation*, *motion capturing*, and *procedural animation* (which includes designing and animation blending). The SmartBody can realize the following types of BML behavior: body posture, body animation, views, head movements, and facial expressions. Most behavior inside the BML events is mapped into a movement controller, which supports one of the animation techniques. The concurrency of the movement controllers is otherwise enabled, but individual movement cannot be realized by using several movement controllers simultaneously. In addition to effective expressive behavior realization, in the SmartBody framework it is also possible to monitor animation state and to use so-called interruption events, by which the execution of current procedure can be interrupted and replaced by a new procedure.

The *RealActor framework* used for the realization of multimodal behavior on the conversational agents and presented by Cereković and Pandžić (2011) and Pejša and Pandžić (2009) is also based on the principle of the realization and animation of BML events (as in the SmartBody framework). It also incorporates the framework for animating virtual characters, named visage|SDK. The basic goal for this framework is to model synchronization between several modalities (BML types and elements), and integration of events that are triggered in the environment. Furthermore, the framework also addresses one of the key issues of the SAIBA framework: the simultaneous realization of BML elements of the same type. In order to solve issues of the SAIBA architecture and BML, they proposed: two-level processing of BML elements; multifaceted movement controllers; use of external functions for control and managing behavior; and use of machine learning techniques for the synchronization of synthesized speech and the co-articulation of lips. Since BML events require adjustments regarding timing between BML elements in the context of a two-level processing of BML elements, they propose the pre-processing step for the detailed specification of time stamps. The RealActor framework, therefore, obtains firstly an animation from the database of animations. Then, during the preparation phase, for each BML element the cross-relationships are established. These cross-relationships and durations of individual animation segments are then used to accurately define the time when each BML element should be actually carried out (animated). To cope with the events from the environment, especially those that are triggered by the co-speakers, the RealActor framework implements functions – for example, in order to stop the current behavior, or to add a new behavior – as a reaction to some event from the environment. The architecture of the RealActor framework needs an external speech synthesizer. Nevertheless, external speech synthesizers in general do not provide complete timing information regarding the synthesized speech. Therefore, the synchronization of speech and co-verbal behavior is carried out using neural networks.

The *Greta framework* presented by Pejša and Pandžić (2009), similarly to the RealActor framework, presents a generally useful and modular architecture for the realization of co-verbal behavior on the conversational agents. It is based on the SAIBA architecture and MPEG-4 standard. Further, for the specification of communicative intents, the descriptive language APML is used. APML can be used to describe the emotions and feelings that are consistent with the condition and emotional state of the agent, and the idea that the agent wants to present in the form of multimodal behavior. The Greta framework is primarily focused on the expressivity of the co-verbal movements and on the synthesis of complex facial expressions. In the context of the synthesis of complex multimodal emotions, the so-called *copy-synthesis approach* was presented. The approach is based on the functional annotations of TV interviews that cover the annotation of communicative acts, emotional stamps and multimodal characters. Altogether, this is then used to drive the synthesis of complex emotions.

Unlike the RealActor framework, the *EMBR animation engine* (Heloir & Kipp, 2009) eliminates the disadvantages of BML procedural descriptions of behavior through the design of an animation level in the SAIBA architecture that is managed by a procedural language, called EMBRScript. The EMBR engine supports the use of absolute timing and absolute space. The basic idea of the EMBR engine is that any animation (BML event) can be described as a sequence of key poses and agent states that occur at specific time stamps. The key poses and states of the agent can then be described using several animation techniques, such as forward kinematics (FK) and inverse kinematics (IK). The transitions between key poses can be smoothed using non-linear interpolation. The conversion of the BML event into EMBR animation is carried out through the conversion of BML elements into EMBR plans of movement, resulting from the static semantic lexicon of the conversational agent. From the viewpoint of BML attributes, they are adaptable in the number of repetitions and in spatial range.

The *Articulated Communicator Engine* (ACE) (Kopp & Wachsmuth, 2004) integrates the animation tool for the behavior realization, which enables the modeling of virtual conversational agents using procedural behavior description language, named MURML. The ACE engine is independent from the graphical platform and is able to synthesize prosodically synchronized co-verbal behavior in the form of multimodal expressions that involve: body movements, gestures of arms and hands, and facial expressions. One of the key features of the ACE framework represents the behavior realization that includes *speech synthesis*, *animation planning*, and *behavior realization*. The ACE engine implements the advanced synchronization techniques and the co-articulation of gestures and speech. Kopp & Wachsmuth presume that some expression can be performed gradually and in pieces. Therefore, each gesture is adjusted to the duration of the corresponding word (or even phrase within the given expressive piece). Transitions of movement and pauses between successive expressions are designed in such a way that the conversational agent is prepared for the synchrony of the upcoming expressions.

DTask & LiteBody (Bickmore et al., 2009) present methods for the development and usage of conversational agents in web applications. DTask is a designer of the dialogue, and is based on a hierarchical decomposition of tasks. The LiteBody represents the web plugin used for behavior realization, which includes a conversational agent, as well as a static set of co-verbal behavior. With the help of LiteBody, we can interpret and animate the co-verbal behavior, described in the form of BML events. The co-verbal behavior that can be realized, however, is limited to lip-sync, gaze, and animation of basic emotions and eye blinking.

EXPRESSIVE CONVERSATIONAL MODEL EVA

The expressive model of co-verbal behavior proposed in this book is able to automatically convert general and unannotated text into co-verbal behavior, composed of non-verbal elements that are associated (correlated) with the verbal behavior (speech). In this way the input text can be represented as multimodal output, composed of speech and visual communication channels. The co-verbal behavior model in Figure 3 also takes care of the synchronization of verbal and non-verbal information that is necessary in order to achieve real naturalness. This is performed both in the domain of the intent, as well as in the time domain. Its architecture also follows the SAIBA concept (Jeremy et al., 2011), since the concept of formulation and co-verbal behavior generation is divided into the following 3 modules: *design and identification of intent* (intent planning), *behavior planning*, and *behavior realization*. As seen in Figure 3, the expressive co-verbal behavior model divides the co-verbal behavior generation process into a generation module and a realization module. This division is based on these facts: speech and gestures are created through the complementary (same) mental processes that function outwards synchronously (McNeill, 2005a, Kendon, 2004), and that the primary aspect of non-verbal behavior is not semantic in nature. Consequently, the gestures contribute mainly in designing and introducing speech content (Herrera et al., 2009). Therefore, the non-verbal behavior is formed simultaneously with verbal behavior (speech). The architecture of the model takes into account the fact that the simultaneousness of several formulations has to be supported. Namely, the synthesis of gestures and speech can be represented as two simultaneous processes, whereby the synthesis of gestures is also based on those features that become available during the speech synthesis process.

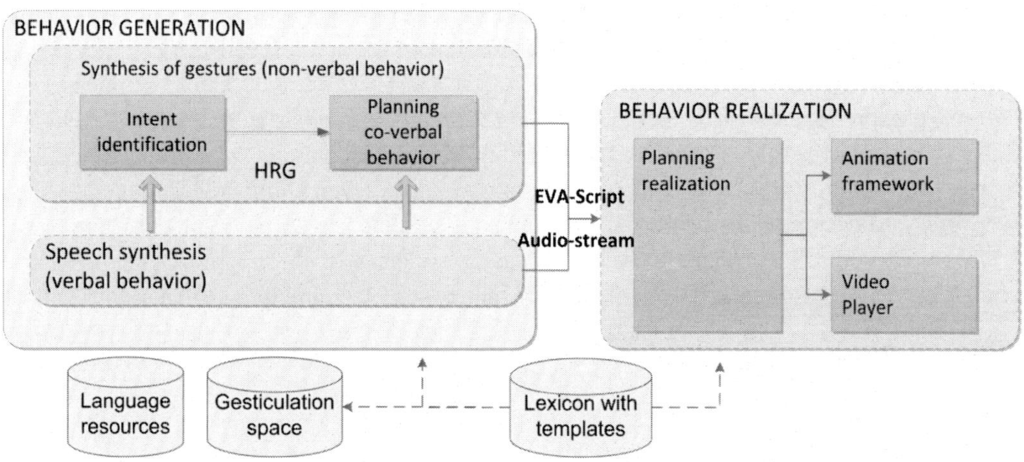

Figure 3. The architecture of the EVA expressive co-verbal behavior model.

The expressiveness represents the way in which the information is presented through the physical realization of the co-verbal behavior (through movement) (Allwood, 2013; Allwood et al., 2007a). The expressiveness of movement is modeled using the following dimensions: *activity* (this models the density of movements), *spatial dimension* (this models the amplitude and the spatial distribution of motion), *time dimension* (this models the duration of movement), *continuity dimension* (this models the internal continuity, and the movement continuity between gestures), *power dimension* (this models the dynamics and the magnitude of movement), and *repeatability dimension* (this models the tendency regarding duplications/replications of consecutive short movements that occur together) (Allwood, 2013; Allwood et al., 2007a). The co-verbal behavior generation module represents that part of the expressive model that takes care of the formulation of speech, the selection of non-verbal elements composed together into gestures, and the synchronization of gestures with speech. The module consists of the following three concurrent processes: *intent identification*, *behavior planning*, and *speech synthesis*. The *speech synthesis* process converts input text into speech. This process in the *co-verbal behavior generation* module represents the source of those linguistic and prosodic features that are used for non-verbal behavior generation. In the *intent identification* process, depending on the content (which may be thought, emotional, or connotative), the possible set of linguistic and prosodic features is defined. The linguistic expressions, regardless of the communication channel through which they are transmitted (e.g., oral, gesticulation, or written), represent some meaningful content or concept. The purpose of the oral content is actually performed by the classification of linguistic expressions into the semiotic classes. The *behavior planning* process involves the prediction and filtering of interpretations of the intent of expressions, and the synchronization of verbal and co-verbal elements regarding time and shape (the so-called life-cycle of the gestures). The algorithms in the *co-verbal behavior generation* module use several linguistic and non-linguistic resources that relate to the generation of both verbal and non-verbal behavior, such as: lexicons, corpora, rules, acoustic database, and machine-learned models, which relate to the synthesis of verbal information, and the gesticular space, rules and lexicon of primes (gesticon), which relate to the synthesis of non-verbal behavior. The results of this module are the procedural description of the co-verbal behavior (which can be converted into animated synthetic behavior), and speech (which represents the verbal behavior). The *behavior realization* module consists of those algorithms and animation methods that are needed for representing the structured co-verbal behavior, generated by the *behavior generation* module, to the user in the form of expressive co-verbal behavior, which is then presented as an animated movement of the virtual conversational agent. Therefore, this module contains: *planning realization* process, *animation framework*, and *player*. The *planning realization* process changes the procedural description of the co-verbal behavior into parallel/sequential transformations' sets of movement controllers. Namely, in the dictionary of shapes, the appropriate procedural template (EVA-script) is selected, added into the animation plan, and then realized.

Chapter 2

A SYSTEM FOR THE GENERATION OF CO-VERBAL CONVERSATIONAL BEHAVIOR

INTRODUCTION

Speech and co-verbal behavior (gestures, facial expressions, emotions) together are generated through complementary thinking processes that appear synchronous (McNeill, 2005a; Kendon, 2004). Therefore, the fusion of algorithms used for speech synthesis and for co-verbal behavior generation into the common processing engine is proposed. The architecture of the system for generating the co-verbal behavior is presented in Figure 4. In this way, we gain efficient and highly scalable architecture, representing actually an extension of the general speech synthesis engine (TTS). The architecture represents a multimodal core, able to convert general and unannotated text into speech, accompanied with corresponding gesticulation and lip movements, which are suitably aligned in order to look natural. The reasons for such design of the architecture are several, but they are mainly arising from the theory behind the correlation of verbal and co-verbal behavior, which says:

1. Part of the thinking processes, which relates to the co-verbal behavior generation is based on lexica and lexical relations. Based on these processes some shapes of co-verbal behavior can be directly related to words, phrases, morpho-syntactic sequences, or sequences of even minor linguistic units, such as syllables (McNeill, 2005b; Esposito Ana & Antonietta, 2011). According to Pierce (Krauss et al., 2011; Atkin, 2010), the intent of such co-verbal behavior can be identified and described by using semiotic classification and semiotic classes. The features of individual semiotic class are identified mainly by words, phrases, part-of-speech sequences, morpho-syntactic characteristics of sentences, and sentence types.
2. The second part of the thinking processes, which relates to the co-verbal behavior generation, is based on paralinguistic and non-verbal information, which is passed by gestures and speech (DeCarolis et al., 2004; Allwood, 2010). Therefore, the intent can also be introduced in the form of those expressions that represent communication concepts, such as speaker exchange, feedback, finding and planning communicative sequence. Such expressions and behavior are formed by using complex communicative mechanisms (functions) that people use during interaction (Allwood,

2010; McNeill, 2005a). The relationship between verbal and co-verbal behavior is established through features, such as: pauses, nasal sounds, speech corrections, interrogative sentences, and linguistic fillers (e.g., hmm ..., ehhh ..., ufff, aaaa etc.) (Kendon, 2004).

In the architecture in Figure 4, the TTS system named PLATTOS is used (Rojc & Mlakar, 2011), although any other TTS system can be used. Nevertheless, PLATTOS is flexible, already modular, and a time- and memory-efficient engine. By using the FSM formalism, the language-dependent resources are separated from the language-independent TTS engine core.

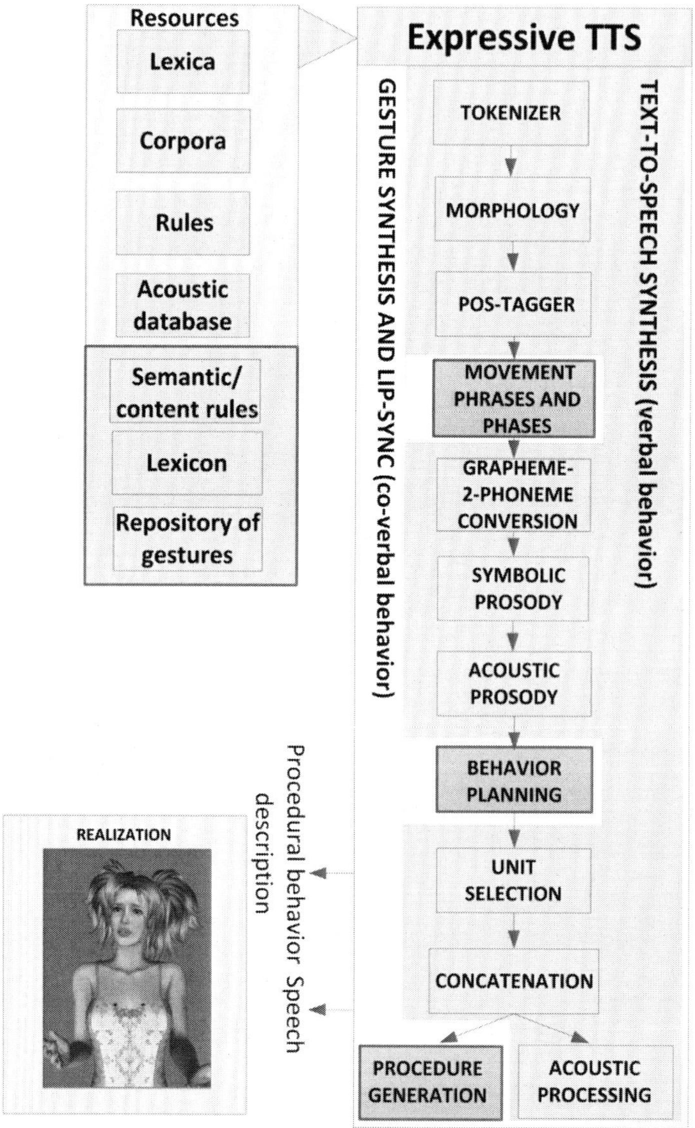

Figure 4. The architecture of the expressive text-to-speech synthesis engine.

The modular TTS architecture allows for the plain integration of new algorithms, and building complex feature structures, in any module. Furthermore, the adding of additional modules and algorithms is well supported by the flexible mechanism of double-linked lists (deques). These general characteristics are also desired for any other TTS system in order to be used efficiently in the proposed architecture.

This architecture can be used for complex and advanced co-verbal behavior generation based on general text. It is able to exploit the knowledge attained in the core TTS engine. Nevertheless, in order to align gestures and speech at both symbolic and temporal levels, the algorithms and modules for co-verbal behavior generation have to be properly fused, able to share data, language-dependent and independent resources, and machine-learned models. Therefore, the architecture of the PLATTOS TTS system has to be extended by the integration of the following modules: *tagger of movement phrases and phases*, *behavior-planning* module, and *procedure-generation* module. The *tagger of movement phrases and phases* is responsible for the definition of the so-called content units (CU) in the text, and for determining their intent. The output of this module then consists of a set of CUs, which represent their possible interpretations and representations in the form of co-verbal gestures. The *behavior-planning* module firstly performs a so-called elimination process for the generated set of possible interpretations. This step is based on features extracted by the TTS engine's *symbolic prosody*, *acoustic prosody*, and *grapheme-to-phoneme conversion* modules. As a result, only those CUs that best represent the intent and the meaning for specific input text are selected. Namely, among the possible definitions of CUs, only those that will actually be involved in the co-verbal behavior realization on the conversational agent (ECA) are kept. Next, for each selected CU and its physical representation, the synchronization procedure is performed, the so-called formal and prosodic alignment. By considering the formal and prosodic consistency of phrases in the CU, the module performs a process, named external synchronization of shape, in order to guarantee the continuity of movement at the boundaries of CUs. The *behavior-planning* module then designs and performs the lip-sync process, which is very important for a higher degree of naturalness of the final multimodal output. In the last step, the *behavior-planning* module takes care of absolute timing when the individual CU and corresponding co-verbal behavior with specified delay and duration are aligned with the temporal characteristics of the synthesized speech signal. At the end, the architecture creates both the XML procedural description of the co-verbal behavior, and corresponding speech signal. Both outputs are provided to the animation framework used for the realization of the co-verbal behavior. In this way, the generated synchronized verbal and co-verbal behavior can finally be represented as a multimodal output.

The proposed architecture serves to extract all of the information about the meaning, intent, shape, and synchronization of co-verbal behavior, fully automatically from general text. Linguistic, morpho-syntactic and prosodic characteristics of speech are accessed by individual modules accessed through the established dequeing mechanism. Those algorithms and modules that are needed for generating a co-verbal behavior (the visual communication channel) are in the architecture based on prosodic and linguistic features, which are provided by the TTS engine. The fusion of the TTS engine and the co-verbal behavior generation part result in better efficiency and better interactive system responsiveness. Further, the architecture also inherits and retains the modular structure, whereby the common processing flow supports the effective use and sharing of resources between algorithms, fast and complex feature sets (as soon as proper data are available), and the optimization of individual processes. Unlike other similar systems, which in general consider TTS engine and co-verbal behavior generation as two independent processes, in this architecture the synthesis of speech and co-verbal behavior description are generated through one common processing stream. In the following subsections those data structures that can be beneficial for the proposed architecture of an expressive speech synthesizer are presented.

THE DATA STRUCTURES FOR THE EXPRESSIVE SPEECH SYNTHESIZER

The architecture presented in Figure 4 can be efficiently and flexibly realized using the following data structures: deques, heterogeneous-relational graphs, and finite-state machines (FSM). The FSMs can be efficiently used, for example, for separating language-dependent resources from the language-independent system core. Within the expressive speech synthesizer, the language-dependent resources are e.g., lexicons, corpora, language rules, acoustic databases, and linguistic rules. Besides, the FSMs also provide the optimal time- and memory-efficient representation of resources. Regarding the co-verbal part, the architecture incorporates language-independent sources, such as lexicon, and gesture database. The concept of deque mechanism can be used to support the flexible integration of new algorithms (or modules) into the common processing flow of the common engine. Further, heterogeneous relational graphs (HRG) can be used for storing and hierarchically relating several linguistic, acoustic, and gesticulation information, which is extracted from the input text (or predicted) during the processing of the general input text. All data can be stored in several relational levels, from the *phoneme* level up to the *movement-phrases* level. The HRG structures can also be used to construct complex features that are needed in accessing patterns in lexicon, or machine-learned models.

The Deque Mechanism

The deque mechanism (Rojc & Kačič, 2007) consists of several individual deques. The deques have been proposed since linguistic elements can be added, or removed at the beginning (head), or at the end (tail) of the queue. In this way, they represent a flexible data structure for transporting several data between the engine's modules. As proposed by Rojc and Kačič (2007), for each individual engine's module, a specific deque is dedicated. These deques are then properly linked into the so-called deque mechanism, which runs all processes in the engine in a successive manner, by performing co-verbal operations and TTS processing steps on the input text. The deque mechanism also supports easy access and tracing of the outputs between individual modules. In this way, the deque mechanism allows flexible extension toward the proposed expressive speech synthesizer's architecture in Figure 4. At least the following deques have to be created:

- tokenizer deque,
- morphology deque,

- POS-tagger deque,
- phrase and phase-tagger deque,
- grapheme-to-phoneme deque,
- symbolic prosody deque,
- acoustic prosody deque,
- behavior planning deque,
- unit selection deque,
- concatenation deque,
- behavior generation deque, and
- acoustic processing deque.

As can be seen in Figure 5, each individual module of the expressive speech synthesizer has its own deque. The mechanism runs the engine through a hierarchy of classes that are derived from the base class, named *ExpTTSEngine*. It is constructed during initialization, when all deques are created, and when reference to the corresponding deque structure is assigned to each individual module. The mechanism then performs the deque filling process within a loop until the *tokenizer deque* is empty (there is no more input text).

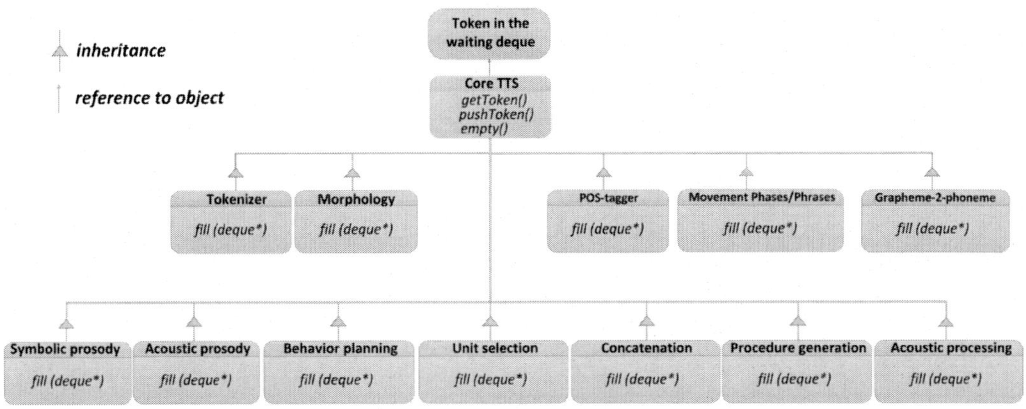

Figure 5. The modular structure of the expressive TTS system.

Naturally, at the beginning all deques in Figure 6 are empty. But during processing the input text, the tokenizer module keeps filling its deque with tokens that represent linguistically meaningful units, until the end of sentence (EOS) condition is detected. Before the next deque in line starts to fill, spaces, ends of lines (EOL), and other special characters that may occur in the general text are eliminated. The subsequent engine's algorithms works in general on complete sentences (not necessarily), which means that they do not do anything until they have in their deque all tokens of the complete sentence. In this way, the deque mechanism moves tokens from one deque into another deque, and the modules' algorithms (using external language resources) are able to generate linguistic, prosodic, acoustic and co-verbal data for a given sentence. When the last module detects the EOS token, the mechanism continues processing the next sentence, again by starting to fill the *tokenizer deque*.

The deque mechanism starts processing by using the reference to *acoustic deque*, and calling the function *getnexttoken*. This function is used for requesting the next element that is stored in the previous deque, where each element represents a token that is extracted by tokenizer module from the input text.

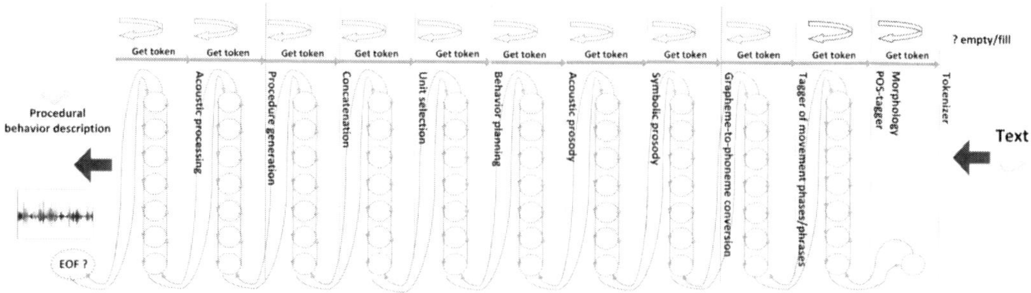

Figure 6. The deque mechanism of the expressive TTS system.

At the beginning, all deques are empty; therefore, the *empty* function in case of all deques returns the condition *true*. Consequently, the request is transferred down to the first *tokenizer deque*. Therefore, the tokenizer module starts filling its deque with tokens (e.g., finite-state machine (FSM)-based lexical scanner, used for parsing text into separators, words, acronyms, numbers, etc., until end-of-sentence or end-of-text conditions are detected). The tokenizer module stops filling its deque when the end-of-sentence condition is met. The last token is, therefore, dedicated token EOS or EOF. By using function *pushtoken (utterance*)*, the deque mechanism then pushes tokens from *tokenizer deque* to subsequent deque. In general, modules can start processing incoming tokens as soon as they are available in their deque. Nevertheless, when algorithms need the whole sentence for processing (usually this is the case), they have to wait until EOS or EOF token is present. For example, the *POS-tagger module* tags the whole sentence, where each word is assigned a part-of-speech (POS) tag that defines its linguistic features (e.g., noun, verb, adjective, case, gender, form, number, etc.). The linguistic features represent the basis for definition of the intent and, for the definition of location and the basic shape of co-verbal gestures. The POS-tagger is therefore followed by *phrase/phase-tagger module*. This module processes the linguistic phrases and identifies content units (*CU*), and corresponding word sequences (those words in *CUs* that coincide with the co-verbal behavior) within them. The phrase/phase-tagger module is followed by the *grapheme-to-phoneme conversion module*. In this module the way in which the input sentence should be pronounced is defined. The *grapheme-to-phoneme conversion module* is followed by the *symbolic prosody module*. This one is used to predict the phrase breaks, and to predict accentuation on the syllable level. The phrase breaks are later involved also in the prediction of segment durations and the duration of pauses in a sentence. This module is then followed by the *acoustic prosody module* that has to predict the duration of pauses and phonemes. When all durations are known, the *behavior generation module* already has available all required features in order to define and describe the co-verbal behavior; namely, the morpho-syntactic features, a set of probable *CUs*, their intent and meaningful words, and corresponding shapes. Further, the phonemic structure, syllable structure, prosodic features regarding segments and pauses (e.g., temporal values), and accentuation are also defined. Thus, in the *behavior generation module* we have to perform the elimination process, shape and time synchronization, and the synchronization of consecutive shapes. In this way, it is possible to determine the complete co-verbal structure, to perform the shape and lip-sync synchronization (regarding visemes), and to define the exact locations of meaningful elements of gestures and their duration, the shape and duration of movements that occur before/after the meaningful shape, and movement that is performed between two consecutive *CUs* that actually contain the co-verbal elements. Further, the *behavior generation module* builds the structure that describes the realization of those co-verbal gestures, which has to perform simultaneously with the generated speech signal. The modules for the selection of acoustic units and for the concatenation of selected acoustic segments follow. In the first one, the most appropriate acoustic units are selected, e.g., diphones, triphones or even larger units (in the case of corpus-based TTS systems). In the second one, the selected acoustic units are prepared for the speech synthesis algorithm, regarding pitch marks. Next, the behavior generation process continues with the *speech-synthesis module*. Here, algorithms such as PSOLA are used (Rojc and Kačič, 2007), whereby the selected units are adjusted according to the predicted acoustic prosodic features (pitch and duration). The last module is used for the generation of procedural descriptions of animation. In this module the adjustment and conversion of predicted co-verbal gestures into a descriptive language is performed, which can be directly used in the realization of movements on a virtual agent. When this is performed for the current sentence, the deque mechanism checks whether there is already an end-of-text token (EOF). When this condition is not yet met, the mechanism starts processing the next sentence; otherwise, the deque mechanism finishes the processing.

Heterogeneous Relational Graphs (HRG)

The *deque mechanism* performs several algorithms on the input sentence, while generating a lot of data, which can be related in many ways. Furthermore, data are also very heterogeneous. The heterogeneous relational graphs (HRG) have already proven to be a very suitable data structure for storing, accessing, relating, reusing, and changing speech-synthesis data (Taylor et al., 2001). The HRG structure can also be flexibly and dynamically built while running the *deque mechanism*, and can be used by any algorithm in any module, regardless of the type of process that the system performs, or data types. Therefore, the HRG structure is recommended to be used also for data that are generated by the expressive text-to-speech synthesizer, and for building complex feature vectors.

The HRG structures are dynamic and can be built gradually when processing the input text. Namely, each algorithm can change, or extend the structure with additional relations, and new elements. The structure consists of nodes, elements, and transitions. Nodes do not contain data, but are used for representing a point in space, and through which the elements are linked. Nodes and transitions define the relation between elements that are storing linguistic information. The relation structures can be trees, lists, or linear structures (Taylor et al., 2001). In the case of lists, the transitions are implemented by complementary pairs such as {*next*, *previous*}; therefore, transitions in a horizontal direction (*forward/backward*) are possible. In the case of trees, the transitions are implemented by complementary pairs {*parent*, *children1*, *children2*, ...}; therefore, transitions in a vertical direction are possible. In general, each element in a list or tree can be linked with several nodes, but each node can belong to exactly one relation level.

In the architecture of the expressive text-to-speech synthesizer, due to new modules, it is necessary to extend the HRG structure as proposed by Rojc and Kačič (2007). Namely, we need additional lists, as well as additional tree structures that are able to store and relate additional non-verbal and co-verbal information that is necessary for new algorithms, such as the synthesis of gestures and lip-sync (Figure 4).

The new HRG structure is proposed in Figure 7. Within the deque mechanism is the reference to the HRG structure given as an argument in the function *fill* that is used for filling deques with tokens (Figure 5). Additional algorithms also have to create several additional relation structures in the form of linear lists and trees (depending on data). Figure 7 presents the complete HRG structure as used in the last module of the expressive text-to-speech synthesizer.

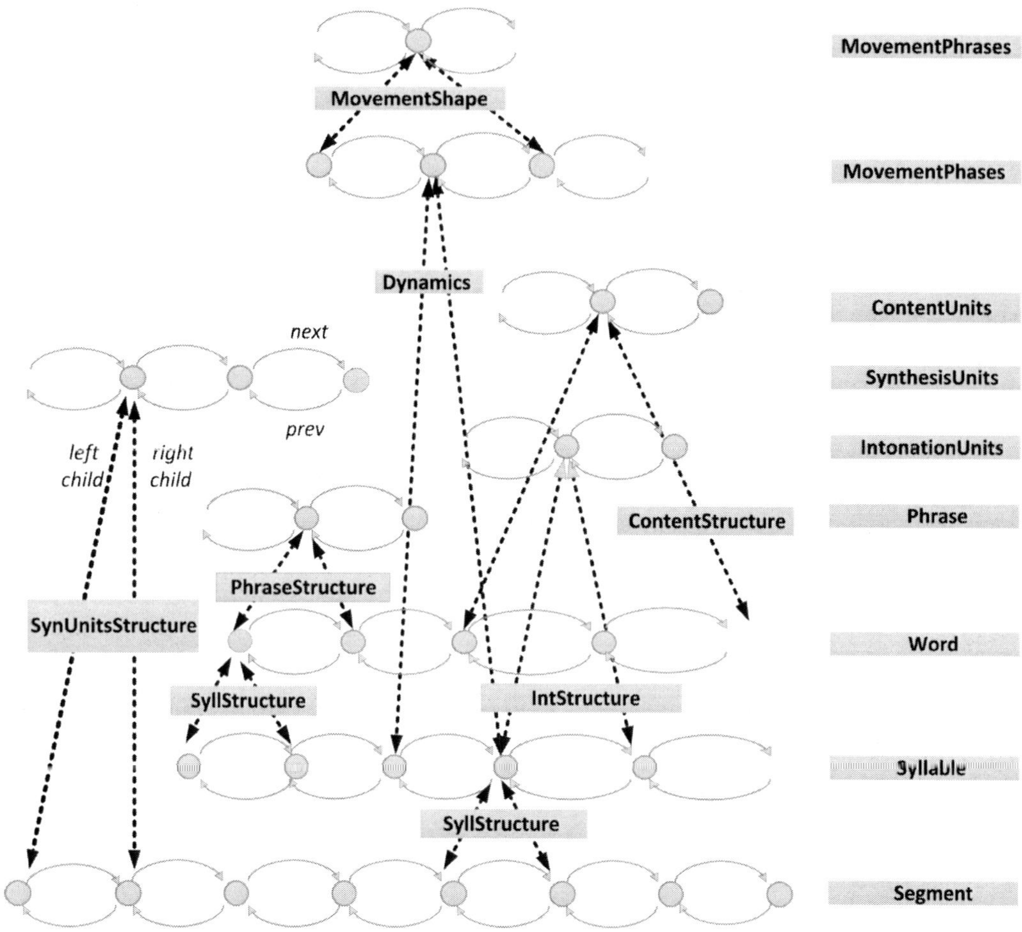

Figure 7. The HRG structure used for storing data and for feature construction in expressive TTS system.

In Figure 7 are relational structures in the form of linear lists, represented as horizontal transitions between states. They are named as follows: *Segments*, *Syllables*, *Words*, *Phrases*, *IntonationUnits*, *SynthesisUnits*, *ContentUnits*, *MovementPhases*, and *MovementPhrases*. Relational structures in the form of trees are then presented with vertical transitions. They are named as follows: *SyllStructure*, *IntonationStructure*, *SynUnitsStructure*, *ProsodicStructure*, *PhraseStructure*, *ContentStructure*, *Dynamics*, *DynamicsExtended* and *MovementShape*.

These relational structures can have a different number of elements, depending on the algorithm. Each element in a list or tree structure can carry several attributes and associated values. They are also added during processing. At the end the elements contain verbal features and those features relating to the co-verbal behavior generation processes. By using linear lists we can establish a relationship between elements within the horizontal relationship levels. In this way, it is possible to pass between current, previous, or next element, by using prefixes *p* (previous) and *n* (next). The tree-based relational structures allow for the creation of additional knowledge that benefits from the vertical relationships between elements in several horizontal relationships. In this way, complex features about the input text can also be built and exploited. For example, in Figure 7 the *MovementShape* and *MovementStructure* relation structures relate the elements in the *ContentUnits* relation structure with elements in the *MovementPhases* relational structure. Therefore, by using tree-based relations, we can assign to individual content unit (CU) those movement phases and shapes that should be carried out within given CU. Furthermore, the *ContentUnits* relation structure's elements are associated with elements in the *Words* relational structure by the *ContentStructure* relational structure. Elements in the *MovementPhases* relational structure are also associated with the elements in the *Syllables* relational structure by the *Dynamics* relational structure. Therefore, by using linear lists and trees in the HRG structure, we are able to create rich additional knowledge regarding the sentence-based co-verbal behavior, and they are also very helpful for performing the synchronization of verbal and co-verbal elements. It is also possible to easily update already created relational structures fully dynamically, which is usually the case with algorithms of the expressive speech synthesizer.

The HRG structure represents a flexible structure for knowledge representation about the co-verbal behavior. In order to access data or create features, the horizontal and vertical relational structures can be used by obtaining those elements and associated attributes' values that we need. In the HRG structure elements are stored representing syllables, words, phonemes, phrase breaks, movement phases, movement phrases, content units, etc. These elements store attributes and associated values such as POS tags, phoneme classes, phrase-break types, phoneme durations, semiotic class, accent, etc. Attributes are best to be named according to the features that are used by individual algorithms. In HRG structure the attribute values can be string, numbers (integer, or floating point numbers), or even objects.

Finite-State Machines (FSM)

Finite-state machines (FSM) represent a mathematical formalism which is very useful in several levels of natural language processing. Key benefits of FSMs are (Rojc & Kačič, 2007; Arnaud, 2000):

- *optimal speed*: time for searching strings is proportional to the length of the input string, and is independent of the size of the FSM.
- *modularity*: different linguistic objects can communicate with each other using operations defined on finite-state machines. A cascade of finite-state transducer can build complex relationships.
- *compactness*: the optimal presentation of resources in terms of size.

- *simple processing*: the construction of finite-state machines can be done using elementary operations, which are very similar to operations between sets. The complexity of operations is well defined, and they are suitable for real-time processing.

The finite-state machine is a directed graph, e.g., with labels on each transition, and with a finite number of states. The FSM machine can be described as follows:

$$K = (\Sigma, Q, i, F, E) \qquad (1)$$

where Σ represents a finite set, called the *alphabet*, Q represents a set of final states, i represents the initial state ($i \in Q$), F represents a set of final states ($F \subseteq Q$), and E represents a set of edges ($E \subseteq Q \times (\Sigma \cup \{\epsilon\}) \times Q$). The finite-state automaton K recognizes the word $\omega \in \Sigma^*$, when:

$$\omega = \varepsilon \text{ (empty symbol) and } i \in F \qquad (2)$$

or

$$\omega = cv,\ c \in \Sigma,\ v \in \Sigma^* \textit{ and automat } (\Sigma, Q, d(c,i), F, E) \textit{ recognizes word} \qquad (3)$$

From the perspective of co-verbal behavior generation, the finite-state machines allow for a compact representation of resources and rules, etc., and in terms of efficiency, the use of FSM is motivated by their time and memory efficiency. Time efficiency is achieved due to determinism; namely, the finite-state automata show linear dependence only at the inputs. Also, memory efficiency is ensured by standard algorithms for minimization. In the proposed architecture, the finite-state machines are used for the separation of language-dependent resources and the language-independent core of the expressive synthesizer, and for a time- and memory-efficient representation of resources that are used by the system.

The Language Resources of the Co-Verbal Behavior Generation System

The architecture of the co-verbal behavior generation system needs external language-dependent resources (as shown in Figure 4 and Figure 8). All these resources are separated from the language-independent core using FSMs. Language-dependent sources are: *corpora*, *linguistic rules*, *semantic/semiotic grammar* and *lexicon*, and *gestures*. The more important language-independent resource is the *dictionary of shapes*. In the dictionary of shapes we store structures of movements that the conversational agent is able to realize, or animate. These are actual descriptions of body movement and body forms, which represent a certain concept of co-verbal behavior (e.g., fist, smile, turning eyes, etc.), and how these can be described as a physical manifestation in the form of articulators (movement controllers). This repository, therefore, depends on the design of the conversational agent, and not the language for which a conversational agent is designed.

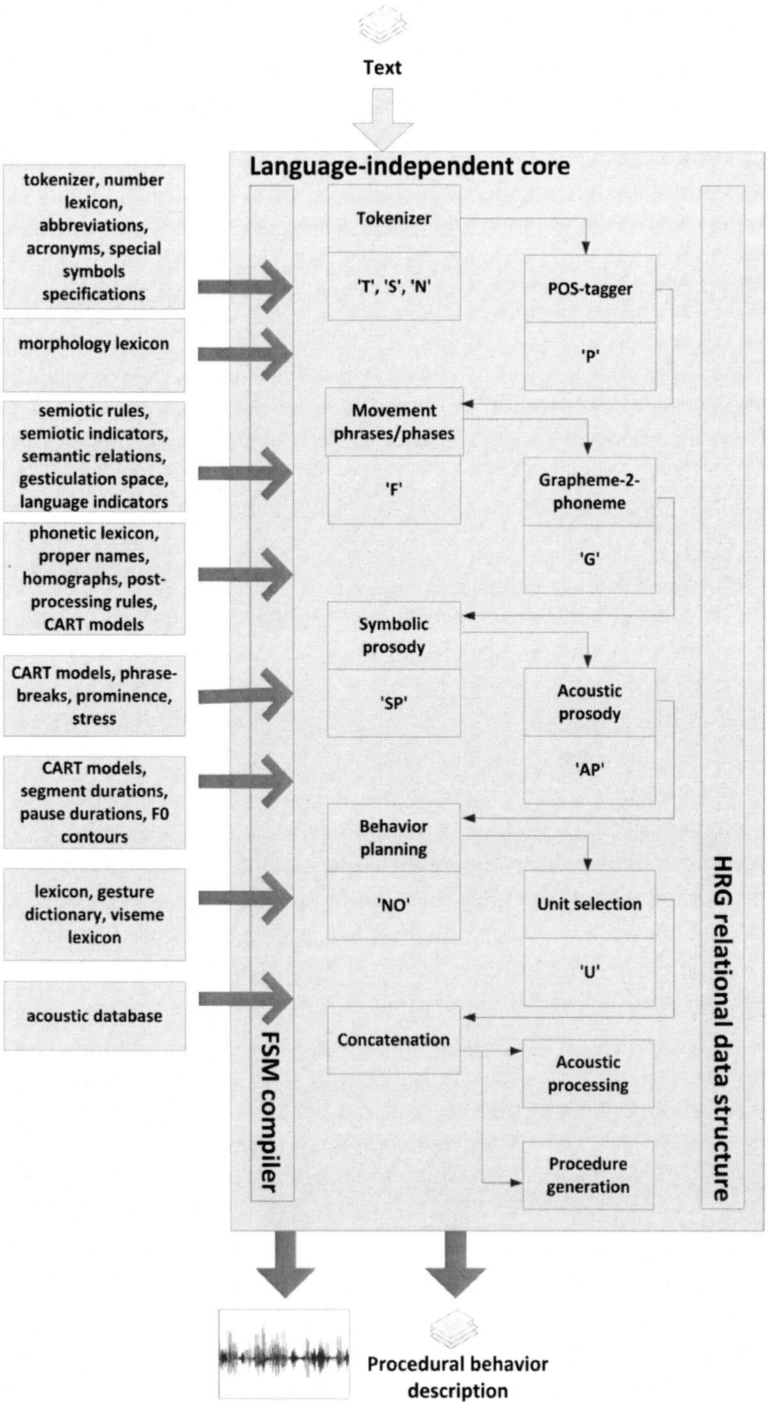

Figure 8. The language resources of the expressive TTS system.

In Figure 8 the resources are integrated into the system using FSMs, where resources are represented as FSM (automata or transducer), or tuple structure, based on perfect-hash automata (Rojc and Kačič, 2007). By using the proprietary *FSM compiler*, we perform off-line the construction of all FSMs and tuples for language resources, such as *regular expressions*, *tokenizer*, etc. In the case of WFSM (weighted FSM), the transitions and/or final states can also be assigned weights (resolving ambiguities, by taking into account heuristics, or machine learning) (Mohri et al., 1996). In *symbolic and acoustic prosody modules*, and in the *co-verbal behavior generation module*, the CART trees can be used for the prediction of phrase-break positions and their type, and for the prediction of the accentuations on words etc., since CART trees are also time- and memory-efficient representations. In addition, they may also be represented as FSMs (Sproat & Riley, 1996).

Further, in the architecture of the expressive TTS system, the following FSMs can be built: FSMs for tokenizers named *T*, *S* and *N*. These can be compiled from the tokenizer's specification, the lexicon for numbers, abbreviations list, acronyms list, and special symbols list. Further, the general text contains many ambiguities (e.g., processing abbreviations, acronyms), and errors (e.g., misspellings, etc.). Therefore, for the TTS engine, the FSM-based spell-checker can also be built (for the automatic detection/replacement of erroneous words with the most probable ones), and FSMs for parsing abbreviations and acronyms, and the processing of special characters. The tokenizer module is then followed by the *POS-tagger*, which can be represented by finite state automata *P*. Additional resources here are, for example, morphological lexicon and linguistic rules. The POS-tagger performs the part-of-speech tagging of general text, where each word is assigned the tag, described according to MULTEXT-East[1] morpho-syntactic specifications (Erjavec, 2012).

The POS-tagger is then followed by the *phrase/phase tagger*. This module uses already assigned morpho-syntactic features in the sentence level, in order to define the so-called CUs that should represent the intents in the general text. According to the morpho-syntactic sequences, the *phrase/phase tagger* selects those sequences and shapes that are best able to describe and present the idea of the meaningful word within a given CU. The needed resources here can be integrated in the architecture as tuple (Daciuk & van Noord, 2004), named *F*. This tuple contains semiotic rules, semiotic indicators, and, when relevant, the semantic correlation between words and intent. This module is followed by the *grapheme-to-phoneme conversion module* that is represented by FSM named *G*. This is actually the finite-state transducer (FST), which is the representation of several language-dependent resources, such as: phonetic lexicons of general words and proper names, homographs, rules for processing phonetic transcriptions, and CART models used for unknown words. In modules for symbolic and acoustic prosody and in co-verbal behavior generation module CART trees are again used. In the expressive TTS system we have to predict the positions and types of prosodic phrases and accentuations to define *CUs*, to define meaningful words and shapes, etc. As presented, the modular architecture that is based on deque mechanism, FMSs, and HRG structure, enable several resources to be flexibly integrated, while preserving the time- and memory efficiency of the system.

In the next chapter, the annotation process based on real multimodal dialogue – through which we are able to build such resources as *dictionary of shapes*, *semiotic grammar*, and *co-verbal behavior lexicon*, named gesticon – is presented in detail. The whole process covers the annotation, definition of annotation scheme, annotation tools, and annotation procedures (descriptions of individual communicative concepts).

---

[1] MULTEXT-East, http://nl.ijs.si/ME/V4/msd/html/msd-sl.html

Chapter 3

THE ANNOTATION AND DESCRIPTION OF CO-VERBAL BEHAVIOR

INTRODUCTION

Those mechanisms that are used during speech formulation, when people are planning, designing, and generating non-verbal movements, represent one of the most important aspects of expressive co-verbal behavior generation. In other words, co-verbal behavior is much more than just a set of synchronous static movements, regarding the manifestation. Co-verbal behavior is namely reflected in the form of a complex, and not yet fully understood set of conscious and subconscious mental processes, which are difficult to describe even with complex and adaptive software algorithms. Therefore, researchers from several multi-disciplinary scientific fields (e.g., psychology, sociology, computer science, etc.) are still analyzing and developing standards for describing the verbal and non-verbal behavior that people perform during natural interaction in greater detail. These descriptions then serve as a basis for the generation and implementation of rules and modeling algorithms that are needed in the model for co-verbal behavior generation. The multimodal annotations represent, therefore, that elementary approach which can be used in the expressive co-verbal behavior generation system, for building language-dependent and language-independent resources.

The multimodal corpora represent a key resource that is needed for both the analysis of human behavior, as well as for modeling the co-verbal behavior and for the realization of behavior on conversational agents (Jokinen & Pelachaud, 2013). The recordings of television interviews and recordings of theater plays represent a relatively reliable source of actual natural co-verbal behavior (Martin et al., 2006b). Nevertheless, these recordings are usually quite formal, and typically do not fully reflect natural spontaneous responses. The main problem of laboratory or artificially obtained corpora represents the level of spontaneity that can be observed during communication. Namely, the everyday natural interaction between people is not asynchronous (Campbell, 2013). The interaction in the dialogue is a well-structured process of so-called *active participation* and includes both active listening and understanding, as well as the active contribution of the content. Therefore, there is the continuous and mutual supervision of attention and mutual planning and developing of themes, from the speaker's as well as from the listener's side. During exchanging information, we are able to detect via the speech channel in the everyday environment a considerable fragmentation and overlapping as a result of poorly structured sentences, ambient noise, mutual completion of statements, accents, denial, etc. Therefore, those interruptions affect successful understanding and communication (Schegloff, 2007). In contrast to formal interviews, non-formal interviews and corresponding corpora typically provide far more authentic relationships between verbal and non-verbal behavior. These corpora can also include phenomena that normally cannot be found in formal corpora (e.g., overlapping, low grammatical regularity, etc.), and consequently describe the whole process around exchanging information in much more dynamic and less predictable ways. In the proposed expressive co-verbal behavior model, the development of a non-formal corpus is therefore proposed, which is based on several TV talk shows in the Slovenian language.

The annotation scheme is represented in general by a set of several tags that are assigned to several data elements. These tags are assigned to data elements so that they reflect different physical, perceptional, or functional features. Therefore, by using categories and their attributes, in the annotation schemes several phenomena being studied can be described. Further, the annotation schemes are in general classified into so-called *functional schemes* and *formal schemes*. The *functional schemes* mainly discuss the functional and non-functional correlations between several information channels used in the dialogue. In most cases, the *functional schemes* do not discuss the shape and the movement dynamics themselves, but they describe the movement only on an abstract level by including its position, direction, and that body part which is actually used in the execution of movement (e.g., head nodding, finger pointing, etc.). The *functional schemes*, therefore, describe the behavior only at the highest contextual level, where we are able to define correlations between individual modalities, which synchronously (simultaneously) appear in the dialogue. These correlations are established based on communicative and uncommunicative dialogue functions, semantic and pragmatic structures, and the personal and emotional characteristics of the speaker/listener. Therefore, the *functional schemes* are one of the best ways of creating rules for modeling the co-verbal behavior. The *formal schemes*, on the other hand, describe the movements' shapes in high resolution. By using them, we are able to define the expressive properties of the observed movement, for each body part. By combining both annotation procedures, we are then able to create a *co-verbal behavior lexicon*, which can also be adapted, by considering the functional role in the dialogue (by considering the context).

For example, the *MUMIM scheme* proposed by Allwood et al. (2007b), is focused on the annotation of the following three communication functions: *feedback*, *speaker exchange*, and *sequencing*. This scheme also describes their relationship with multimodal elements in the dialogue. Further, Jokinen (Jokinen, 2009) presents hardly noticeable features (the so-called *subtle cues*), which are expressed in the form of gestures, facial expressions, and eye-gaze, and which represent that multimodal inventory which people use for *feedback* or during dialogue management. Bergmann (Bergmann & Kopp, 2010) discusses the relationship between contextual factors (the reference features, and discourse) and gestures. Furthermore, she classifies the multimodal elements into *systematic* (distributed between speakers), and *unique* (specific to each individual) ones.

Quite the opposite can be said in the case of *formal schemes*. These schemes are mainly focused on a detailed analysis and description of the shape, and the internal dynamics of the movement, while the relations with the functionality and the intent for using some movements in the dialogue are rather limited. Specifically, the movement's shape is usually described through the spatial characteristics of the movement regulators, while the movement dynamics is described by a temporal description of the changes in the movement's spatial characteristics. The FORM scheme presented by Martell (2005) is one example of a *formal scheme*. It considers those most exposed body poses (key poses) that are observed during the propagation of each movement. By considering the observed segment of movement, the key spatial poses of the observed body part are first defined and temporally described. In these identified key poses the spatial characteristics of those regulators of movement that are involved in the generation of the observed pose are then accurately identified. Furthermore, these individual key poses are then bound into an annotation graph, which enables the integration of communication rules. The FORM is limited primarily to manual gesticulation and the annotation of hand shapes. The same is true for the annotation scheme, named COGEST (Trippel et al., 2004). This scheme even further distinguishes between static (poses, and hold movements) and dynamic movements (those movements where both the source and trajectory can be determined). The descriptions of shape in high resolution, that are possible using a *formal scheme*, are then reflected in the expressiveness of modeling the artificial behavior, and in very time-consuming analysis and development of *co-verbal behavior lexicons*. Kipp et al. (2007b) also propose an annotation scheme for describing co-verbal gestures. Their approach is based on the fact that co-verbal gesticulation between speakers does not differ only in regard to intent and the instant when gesticulation is issued (namely, why someone gesticulates, and where within the sentence they actually gesticulate), but also in regard to the shape that is used during the gesticulation. Therefore, for the annotation scheme the speaker's style is also described. Further, the gesture is described in the form of gesticulation units (so-called *G-units*) (McNeill, 2005a; Kendon, 2004; Kita et al., 1998), which consist of *gesticulation phrases* and *phases*. The *gesticulation phases* are analogous to the *movement phases* of Kita et al. (1998), and are described as:

- *The stroke phase* F_S: a movement phase in which the gesture's dynamics and shape are manifested with highest clarity. This is part of that movement which is also manifested with most energy. The F_S represents the gesture's core and is the most relevant reflection of the intent.
- *The preparation phase* F_P: a movement phase that is always located before the stroke phase F_S. It represents the preparation and placement of body parts in the initial manifestation of the F_S. Usually, it can be observed as that movement which possesses less energy.
- *The retraction phase* F_R: is part of that movement which leads body parts involved in creating physical manifestations into a relaxed (elementary) state. This state usually follows the stroke phase F_S, or the retraction phase F_R, and is in general maintained for any length of time. The retraction phase F_R can be followed only by the next preparation or stroke phase.
- *The hold phase* F_H (*pre-stroke-hold* F_{HS}, or *post-stroke-hold* F_{SH}): is part of that movement which occurs at the end of the stroke phase F_S or just before the beginning of F_S. F_H is represented as a shorter withleding of the physical manifestation.

The spatial form of motion is described by Kipp et al. (2007b) as a set of abstract body configurations that occur at the beginning, or at the end, of the preparation phase F_P. Here, the abstract description of body configurations is further enriched using the tool for the specification of 3D poses. In this way it is possible to describe the individual configuration in the form of spatial configuration of *movement controllers* (*articulators*). The annotation schemes may, therefore, contain several numbers of levels, which can be used for describing the observed phenomena. Nevertheless, the annotation schemes may also contain only one level for describing the in-depth analysis of analytical categories. Their main purpose is to describe phenomena using analytical categories and those associated attributes which reflect the issue under consideration. In general, each annotation scheme addresses the following issues (Jokinen & Pelachaud, 2013):

- the identification of those elements that are relevant from the communicative point of view;
- the data analysis and definition of boundaries of these elements; and
- the correlation of those relationships which relate these elements in different annotation levels.

THE METHODOLOGY FOR MEASURING THE RELIABILITY OF THE ANNOTATION SCHEMES

The agreement regarding the coding represents a set of methodological recommendations by which it is possible to evaluate the suitability of annotated data and to ensure the consistency and reliability of annotations. In these recommendations those conditions and restrictions with which different annotators have to comply during the annotation of individual elements are defined (Cavicchio & Poesio, 2009). By using the statistical methods, which are part of the agreement regarding the coding, the reliability of the annotated data can be evaluated by considering the agreement between annotators (e.g., how many times the annotators assign the same category to the same element). The *agreement rate* without coincidences can be measured using the following Cohen's kappa coefficient (Cavicchio & Poesio, 2009):

$$\kappa = \frac{P(A) - P(E)}{1 - P(E)} \quad (4)$$

where *P (A)* represents those proportions of elements about which the annotators are agreed, and *P(E)* represents the hypothetical (expected) probability of their agreement. For example, if the annotators completely agree, then the value of kappa is 1. When the annotators do not agree at all, the value of kappa is 0. Further, on real data, the value of a kappa coefficient above 0.8 indicates almost perfect agreement between annotators; the values between 0.6 and 0.8 signify considerable agreement; the values between 0.4 and 0.6 indicate moderate agreement; and values between 0.2 and 0.4 denote slight agreement (Jokinen & Pelachaud, 2013). When the kappa reaches a value of 0.6 or more, the condition regarding the reliability of annotated data is already achieved.

In the case of dialogue annotations, the κ value, due to irregularities in communication, overlapping speech, unfinished and inserted sentences, and the subjectivity of annotators, often has quite low values. The annotator can, for example, also reflect the tendency of annotating elements with a particular category (e.g., he perceives deictic gestures more likely as iconic gestures, and therefore annotates them more often). The probability of random agreement between annotators regarding the selection of such category P(E) is, therefore, increased. Consequently, the general agreement measured by κ is decreased. Therefore, alternative statistical methods for measuring the reliability of annotated data have been proposed. One of the most commonly used is Krippendorff's α coefficient (Fabri et al., 2007) which, in the calculations of reliability, also takes into account the bias of the distribution of categories. Krippendorff's coefficient is defined as:

$$\alpha = 1 - \frac{D_o}{D_e} \tag{5}$$

where D_o describes the actual disagreement about the described values of the elements, and D_e describes the expected disagreement, in the case where annotators annotate elements randomly, and without considering their actual characteristics. The α coefficient can be used on incomplete data, and on any set of values and metric types (binary, nominal, coordinate, polar, interval, etc.). Further, the advantage of the α coefficient is that the subjectivity of the annotators is taken into account, and that the calculated reliabilities can be compared between different types of annotations with an unequal size of patterns.

Tools for Tagging the Co-Verbal Behavior

The annotation schemes are based on different communication theories and are established on the basis of real data. The multimodal annotation also includes several independent data streams and elements that we can observe, describe, and relate using the annotation scheme. Therefore, the annotation tool must in general support the analysis and processing of multimodal information, and the fusion of multimodal input streams (e.g., speech, gestures, facial expressions, etc.). Below those tools that are usually proposed and used for performing annotation and transcriptions are briefly described.

Praat

Praat[1] is a tool used for the analysis and synthesis of speech (Boersma & Weenink, 2013). By analyzing speech in Praat, we are able to annotate speech segments and transcribe individual spoken words. The transcribed text and corresponding timestamps are stored into files. Praat is otherwise primarily intended for the analysis of the phonetic characteristics of speech. Regarding the analysis and speech synthesis, therefore, supports a wide range of tasks, e.g., spectral analysis, formant analysis, articulatory synthesis, Klatt's acoustic synthesis, etc. In addition to speech analysis, we are able to perform probabilistic and statistical processing, using methods such as multidimensional scaling, component analysis, discriminant analysis, etc. The transcription and text analysis is otherwise feasible in the form

[1] http://www.fon.hum.uva.nl/paul/praat.html.

of annotated intervals and corresponding timestamps, and the phonetic alphabet, but it is difficult to observe each description within the transcription. Praat also does not allow for analyzing the overlapped speech; namely, when two or more speakers talk simultaneously. Nevertheless, the main advantage of the tool is its compatibility with a wide range of other annotation tools, which are generally used for the annotation of discourse.

Transcriber

Transcriber[2] (Geoffrois et al., 2000) is another annotation tool that is used for the transcription and annotation of speech signals. It is primarily designed for research in linguistics. In general, it supports multi-layer hierarchical segmentations, the annotation of entities using labels, management of the list of speakers and topics, and observation and relating the overlapped speech. The user interface of the tool comprises: *signal editor*, which is used for the analysis of speech waveforms and their segmentations; and *text editor*, which is used for creating, displaying, and correcting transcriptions. Transcriber is a tool primarily intended for transcribing the speech signal into text. Like the Praat, it is not most suitable for the annotation of discourse and conversational dialogue directly.

Anvil

Anvil[3] is a tool for the annotation of video data (Heloir et al., 2010). This tool supports the manual coding of those phenomena which appear in the video data, usually in several layers and in some chronological time sequence. The official website says that the tool was developed for the research of human gestures in 2000, and that it has been used in several studies that relate to e.g., human-machine interaction, linguistics, ethology, anthropology, psychotherapy, virtual agents, computer animation, and even oceanography (Kipp, 2011).

The user has to define a coding scheme before he actually starts annotating data. The user is able to directly create this scheme using the XML editor, or by using the GUI, which is part of the Anvil tool. The structure of the coding scheme is based on tracks, attributes, and their values. In Anvil, the track (also layer, or level) represents a container for each type of information (e.g., *movement phase*). Further, each track can contain several elements that can be edited and filled in terms of pairs of attributes/values. The annotation within individual tracks never overlaps. Version 5.0 already supports even relationships within individual tracks, in order to allow the user to code the major entities (e.g., *gesture*), and then split each entity into separate tracks (e.g., into *movement phases*). Several tracks can also be joined into sets by taking into account their semantic properties (e.g., joining tracks that refer to linguistics, or joining those tracks that refer to gestures). Further, the user can also insert instructions for coding and documentation during the development of specifications that can then be accessed during annotation. To each track's attribute that is documented, a small question mark is assigned; when the user clicks on it, the documentation for corresponding

[2] http://trans.sourceforge.net/en/presentation.php.
[3] http://www.anvil-software.org/.

attributes is shown, together with associated tags. The user is able to generate the specifications as a set of HTML files, by selecting *Edit→ Create Coding Manual*. In order to read specifications, any browser can be used. The Anvil also supports the inclusion of those annotation files that were generated in other tools, such as: in PRAAT (*TextGrid* file), or in ELAN (also annotation tool), in order that the user can view, modify, or analyze data using the Anvil tool.

Elan

ELAN[4] (EUDICO Linguistic Annotator) is a tool for the multi-level annotation of video and/or audio data that has been developed at the MPI institute (Max-Planck-Institute) (Sloetjes & Wittenburg, 2008). It is developed in JAVA language and can be used on Windows, Macintosh, and Linux. The tool integrates a data model that includes time information and is stored in XML format. The tool is most often used for annotating digital audio and video data. The tool has been developed for the analysis of sign language and gestures. However, the tool can be used efficiently for analyzing corpora from different media (containing video and/or audio data), and for annotations and their documentation. Basically, ELAN enables the user to relate annotations and media streams, to relate annotations with other annotations, as well as to specify the relationships between any annotation layers. Further, the ELAN interface can display up to four video and/or audio data, and provides numerous presentations of annotations. The ELAN supports a large character set, plus inclusion and exportation into many formats. The ELAN also supports the inclusion of those transcriptions that were created in other tools, and to relate them with media data within ELAN. The ELAN can also adjust the files from other tools, such as Transcriber and CHAT. In particular, it is easy to import from Transcriber. In ELAN a lot of features that can save time are also embedded, e.g., rapid segmentation (similar to the one available in Transcriber), although this is a relatively new feature. This feature allows the users to listen to the media stream and to annotate (rough) boundaries of, for example, intonation units, or those positions where exchanges of speakers occur, significantly faster. The users can decide whether the annotation should be performed by a single key press (for adjacent annotations), or by two key presses (for non-adjacent annotations). When the rough boundaries are defined, more precise adjustments can be performed using the mouse. Other features that can also save a lot of time include tokenization, filtering, and copying of tracks.

The EVA Scheme for Annotating Co-Verbal Behavior

The main objectives of the annotation scheme proposed in this book are the following:

1. to identify the relationship between the morpho-syntactic characteristics of the verbal information, and the intent of the corresponding content units (CU) that are comprised of verbal and co-verbal behavior;

[4] http://www.lat-mpi.eu/tools/tools/elan.

2. to identify the occurrence of used poses and shapes, and their relationship with the morpho-syntactic and prosodic features of verbal information. Namely, to determine where we gesticulate, and how the gesticulation is actually structured; and
3. to describe the identified movement shapes with high resolution. Namely, to determine how we actually gesticulate.

The EVA scheme is based on the fusion of functional and descriptive annotation scheme, with the aim of describing human co-verbal behavior as a relationship between the morpho-syntactic and prosodic features of verbal behavior, and the structure and shape of co-verbal movement. The formal model of this annotation scheme is presented in Figure 9. As can be seen, the EVA scheme is a multimodal annotation scheme that consists of three levels. The corresponding topological model of the scheme is presented in Figure 10. The highest (first) level consists of elements named *Text* and *Body Parts*. The element *Text* can be described with morphological characteristics defined in the word and sentence levels, and with prosodic features. In the *sentence level*, the text is presented as a sequence of words (so-called transcription) and corresponding sentence type (e.g., narrative, interrogative, imperative, optative, and exclamation sentence). In the *word level*, each word is assigned its part-of-speech based on MULTEXT-East morpho-syntactic specifications. The corresponding speech characteristics are also described in terms of prosodic features, intonation, and accentuation.

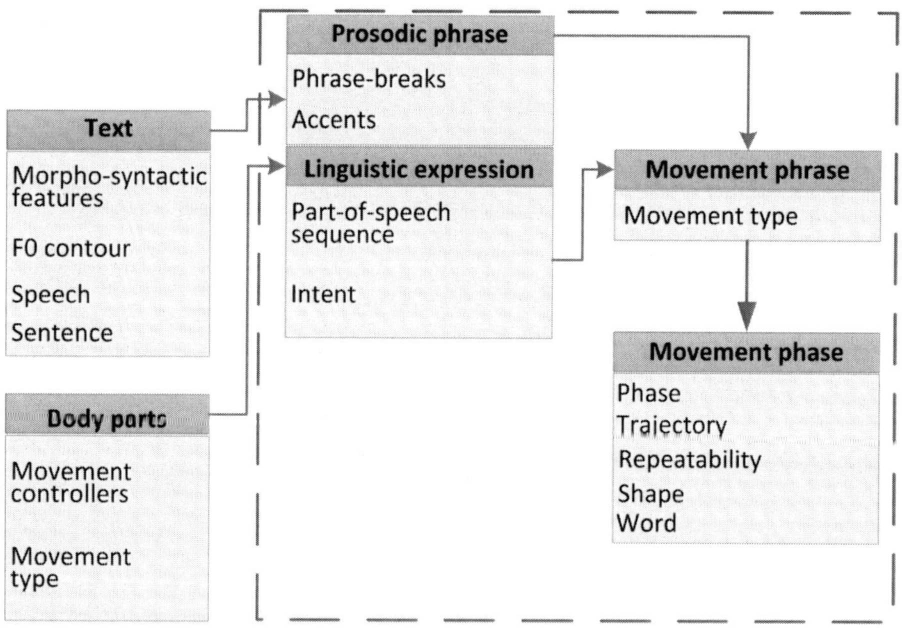

Figure 9. A formal model of the EVA scheme.

For describing text features, *Transcriber* (for transcription of speech into text), *Praat* (speech signal analysis), and proprietary *POS tagger* (morpho-syntactic features) have been used. The element *Body Parts* represents the structure of the object by which the physical manifestation of the movement (the co-verbal behavior) is carried out. Our work is based on a multipart assumption, according to which the body can be divided into the following parts: *head, face, left arm, right arm, left hand, right hand*, and *torso*.

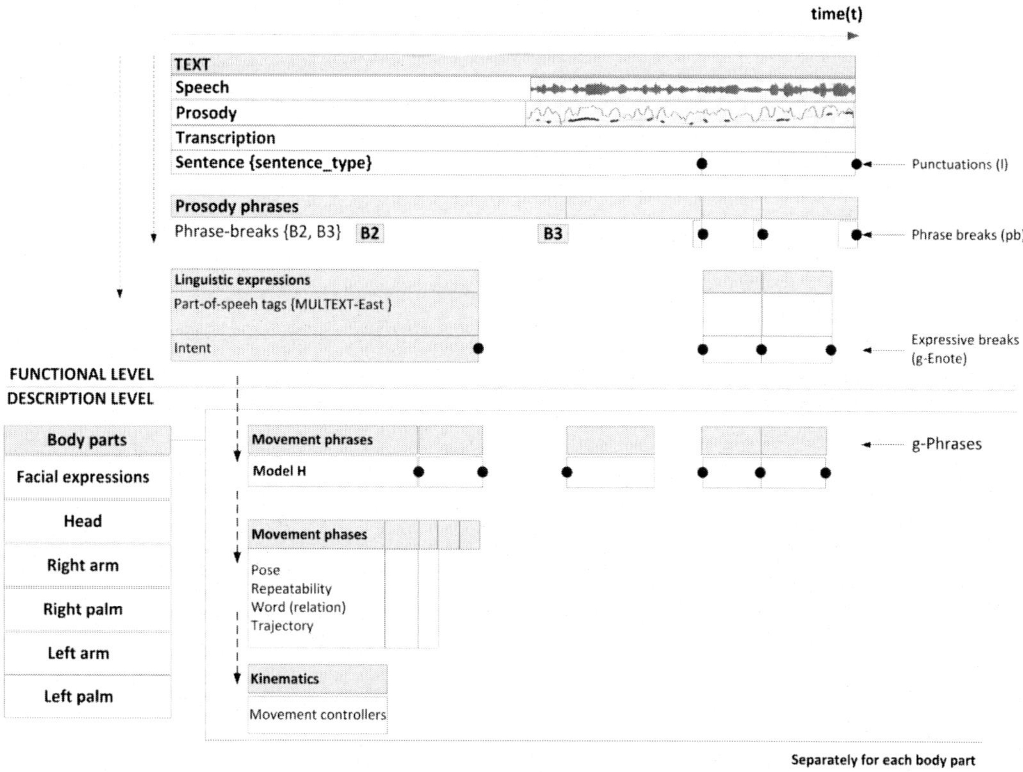

Figure 10. The topological model of the EVA scheme.

Each body part contains a set of unique *movement controllers* (these are articulators, such as joints and skeletal structures, blend shapes, etc.) that can be configured in order to render shapes, poses, and expressions on the conversational agent's articulated model.

The EVA scheme is used to analyze and describe the following co-verbal elements:

- *views and head movements:* a description of positions and orientations of head and eyes,
- *facial expressions:* the physical configurations and positions on the face (e.g., smile, astonishment, emotions, etc.),
- *hand gestures:* the physical configurations and positions that are carried out with arms or hands,
- *posture:* the physical configurations that combine the simultaneous movements of several body parts (e.g., *torso*, *arms*, *head*).

At the *functional level* (the first level) of the EVA scheme, the general characteristics of the observed co-verbal behavior are annotated. Here, the input text is split into verbal (speech and corresponding transcriptions) and co-verbal behavior (movement, gestures, and poses that are carried out simultaneously with speech). The second level can then be used for a functional description of the text. At this level, it focuses primarily on the characteristics of verbal behavior. The level contains two types of elements, named *linguistic phrase* and *prosodic phrase*. The *linguistic phrase* represents any sequence of words that is defined by prosodic phrase boundaries. The prosodic phrase boundaries can be defined by considering the punctuations, pauses, accentuations, and linguistic and intonation rules. The *linguistic phrases* are, therefore, sequences of several prosodic phrase boundaries that can be labeled as, for example, B2 (for minor phrase breaks), or B3 (for major phrase breaks) (Rojc, 2003). In Figure 10, the more emphasized prosodic phrase has at the end label B3 (this is also the end of the sentence). At the end of the minor, intermediate *linguistic phrases* (usually within the sentences) the tag B2 is used.

Furthermore, the *linguistic expression* is defined as that part of the *linguistic phrase* where the movement (gesticulation) is carried out simultaneously with speech. Therefore, the *linguistic expression* may be a part of the *linguistic phrase* (identified by B2), or it may encompass even the complete *linguistic phrase* (identified by B3). The boundaries of *linguistic phrases* and *linguistic expressions* do not need to be matched, and the *linguistic expression* can be stretched also beyond the boundaries of the *linguistic phrase*. Nevertheless, the main goal of the annotation scheme is to analyze in detail the concurrency and the synchrony of verbal and co-verbal behavior. Therefore, in the analysis only those segments in recordings that represent and describe simultaneous verbal and co-verbal behavior are studied. In doing so, the *linguistic expressions* are always positioned within the *linguistic phrases*. Furthermore, each *linguistic phrase* may contain one or more *linguistic expressions*. When *linguistic expressions* are annotated, the morpho-syntactic characteristics of the text (on words, and on sequences of words) which the expressions include, are described. Additionally, the intent for each *linguistic expression* (by considering the semiotic categories), or the content that the speaker wanted (speaker, listener) to present in the form of simultaneous verbal and co-verbal behavior, is annotated. The vertical arrows in Figure 10, therefore, relate the observed and described features to the time line. The annotation scheme's description level serves for the annotation of expressivity and for describing shapes, poses, and movements that happen within the individual *linguistic expressions* in great detail. The structure of the shapes and movements is described separately for each body part.

The movement of the observed body parts within each linguistic expression is described in the form of the following elements (Mlakar et al., 2012): *movement phrases* (gesticulation phrases), *movement phases* (McNeill, 2005a; Kendon, 2004), and the spatial mesh configuration of the movement controllers that are involved in the realization of the conversational agent. The *movement phrase* describes the entire course of the co-verbal behavior that is realized in specific *linguistic expression*, which always contains the *stroke phase*, and optionally the *preparation phase*, *hold phase*, and *retraction phase*. The *movement phrases* are related to the *linguistic expressions* in the co-verbal behavior level. The *linguistic expression* can also be defined by considering the *movement phrases* and *movement phases*. Namely, the *linguistic expression* is the co-verbal sequence within that *linguistic phrase* which contains at least one *movement phrase* and at least one *movement phase* (and at least one *stroke phase*). The *movement phrase* is described in the annotation scheme by the type of movement and by the abstract description of shapes and poses (e.g., smile, hand shape forming a cup, hand shape forming a fist, amazement, etc.). The individual *movement phase* within the *movement phrase* then describes the temporal characteristics and repeatability of shapes and poses, and the actual configuration of movement controllers in descriptive and/or abstract form (McNeill, 2005a; Kendon, 2004; Kita et al., 1998). The individual *movement phase*, therefore, keeps a set of those *key poses* for a particular body part (the configuration of movement controllers) that appear on its boundaries, together with the amplitude of the pose and shapes, handedness (by using left, right, or both hands), and the trajectory of movement (e.g., linear or straight line, ellipse, or triangular path). In general, co-verbal behavior can be presented in the form of the following relationships (Pavlovic et al., 1997):

$$H = T_m G \quad (6)$$

$$V = T_{vm} G \quad (7)$$

$$V = T_{vm}(T_m G) = T_{vg} G \quad (8)$$

$$\hat{G} = T_{vg}^{-1} V \quad (9)$$

The transformation *T* can be understood as a set of different models (or configurations of movement controllers). T_{vm} then describes a model of visual representations regarding the movement *H*. Furthermore, T_{vg} describes how a set of visual representations *V* for the selected gesture *G* is created. The models are in general parametric and belong to their own parametric space M_τ. Therefore, the *functional level* of the presented annotation scheme relates gestures *G* to their visual representations *V*, using the gesticular model T_{vg} (equation 9). The realization of the individual gesture (the co-verbal movement) is represented as a trajectory in the parametrical space of the model; for example, the realization of gesture by the movement of arms and hands where the arm position, hand position and its shape describe the trajectory in the 3D space.

Annotating the Functionalities in the Text

The functionality in the text specifies the *intent* that represents the base for co-verbal behavior generation, including both verbal and co-verbal representation of information. The objectives of the functional annotation level in the text are:

1. to identify a set of those morpho-syntactic sequences by which we are able to determine the *intent* of linguistic expressions,
2. to identify the dependency of linguistic expressions from the sentence type, and
3. to identify a set of conditions for the appearance of specific co-verbal movement in dependence of the *intent*, the morpho-syntactic sequences within the linguistic expression, and the prosodic features (e.g., prosodic phrase break types and positions, accentuations, etc.).

Therefore, the *functional level* in the annotation scheme is used to describe the characteristics of gesticular parametric space M_τ, through which the gesture *G* can be defined as a sequence of shapes, poses, and transitions on some body part that is carried out as a result of a specific *intent* that the speaker/listener wanted to express. For the description of verbal behavior's functionality that is defined by the *intent*, it is proposed that linguistic expressions are annotated in the form of *semiotic categories*. Therefore, the parametric space M_τ is defined based on Peirce's semiotic categories (Atkin, 2010) and based on the meaning of movement performed in the dialogue that is required to be presented. The features stored in the parametrical space M_T are prosodic (e.g., accents, intonation) and linguistic (e.g., morpho-syntactic sequences, phrase breaks). The gesture G in equation 9 is, therefore, defined as a co-verbal expression, which is a function of phrase-break boundaries, sentence type, accents, and morpho-syntactic sequences in the text that are simultaneously accompanied with the gesture. In this context the concept of gesture G is used as any movement/sequence of poses that is simultaneously accompanied by the speech. Therefore, the gesture G includes hands, arms, head, views, facial expressions, and emotions. The model of expressive co-verbal behavior that is proposed in the book defines the following classes in the semiotic space M_T:

The iconic gestures are used in dialogue mainly for outlining concrete entities and actions. For example, the physical outline (performed by using both hands) of clinging and curving, while uttering this word phrase: *I have curved the pipe.* The iconic gesture acts as a reference symbol that presents the formal and structural similarity of the event/object that someone is talking about. The classification of iconic gestures is further extended by the concept of *metonymic gestures* (Koutsombogera & Papageorgiou, 2012; Beattie & Shovelton, 2002). These are used to describe the spatio-temporal characteristics of entities and actions (e.g., the size, shape, direction, and movement speed, etc.). Furthermore, *metaphorical (qualitative) gestures* are used in the dialogue to present some abstract usage of shapes in space. In this context, the metaphorical gestures are used to represent some abstract contents, where the abstract concept/object itself is presented by gestures to indicate it having actual form and actually occupying some space. For example, the speaker performs a posture like a clinging object, regardless of whether the object has any physical meaning (or shape), or represents just an "idea" or "memory." The iconic gestures (mainly outlines) often represent the semantic relationship between verbal and co-verbal information, and are usually synchronized with the words (Koutsombogera & Papageorgiou, 2012).

Among **deictic gestures** (Krauss et al., 2000) are classified those body movements that lead the listener's view into a desired direction (the so-called *pointing gestures*); namely, those gestures that represent determination, or reference to someone, or are indicators for speaker exchange (*index gestures*), and those gestures that represent *counting* and *enumeration*. Typical representatives of *pointing gestures* in the deictic dimension of the gesticulation space include e.g., stretched index finger and opened hand. By using *pointing gestures*, we are usually trying to locate entities and actions in the space that is around us. Most *pointing gestures* used in dialogue, for example, don't show the direction in which the physical objects really are, but are used in the sense of localizing something abstract (e.g., in the expression *somewhere there*, the word *there* does not define the exact position in space; and, in the expression *ancient history*, the expression does not actually represent physical space); this has been defined by Bühler as *deixis at Phantasm* (Bühler, 1982). The typical representatives of *index gestures* are, therefore, an opened hand that is oriented toward the speaker (*yours*, *what do you think?*), and the hand that is placed on the upper part of the chest (*my*, *mine*, etc.). The *deictic gestures* can also include concepts such as counting and enumeration. These gestures typically represent the so-called beats, where the individual gestures are cyclically repeated (e.g., in a similar shape, when counting *1, 2, 3, 4, 5, ...* ; alternating left and right arm (hand), e.g., *first, second, third, ...* or even in a related form, e.g., television, radio, internet, ...).

The adapters (manipulators) are those gestures that are used to address/outline the verbal behavior, together with possible interruptions. Most frequently, interruptions in speech are used when the speaker is searching for a word/words in his own vocabulary, is thinking, or is hesitating. In general, *linguistic fillers* trigger such co-verbal behavior (interjections, such as *hm ..., oh ..., aaa ...,* etc.). Furthermore, co-verbal manipulators are typically well synchronized with the verbal behavior when talking. Often, manipulators are also known as *search gestures* and are in general used to gain some time, in order to find the most suitable shape for representing information, e.g., searching word/word phrases (Esposito. et al., 2001). The shapes for these movements are, for example, oscillatory movements of the arms around the hold shape. During the oscillatory movement, the shape of the hands in general does not change (e.g., scratching the scalp, swinging arms up and down, etc.). The *linguistic phrase* that follows the movement usually represents some response to the search action (the speaker has found a proper solution), and is usually accompanied by co-verbal behavior (e.g., *hm ... [silence], of course*). The *beats* are part of those manipulators that, in a given time interval, outline evenly repeated movements, which can actually be seen as a physical manifestation of rhythm. The spontaneous beats are an integral part of the paralinguistic context of the co-verbal behavior. Usually, the strokes accompany the speech spontaneously. In the scope of the dialogue, the beats are used primarily for maintaining the attention, and are intended primarily to the listener (Biau & Soto-Faraco, 2013). By using beats, the speaker modulates the speech and keeps the listener's attention and the dynamism of the communication.

The symbols include conventional signs and emblems, e.g., a thumb that is stretched up (as a sign of agreement), or a stretched index and middle finger (as a sign of peace or victory), etc. The symbol has a defined meaning also without any verbal information; therefore, the listener does not need any verbal context. The emblems are also very culturally dependent. When using symbols as part of co-verbal behavior, we are usually considering the semantic correlation *one-on-one*, where the shape and the movement structure directly represent a verbal representation of a symbol (*peace*, *ok*, and *goodbye*). The shape for the symbol can be further modeled according to the amplitude (strength) (e.g., the gap size between the index and middle finger, the dynamics of gesticulation, etc.).

The Analysis and Annotation of the Temporal Structure of Movement

The temporal structure of movement can be defined right after the movement phrases and phases are identified (McNeill, 2005a; Kendon, 2004; Kita et al., 1998). By the description and analysis of the temporal structure of movement in the form of movement phrases and phases, and logical relations between individual levels, we are able to analyze and define the following:

1. the set of types of movements that depend on the *intent*, and its morpho-syntactic sequences and prosodic features,
2. the set of movement structures, and
3. the set of morpho-syntactic indicators that depend on the intent, and its morpho-syntactic sequences and prosodic features.

Mostly the *intent* of the co-verbal behavior is expressed through a stroke phase F_S and through the retention of shape, which follows the stroke phase (represents the hold phase F_{SH}). The hold phase still represents the core of the *intent*, and represents the part of the semantically most important segment of movement (McNeill, 2005a; Kita et al., 1998). This phase is fully perceptional, since in the dialogue this is actually a movement without a direct meaning from the semiotic's perspective. Nevertheless, in the hold phase the parts of the body are not completely static (Esposito et al., 2002).

Furthermore, the presence of the hold phase before the stroke phase F_{HS} usually means that the idea that the expressive co-verbal behavior is reflecting has been formed in advance. The theory about dialogue says that the coordination between the syllable/word and gesture is planned at the start, while the information is presented at the end of the sentence (Ruiter et al., 2012). On the other hand, the hold phase that is carried out after the stroke phase represents the binding, causing fixations, and additional emphasis on the significance (Nobe et al., 1998). The movement that is carried out before or after the semantically most important segment of movement is particularly important, in order to ensure the proper internal continuity of movement, the dynamism of gestures, and credible perception. Different gestures generally differ in the synchronization method used, with different linguistic and prosodic elements (Kendon, 1980). And events on the gestures' boundaries may indicate several mental processes, such as *thinking*, *discussion*, *hesitation*, etc.

During annotation, firstly movement phrases and those segments are annotated within individual *linguistic expressions*, where the movement is most prominent, the so-called stroke phase F_S. And then the hold phase around the stroke phase is annotated, if it exists. At the end the preparation F_P and retraction phase F_R are annotated.

During annotation it is often the case that it is impossible to distinguish between the stroke phase and the preparation phase, or it is not possible to claim that the preparation phase exists (or does not exist). In this case, we assume that the movement belongs to the stroke phase F_S. In the EVA annotation scheme, the description and analysis of the temporal structure of movement represent the definition of a set of possible movement models H (equation 6), by which we are able to represent some gesture G. As can be seen in Figure 7, the *movement phrases* and *phases* hierarchically belong to the co-verbal expression (gesture G). Therefore, the temporal structure of movement can be understood as a movement model H, where H can be described as:

$$\hat{H} = T_{vm}^{-1} V \tag{10}$$

And gesture G can be described as:

$$\hat{G} = T_{m}^{-1} \hat{H} \tag{11}$$

Obviously, the movement model H may be represented as a transformation of the visual presentations, and can be formed independently of the gesture. And in equation 11 H is then related with gesture G via inverse transformation T_m. In this way, these equations also follow the hypothesis regarding the separate analysis of functional relationships of the text and shapes.

The Analysis and Annotation of Shapes and Spatial Configuration

Co-verbal behavior is represented as the movement of body parts in 3D space and the corresponding rendering of body shapes and expressions via the configuration of movement controllers. The description of gestures must, therefore, reflect the time and spatial characteristics of the gesture (how the gesture is performed) and the individual body parts (or movement controllers), which depict the gesture. As can be seen in Figure 10, during annotation the time and spatial characteristics of the gestures are described only abstractly, regarding the space in the level of body parts (e.g., the position of the hands, the hand orientation, the abstract shape of the hand, the position and orientation of the arm, etc.), and annotation in the form of detailed description of the kinematics in the form of the configuration of movement controllers that are based on 3D models (the approach that is based on 3D models and on movement controllers of the skeleton (Morge et al., 2011)). The main purpose of describing the shape and spatial configuration is to define: (a) the context-independent dictionary of expressive shapes (Figure 4); (b) the visual shapes *V*, which the conversational agent is able to realize, and for which the transformation T_{vm} (or T_{vm}^{-1}) can be defined and which is also conditioned with logical relations and features of its own parametric space in the level of movement phrases and phases.

Table 1. The abstract dimensions used for describing the shape

Body part	Dimension
Arm	Height
	Distance
	Radial orientation
	Swivel
	Forearm orientation
Hand	Hand orientation
	Shape of fingers and hand
Head (view)	Orientation
Facial expressions	Expression or emotion
	Amplitude (1-10)

As can be seen in Figure 10, the element *V* is described based on the *shape/pose similarity* (by using the *Hamming distance* in order to measure the similarity, as proposed by Hogrefe et al. (2011)), *repeatability*, the *body part* to which it belongs, *trajectory*, and *kinematics* (the description of the configuration of movement controllers (optional). The description of the shape and spatial configuration is done for each body part separately in the level of movement phases. When analyzing and describing the poses, we restrict ourselves to the annotation of those pose attributes that can be observed on the boundaries of the movement phases. The transition between poses is then described by motion trajectory, which defines whether linear transition (a straight line), elliptical, or rectangular transition (consisting of vertical and horizontal displacements) is performed.

The attribute *shape* represents an abstract position, orientation, and handedness (if such exists) of the observed body part in 3D space at the boundaries of movement phases. The arm position is described in 3D space similar to that proposed by Kipp et al. (2007b); namely, in dependence on the hand. Table 1 shows all of the abstract dimensions used for the description of the shape, in dependence on the body part. Additionally, a realization of these abstract dimensions for some abstract description of the shape of the arm in 3D space is presented (Figure 11).

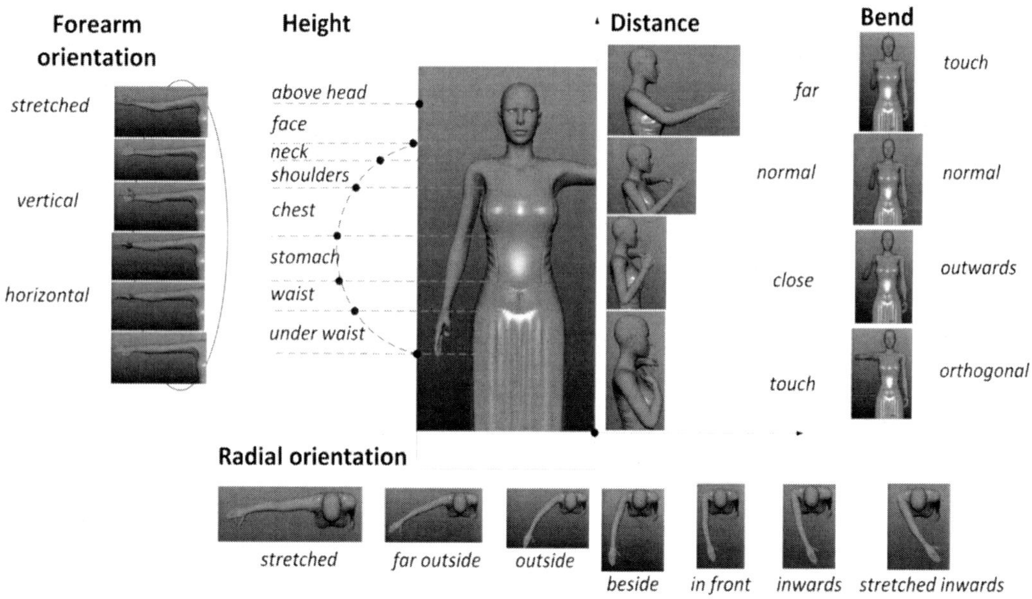

Figure 11. The abstract dimensions used to describe the shape of the arm.

Shapes and arm positions are described using the attribute *height*, which describes the height of the hands in relation to the body (e.g., hands within the face region, within the stomach region, or within the shoulder region etc.). The second dimension for describing the arm is the attribute *distance*, which describes the distance between the hands and the body (the *z* axis in 3D space) (e.g., *touch*, *close*, *normal*). The third dimension for describing the hands is the attribute *radial orientation*, which describes the position of the hands in relation to the *y* axis in 3D space, where the referential point represents the middle of the body (e.g., *inwards*, *outwards*, *in front*, *aside*). The attribute *bend* is the fourth dimension, which is related to the configuration of the shoulder and the shape that can be formed by various shoulder configurations (e.g., *orthogonal*), or how close the body is to the elbow for some shoulder configurations. The orientation of the forearm mainly affects the final orientation of the hand (e.g., *vertical*, *horizontal*, *stretched*). The hand is described by considering its orientation, dimension (similar to the case of forearm orientation), and shape of the fingers and hands, where the *Ham-No-Sys notation* (Hanke, 2004) is used. This notation is the so-called alphabet for describing the characters in the phonetic level, or its derivation *SignPhon* (Crasborn et al., 2000). The shapes of poses which are carried out by the head are estimated in relation to the position of the eyes and the orientation of the eye-gaze (e.g., *look_left*, *look_right*), and slope (e.g., *forward*, *backward*). In this way we can describe movements such as shock, shaking, etc.

The *similarity* of the poses and shapes represents a measure of how similar the configurations of the observed body part actually are. The lexical similarity is particularly important for co-verbal behavior analysis, which is carried out using hands and facial expressions. The similarity of gestures and poses is defined by *Hamming distance*, as proposed by Hogrefe et al. (2011); this is used as a quantitative measure for the evaluation of the common features of two observed poses. The Hamming distance is basically a function that measures the symmetrical difference between two polygons, but only those regions that belong to only one (i.e., are not included within their intersection). If the two polygons are exactly the same, there are no such areas, and the Hamming distance is equal to 0. In other words, the more similar the two polygons, the smaller the Hamming distance. In the case of manual gesticulation, the Hamming distance can be extended and used for both analytical and subjective estimates regarding the similarity of gestures via:

- the shape and orientation of the hand on the final boundary of the movement phase,
- the height, distance, radial orientation, bending, and orientation of the forearm,
- the repeatability,
- the movement trajectories within the movement phase,
- the handedness (use of one or both hands), and the distance between the hands.

A similar process can also be used for the head, facial expressions, and emotions, or for any body part with a final set of abstract shapes. For example, the similarity of facial expressions and emotions can be measured by observing the activity of facial action units, and MPEG-4 facial action parameters (FAP) (Petjan, 2005), and their representations in the laboratory environment (e.g., MMI database of facial expressions (Pantic et al., 2005), Cohn-Kanade (Lucey et al., 2010), CBCL Face Database[5]). By using the presented description of poses at the boundaries of individual movement phases, we are able to form a reliable set of visual shapes *V*, which can be displayed and used by the conversational agent as part of the expressive co-verbal behavior. Each element from *V* can be represented as:

$$V = (shape, \{dimension1, dimension2, dimension3, \ldots\}) \tag{12}$$

where *V* represents the class of time- and function-independent spatial configurations of poses that are closest to each other (according to Hamming distance). By using the transformation T_{vm}^{-1}, we are able to move the class into a corresponding movement phase and phrase, and we are able in this way to create the co-verbally synchronized movement model *H*, which is represented as a sequence of movement phases, where the shapes *V* are realized. Therefore, the equation 10 can be written as follows:

$$\hat{H} = T_{vm}^{-1}V = T_{vm}^{-1}(V,V,V,\ldots) \tag{13}$$

[5] http://cbcl.mit.edu/software-datasets/FaceData2.html

The Analysis and Annotation of Kinematics

Similar to the abstract concept for describing positions in 3D space is a description of the pose using the configuration of movement controllers dependent from the body part being observed. Additionally, the description of the kinematics is also affected by the type of 3D model for which the movements are described. Nevertheless, in the EVA annotation scheme, only the description of the kinematics of movements expresses the dependence of the 3D model by which the gestures and co-verbal behavior can be realized. The 3D volumetric mesh models that support skeletal structures are most commonly used for the realization of co-verbal behavior. The movement controllers in the volumetric mesh models are presented in the form of skeletal structures and joints (bones/joints), and in the form of animated shapes (blend shapes/morphed-shapes). The advantage of volumetric mesh models is the minimization of those parameters that we have to describe for the definition of configuration.

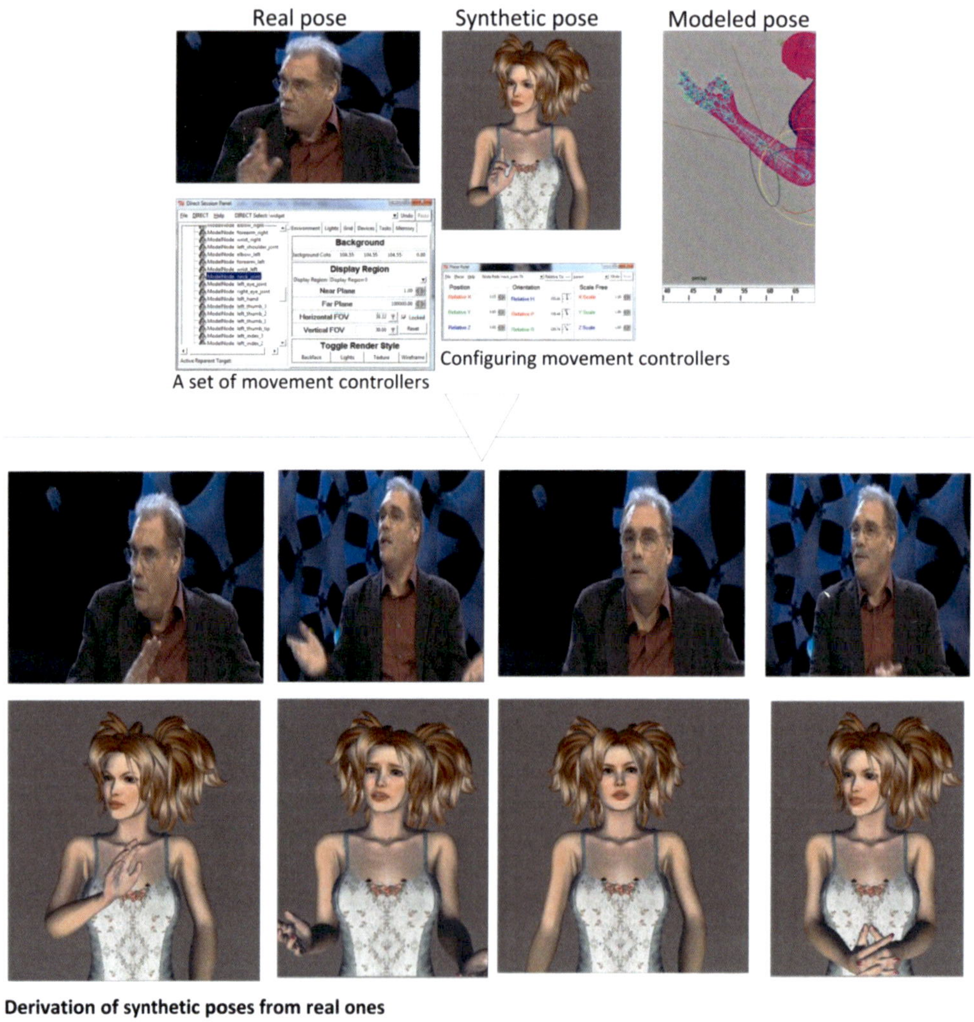

Figure 12. The description of kinematics based on subjective adjustments.

The description of kinematics is otherwise an optional part of the analysis and description of the co-verbal behavior. It is proposed that it is carried out directly on the conversational agent that will realize the movements. In this way, a set of realistic visual representations *V* can be created, without any additional work. The way in which the description of the pose can be performed, as well as the virtual conversational agent's adjustments to the observed shapes of individual human body parts, is presented in Figure 12.

For a description of the kinematics of shapes with a high resolution, that body part which is being observed and described is selected first. In other words, the available movement controllers are conditioned by the body part. For example, when describing hands, the available movement controllers would be in the form of joints and bones (e.g., shoulder joint, elbow joint, forearm joint), and when describing the hands the available joints and bones by which we can create hand shapes are used (depending on the used skeletal model). For each body part we have access to the referential visual forms *V*, which have been previously described. By using these visual forms, we can set the basic configuration of movement controllers, and can then adjust by using the attribute *power*, or even directly through value adjustments of each attribute (e.g., HPR values in the case of joints and bones). Furthermore, in Figure 12 the pose/shape *V* is adjusted with the observed pose directly on the conversational agent. Additionally, the figure demonstrates the importance of the description of kinematics. The individual pose that the agent will have to realize in other sequences and gestures can be very thoroughly adjusted to the realistic representation. In this way we are able to form different time- and function-independent classes of visual representations that contain elements that are close regarding the similarity measure.

The description of kinematics is otherwise quite a time-consuming process. The accuracy, quality, and flexibility of the co-verbal behavior, however, compensate for the complexity of the proposed descriptions (or synthetic poses, derived from the real ones, as shown in Figure 12). In addition, each element *V* can be reused in the description of the other movement model *H* which is carried out by a different transformation, *T*. In this way, the conversational agent will be able to realize the co-verbal behavior by using the same set of highly realistic visual representations, *V*, which can differ in several dimensions of expressivity. Furthermore, by using the transformation T_{vm}^{-1}, the agent is able to adapt the shapes that are realized at the boundaries of the preparation and retraction phases. And according to the co-verbal behavior features, the agent is able to adapt not only the meaningful part of the co-verbal behavior, but also the context that defines how to obtain the meaningful part, and how to adjust the co-verbal behavior, when the meaningful part is completed. In order to minimize the time needed for the EVA annotation concept, several 3D modeling tools can be used for defining and encoding expressions, such as: Maya3D[6], Daz4D[7], Blender[8], etc. Namely, by using these tools on some presentation of an agent in the 3D environment, we are able to adjust the shape/pose to the observed real shape/pose (modeled pose in Figure 12), and to export it as a procedural shape, pose, or even animation into *co-verbal behavior lexicon*.

---

[6] Maya3D: http://www.autodesk.com/products/autodesk-maya/overview.
[7] Daz3D: http://www.daz3d.com/.
[8] Blender: http://www.blender.org/.

Chapter 4

MARKUP LANGUAGE FOR THE SPECIFICATION OF SHAPES, POSES, AND BEHAVIOR OF CONVERSATIONAL AGENTS - EVA-SCRIPT -

INTRODUCTION

In multi-modal systems where the co-verbal behavior has to be represented by some synthetic movement of body parts on an embodied conversational agent (ECA), abstract description languages such as BML (Vilhjalmsson et al., 2007), MURML (Kransted et al., 2002), EMBRScript (Heloir & Kipp, 2009), APML (DeCarolis et al., 2004), etc. are needed in order to describe the relationship between the specification of the co-verbal behavior design and its realization on an ECA. The final form of co-verbal behavior is in such cases generated during the realization phase through conversion of the abstract descriptions of movements into animation descriptions that the virtual agent can then reproduce and manifest. Nevertheless, based on theory about conversational agents and co-verbal behavior, it would be better to design such descriptive language that would relate verbal and co-verbal behavior through the *absolute timing* and *offsets*, considered as delays. Then, instead of establishing a complex synchronization point, we can just decide to let the gesture start with an offset *t*. Therefore, unlike the other high-level descriptive languages mentioned above, a novel description language, named EVA–Script, is proposed, which segments the co-verbal behavior according to the body part, and presents it as an event.

The EVA-Script, as well as EMBRScript, originates from the fact that the description of the co-verbal behavior should already be provided to the realization framework in a form that the framework understands. But the EMBRScript represents the language that converts the abstractness of languages, such as APML and BML, into procedural animation. Therefore, the abstract description of movements is converted into procedural equivalents, and the relative timing used for such a synchronization process, which is based on the concept of absolute time (i.e., the actual overall duration, rather than considering start and end times on the timeline). On the other hand, the EVA-Script is a so-called *transformation language* which not only describes the co-verbal behavior design and synchronization process in the absolute time domain, but can also be used to simultaneously describe shapes and poses in the *co-verbal behavior lexicon*. Furthermore, EVA-Script can be created in real time during the speech synthesis process, where for each text sentence both speech signal and co-verbal behavior description are outputs that are available to some realization framework (both with the common timeline and perfectly synchronized). In this way, the *co-verbal behavior lexicon* does not need to include any functional (semantic/semiotic) relationships between speech and co-verbal behavior, nor the timing information or description regarding the internal continuity of gesture and overall (external) continuity of the generated sequence of co-verbal behavior.

EVA-Script

For expressive description and the definition of shapes *V*, poses *P*, and co-verbal behavior, a flexible markup language named EVA-Script (Mlakar & Rojc, 2011a) has been designed. The EVA-Script can fulfill several dimensions of expressivity (Bevacqua et al., 2007). The EVA-Script considers the description of shape/pose in the *co-verbal behavior lexicon* only in the context of spatial dimension and as an XML block that holds the movement controllers (the so-called *degrees of freedom* - DOF). The other expressive dimensions, such as *activity*, *temporal distribution*, *continuity*, *amplitude*, and *repeatability*, are in EVA-Script referring to the definition of different movement models *H*, and the formulation of co-verbal behavior. The description of the co-verbal behavior in EVA-Script is represented using an EVA event, which includes XML tags and attributes. In the EVA-Script and EVA-framework (the framework for animation realization) animation (or the co-verbal behavior, the movement) is, in general, defined as an EVA-Script event, which has its own locally defined duration. In view of this, absolute timing is proposed, whereby the temporal basis represents that moment when the EVA-framework receives the EVA event. Namely, all of the required temporal information within an individual EVA event applies only to this EVA event; therefore, it can be given absolutely. When the EVA-framework accepts a new event, it properly resets its temporal basis.

For expressive description of poses, shapes, and co-verbal behavior, the EVA-Script defines several XML tags and attributes, which can be used in a procedural level in order to describe spatial (in terms of structure or amplitude), dynamic, and temporal parameters of poses, gestures, and co-verbal behavior. Table 2 describes the formal syntax of the EVA-Script scheme.

Table 2. The formal syntax of the EVA-Script scheme.

Element	*Attribute*	*Description*
<speech>	***this tag defines a procedure for visual speech synthesis***	
	expression	
	the facial expression that has to be visualized simultaneously with speech, and only during speech,	
	amplitude	
	the desired intensity of the facial expression's shape, that is simultaneous with speech,	
	initialDelay	
	the initial delay of speech, lip-sync, and facial expression that is simultaneous with speech,	
	tts_document	
	the sound file that contains synthesized speech for specific EVA event,	

Element	*Attribute*	*Description*
<viseme>	***this tag defines the visual representation for a specific phoneme, the co-articulating element***	
	id	the id of the shape that is used to find the corresponding phoneme's template for visualization, which is stored in a *co-verbal behavior lexicon*; or can already represents the template itself, when the configuration is described,
	amplitude	the desired intensity of the shape,
	durationStroke	within this time, the viseme's end shape for some phoneme is reached (depends on the intensity),
	durationRetraction	the time that is needed in order that the viseme's end shape is transformed into a neutral pose (when its effect on the facial region is neutralized),
	offset	this represents a temporal value that should be available for overlapping two consecutive visemes (to shift for specific time the current viseme into the previous one),
<fgesture>	***this tag defines the facial expression, including emotions***	
	id	the id of the shape, which is used to find the corresponding template stored in the *co-verbal behavior lexicon*; or can already represent the template itself, when the configuration is described,
	type	whether the procedural description defines the emotion, or facial expression,
	amplitude	the global intensity of the visualized shapes defined within this tag,
	repetivity	how many times the procedural description, defined within this tag/template, should be repeated (including temporal intervals),
	complexity	does this facial expression/emotion represent a basic expression/emotion (*B*), or concept of masking (*M*), or overlapping (*S*),
	blending	the weight measure (used for blending), which defines the desired effect in those regions that are affected by several *<fgesture>* tags,
	initialDelay	the initial delay before executing the procedure is measured from the time instant when the EVA event should start,
	durationStroke	the available time for the realization of the procedure,
	durationRetraction	how much time is available for the end shape of the stroke phase to be transformed into a neutral shape (when the effect on the face is neutralized),
	durationHold	how much time, after reaching the end shape during the stroke phase, the procedure's affect should be maintained,
<bgesture>	***this tag defines those elements that carry out physical transformations (poses), but are not part of the facial expressions (e.g., head, arms, hands)***	
	name	the name of the shape used for finding the appropriate template that is stored in the *co-verbal behavior lexicon*; or can represent the template itself, when the configuration is described,

Table 2. (Continued)

Element	*Attribute*	*Description*
	body_part	that part of the conversational agent's body that is managed within this procedure (e.g., head, right arm, right hand, left hand, left hand),
	intensity	the global intensity of the visualized shapes contained within this tag,
	repetivity	how many times the procedure defined within this tag/procedure should be repeated (including temporal intervals),
	initialDelay	the initial delay (a global influence) before executing the procedure, measured from the time instant when the EVA event should start,
	durationStroke	how much time (global) the procedure has available in order to be performed,
	durationRetraction	how much time (global) is needed for the end shape of the stroke phase to transform into a neutral shape (its effect on the body is neutralized),
	durationHold	how much time, after reaching the end shape during the stroke phase, the effect of the procedure has to be preserved,
	trajectory	the name of the parametric curve that is stored in the *co-verbal behavior lexicon*, and is used for the calculation of inverse kinematics, in order to determine the intermediate configurations between the initial and excited state,
<parallel>	***this tag defines the simultaneous animation of those movement controllers stored within this tag,***	
<successive>	***this tag defines the consecutive animation of those movement controllers stored within this tag,***	
	repetivity	how many times the procedural description stored within this tag/template should be repeated (including the temporal intervals),
	durationHold	how much time, after reaching the end shape described within this tag, the effect of the procedure has to be maintained,
<FAP>	***these tags are used in order to define a configuration of a complex/elementary movement controller. The FAP (always within tags <fgesture>) is used in order to describe the configuration of facial expressions and visemes,***	
	name	the name of the elementary movement controller; or the name of a complex movement controller (e.g., the templates in the *co-verbal behavior lexicon*),
	type	the type of configuration that the movement controller should perform (e.g., *HPR* configuration for rotation of joints, *X* configuration for translation of animated shapes, or *empty* configuration in case this is the template),
	value	the desired configuration that the movement controller should perform,
	amplitude	the desired intensity used for the template stored within these tags (it is used only in the case when the FAP describes a complex motion controller),
	complexity	

Element	*Attribute*	*Description*
		whether the facial expression/emotion represents a basic expression/emotion (*B*), the concept of masking (*M*), or overlapping (*S*). It is used only in the case when the FAP represents a complex movement controller,
	blending	a weighted measure for blending defines the desired effect of the procedure in those regions that are simultaneously affected by several *<fgesture>* tags. This value is used only in the case when the FAP represents a complex motion controller,
	durationStroke	how much time the elementary/complex motion controller has available, in order to reach the configuration value that is defined within the <FAP> attribute *value* (this depends on the intensity),
	durationRetraction	how much time the elementary/complex motion controller has available in order to move from its end shape into a neutral shape (the effect on the facial region is neutralized),
	durationHold	how much time after reaching the end shape the effect of the procedure has to be maintained for, given FAP configuration,
	initialDelay	desired delay before executing the elementary/complex motion controller. It is measured from the first occurrence of this tag.
<BAP>		***these tags define a configuration of complex/elementary movement controller. BAP is used to describe the configuration of body expressions (always within tag <bgesture>)***
	name	the name of the elementary movement controller; or the name of the complex movement controller itself (e.g., templates in the *co-verbal behavior lexicon*),
	type	the type of configuration that the movement controller should execute (e.g., *HPR* configuration for the rotation of joints, *X* configuration for the translation of animated shapes, *empty* configuration in the case of template),
	value	the name of the configuration that the movement controller should perform,
	amplitude	the desired intensity of that template which is written within this tag (it is used only when BAP represents a complex motion controller),
	durationStroke	how much time the elementary/complex motion controllers has in order to reach the configuration value specified within the <BAP> attribute *value* (depends on the intensity),
	durationRetraction	how much time is needed for the elementary/complex motion controller to move from its end shape into a neutral shape (the effect on the facial region is neutralized),
	durationHold	how much time, after reaching the end shape, the effect of the procedure has to be maintained for the given BAP configuration,
	initialDelay	desired delay before executing the elementary/complex movement controller. It is measured from the first occurrence of this tag,
	interpolation	this represents that kinematic curve which has to be used for the automatic calculation of intermediate configurations during the transition from the current state into the excited state, or the state that is described by the <BAP> attribute *value*. It depends on the animation framework. The EVA-framework currently supports three types of interpolation: *EaseIn*, *EaseOut*, and *EaseInOut*,

Table 2. (Continued)

Element	*Attribute*	*Description*
	view	how to orient eyes during head movements. The value *auto* is used when automatic adjustment of eyes should focus into the center of the screen. Then value *track* is used when eyes and head have to be oriented toward some object's position that is specified in the <BAP> attribute *focus*. The value *direct* means to orient eyes and adapt them by considering some point in the area, as specified in the <BAP> attribute *focus*. The *empty* value is used when the forward kinematics mechanism has to be considered without any adaptation. The attribute is used only then, when <BAP> or template includes the neck joint movements.
	focus	this attribute stores those values that are dependent on the <BAP> attribute *view*. When the *view* has value *track*, the *focus* value represents the name of the object (e.g., the mouse pointer). And when the *view* has value *direct*, then the *focus* value is defined by 3D coordinates of the conversational agent's area (as *vector (x, y, z)*),
	trajectory	the name of the parametric curve that is stored in the dictionary of *co-verbal behavior lexicon* and is used for the calculation of inverse kinematics in order to determine the intermediate configurations between the start and the excited state. It is used exclusively for modeling the movement of arms and only then, when <BAP> defined use of some template.

The formal syntax and the structure of the description for pose, movements, and movement models *H* support different dimensions of expressivity. The attributes in different hierarchical levels (for different elements) can be used for adjusting the temporal, spatial, and dynamic characteristics, including *continuity* and *repeatability*. In general, three types of behavior can be described: *speech*, *facial expressions*, and *emotions*, and also those body movements that have hierarchical structure.

The **first type of behavior** describes those shapes, poses, and transitions that relate to pronunciation and co-articulation. The complex and elementary controllers are combined in the XML block that is enclosed by tag *<speech>*. Furthermore, each EVA-Script event can contain exactly one such block. The *<speech>* tag includes those global attributes that affect the co-articulation of the entire viseme sequence, described within this tag. As seen in Table 2, these attributes are:

a) *expression* and *amplitude*: describe the occurrence of facial expressions and the amplitude of these during the visualization of the pronunciation (the *expression* affects the pronunciation only during speech, and ends when there is no speech),
b) *tts_document*: describes the speech source (e.g., the audio file), and
c) *initialDelay*: describes how much time after the occurrence of the event the speech and lip-sync processes should start.

Furthermore, the co-articulatory parameters are also stored within tag *<speech>*. They are in general contained within sequences of tags *<viseme>*. Namely, the individual *<viseme>* tag contains attributes such as: *id*, *amplitude*, *durationStroke*, *durationRetraction*, and *offset*. With the attribute *id*, we can identify the specific template that is stored in the *co-verbal behavior lexicon*, where the corresponding shape represents a visual representation of the phoneme. By the attribute *amplitude*, the intensity of the viseme can be defined; namely, how distinctively a visual representation of the phoneme should be carried out. In this case the values for the attribute have to be on the interval [0, 1]. The temporal description of the phoneme's visualization can be performed using attributes such as: *durationStroke*, and *durationRetraction*. By the attribute *durationStroke* we are able to define the time when the viseme should reach the end shape (this depends on the *intensity*), and therefore for how much time the specific template, modulated by the *amplitude* value, should be executed. And by the attribute *durationRetraction* we are able to define the time when the effect of the viseme should be neutralized; namely, how much time is needed for transforming the viseme from its end shape into a neutral shape. The attribute *offset* represents that co-articulation parameter which can be used for specifying the start and the duration of the simultaneous effect of two consecutive visemes on the face region. Therefore, this defines how much time is available in order to simultaneously decrease the effect of the prior viseme, and to increase the effect of the next viseme.

The **second type of behavior** describes shapes, poses and transitions for facial mimics, facial expressions, and emotions. Elementary and complex controllers for this type of co-verbal behavior are merged within the XML block, enclosed by the tag *<fgesture>*. Individual EVA-Script events may include one or more *<fgesture>* tags. However, all individual blocks are executed simultaneously. Therefore, the facial expressions described within these tags appear on the face simultaneously. The effect of individual facial expressions, or the corresponding weighted measure, is described by the attribute *blending*. When there are simultaneous tags *<fgestures>* in a template, the animation framework should execute them simultaneously. When more elementary movement controllers have to model the same area of the body simultaneously, or several procedures have to set the same movement controller simultaneously, the technique for blending shapes has to be used, whereby each tag *<fgesture>* contributes to the visualization of the end shape. Each effect can be defined by using some weighted measure, which can be set with the attribute *blending*. As seen in Table 2, the basic attributes for the *<fgesture>* tag are:

a) *id*: the name of the shape that is used in order to access the corresponding template stored in the *co-verbal behavior lexicon*, or a name of the template when a configuration describes a shape (the pose) in the *co-verbal behavior lexicon*,
b) *type*: the type of configuration that describes the procedural description; can represent the emotion, or facial expression,
c) *amplitude*: describes the global intensity of those shapes that are contained within the *<fgesture>* tags. This attribute is taken into account only when the *<fgesture>* tag or *<FAP>* tag already represents a complex motion controller. Only then are the values of elementary motion controllers properly modeled by considering this attribute,
d) *repeatability*: defines how many times the procedural description within individual tags should be repeated. Each iteration also takes into account the temporal characteristics (attributes such as *durationStroke*, *durationRetraction*, and *durationHold*),
e) *complexity*: defines whether the facial expression/emotion represents a basic expression/emotion (*B*), the concept of masking (*M*), or overlapping (*S*),
f) *blending*: this is a global weight used for the blending process, which defines the effect of elementary controllers in the procedure on those face regions where there is a concurrent effect of several *<fgesture>* tags,

g) *initialDelay*: defines how much time after the EVA event this procedure should be carried out,
h) *durationStroke*: defines that global time which is available in order that all hierarchical levels within the procedure are carried out. After the time expires, the last state of the movement controllers is always shown. When the <FAP> or <*fgesture*> tag represents a complex motion controller, the duration of the template, as well as individual sequences within it, is adjusted accordingly,
i) *durationRetraction*: defines that global time which is available in order that elementary/complex motion controllers within the procedure pass-over from the end shape, as described in the procedure, into a neutral state (the effect on the face region is neutralized). When the <FAP> or <*fgesture*> tag represents a complex motion controller, the duration of the template, as well as individual sequences within it, is adjusted accordingly,
j) *durationHold*: defines how much time after reaching the end shape of the last configuration described within the individual tags the effect of this shape should be maintained.

The individual tag <*fgesture*> directly represents a complex motion controller (the call of the template that is stored in the *co-verbal behavior lexicon*), or in fact represents a procedure that describes the simultaneous and consecutive configuration of the conversational agent's face via complex and elementary movement controllers. When the <*fgesture*> tag represents a procedural description, it contains at least one block that is enclosed by the <*successive*> or <*parallel*> tag. The <*successive*> tag ensures that individual complex/elementary movement controllers that are contained within the block are carried out successively. This means that the next configuration of the movement controller is carried out only after the execution of the preceding one is finished (this includes all of the movement phases, such as *stroke*, *retraction*, and *hold*). The <*successive*> tag may contain two attributes, *repeatability* and *durationHold*. The *repeatability* attribute defines how many times the procedural description included within the block should be repeated, and the *durationHold* attribute defines how much time after the execution of the procedure within the block the effect of the end configuration should be maintained. When some part of the gesture, e.g., shape or pose, requires that individual complex/elementary movement controllers are carried out simultaneously, they should be specified using the <*parallel*> tag.

The *third type of behavior* relates to describing the shapes, poses, and transitions that relate to those gestures and movements which are performed in non-face regions (e.g., hands, head). The elementary and complex controllers that belong to this type of movement are fused in the XML block that is enclosed by <*bgesture*> tag. Each EVA event can contain several <*bgesture*> tags. When there are several simultaneous <*bgesture*> tags, they are considered simultaneous (similar to <*fgesture*> tags). However, in the case of body movements, the simultaneousness does not mean blending effects in common regions, but only the simultaneous realization of several procedures for different body parts. The EVA-Script currently supports specifying up to five body parts that can be described using the <*bgesture*> tag's attribute, named *body_part*. These body parts are: *left arm*, *left hand*, *right arm*, *right hand*, and the *head*. Furthermore, the EVA-Script allows the definition of only one *body_part* attribute within the individual EVA event. In other words, we cannot move an arm simultaneously left and right. And when the same *body_part* attribute appears several times, only the last <*bgesture*> tag is ever taken into account. As can be seen in Table 2, the <*bgesture*> tag is described by the same attributes as the <*fgesture*> tag. Nevertheless, the <*bgesture*> tag does not support attributes such as *blending* or *complexity*. Furthermore, within each <*bgesture*> tag, there must be at least one block enclosed by a <*successive*> or <*parallel*> tag (when it presents a procedural description).

The individual complex/elementary movement controllers are in the context of EVA events given in the form of <*FAP*> tags. The <*FAP*> tags in the procedure description define the configuration of the complex/elementary movement controller. The <FAP> tags (which are always in the XML block that is enclosed by the <*successive*> or <*parallel*> tag, and in the XML block enclosed by <*fgesture*> tag) are used to describe the configuration of facial expressions and viseme templates. The individual FAP tag can be configured using the following attributes: *name*, *type*, *value*, *intensity*, *complexity*, *blending*, *durationStroke*, *durationRetraction*, and *initialDelay*. The attribute *name* is used for the elementary movement controller, or as a designation of the complex movement controller (to access the template in the *co-verbal behavior lexicon*). By using the attribute *type*, we are able to describe the type (dimension) of the configuration that should be carried out by the controller (e.g., *HPR* is used for the rotation of joints, *X* is used for the translation of animated shapes, and *empty* value is used for templates). The attribute *value* describes the values of that configuration which the movement controller should apply. The attribute *amplitude* describes the intensity of that template which is described within the tag (it is used only when <*FAP*> represents a complex motion controller). The attribute *complexity* describes whether the facial expression/emotion represents a basic expression/emotion (*B*), masking (*M*), or overlapping (*S*). It is used only when <*FAP*> represents a complex motion controller. The attribute *blending* describes the weighted measure that defines the effect of the procedure in those regions that are affected concurrently by several complex movement controllers. This attribute is used only when <*FAP*> represents a complex motion controller. The temporal attribute *durationStroke* specifies the duration for the elementary/complex motion controller to take the configuration value specified within the attribute *value* (depending on the *intensity*). When the <*FAP*> should realize some template (the complex motion controller), the template's duration and the duration of its individual sequences have to be appropriately adjusted by considering the global stroke duration, and the value of the <*FAP*> attribute *durationStroke*. The *durationRetraction* specifies how long after reaching the end shape, according to the given <*FAP*> configuration, the effect of the procedure has to be maintained. When the <*FAP*> executes the template (a complex motion controller), the template's duration and the duration of its individual sequences have to be appropriately adjusted according to the global retraction duration and the <*FAP*> attribute *durationRetraction* value. The attribute *durationHold* defines how long the end shape should be maintained after reaching the end shape. The attribute *initialDelay* specifies the desired delay before the shape is realized through the elementary/complex motion controller, and is measured from the start time of the <*FAP*> tag. In the case of consecutive realization, this attribute represents the hold before stroke (pre-stroke-hold) situation, and in the case of simultaneous realization this attribute represents the hold in relation to the occurrence of the <*parallel*> tag.

Similarly, as in the case of the <*fgesture*> tag, within the <*bgesture*> tag the selected configuration of the body can also be represented with <*BAP*> XML tags. The individual <*BAP*> tag can be described with the same attributes as the <*FAP*> tag. Nevertheless, the

<*BAP*> tag does not support attributes *blending* and *complexity*. As can be seen in Table 2, the <*BAP*> tag supports the following four attributes:

a) *interpolation*: this attribute describes a kinematic curve, which is used for the automatic calculation of intermediate configurations, when passing from the current into the excited state, or into some state that is described in the *value* attribute. The interpolation is dependent on the conversational agent's framework. The EVA-framework currently supports three types of interpolation: *EaseIn*, *EaseOut*, and *EaseInOut*.
b) *view*: this attribute specifies the orientation of view during head movements. The *auto* value specifies the automatic adjustment of eyes, when they are oriented into the center of the screen. The *follow* value specifies the orientation of the eyes and the head by considering the position of the object that is specified in the *focus* attribute of the <*BAP*> tag. Furthermore, the *direct* value specifies that the eyes have to be oriented and adapted toward some point in the area that is given in the *focus* attribute of the <*BAP*> tag. And the *empty* value of this attribute specifies that the forward kinematics mechanisms, without further adaptation, should be considered. This attribute is used only when <*BAP*> or the template include the movement of the neck joint.
c) *focus*: this parameter specifies those values that are dependent on the *view* attribute of the <*BAP*> tag. When *view* has the value *follow*, the attribute *focus* represents the name of the object (e.g., the mouse pointer). And when *view* has the value *direct*, the attribute *focus* is described by 3D coordinates in the area of the conversational agent (*vector (x,y,z)*),
d) *trajectory*: this attribute describes a parametric curve, which is stored in the *co-verbal behavior lexicon* and is needed when calculating the inverse kinematics, used for determining the intermediate configuration between the start and the excited state. It is used exclusively for modeling the arm movements (only when <*BAP*> represents the realization of the template).

By using the proposed formal scheme for the procedural description of the co-verbal behavior, we are able to accurately and with high-resolution describe even complex structures and shapes that can be observed in any multimodal corpora. The proposed EVA scheme supports absolute timing in order to define e.g., that individual time runs from the time instance of the EVA event, or from the first occurrence of some tag, within which it is stated. In the following chapter we will present the temporal and contextual independent descriptions of individual shapes and poses by using EVA-Script that the conversational agent is capable of rendering and animating.

Chapter 5

DESCRIPTION OF MOTORIC CAPABILITIES OF CONVERSATIONAL AGENT

INTRODUCTION

The main problem of abstract descriptive languages represents a functional dependency of movements' descriptions from their use, the relative timing, and the expressive conception of behavior. In the EVA-Script we distinguish between poses, shapes, gestures, and movements. The *pose* represents the functional and temporal independent visual shape V (see equation 12), which does not carry any meaning (e.g., fist, shrug, shaking, gesticulation, etc.). The concatenation of several poses sequentially (and transitions in between) in the form of movement phases (and movement phrases) then results in a movement model H (see equation 13), or motion. The movement model H represents a complex set that consists of sequences of poses and transitions in between, which is according to some desired temporal structure in the form of movement phases and phrases presented (by using transformation T_{vm}) as a movement (a sequence of physical manifestations). Even the movement itself (without the context) does not add any meaning to verbal communication. Therefore, the movements, shapes, and poses are the so-called *elementary units* that the co-verbal behavior generation module has to understand.

In order that movement can represent additional meaning during communication (or represent the added value), the *context* or the *intent* also has to be added. This is carried out using the transformation T_m (or T_m^{-1}) (equation 11) which actually converts movement into a gesture. Therefore, the movement (movement model) is generally represented as a sequence of poses and transitions, and the gesture as a movement that is related with some meaning and intent. The *co-verbal behavior lexicon* in this way represents a set of shapes V^* and poses P, which can be arbitrarily mutually combined. In order to design the appropriate *co-verbal behavior lexicon*, it is important to consider the following:

a) the conversational agent has to understand and be able to realize the descriptions of poses and shapes in the dictionary,
b) descriptions in the dictionary have to be independent from each other, in order that they can be mutually arbitrarily combined into several hierarchical structures (e.g., a fist can be represented as an elementary unit, or also as a set of poses of individual

fingers; a stretched palm can be represented as an elementary shape, or also as a set of hand and arm shapes; a symbol for peace can be represented as an elementary unit, or also as a fist with extended middle finger and index finger, etc.),

c) it must be possible to arbitrarily address individual entries in the dictionary based on the structure, duration, and amplitude,
d) movement model *H*, which can be formed by a combination of several elements *V*, can be addressed in *spatial* (structural) and *time domains*, and in the domain of internal and external continuity. Similar intent can be expressed for several acoustic prosodic features for speech.

In general, the abstract descriptive languages define animation as a set of abstract relationships between several elements that are related through relative timing (e.g., movements *A* and *B* should start at the same time), and through complex synchronization points. In this way, the movement cannot be presented as a hierarchical set of parallel and sequential movements of individual body parts, but only as a set of templates that contain relatively static spatial configurations, which can be made expressive mainly by changing duration (and in the case of emotions, also by changing *intensity/amplitude* attributes). Furthermore, definitions of shapes/poses and gestures do not preserve high resolution, and the gesture is often defined by a pre-prepared animation segment that already specifies intent as well (e.g., the repetition of movement in the case of *cyclic gestures* usually represents the repetition of an identical cycle over and over again, without the possibility of divergence in growth). Through the design and development of EVA-Script and the concept of context- and time-independent motor skills, a set of available shapes and movements can be physically separated from the context-dependent lexicons. This makes it possible for individual entries in the *co-verbal behavior lexicon* to reflect several expressive characteristics of movement and reuse them in different psycho-sociological contexts that we want to present through the multimodal interfaces. Further, the EVA-Script not only supports the one-to-one correlation; namely, when some abstract shape can be described by only one procedural specification. Instead, in the *co-verbal behavior lexicon* all abstract shapes can be represented by representative classes of shapes, which include similar candidates of *V* (based on Hamming distance). In order to present the co-verbal behavior as behavior that depends on the given time instant (e.g., the environment, emotions, and speech), and includes at the same time concepts of cultural diversity, then the *co-verbal behavior lexicon* also has to support flexible expressive adjustments of hierarchical structures of poses, and the generation of expressive movement models *H*, which can be formed by any combination of (adapted) elements. By using the proposed *co-verbal behavior lexicon*, the individual poses, shapes, can be moved closer to those shapes that have been annotated in the communicative dialogue's multimodal database.

Abstract languages do not usually consider co-verbal behavior and speech as a common process. Instead, they are considered as two separate processes, which are then related through the synchronization points and the intent. In general, it is assumed that a speech signal is already available and, therefore, it is only necessary to pre-process (transcribe it) it and annotate the corresponding text. Furthermore, the time instants for co-verbal behavior are usually defined in the form of XML structures, where it is exactly specified e.g., how long before or after the specific word/syllable position the behavior should be carried out, and its desired duration. In this way, abstract languages fulfill a more general usability, which is unfortunately often reflected in the larger complexity of the schemes, in laborious changes and improvements, and in the lower resolution and adaptability of gestures to individual (existing and novel) concepts which affect the movement.

The shapes in the co-verbal behavior lexicon are defined as a set of procedural descriptions of configurations *V* for different movement controllers *M* that are involved in the rendering of some pose (equation 12). Here, *V* represents a class of similar (based on Hamming distance) descriptions for specific poses that belong to a specific body part. An individual class of similar descriptions is semantically/semiotically related with the abstract shape (e.g., fist, out-stretched hand, slope, etc.). Each class *V* is in this way represented as an associative object that is accessible through the semantic/semiotic descriptions of *V*, while the corresponding values are represented as a list of similar EVA-Script templates. Furthermore, the individual description of the pose represents an object that is accessible through a sequence of abstract dimensions of description of the shape, while the corresponding value is a list of movement controllers *M* and their configuration used for the recreation of the shape. Each movement controller *M* may represent an elementary movement controller (e.g., joint, animation of the shape), or one of the possible configurations of the pose (which may be similar or not). The shapes in the co-verbal behavior lexicon are thus represented as a hierarchically structured tree, which contains hierarchically ordered lists of associative objects, where the number of hierarchical levels can be arbitrary. The representation of shapes in the co-verbal behavior lexicon is shown in Figure 13.

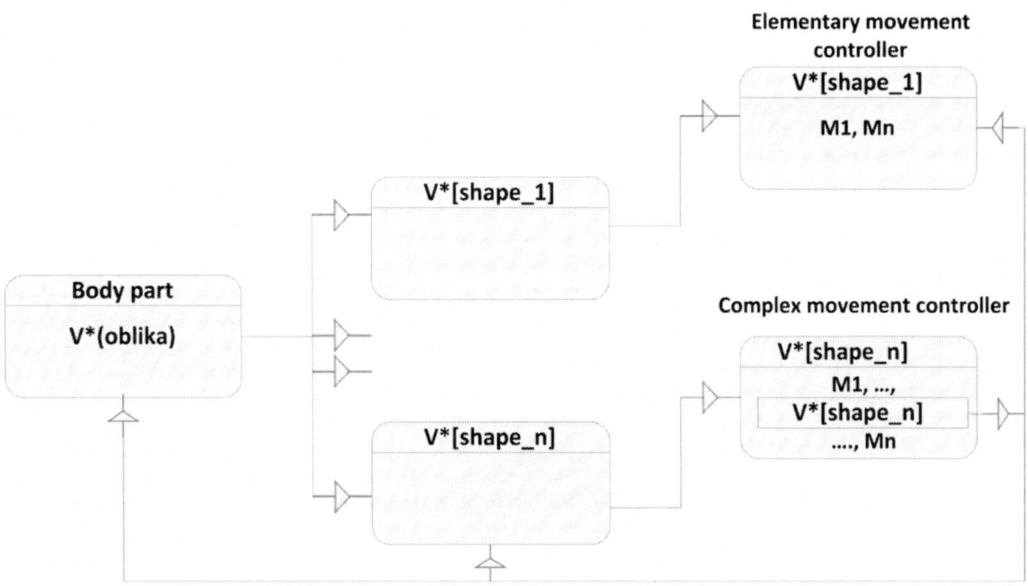

Figure 13. The formation of shapes through the arbitrary number of levels.

Each element *V* can be described as follows:

$$V^*(shape_i) = \{M1:value, M2: shape (\{M11: value, M12: value\}),\ldots\} \quad (14)$$

Each body part may contain a different number of classes *V**. $V^*(shape_i)$ in Figure 13 is a class of visual representations, which depends on the shape. Furthermore, each $V^*(shape_i)$

class can contain any number of similar visual shapes that represent the same abstract shape. For example, the fist shape (based on sign notation *Ham-No-Sys* 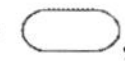, or as *A1* based on *SignPhon* notation) can be represented as a configuration of joint fingers. Elements of the class *V*(fist)*, preserve the basic shape of the fist, together with minor variations regarding the intensity of the joint fingers (e.g., open fist, a raised little finger). In this way, we are able to obtain *n* non-uniformly designed fists, although their baseline configuration still fits to . As can be seen in Figure 13, each shape can be represented as elementary and can be described using elementary motion controllers, or even complex, when in the description of the shape both elementary and complex shapes are included; for example, the derivation of several hand configurations from the fist shape by only adjusting the position of the thumb (e.g., the stretched thumb, which may represent *Ham-No-Sys* signs such as ).

In this way, by using a minimal set of elementary shapes and with only minimal adaptations, we are able to design a wide range of complex movement controllers for a given body part. Therefore, with relatively little effort we are able to form a large repertoire of movements that the realization entity can manifest. When binding different body parts into complex pose *P*, the hierarchical structure of the proposed shapes is even more important. Namely, each pose *P* can be composed by binding several classes V^* $(shape_i)$ and associated elements. In this way, the pose *P* (which is still element *V*) can be defined as a set of *V*(shape)*, where each shape belongs to the corresponding body part:

$$P = V^*_{part}(shape_i) + V^*_{part}(shape_j) + \ldots \tag{15}$$

where V^*_{part} $(shape_i)$ represents the selected pose on a selected body part, and the + sign defines the simultaneous manifestations of these poses. In this way we can represent the complex pose *out-stretched hands* as: a stretched-out hand, a stretched fist, etc. Similarly, we can define the complex pose *stretched hands* as: simultaneousness of the pose for out-stretched left fist and of the pose for out-stretched right fist. The complex poses without additional design/annotation even further extend the set for realization entity by considering the stochastic nature of human gestures, which says that in general there is no gesture that would be even under the same conditions and in the same parametrical space carried out by using the same shapes and same movement (Pavlovic et al., 1997). In the scope of the proposed shapes of the co-verbal behavior lexicon, we define the following four classes of visual representations:

- V^*_{head}: this class combines those poses and gaze that are created by using elementary movement controllers that belong to the head region (e.g., neck joint, eyes and eyelids, etc.),
- V^*_{face}: this class combines those poses that are created by using elementary motion controllers that belong to the face region, including visemes (visual representations of phonemes),
- V^*_{arm}: this class combines those poses that are created by using elementary motion controllers that belong to the regions of the left and right arms,
- V^*_{hand}: this class combines those poses that are created by using elementary motion controllers that belong to the regions of the left and right hands.

In addition to the extended basic set, the individual poses in class V^*_{part} *(shape)* serve as indicators of the space in which the gestures are performed. Namely, people are able to gesticulate only within certain restrictions. For example, for gaze and head movements, these restrictions are determined by the muscles of the neck. Therefore, the neck can be moved only to a certain extent. A similar issue can be observed in the case of finger joints. Furthermore, when observing hand and arm gestures, there is an evident tendency that they are performed in a specific space and by following certain patterns. By using the proposed concept of hierarchical shapes, we are able (based on real movements, and annotated using EVA-Script annotation scheme) to simultaneously evaluate and adapt both of the spaces as poses that belong to a given class *V*. Also, for complex poses it is assumed that modeling and access to $V^*_{part}(shape_i)$ is possible, independently from the other poses for other body parts. Therefore, within the complex pose *P*, the amplitude (as one of the components of expressive movement) of the individual component (body part) can be set independently (or even by using a common amplitude coefficient). Furthermore, the movement in the context of co-verbal behavior lexicon can also be represented in the form of movement model *H* (as a sequence of poses, with corresponding timings of transitions between poses, and interpolation methods). In addition, such movement *H* is not created by using movement phrases that are dependent from the text (equations 10 and 13), but as a sequence of end poses, which are performed by following the temporal conditions and the interpolation curve, as annotated in the multimodal database. Even these movement models can be made expressive in a flexible way.

How to Describe the Expressive Shapes and Poses

The conversational agents are usually designed by 3D volumetric mesh models that support rendering based on skeletal structures, animation of shapes, and other movement controllers (e.g., muscles). From the perspective of co-verbal behavior, the significant shapes occur on the boundaries of the movement phases, as *key poses* (key shapes). Therefore, it is proposed that the shapes in the co-verbal behavior lexicon (the visual representations *V*) are designed in form of corresponding elementary (and complex) movement controllers. In this way each shape *V*, as observed on the boundaries of movement phases, may be defined as: (1) new configuration of elementary controllers, or (2) as an extension of existing shapes ***V*** which adjust only particular elementary controllers (see Figure 16). The repository then contains these definitions specified in EVA-Script descriptive language and groups them into particular classes and subclasses (e.g., fist, tight fist, fist with hidden thumb, etc). Nevertheless, the individual poses and shapes may also be described in any other descriptive language. In general, the conversational agents that are based on the MPEG-4 standard define the individual shapes/poses by using the MPEG-4 standard, which defines animation parameters for the body (BAP), or are based on the standard which defines facial animation parameters (FAP). These animation parameters (similar to those in EVA-Script) are based on the configuration of the joints within the skeleton and on the animation shapes of facial points. When describing movements using the EVA-Script, some BAP and FAP parameters are actually mapped into HPR rotation of joints and chains, and translations of animated shapes. And individual DOFs (degree of freedom) are described as final values or by amplitude in the interval (0, 1]. In the co-verbal behavior lexicon the EVA-Script is used because the scripts can be directly animated on the conversational agent using the EVA-framework. Furthermore, at the same time, for the modeling of shapes tools for 3D modeling (e.g., Maya 3D, Blender, etc.) can be used for exporting shapes directly into the co-verbal behavior lexicon. In this way, the realization of the co-verbal behavior may be animated via several animation frameworks and, without the need for additional compilers or special transformations. The following subsections present the way in which the co-verbal behavior lexicon can be created using the EVA-Script descriptive language and the shapes and poses in the multimodal corpus of real and spontaneous co-verbal behavior that are annotated according to the EVA annotation scheme.

How to Describe the Spatial Configurations of Body Parts

The spatial configurations of poses are described by configurations of joints (bones), where a joint represents such a node within a skeletal structure (see Figure 14) that keeps information about a topological structure of the agent. Each joint has a three-dimensional transformation (which includes its position, scale and orientation), and an optional parent joint. Each joint in the skeleton is also associated with some portion of the character's visual representation (the points in the mesh). The joints form a hierarchy (skeleton). The full transform of a child node is the product of its parent transform as well as its own transform. In addition to 3D transformation each joint is also identified with several restrictions regarding flexibility (DOF - degrees of freedom). For instance, the movement of most joints that bind the wrist is, therefore, rather limited. The same applies to those joints which belong to the metacarpal or to the joints in the neck region. However, DOF differ depending on the body part.

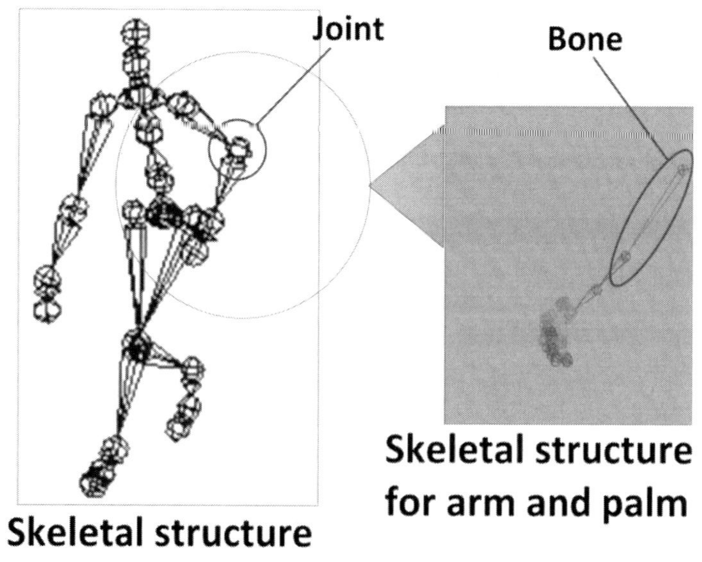

Figure 14. The skeletal structure of the conversational agent.

Since the DOFs differ depending on the specific body part the kinematic restrictions must reflect that and must be based on the actual body part (Singh et al., 2013). These restrictions can be static or dynamic. The *static restrictions* refer to the rotation of joints (the minimum and maximum possible rotations) and the *dynamic restrictions* refer to those that arise from relations with adjacent joints in the skeletal chain (e.g., inner dependency of DIP and PIP joints of fingers) (Pavlovic et al., 1997). The spatial component of the pose that is described in the form of elementary joints (and bones) is usually presented by the configuration of 3D rotational vectors R_V, as follows:

$$R_V = R(\alpha,\beta,\gamma) = R_z(\alpha)R_y(\beta)R_x(\gamma) = (H,P,R) \tag{16}$$

where H – heading, P – pitch, and R – roll. Here, the rotation vector R_V represents a spatial configuration in the Euclidian space. H represents a rotation by an angle α around the z-axis, in the counterclockwise direction (or the vector (0, 0, 1)). Further, x and y components are adaptable, and z is constant. Therefore, H can be represented by the following rotational matrix:

$$H = R_z(\alpha) = \begin{matrix} \cos\alpha & -\sin\alpha & 0 \\ \sin\alpha & \cos\alpha & 0 \\ 0 & 0 & 1 \end{matrix} \tag{17}$$

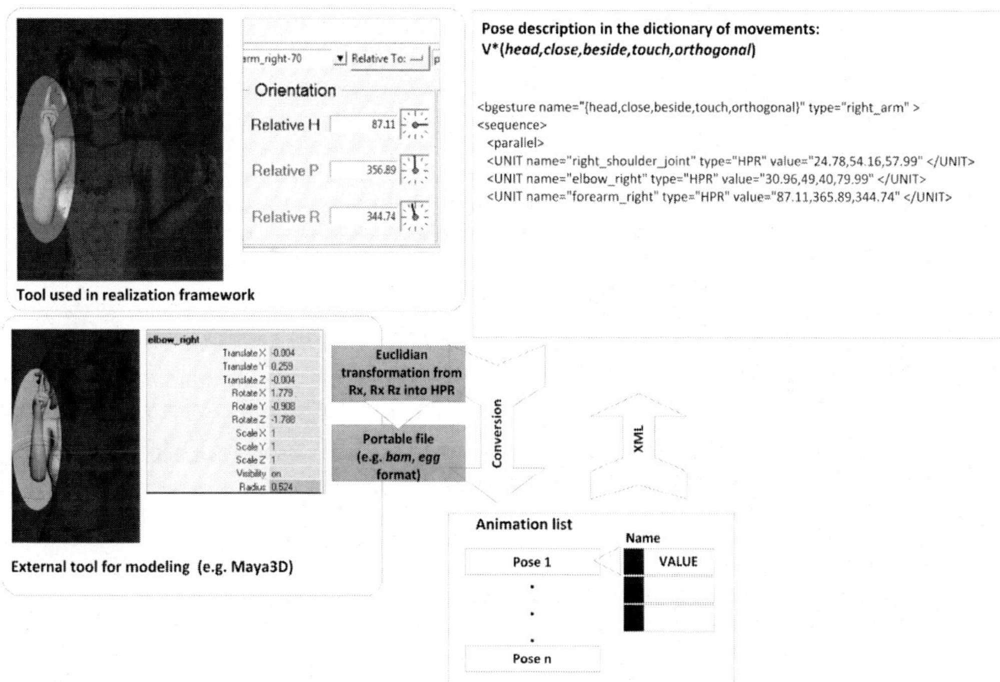

Figure 15. The conversion of the selected pose into an entry in the co-verbal behavior lexicon.

The pitch parameter P represents a rotation around the y axis by an angle β, and also in the counterclockwise direction (or vector (0, 0, 1)). The x and z components are adaptable, but y is a constant.

The parameter P is calculated by the following rotational matrix:

$$P = R_z(\beta) = \begin{matrix} \cos\beta & 0 & \sin\beta \\ 0 & 1 & 0 \\ -\sin\beta & 0 & \cos\beta \end{matrix} \qquad (18)$$

The roll parameter R represents the rotation around the x axis by an angle γ in the counterclockwise direction (or vector (1, 0, 0)). The components y and z are adaptable, but x is a constant. The parameter R is calculated by the following rotational matrix:

$$R = R_z(\gamma) = \begin{matrix} 1 & 0 & 0 \\ 0 & \cos\gamma & -\sin\gamma \\ 0 & \sin\gamma & \cos\gamma \end{matrix} \qquad (19)$$

In order to describe the spatial configuration of individual pose in the regions of arms, hands and head, in general a skeletal chain has to be defined, and an appropriate rotation vector in the form of *HPR* (*Rv = (H, P, R)*, see equation 16) to individual elementary motion controller has to be assigned. As in the case of annotation (Figure 12), also the spatial configuration is designed and modeled directly on the conversational agent. Further, that individual elementary motion controller which belongs to the selected skeletal chain has to be selected from a set of motion controllers. The joint configuration is set by using the graphical interface used for configuring the elementary motion controller that is available in the EVA-framework, or by using some external tool for 3D modeling (Figure 15). The observed pose described in EVA-Script descriptive language is then transferred into the co-verbal behavior lexicon.

When a pose is described using the EVA-framework, the XML syntax is written manually. Firstly, the *<bgesture>* block with attributes *body_part* and *name* is created. For example, a pose in Figure 15 is a pose of the right hand; therefore, the attribute *body_part* has value *right_arm*. And the value for the attribute *name* is created that is based on the abstract conception of dimensions used for the description of the shape in dependence on the body part (see Table 1). Since in this case the body part is *arm*, the *name* of the pose is determined after the *model* {*height*, *distance*, *radial orientation*, *bending*, *orientation of the forearm*}. Therefore, in Figure 15 we have {*head*, *close*, *on the side*, *touch*, *perpendicularly*}. When designing the pose, where it is assumed that there should be simultaneous rendering of the shape through the movement controllers, the actual configuration has to be described within the XML block *<parallel>*. Further, the individual movement controller has to be described by using the *<BAP>* tag with attributes *name*, *type* and *value*. The attribute *name* represents the actual name of the individual elementary movement controller within the articulated 3D model of the conversational agent. In Figure 15 the movement of the right hand is described; therefore, the attribute *name* has to be, for example, *right_arm_joint*, *right_elbow*, *right_forearm*. The attribute *type* then describes the dimension of the configuration that the controller should execute. In Figure 15, the configuration of the joints which are controlled by rotational vectors is described. Therefore, for *type* we have *HPR* value. Besides the right hand, the pose in Figure 15 is designed also by using the right hand. Therefore, similarly as for the arm, the configuration of the right hand also has to be described as a spatial configuration of joints (BAP tags) that belong to the hand region (e.g., DIP, PIP, wrist, etc.) and combined within the tag *<bgesture>*.

The description of the configuration of movements by the EVA-framework is still relatively complex and quite time-consuming. The same holds true for the direct transfer of poses from the conversational agent into the co-verbal behavior lexicon. As a result, the proposed design of the co-verbal behavior lexicon and the EVA-Script support and define how to transfer poses and movement models directly from 3D modeling software (see Figure 15) into the co-verbal behavior lexicon. In this case, the lexicon is created by designing actual poses in some external tool used for 3D modeling (e.g., Maya 3D, 3D Blender) that are then stored as *poses* or *key frame animations*. By using the interfaces for export, the record of the selected frame (which contains the shape with semantics and a format that is understandable to the conversational agent) is converted, wherein the Euclidian transformation and the interpolation from the environment's 3D space into the 3D space of the movement realizer are performed (see equations 17, 18, 19). In this case these are so-called *egg*[1] files. The content of the *egg* file can be converted into a shape described in EVA-Script descriptive language by using the proprietary conversion tool in the EVA-framework.

In order to perform the conversion from the 3D environment into EVA-Script format, firstly the input *egg* file is parsed and all the semantic elements are extracted. The structures and the record of the animation frame in *egg* format (semantics) expect that the key information about the pose is located within elements *EggTable* and *EggGroupNode*. Further, the individual element *EggTable* may encompass one or more elements *EggGroupNode*. Similarly, the individual element *EggGroupNode* can encompass one or more elements *EggTable*. Therefore, the content has to be parsed by using the following recursive method:

$$f(i,e) = \begin{cases} e.process; \text{if e.type= EggTable} \\ f(i,node); \text{if e.type= EggGroupNode} \end{cases} \tag{20}$$

Namely, in the list the following two types of elements are searched: *EggTable* and *EggGroupNode*. The arbitrary number of hierarchical levels can be considered. One of the levels (usually the last one) contains the element *EggTable* which actually keeps the content about the shape. The content of the *EggTable* is then processed further, in order to extract the 3D rotation vector. It is stored into a temporary hash table that keeps the value of the individual elementary movement controller and can be accessed through his name (as defined in the skeletal chain of the articulated 3D model of the conversational agent). This two-dimensional list is then stored in a list of animations. When storing the description of the pose/animation in EVA-Script format, each entry in the list of animations represents one pose, and the content of the pose of the skeletal chain of the movement controllers (and values) that are involved in the manifestation of the shape.

[1] http://en.wikipedia.org/wiki/Python_eggs.

Each entry in the list of animations is placed within its EVA-Script block *<successive>*, while the description of the pose is placed into a set of *<BAP>* tags, with assigned attributes *name*, *type* and *value*. When the attribute *name* represents the key in hash table, the attribute *value* represents the value that the key keeps (e.g., *hash_table[key]*), and the attribute *type* is determined based on the configured belonging of elementary movement controllers to an individual body part.

The proposed co-verbal behavior lexicon, in addition to elementary movement controllers, also uses complex movement controllers, which actually represent the call of that template which is already stored within the co-verbal behavior lexicon. By using already designed templates, the design of the new pose can be performed by using the existing one and by addressing those individual elementary controllers that actually differ regarding the configuration. Figure 16 shows how to derive the hand shapes by using the existing templates (complex movement controllers), and the corresponding XML notation in the EVA-Script format.

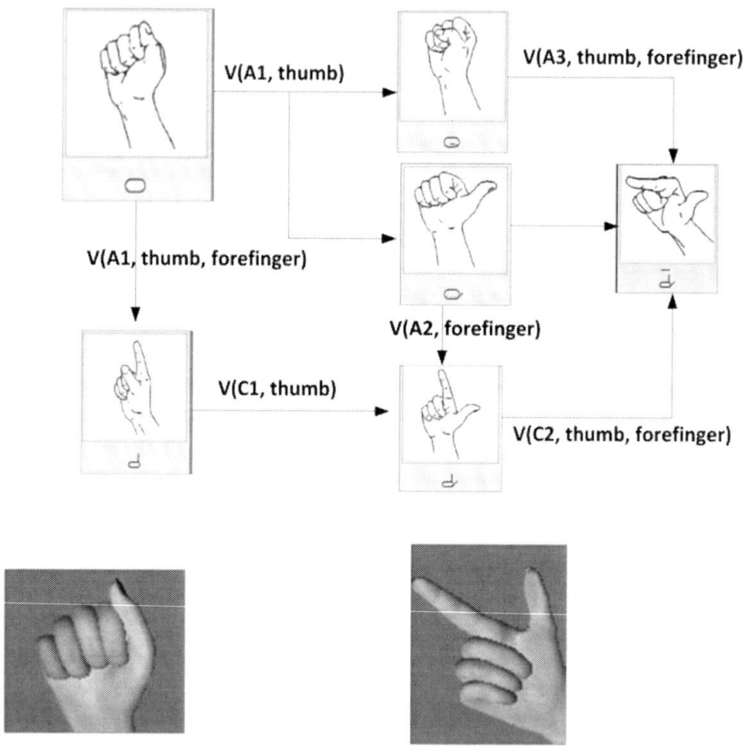


```
<bgesture name="A1" type="left_hand" >
  <sequence>
    <parallel>
      <UNIT name="thumb_TM"
      <UNIT name="thumb_MCP"
      <UNIT name="thumb_IP"
      .
      .
      .
```

```
<bgesture name="A1" type="left_hand" >
  <sequence>
    <parallel>
      <UNIT name="forefinger_TM"
      <UNIT name="forefinger_MCP"
      <UNIT name="forefinger_DIP"
      <UNIT name="forefinger_PIP"
      <UNIT name="thumb_TM"
      <UNIT name="thumb_MCP"
      <UNIT name="thumb_IP"
```

Figure 16. The derivation of the pose or shape.

In Figure 16 there are different and multi-level derivations of hand shapes that are based on the complex motion controller named *fist* (*A1*). The *fist* is described by the configuration of elementary controllers that belong to the palm region (of the individual fingers):

V(A1) = ({thumb_TM: (H,P,R), thumb_MCP:(H,P,R),...,
pinkie_PIP: (H,P,R) }) (21)

Instead of *fist* versions with type *A3* or *A2* (see Figure 16) being only defined in the form of elementary controllers, they can also be derived using complex controllers and presented as follows (equation 14):

{M1: A1, thumb_TM: (H,P,R), thumb_MCP:(H,P,R)} (22)

where a shape for fist *A1* is presented by the modulation of thumb. Similarly, the pose *C2* can be described as a pose *C1* by the modulation of the thumb, or as a pose *A1* by the modulation of the thumb and index finger. The derivation is also reflected in the formal description of the pose, where the pose *C2* is represented as a simultaneous modulation and not in the form of elementary movement controllers. The description of the shape *A1* (the *<bgesture>* element within the EVA-Script block *<parallel>*) is followed by elementary controllers (the *<BAP>* elements), which modulate the shape *A1*. In a similar manner, complex poses *P* and movement models *H* can also be created and not just different shapes.

How to Describe Trajectories

The proposed co-verbal behavior model is based on the description and realization of key poses (final shapes) that occurred at the boundaries of movement phases. The actual realization of key poses, (the animation of the movement model) however, represents a transition from the previous (initial) shape into the shape described by the key pose. This transition is represented by a movement model, *H,* which defines the actual transformation between the shapes (poses). In the model the transformation T_{vm}^{-1} contains the timing information and the kinematic interpolation used for the automatic determination of intermediate frames as part of *key frame animation*. In the case of gestures which are performed with arms, the transformation T_{vm}^{-1} also contains the *trajectory* of the transition. The trajectory of the transition actually represents a curve that the movement controller (or the observed body part) outlines during the transition from the initial pose P_S into the end pose P_E for a given movement phase. Therefore, the movement is not only carried out by interpolating the increased/decreased configuration values of movement controllers in the individual animation frame, but is also carried out by following some movement trajectory in 3D space (the so-called *motion-path*).

In the expressive co-verbal behavior model, we are primarily interested in that trajectory which is in 3D space described by the hand (e.g., the path that is performed by the hand when moving from the initial pose P_S into the final pose P_E). Namely, by using mechanisms of inverse kinematics, it is possible (based on the predicted spatial positions of the hands) to automatically calculate the appropriate positions and configuration of movement controllers which handle the arm (e.g., automatically configure parent joints of the wrist joint). The arm gesture can be understood as a movement with meaning, which is performed by using the arm (and may also include the palm). When using it, we wish to express our emotion or attitude toward the discussion's topic or to illustrate (to emphasize, to outline, etc.) the information (the communicative goal). Within this context the arm gesture can even substitute the speech, or may just be used simultaneously with speech as an additional, speech synchronous communication modality (Nam & Wohn, 1996). When observing and annotating the co-verbal arm movements (the expressive shapes and poses) as key poses at the boundaries of movement phases, there is a problem regarding expressing the communicative intent/idea through the spatial structure and spatial configuration of the arm. Namely, the communicative intent does not reflect itself only in the form of key poses, but also in the way the movement from the pose P_S into the pose P_E is actually performed within a specific amount of time. The trajectory that the hand performs during the transition from P_S into P_E is one of the most important components regarding the manual gesticulation. By using the trajectory that is outlined by the palm, we are able to show numerous communicative concepts, such as the outlines of objects, actions, concepts and feelings, diversity, dynamics in behavior, etc. (Nam & Wohn, 1996; Rieser et al., 2012).

When describing the trajectory, the main problem represents the spatial complexity (similarity and diversity) of the specific trajectory that can be outlined by the speaker's hand within a communicative dialogue. The reason for the spatial complexity lies primarily in the flexibility regarding the movements of the human arms in 3D space which result in the high rotational and translational diversity of transitions between two key poses.

Therefore, accurate descriptions of trajectories using configurations of movement controllers (not just at the boundaries of the movement phases, but also in all intermediate frames - the so-called direct description of the procedural animation) are inappropriate and infeasible in terms of time. As a result, the proposed co-verbal behavior model uses parametric trajectories which include poses for just a few key points of the prime movement trajectories (or *movement primes* such as linear, arc, chair, roof, spiral). Furthermore, at each such key point the configuration of movement controllers is described only at the abstract level, e.g., in the form of the hand position in 3D space depending upon the position of the hand and body (see Table 1).

Figure 17 outlines some of the *movement primes*. As can be seen, for a description of the trajectory two basic primes are defined, which are called *linear prime* and *arc prime*. The *linear prime* describes all those transitions where the hand actually describes a straight line in space. Since in the case of linear transitions there are no changes in direction, the trajectory can be fully described by only two key points, i.e., the initial and the final positions of the hand. Thus, the trajectory can be described with the abstract spatial configuration of the arm at the start (with pose P_S) and at the end (with pose P_E) of the given movement phase. And the *prime arc* describes all those transitions where the hand outlines an elliptical trajectory, in which up to two changes of direction occur, e.g., downwards and from left to right. For the description of this prime, three key points are needed: the arm configuration at the start of the movement phase (with pose P_S), the arm configuration when the direction changes (with pose P_I), and the arm configuration at the end of the movement phase (with pose P_E). When the hand outlines a trajectory that contains more than one change of direction, then the movement trajectory is composite. In this case, descriptions for the initial, final, and intermediate configurations are needed (at all those positions where there is a change in direction). For example, for the description of the composite prime of type chair (see Figure 17), three to five key points are needed. The composite prime can be, for example, described in the form of two linear primes, or as a combination of two linear primes and one prime *arc*, etc. Irrespective of the complexity of the composite prime (regarding the number of positions at which the direction of movement changes), any movement's trajectory can be represented by a set of basic primes.

The number of key points depends on the number and type of basic primes which compose the specific complex prime. Furthermore, a composite prime with a large number of key points is spiral. The spiral is often used at the end of enumeration (e.g., in the verbal phrase: *and so on*), or as a manipulator during the search phase (e.g., in the verbal phrase: *I mean ... that ... hm ...*). The complexity of the spiral depends on the number of its curves. Namely, each turn of the spiral can be described by three arcs, or as a sequence of seven abstract configurations in seven intermediate points.

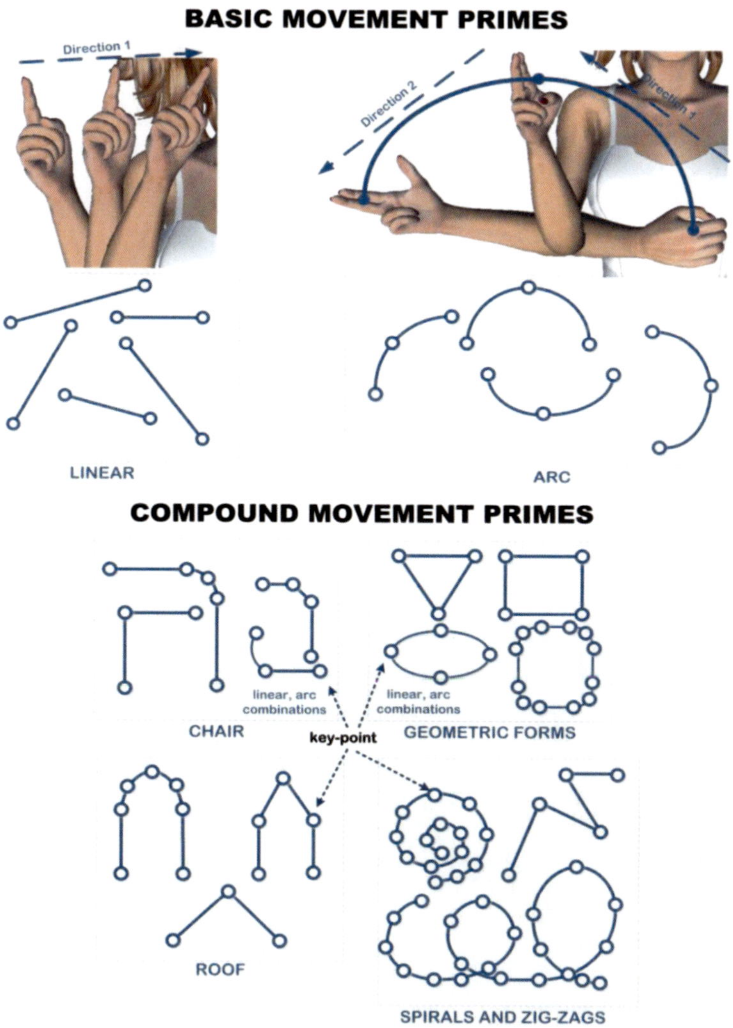

Figure 17. The basic and composite primes of movement trajectories.

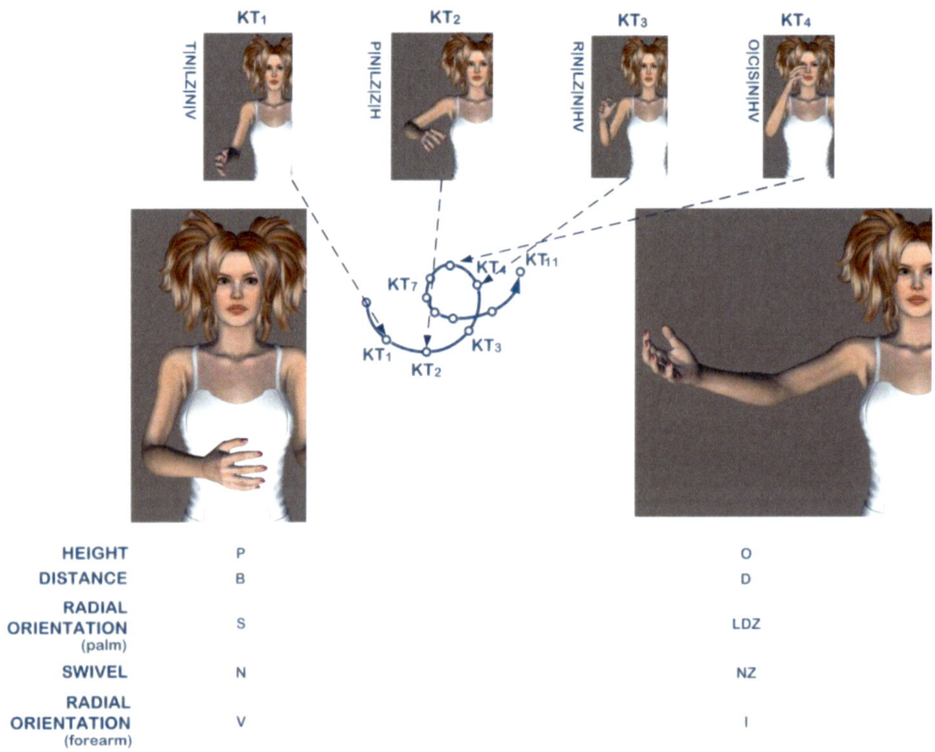

Figure 18. The description of the spiral transition between poses using the intermediate key points and primes.

Let *T* represent a spiral (see Figure 18), which consists of two curves (1 complete and 2 half). It describes the transition from the pose P_S = *{P|B|S|N|V}* into the pose P_E = *{O|D|LDZ|NZ|I}*. *T* can be described as a transition which is carried out using the four arcs that are defined by 9 key points. The first key point KT_0 represents the configuration of the start pose. The second key point KT_1 describes the configuration when the palm is located in the abdomen region (T), the distance from the body is *normal* (N), the radial orientation is *left-outside* (LZ), the bend is *normal* (N), and the orientation of the forearm is *vertical* (V).

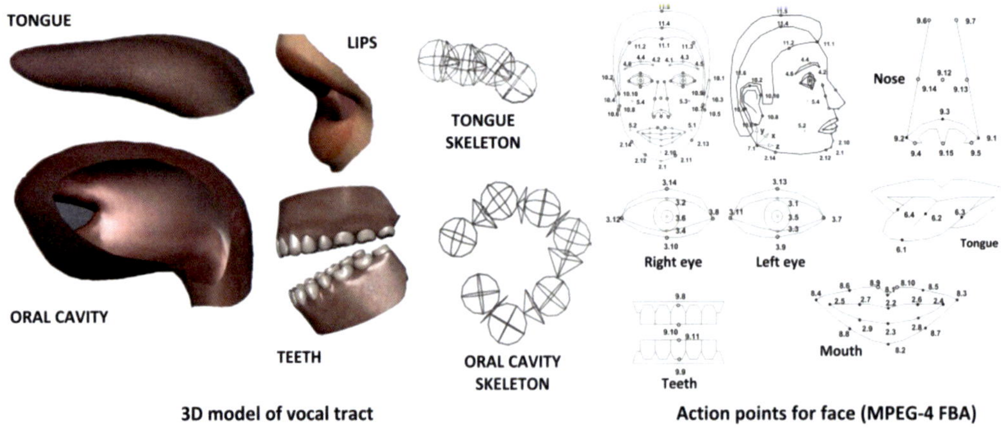

Figure 19. The EVA ECA's 3D model of the vocal tract.

In this way, the key point KT_I can be described abstractly as KT_I = *{T|N|LZ|N|V}*. Similarly, remaining key points K_i can also be described. The trajectory *T* is parametrically described as a sequence of key transitions, defined by using the shape of the basic prime and key points that define the prime. If the prime is linear, then the key transition is described as follows: *KP* = *{linear, [KT_S, KT_E]}*. However, when the transition is in the form of an arc, the *KP* is described as: *KP* = *{arc, [KT_S, KT_I, KT_E]}*, or as a sequence of three key points (start, intermediate, and end). The key transition of type *arc* must contain at least three key points, since it is realized by interpolation using Bezier curves (Farin, 1997) within the EVA-framework.

How to Describe a Viseme

Visemes represent the visual rendering of phonemes in the vocal tract region. Namely, the pronunciations can be represented by the movement of the vocal and nasal tracts. In the context of animation, the visemes are represented, therefore, in the form of 3D models of the vocal tract. As suggested by King and Parent (2001), the 3D model of the vocal tract is further divided into the following 6 regions: *teeth* (upper and lower), *lips* (upper and lower), *oral cavity*, *tongue*, and *epiglottis*. The research in the field of audio-visual speech intelligibility shows the importance of the information that is provided by performing the co-articulation of the lips, especially when the verbal information is of inferior quality. Those elements of the facial region that include the vocal tract are able (when there is no speech, or it is unintelligible) to provide up to two-thirds of the missing information. Half of this missing information is provided by the outer part of the face (lips, cheekbones), while the other half is given by the internal part of the face (mouth, tongue, and teeth) (King & Parent, 2001). The appropriate level of intelligibility can only be achieved by a carefully engineered 3D model of the vocal tract, which allows a coherent visual representation of the speech signal and animation in the form of co-articulation (Zorić & Pandžić, 2006). The EVA ECA's 3D model of the vocal tract in Figure 19, therefore, includes the following 6 regions: *teeth* (upper and lower), *lips* (upper and lower), *cheekbones*, *nasal region*, *tongue*, and *oral cavity*.

In the EVA 3D model of the vocal tract, individual regions are modeled in the form of meshes, with appropriate skeletal structure added. In Figure 19 the mesh structures (with textures) of the individual regions and associated skeletal chains are shown. To the upper and lower teeth are each one added one joint, whereas the final joints of the skeletal chain of the oral cavity also affect the modulation in the region of the lips. The defined joints for the tongue represent the minimized set of movement controllers that results from the definition of the parametric 3D models of the tongue. In Figure 19 (right) the definition of facial points according to the MPEG-4 FBA standard is also shown (Pobar & Ipšić, 2012; Petjan, 2005). With the definition of the 3D model of the vocal tract we are able to describe particular phonemes as a combination of modulation of the vocal tract region and cheekbones in the form of animated shapes (MPEG-4 visemes, and MPEG-4 FAPs (facial points)) and skeletal deformations. When describing visemes' shapes, the MPEG-4 definitions of viseme shapes and extended *Preston-Blair* phonemic series are used. The MPEG-4 FBA standard defines those parameters that are used for modeling the face of the virtual agent. The MPEG-4 sets of facial parameters are classified under FAP (facial action points). The individual parameters modulate specific face regions. The standard defines 66 elementary FAP parameters that describe the distances between key facial characteristics. In addition to the elementary ones, the MPEG-4 standard defines 14 high-level FAPs for descriptions of visemes, and 6 FAPs for descriptions of the elementary facial expressions (emotions). Based on the 3D model of the vocal tract and MPEG-4-based visemes, templates of visemes for the conversational model can be created that are not based only on lip modeling, but also on the modeling of the teeth and tongue. By using 14 visemes, as defined by the MPEG-4 FBA, a visual representation of all the English phonemes can be presented. Nevertheless, the MPEG-4 FBA set of visemes is not sufficient for several other languages. The visemes are obviously language-dependent and, therefore, only a partial overlap with the English set can be provided. As with, for example, the Croatian language (Petjan, 2005), it is also necessary to figure out the maximal possible overlap for other languages and check the possibilities to map non-existing phonemes to the best approximation that can be found in the database.

Table 3. The mapping of Slovenian phonemes and visemes

Phoneme	Word	Viseme
a:	mama (*eng:* "mother")	aa
a	pas (*eng:* "belt")	aa
i:	pila (*eng:* "drinked")	ih
i	sir (*eng:* "cheese")	ih
e:	pet (*eng:* "five")	e
E	zelen (*eng:* "green")	e
O:	voda (*eng:* "water")	oh
o:	pot (*eng:* "path")	oh
u:	suša (*eng:* "drought")	ou
dZ	džungla (*eng:* "jungle")	ch
j	jasno (*eng:* "clear")	ih
k	kod (*eng:* "where")	kk
g	kdaj (*eng:* "when")	kk
r	res (*eng:* "really")	rr
s	sin (*eng:* "son")	ss

Table 3 maps the Slovenian pronunciations of phonemes and associated visual representations (visemes) which were defined in the context of the co-articulation model. The starting point of these mappings represents the established phonetic theory in Slovenian grammar (Toporiščič, 2000), which considers the pronunciation of individual phonemes which are represented by 25 letters. For example, the phonemes /k/ and /g/ are in general pronounced the same; therefore, they can be mapped to the same visual representation, named /kk/. Similarly, letters such as /š/, /č/, /ž/, and /dž/ can be mapped into viseme /ch/. Individual descriptions of visemes (or the configuration of elementary movement controllers) are similar to poses for hands, arms and head stored in the co-verbal behavior lexicon in the form of time- and context-independent templates that the agent is able to manifest. The description of the shape is written in XML notation in the EVA-Script format.

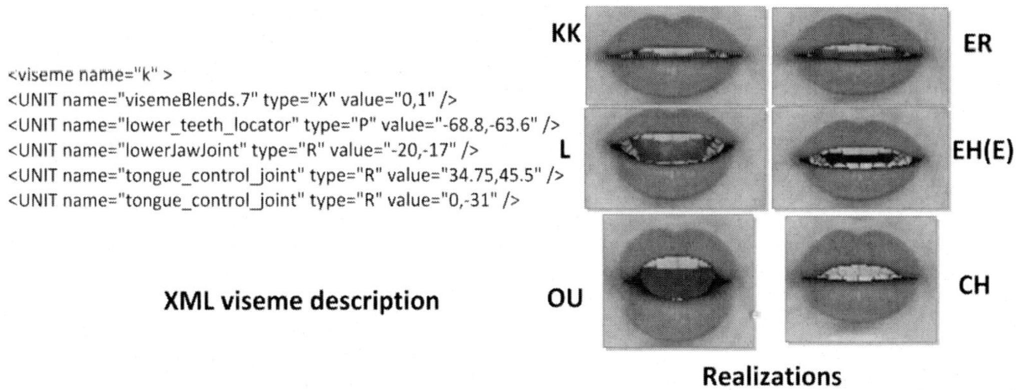

Figure 20. The description of visemes in EVA-Script format (*left*), and their visualization (*right*).

In Figure 20 (left) a description of the viseme /kk/ in the EVA-Script format is presented. It is virtually identical to the description of the pose for the hands, arms, or head. The configuration of local motion controllers that affect the physical manifestation can be described within the *<FAP>* tags, where the transformation type and value are defined. Unlike descriptions of poses for hands, arms and head, when describing the visemes their minimum and maximum values for each movement controller also have to be given. For all *<FAP>* tags within the *<viseme>* tags, a simultaneousness of modeling is assumed for that region of the 3D model which the motion controller includes. Figure 20 (*right)* shows the actual results of the physical manifestations of isolated visemes as those shapes that the conversational agent can present in the face region (or in the vocal tract region).

How to Describe the Facial Expressions

Natural expressive behavior also includes the expression of mood, attitude toward a specific theme and attitude toward one's own emotional state. In general (based on the theory of discrete emotions (Ekman & Friesen, 1982)), people are able to express six *basic emotions* that can be recognized in several cultures and are mutually discrete, since they can easily be distinguished from each other. The basic emotions differ in terms of facial configuration, as well as in those biological processes that form them. In addition to basic emotions, people also express their condition, their attitude toward a specific theme, and their attitude toward their own emotional state by using *complex emotions* that cannot be directly attributed solely to one of the basic emotions. Therefore, the complex emotions are usually described using dimensional models that try to describe the neuro-psychological closeness of the condition (feeling, attitude) and the contraction of muscles in the face region through the concepts of overlapping and masking of basic emotions. On the conversational agents, for the definition and synthesis of emotions VAD models (Circumplex) (Rubin & Talerico, 2009), PANA (Bales, 2001), and PAD (Bales, 2001) are mostly used.

The facial expressions represent a set of complex and elementary motion controllers, which may simultaneously affect the common sub-regions in the face. The lip synchronization, for example, affects the shape of the face in the vocal tract region, which includes the lips and surrounding area. The facial expressions and emotions affect the face as a whole (including the individual segments of the vocal tract). Therefore, it is quite natural that the speech is present simultaneously with the facial expressions, such as a *smile*, or *astonishment* in the region of the eyes, etc. It is also fully natural for speech to be present simultaneously with those complex emotions that are expressed by the blending of different shapes (expressions) in the facial region (Martin et al., 2006a).

Complex emotions/expressions are classified as *superimposed (overlapping)*, and *masked* (Ahn et al., 2013). Often people do not want to show some emotion or attitude that they actually feel. These are called *masked emotions*. The masking is usually the consequence of some social norm (Tsapatsoulis et al., 2002). On the other hand, overlapping is present when two emotions are evenly expressed. Ekman (Ekman & Friesen, 1969) defined the following six basic emotions: *anger*, *disgust*, *fear*, *joy*, *sadness*, and *surprise*. According to the literature (Martin et al., 2006a; Tsapatsoulis et al., 2002) and observations from the annotations of EVA multimodal corpora, it can be concluded that there is indeed a wider range of emotions which extends the basic emotions into contexts of superimposed and masked feelings, such as: *disappointment*, *masked satisfaction*, *despair*, *pride*, *sarcasm*, etc. In order to represent these complex emotions as a set of blended elementary emotions and through animation blending techniques, we have to first identify the *similarity measure* between complex and elementary emotions. In this way we indentify the most expressed primary emotion and all other emotions that complement or overlap the most expressed one. For this task a concept of evaluation of similarity of emotions and expressions through *Hamming distance* is used. This concept is quite similar concept to the one used for the description of shapes and spatial configurations of the arms, hands, and head. Namely, the similarity of emotions and expressions is measured according to the *FAP* distribution in the face region. In the expressive model of the co-verbal behavior, the emotion/facial expression is defined as a shape in the face region V_{face} and composed of elementary movement controllers that are based on the FAP facial parameters. Let the facial expression (emotion) E_i represent the effect of FAP parameters in the face region, where E_i contains the FAP parameters F_i of all sub-regions of the face. Each F_i, therefore, represents a unique segment in the face region, which can be used to modulate the facial expression (e.g., eyelid, left angle of the left eyebrow, right angle of the right eyebrow, etc.). Thus, each E_i can be represented as: $E_i = \{F_i^{E_i}, i = 1...n\}$. The blending of facial expressions can then be presented as the simultaneousness of expressions E_i and E_j, which effectively means that there are face regions and facial parameters that the facial expressions are trying to create simultaneously. Therefore, *masked* (*M*) or *overlapped* (*S*) expressions can be described as: $\{F_i^{(E_i,E_j)}, i = 1...n\}$. In this way, by using only six basic Ekman emotions, the dominant influence can always be defined; i.e., whether $F_i^{(E_i,E_j)}$ belongs more to the facial expression E_i or E_j.

Let E_u represent one of the basic emotions, and E_i the observed overlapped or masked facial expression. When describing the observed facial expression, the goal is to describe E_i as a function of the basic emotion E_u (to which basic emotion it is most similar) and to obtain corresponding parameters, which can be used to modulate it (the FAP parameters that can be traced and are not consistent with the basic emotion). For each E_u those intervals can be defined which describe all plausible (credible) presentations of the specific emotion. For each $F_i \in E_U$, therefore, such a numeric interval can be defined that captures the credible values of the parameter in the context of basic emotion E_u. The observed facial expression E_i can be visually compared with each basic emotion $E_{u,}$ counting how many characteristics of the E_i differs from the one of plausible representation of E_u. As a basic $E_{u,}$ that one is selected whose Hamming distance is the lowest (E_i and E_u differ in the smallest number of FAP parameters $F_i^{E_i}$). For the modulation of basic emotion E_u, the next basic emotion E_u is selected that poses the minimal Hamming distance. The observed expression, therefore, can be described as $E_i = \{E_U^i, E_U^j, F_i^{E_j}; i = 1...n\}$, which represents a blending function of two primary emotions E_U^i, E_U^j, and FAP parameters $F_i^{E_j}$, which are modulated by E_U^j.

Chapter 6

CORRELATING SHAPES AND SEMIOTIC INTENT

INTRODUCTION

The set of shapes that an agent can present in fact represent a set of concepts that can be animated on the corresponding 3D model of the conversational agent. However, the shapes themselves do not bare meaning or the *intent*. In order to add meaning (the intent) to shapes and to be able to convert them in the co-verbal behavior (gestures), we introduced the following two transformations: T_{vm}^{-1} (equation 10), and T_{m}^{-1} (equation 11). Both transformations represent correlations that can be used to relate verbal and non-verbal behavior. The first one defines the movement model and the second one the gesture. The co-verbal behavior lexicon and grammar then represent the external resources for the proposed architecture, as outlined in Figure 4. Both are needed for the generation of expressive co-verbal behavior. By using the lexicon, the relationships between the morphology (and semiotic properties) of input text and the co-verbal behavior lexicon can be established. Moreover, the grammar also establishes and maintains the dynamic rules which represent the co-verbal behavior as a function of the input text.

THE CLASSIFICATION OF THE INTENT USING SEMIOTIC GRAMMAR

Semiotic grammar represents a set of rules by which we are able to predict (based on the morphological characteristics of the input text and prosody) *n*-possible interpretations of the intent on the individual segments in the input text. The intent is defined in the form of semiotic classification. The main issue in the case of semantic relations is to maintain the explicit correlation between content and gestures, especially in large semantic spaces. Consequently, very large databases that store the correlation between the statements are needed in order to plan and synchronize the gesture models *G*. Most existing co-verbal lexicons used in HMI are based solely on semantics. These lexicons form domain-specific grammars, which are mostly suitable for the realization of the co-verbal behavior that is based on a pre-defined or pre-known context (word sequences contained in the database), and already annotated and pre-prepared text. When the co-verbal behavior is defined exclusively in the semantic space, the algorithm that predicts the behavior has to be familiar with the semantic meaning of that word sequence where the behavior occurs. The proposed EVA grammar, however, keeps a set of patterns that associate the morpho-syntactic sequences with the semiotic classes and semiotic subclasses (based on the so-called semiotic classification) in an unrestricted semiotic space. Furthermore, the understanding of the text and the intent is not based on the semantics of the key word (or key sequences) and their semantic meaning. Instead, a more general correlation between text and gestures is based on the semiotic features of phrases, on the morpho-syntactic structure of the text, and on the prosodic features of the spoken content. By considering that the morpho-syntactic space, e.g., for the Slovenian language, contains a much smaller set of possible morpho-syntactic sequences of part-of-speech tags than the semantic space with a vocabulary of more than 300,000[1] words, then the semiotic presentation of the intent (as relations dependent on the morpho-syntactic sequences) can significantly reduce the size of the knowledge database that is needed to classify the phrases. The EVA grammar is represented as a parametric space of the intent M_τ (see Figure 1), which defines the following four semiotic classes: *iconic*, *deictic*, *manipulative* (adapters), and *symbolic*.

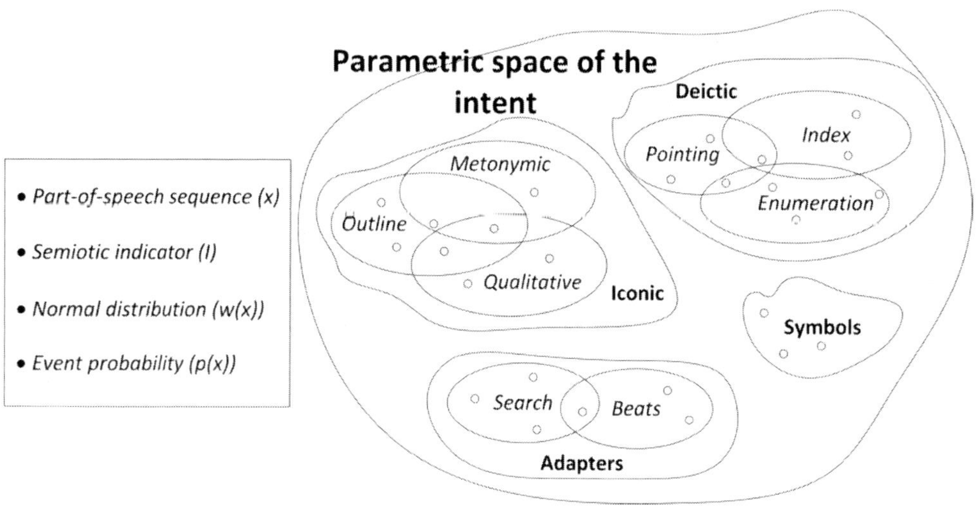

Figure 21. The semiotic space represented as parametric space of the intent.

As seen in Figure 21, the individual semiotic class consists of several subclasses. The *iconic class* consists of the *outline*, *qualitative*, and *metonymic* subclasses. The *deictic class* then consists of *pointing*, *index*, and *enumeration* subclasses. Furthermore, the *adapters class* consists of *search*, dialogue *management* (for dialogue management through communicative functions, e.g., exchange of speakers), and *beats* subclasses. The *symbolic class* does not contain any subclasses, since the symbols are explicit semantic representations, and as conventional signs they already express the intent independently from the accompanying verbal information. The individual semiotic subclass contains elements (rules) that can be used in order to identify the subclass. In order to determine the intent of linguistic expressions within the input text, the research published by Allwood (2010), McNeill (2005a), Bühler

[1] Besede slovenskega jezika, http://bos.zrc-sazu.si/sbsj.html.

(1982) and Yap et al. (2011) and the analysis of the EVA multimodal corpus has been considered, and then the following set of attributes has been identified and defined:

- *M – the morpho-syntactic sequence*: represents the sequence of POS tags that are encoded, e.g., by MULTEXT-East morpho-syntactic specification,
- *I – the semiotic indicator of the POS morpho-syntactic sequence*: represents the semiotic core, e.g., the morpho-syntactic tag of that word which identifies the co-verbal shape or is the most responsible for the outline of the shape,
- $\omega_s(x)$ *– the normal distribution of the morpho-syntactic sequence*: represents the distribution of the POS sequences for the specific semiotic class/subclass,
- $p_s(x)$ *– the probability of selecting the specific semiotic class*: represents the distribution of selecting the specific POS sequence between semiotic classes/subclasses.

The morpho-syntactic sequence x can be represented as a sequence of POS tags $X_1, \ldots ,$ X_i. Furthermore, the individual part-of-speech tag X_i is described by a set of attributes, e.g., *{class/type, person, gender, number}* for nouns. When the attribute value for a given part-of-speech does not exist, then its value is represented by - sign. Therefore, nouns can be represented, e.g., as *{N, c|p, -, m|f|n, s|p|d}*, verbs as *{V, m|o|c, 1|2|3, s|p|d}*, adjectives as {*A, f|s|o,-, m|f|n, s|p|d* }, numerals as {*M, c|o|m|s, m|f|n, s|p|d* }, conjunctions as *{C, c|s, -,-,-}*[2], etc. Features that belong to the entries in the semiotic grammar are obtained through the annotation of communicative dialogue in the level of *functional annotations*. Furthermore, the *intent* of the text can be identified in the form of the following vector ***M****={x,* ***Z****}*, wherein **Z** $=\{S,I,\omega_s,p_s\}$ represents the parametric description of the semiotic class (sub-class). In this way, the semiotic grammar with a parametric description for each morpho-syntactic sequence X can be represented by the following tuple $T^{i,j}:(X_1\times X_2\times\ldots\times X_i)\rightarrow(S\times I\times\omega_s\times p_s)$, where the tuple $T^{i,j}$ describes the following function:

$$(X_1\times X_2\times\ldots\times X_i)\rightarrow Z^j \tag{23}$$

where $X_1\times X_2\times\ldots\times X_i$ represents the i so-called word columns with POS tags (representing morpho-syntactic sequences X – each column contains hash numbers), and Z a sequence of the j so-called data columns (representing S, I, ω_S, p_S – each column can contain either integers or real numbers (Daciuk & van Noord, 2004). The function in equation 23 in this way maps each morpho-syntactic sequence M into the corresponding unique *n-tuple* of integer and real numbers. For example, the POS tags in columns $X_1\times X_2\times\ldots\times X_i$ represent the morpho-syntactic sequences, such as: *{R,A,N}, {Pr,V}, {Ps, N}*, etc. And data columns Z^j keep the corresponding intent in the following format *{semiotic class S, semiotic indicator I,* ω_s*,* p_s*}*. Here, the probability $p_s(x)$ represents the probability of selecting a semiotic class

[2] The character '|' represents all possible attribute values according to the *Multext-East* specifications.

for a given morpho-syntactic sequence M, and is evaluated based on annotated multimodal data. It is defined as a function of the normal distribution of the morpho-syntactic sequence $\omega_s(x)$ for given semiotic class S and the distribution of the morpho-syntactic sequence according to the parametric space M_τ, where $S \subseteq M_\tau$:

$$p_s(x) = \frac{\omega_s(x)}{\sum_{j \in G} \omega_j(x)} \tag{24}$$

$$\omega_s(x) = \frac{1}{\sigma_S \sqrt{2\pi}} e^{-(x-\mu_S)^2/2\sigma_S^2} \tag{25}$$

Namely, the normal distribution of the morpho-syntactic sequence X, $\omega_S(x)$, is within the semiotic class S, modeled as a Gaussian function with a mean value μ_S, and co-variance σ_S^2. As seen in Figure 21, within each semiotic class the existence of those morpho-syntactic sequences are assumed that are able to identify several related interpretations of the intent (the internal overlapping of the sub-classes). By using the normal distribution $\omega_S(x)$, we are able to quantitatively define the POS sequence to a specific semiotic class/sub-class. Furthermore, the probability $p_S(x)$ is then defined by considering the normal distribution of the morpho-syntactic sequences (events x) within the semiotic space, and tells us the probability of the sequence x representing the given semiotic class. When annotations do not result in some relations between the morpho-syntactic sequence x and specific semiotic class S, then this probability has zero value. By $p_S(x)$ the overlapping between the semiotic classes can also be considered; namely, when a specific morpho-syntactic sequence can be a member of two different semiotic classes. This means that a given sequence can define two different intents. In this way, the $p_S(x)$ and $\omega_S(x)$ can be used for selecting the most appropriate interpretation, when there is an overlap between sub-classes within the same semiotic class S, or also between different semiotic classes S. The number of the i columns with POS tags is fixed by the longest morpho-syntactic sequence x which identifies the intent in the multimodal database and used in the semiotic grammar, while the number of data columns is 4. The proposed semiotic grammar is represented in the form shown in Figure 22.

The values in the POS columns in the semiotic grammar table (see Figure 22) are represented by hash numbers that are determined using perfect-hash automata. Namely, the POS columns are represented by *i perfect-hash automata* (one per each word column), where each column is presented with its own automata. In this way the *i'th* deterministic acyclic finite-state machine accepts all POS tags within the *i'th* column. And each transition in the perfect hash automaton has an assigned integer value. If the POS tag represents the *k'th* tag within *i'th* column, then the sum of these integer values along the selected path N represents value k. The hash key can be (based on path N) described as $N(X_{ki})$, and the time complexity of the calculation can be defined as $O(|X_{ki}|)$ (Daciuk & van Noord, 2004). In this way all POS tags within a specific column are represented with corresponding unique hash keys, resulting in the table shown in Figure 23. Finally, a tuple structure can be compiled from the table in Figure 23, consisting of $i+j$ columns. Since each sequence $X_1, \ldots, X_i$ is converted into hash keys $N(X_1) \ldots N(X_i)$, it can be said that each sequence has unique entry and data in the tuple, and can be defined as $N(X_1), \ldots, N(X_i) \rightarrow z_1, \ldots, z_j$.

Word columns (x)			Data columns S	I	w	p
R	A	N	I{qualitative}	A	0.42697	0.512
N	N	N	D{enumeration}	N	0.71303	
V	V	-	D{enumeration}	V	0.53032	
N	-	-	I{outline}	N	0.27303	
V	-	-	I{outline}	V	0.12303	
Pi	N	-				
V	Ps	N				
Pk	N	-				

Figure 22. The semiotic grammar table containing the morpho-syntactic sequences and associated data.

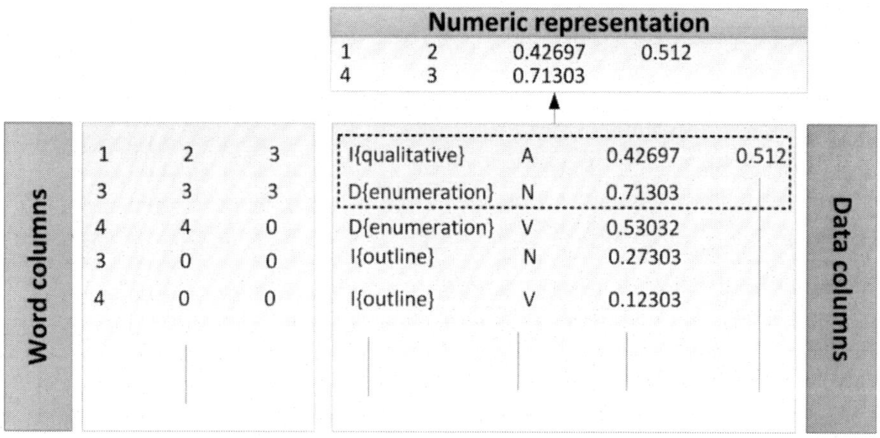

Figure 23. The data structure of semiotic grammar.

As seen in Figure 23, all values in columns are represented with numeric values, since sets of semiotic classes and morpho-syntactic tags are final. After all data in the semiotic grammar's table have been represented with numeric values, it is still important that these values are represented with a minimal number of bytes, in order that the final tuple size can be minimal. Additionally, a numeric representation can be made system-independent. At the end the tuple is presented in the form of a compact table and i perfect-hash automata, which can be used for the conversion of entries into hash keys and vice versa. When accessing data, for each POS sequence a sequence of hash keys is used for obtaining the corresponding semiotic pattern. The time complexity can then be described as $O\left(\log\left|T^{i,j}\right|\right)$; therefore, it is proportional to the logarithm of the number of entries in the tuple.

In the grammar table there are also the probabilities of selecting the specific semiotic class $p_S(x)$ and the normal distribution of morpho-syntactic sequence $\omega_S(x)$ that are represented as real numbers. Real numbers consume more bytes than integers. Therefore, the compact representation of the real numbers is desired, since in real communicative dialogues lots of possible morpho-syntactic sequences can result in lots of entries in the semiotic grammar and circumstantially in large tuple sizes. Furthermore, real numbers are considered to be system-dependent, since different platforms represent real numbers with different resolutions. As a result, the transfer of data between platforms often leads to a loss of precision. Therefore, it makes sense to represent values for $p_S(x)$ and $\omega_S(x)$ in a more compact form. A real number can be represented in a more compact form when it is presented in the form of a normalized mantissa m and exponent t, where it is: $r = m \cdot 2^t ; |m| \leq 0.5 \vee m = 0.0$. Let $\hat{m} = a_0.a_1...a_n = \sum_{i=0}^{n} a_i \cdot 2^{-i}$ represent the mantissa m. Then the resolution of the real number can be described as follows: $2^{-n-1}; |\hat{m} - m| < \varepsilon$. For the presentation of the mantissa with a resolution of ε, we then need only ([n/8] + 1) bytes. And the exponent can be represented using only 1 byte (Daciuk & van Noord, 2004). This results in a more compact form of semiotic grammar. At the end, the semiotic grammar is represented as a tuple, which accepts the input morpho-syntactic sequences and returns associated parametric descriptions of the possible interpretations $Z^* = \{Z_1,..,Z_i\}$, where $Z = \{S, I, \omega_S, p_S\}$. The semiotic grammar is designed based on annotations of communicative dialogue, taking into account the data contained in the functional level of annotations. Furthermore, the functional descriptions within an individual phrase relate to POS sequences with a corresponding semiotic class S ($S \subseteq M_\tau$), and at the same time define the morpho-syntactic and ortographic designation for semantic indicator I. Therefore, when designing it, firstly the morpho-syntactic sequences x have to be created, as entries for the semiotic grammar. Then for each morpho-syntactic sequence x, the following data has to be assigned based on annotations:

- S: semiotic class,
- I: semiotic indicator,
- $\omega_S(x)$: the normal distribution of the morpho-syntactic sequence x within the semiotic class S, which is estimated using the equation 24,
- $p_S(x)$: represents the probability of selecting a semiotic class for a given morpho-syntactic sequence x, and depends on the internal distribution of occurrence of the morpho-syntactic sequence x, within the selected semiotic class S, and the internal distribution of the occurrence of a morpho-syntactic sequence x in other semiotic classes (subclasses) (equation (3)).

Relating Shapes and Intent through the Co-Verbal Behavior Lexicon - Gesticon

Schegloff (Schegloff, 1985) described the co-verbal behavior lexicon, or the lexical affiliation as 'words of words,' i.e., words (phrases) which can best represent the meaning of gestures; namely, as a semantic relationship between a gesture and a word (or phrase). Typically, these relationships are established through the pronouns (e.g., *my*, *yours*, *you*, etc.), nouns, or adjectives. However, often such morpho-syntactic sequences can be observed in co-verbal behavior, when it is difficult to define the lexical affiliation (e.g., *red church*), or the meaning of the gesture is represented by several morpho-syntactic sequences (e.g., *so many*). In the proposed co-verbal behavior model, the co-verbal behavior lexicon (gesticon) maintains the correlation between verbal (text) and non-verbal behavior (gestures) through semantically independent *intents*. However, the semiotic correlation may also include semantic exceptions for emblems and gestures with high semantic dependency (e.g., negation and head shaking, confirmation and nodding). It is assumed that the gesture's *intent* can be presented in the form of semiotic categories and subcategories that are defined by morpho-syntactic sequences. In general, one morpho-syntactic sequence can belong to one or more *intents*. The accurate definition of the intent for a given morpho-syntactic sequence can be defined using semiotic indicators (these are the carriers of the *intent*). The lexicon is then represented as a set of semantic relations (Yap et al., 2011; Schegloff, 1985). In the case of *iconic gestures* and *symbols* it is possible to find an explicit temporal and formal correlation between speech and the presented behavior (Krauss et al., 2000; Yap et al., 2011). And the same can also be applied to *symbolic gestures* (*emblems*) and *deictic gestures*. The semantic correlation between shapes (gestures) and verbal information may, as in the case of grammar, require a wide range of knowledge resources and a huge semantic database where such relations are established and maintained.

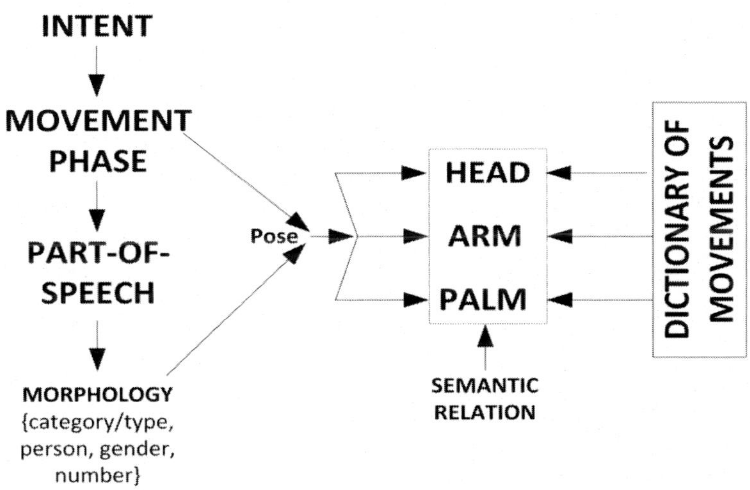

Figure 24. The co-verbal behavior lexicon – EVA gesticon.

The EVA gesticon is based on semiotic correlation rather than semantics. It can be considered also from the point of view of the interpretation of the gesture (see Figure 24).

Namely, the shape, pose, and movement represent those elementary units, which themselves do not carry the meaning, and do not represent any semantic contribution (with the exception of the *emblems*). The gesture can therefore be defined as an application of the sequence of shapes, poses, and movements in a given semantic context or, in regard to EVA gesticon, with a specific *intent*. In other words, gestures are shapes and trajectories that accompany the verbal behavior, and are dependent on the verbal behavior intent. Since the intent is defined in the semiotic space, the EVA gesticon can also be represented as a set of relations in the parametric space of the intent independently of the semiotic features of the text (or meaningful words). The pose (see equation 15) represents one of the possible configurations that contain a set ***V* (shapes)***. In the case of the EVA gesticon it is assumed that the selection of the pose (and shape) depends on:

a) *intent* (semiotic class *S*),
b) *movement phase*, in which it manifests itself (*F*),
c) *part-of-speech tag* of the word carrying most meaning (POS tags, *M*),
d) *semantic relationship* (when one exists).

The EVA gesticon, therefore, represents such a knowledge database which, for given *intent*, *movement phase*, *part-of-speech category* and *morpho-syntactic characteristics*, defines the possible set of poses ***P***, or shapes ***V****, depending on the body part, by which the specific word (phrase) can be visually represented. Furthermore, in EVA gesticon a relationship (in the form of trajectory) between the pose in the stroke phase F_S and the preparation F_P and retraction phases F_R is also established. By these trajectories, the possible context (the dependence on the previous/next shape) and a set of transitions between individual shapes (creating movements) are also defined. The semantic correlation is essential especially when we are selecting the shape (gesture) in the context of semiotic sub-classes, such as: *outline* and *metonymic gestures*, and *emblems*. The sequences within these semiotic sub-classes actually represent some concepts that exhibit a high semantic correlation between the actual meaning of a word and the co-verbal behavior represented while speaking them (e.g., to illustrate something round, showing *peace* sign, showing the *ok* sign while saying: perfect, etc.). By using the semantic correlation, therefore, the goal is to prevent inconsistencies regarding shapes and verbal meaning, such as demonstrating confirmation in the following phrase: *of course I can write*, while moving the arms and head to actually illustrate negation.

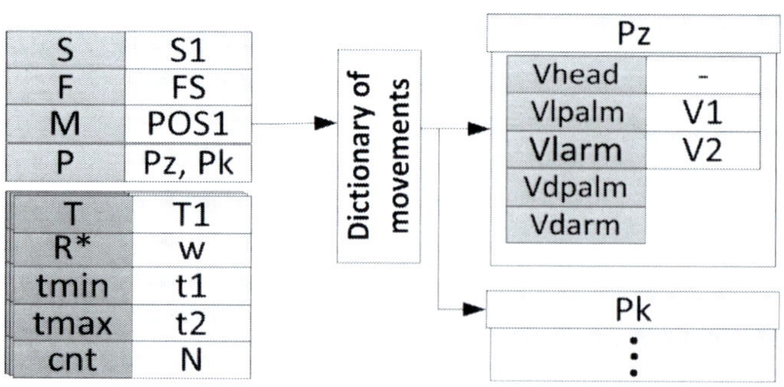

Figure 25. The entries in the EVA gesticon.

As in the case of semiotic grammar, the entries for EVA gesticon are also created based on the annotated multimodal data. Each entry in the semiotic lexicon is unique, where the individual entry L_i can be represented as the following tuple $(S_i \times F_i \times M_i) \rightarrow \{P, T, R^*, t_{\min}, t_{\max}, cnt\}$ (see Figure 25), i.e., as $\boldsymbol{L} = \{x, \boldsymbol{Z}\}$. Here, the $x = (S_i \times F_i \times M_i)$ represents a sequence for lookup into semiotic lexicon, and $Z = \{P, T, R^*, t_{\min}, t_{\max}, cnt\}$ the corresponding data. Here, the pose P is defined as a pair, which is composed of the initial and final poses, $P = \{P_S, P_E\}$. The R^* then represents those words which they represent by the transition between poses (movement model H) $P_S \rightarrow P_E$ of the observed person (EVA Corpus). Furthermore, the $t_{\min}$ and $t_{\max}$ represent the minimal and the maximal times that the persons have spent in the communicative dialogue in order to perform the pose, and the *cnt* number tell us how many times the given pose occurs for these specific features: S, F, and M. T represents the parametric trajectory of the transition that the observed persons have performed with their hands in the communicative dialogue between $P_S \rightarrow P_E$. When the pose $\boldsymbol{P_i}$ is defined as a pair $\{P_S, P_E\}$, it is best to use those animation procedures which are based on transitions between the initial pose P_S and the final pose P_E, or the so-called *key frame animation*. Namely, when animating the movement model H, the re-configuration of individual movement controllers is carried out automatically and not necessarily linearly (following the straight line).

The parametric trajectory T, therefore, takes care of a smooth transition, which includes the *route planning* using the movement trajectories and inverse kinematics. For proper definition of the movement model H, in addition to poses P_S and P_E, the corresponding movement trajectory also has to be known (when moving arms). Of course, the selected pose P can also be presented as a procedural description or even as a pre-recorded animated segment. In this case it is not necessary to have one available or to know the movement trajectory (since it is already defined within the procedure or animation). In general, it is valid that each such pose pre-defines the preparation F_P and stroke phase F_S which, while reducing the complexity of the algorithm at the level of defining shapes, nevertheless increases the amount of work that we need to invest into the design of the co-verbal behavior lexicon and to ensure the interconnectivity of gestures. Each entry in the EVA gesticon, therefore, represents a transformation of annotated data into a minimal and ordered set of attributes, by which we are able to obtain for given intent, movement phase, and morpho-syntactic tag of the semantic word: a set of poses, corresponding trajectories, semantic exceptions, minimum and maximum durations, and repeatability of the pose.

In the proposed expressive synthesizer, each pose $\boldsymbol{P_i}$ is defined as a pair $\{P_S, P_E\}$, while the algorithm automatically defines all the necessary movement models, including all movement phases (preparation, stroke, retraction, and hold). During the conversion of annotated data into entries for the semiotic lexicon L_i, shapes and gestures are related with *functional* and *descriptive levels* of the annotation scheme (see Figure 10). The functional level defines the intent S and morpho-syntactic code of the word M. In the *descriptive level*, we represent the correlation between shapes (consisting of the pose at the left and right boundaries of the movement phase), repeatability, and minimal and maximal temporal characteristics of the phase. The conversion of annotated data into the L_i entries for the EVA gesticon is performed using the following procedure:

1. Check if a combination $\{S, F, M, P\}$, already exists in the semiotic lexicon. Here, the P_S represents the pose at the beginning of the phase, and P_E represents the pose at the end of the phase (see equation 15). The similarity is evaluated by taking into account the Hamming distance.
2. If such an entry L_i is already present in the EVA gesticon, then add to the set: word w, trajectory T, adjust correspondingly both t_{min}, t_{max}, and increase the repeatability cnt for 1.
3. If there is no such entry L_i yet, then a new entry (see Figure 25) is created for storing the intent S, the movement phase F, the morpho-syntactic description of the word M, and the pose P as a pair $\{P_S, P_E\}$. The pose P is also added into EVA gesticon, if it does not yet exist.
4. For each new entry L_i in the EVA gesticon, we add into the set the word w and trajectory (e.g., linear, cyclic, etc.), while adjusting both t_{min}, t_{max} in order to be equal to the duration of the observed movement phase.

Word columns (x)			Data columns					
			P	T	R*	tmin	tmax	cnt
S1	FS	Pi	P1	T1	w	t1	t2	n1
S1	FS	Pi	P2	T2	w	t1	t3	n2

Figure 26. The entries L_i in the semiotic lexicon.

As can be seen in Figure 26, the individual entry L_i in the semiotic lexicon is represented in the form of tuples with several columns. The so-called word columns are in this case defined by S, F, and M, while the data columns represent P, T, R, t_{min} and t_{max}, and cnt. Here, S_i represents the finite set of semiotic intents that are defined using semiotic classes and subclasses (the parametric space of the intent M_τ - Figure 21); F_i then represents the finite set of movement phases $\{F_S, F_P, F_R\}$, and M_i the set of morpho-syntactic tags. Thus, the individual entry L_i can be represented as $T^{i,j}:(S_i \times F_i \times M_i) \rightarrow \{P, T, R^*, t_{\min}, t_{\max}, cnt\}$. As in the case of semiotic grammar, the EVA gesticon can also be represented in a more compact tuple structure by using perfect-hash finite automata. The word columns $X_1 \dots X_j$ are converted into corresponding hash keys $N(X_1) \dots N(X_j)$. Values in data columns are also mapped into $z_1, \dots, z_j$, wherein the integer and real numbers are represented by the minimum necessary number of bytes, depending on the desired accuracy. In Figure 26 there are two sequences, each one with an associated unique pose. Let S1 represent a semiotic class titled *pointing*, *FS* the stroke phase F_S, and *Pi* the part-of-speech tag $\{P,d,-,n,s\}$[3]. The word sequence x for the tuple, therefore, represents the following pattern: $(S1 \times FS \times M1)$.

[3] MULTEXT-East: *pronoun, dative, neuter, singular*.

After the lookup, the semiotic lexicon *L(x)* returns two sets of values:

set 1: {P1{P_S, P_E}, *arch*, *to (eng. this)*, 100, 150, 3 }
set 2: {P2{P_S, P_E}, *linear*, *to (eng. this)*, 80, 120, 7 }

Let $P1.P_S$ represent the following starting pose, which is described according to the position of the arm in Figure 27 as $R|B|S|O|H$: where *R* is used when the palm position is - *in the height of the shoulders*, *B* is used when the distance from the body (torso) is - *near*, *S* is used when the radial orientation of the palm is - *in front of*, *O* is used when the position of the arm regarding the swivel is - *orthogonal*, and *H* is used when the orientation of the forearm is - *horizontal*. $P1.P_S$ also includes the shape of the palm.

$P1.P_E$ then represents the final pose for *P1*, which is described according to the position of the arm in Figure 28 as $C|D|LZ|O|V$: *C* is used when the palm position is - *in the height of the chest*, *D* is used when the distance from the torso is - *far*, *LZ* is used when the radial orientation of the palm is - *left outside*, *O* is used when the position of the arm regarding the swivel is - *orthogonal*, and *V* is used when the orientation of the forearm is *vertical* (V). $P1.P_E$ also includes the shape of the palm.

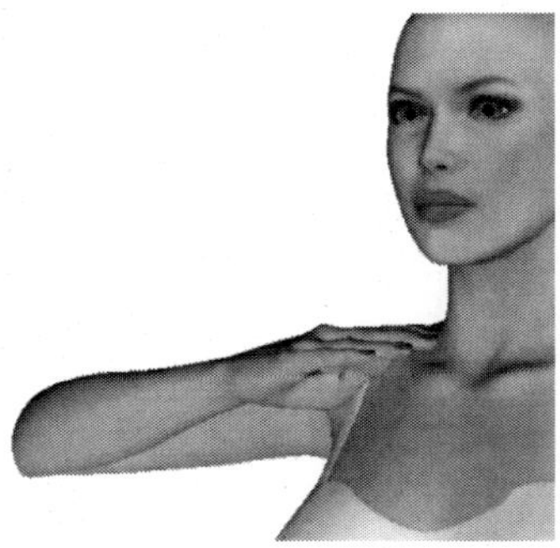

Figure 27. Pose $P1.P_S$ is described as $R|B|S|O|H$.

Figure 28. Pose $P1.P_E$ is described as $C|D|LZ|O|V$.

Furthermore, the realization time of the pose *P1* is defined by the interval [100, 150]. In the EVA Corpus it was annotated that transition $P1.P_S \rightarrow P1.P_E$ actually represents an outline of the ellipse (or at least part of the ellipse) that happened on the word *to* (eng. *this*). Further, in the EVA Corpus, the pose $P1\{P_S, P_E\}$ was observed three times for the following combination $(S1 \times FS \times M1)$. Similarly, the initial pose of the pose 2, $P2.P_S$ can be described by the position of the arm in Figure 29 as G|B|S|N|V. Here the shape of the hand is neutral.

Figure 29. Pose $P2.P_S$ described as G|B|S|N|V.

The final pose of the pose 2, $P2.P_E$ can be described by the position of the arm in Figure 30 as *C|D|LZ|N|I*: *C* is used when the position of the arm is: in the *height of the chest*, *B* is used when the distance of the palm from the body is - *far*, *LZ* is used when the radial orientation of the palm is - *left outside*, *N* is used when the position of the arm regarding the swivel is - *normal*, and *I* is used when the orientation of the forearm is - *stretched*.

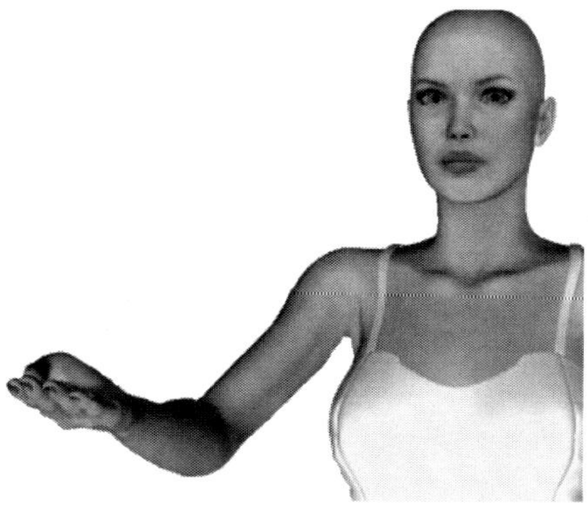

Figure 30. Pose $P2.P_E$ is described as *C|D|LZ|N|I*.

In the EVA Corpus, the pose *P2* was observed seven times with the realization time in the interval [80, 120].

Chapter 7

ALGORITHM FOR THE AUTOMATIC GENERATION OF EXPRESSIVE CO-VERBAL BEHAVIOR

INTRODUCTION

The expressive co-verbal behavior algorithm, which is proposed in this chapter, has to automatically convert general text (sentences/statements) into a communicative act. In this way, more natural interaction can be achieved that favorably affects the cognitive process of the listener (the person you address) regarding understanding, and the cognitive processes of the speaker. Additional information presented by synchronous multimodal signals, so-called synchronized verbal and co-verbal behavior, is not only more understandable, but is also able to establish a social relationship between speakers and listeners. In order to achieve the acceptable naturalness, a proper consistency relationship that reflects the intent of the presented information has to be established between the speech and the co-verbal behavior. The main issues that the algorithm considers are pragmatic in nature (Allwood, 2013; Esposito Ana & Antonietta, 2011), resulting both from the nature of the gestures as well as from the nature of the unannotated text:

1. Gestures do not have "syntax" such as e.g., language. Therefore, the shape and the way in which they are performed do not follow any e.g., well-defined linguistic rules.
2. General unannotated text does not contain any broader context regarding the intent. Therefore, it is not possible to define shapes and timings for the movements of body parts (or timestamps for when the co-verbal behavior should occur, or should be completed) directly.

In order to tackle these problems, a novel algorithm for the automatic generation of expressive co-verbal behavior is presented. This algorithm is able to create co-verbal behavior by considering: *the synchronization of the intent and shape*, *the synchronization of several movements*, and *the prosodic and timing synchronization regarding speech and gestures*. Its functional scheme is presented in Figure 31. As can be seen, the algorithm is carried out in the following phases:

- *classification of the intent*: the input for this phase represents POS-tagged text and semiotic grammar. Further, in the POS-tagged text, several morpho-syntactic sequences have to be checked, since these sequences can provide possible semiotic interpretations of the intent on the general (unannotated) text/statement. Further, in this phase an additional level in the HRG structure is created, named *ContentUnits*. It is used for storing created *CU* (content unit) elements used for storing semiotic classification of the intent and cores of meaning (these are those words that actually induce the shape in the stroke phase F_S), and are the result of the semiotic analysis based on semiotic grammar. As can be seen in Figure 7, each *CU* element is associated with the corresponding word sequences to which they belong (through the tree-based relationships). Any statement/text can have several interpretations and its own cores of meaning. Further, statements/text can partly or fully overlap and therefore introduce ambiguities and a number of inconsistencies.

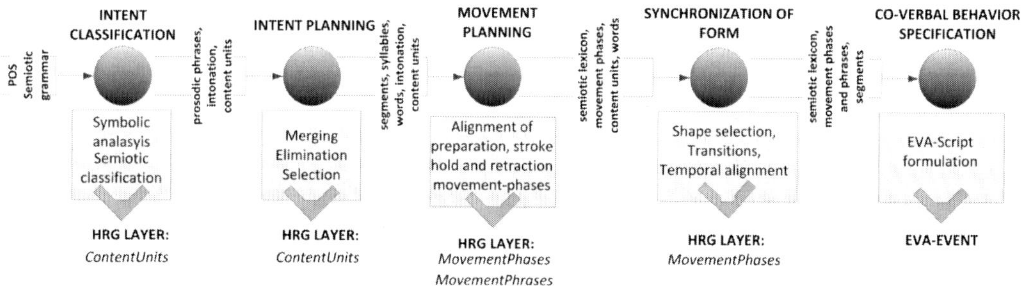

Figure 31. The functional scheme of the algorithm for the automatic generation of co-verbal behavior.

- *planning of the intent*: in this phase the inconsistencies and ambiguities are resolved using several methods, such as: *integration*, *elimination*, and *selection*. The input of this phase represents several possible interpretations stored in the relational structure *ContentUnits*, and several prosodic features regarding speech (prosodic phrase-breaks, and accents). The latter have to be provided by the core TTS engine. The result is a uniquely defined sequence of local intents without overlap or ambiguities.
- *planning of the movement*: by considering an unambiguous defined sequence of local intents, the structure of the movement in the form of movement phases can be defined, but still independently of the temporal characteristics of the speech. Namely, the structure of the co-verbal movements depends primarily upon:

  a. *semiotic intent*,
  b. core of meaning,
  c. most accentuated positions in the text (within each *CU*), and
  d. intonation of individual words within each CU.

Based on these features, the *movement phases* and *phrases* can be defined. Therefore, two new relational structures in the HRG structure are created, named *MovementPhases* and *MovementPhrases*. The first one stores the phase elements that are also related with words' syllables of the current sentence (including silence) through the *Dynamics* tree-based relational structure.

- *the synchronization of the shape*: in this phase, for each *movement phase* the selection of shape and transition has to be carried out. The selection of shape and transition depends on:

    a. the movement phase,
    b. the intent stored in each *CU*,
    c. the duration of those words (syllables and segments), where the co-verbal behavior should be carried out, and
    d. the semiotic lexicon *L*.

    This phase updates elements in the *MovementPhases* relational structure, and defines for each one the body poses at its left and right boundaries, their duration, and the trajectory between the initial and final body poses.

- *the generation of co-verbal behavior*: in this phase the HRG structure is converted into a form that the conversational agent understands and is able to realize. Therefore, the algorithm has to convert the complete HRG structure into a so-called ECA event (or EVA event) that is described in the form of some descriptive language (e.g., EVA-Script) (Mlakar & Rojc, 2011a; Mlakar & Rojc, 2011b).

PHASE I : THE CLASSIFICATION OF THE INTENT

In the first phase of co-verbal behavior generation, the symbolic text analysis is carried out. It is performed in a module named *phrases and phases tagging* (see Figure 4 and Figure 8). Previous modules and external resources have to provide this module with the morpho-syntactic sequences and semiotic grammar. As seen in Figure 4, several modules of the core TTS system are used in order to provide the resources needed for the automatic co-verbal behavior generation modules, where the proprietary PLATTOS TTS system is used as the core TTS system (Rojc, 2003), and is based on flexible and efficient architecture, and already supports HRG structures. Therefore, the fusion of additional co-verbal behavior generation modules has been straightforward and simple. Nevertheless, any other TTS system can also be used with the proposed algorithm, when it is possible to provide data in the form of HRG structure for co-verbal behavior generation modules.

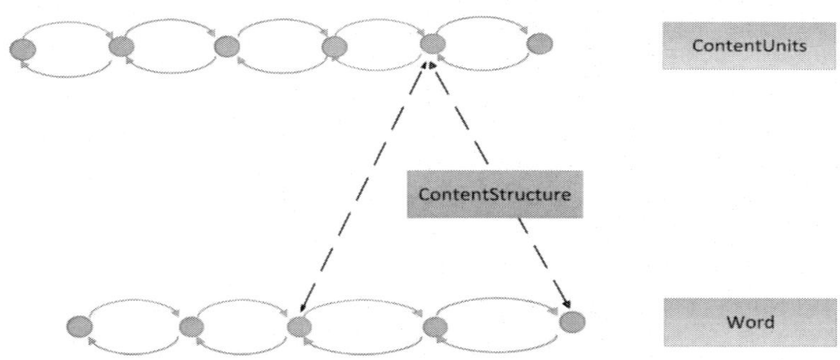

Figure 32. The HRG structure and significant relational structures for Phase I.

In this way, the morpho-syntactic sequences in the sentence level are provided by the following modules: *tokenizer*, *morphology*, and *POS tagger*. Furthermore, by using the morpho-syntactic information and semiotic grammar, all possible interpretations of the POS tags in the input text are identified in order to perform the classification of the intent by defining the semiotic classes and corresponding cores of meaning. The lookup procedure is performed into the semiotic grammar, which is stored in the form of tuple data structure, and serves for the mapping of individual morpho-syntactic sequences detected in the input text, into a corresponding parametric description of the semiotic class (subclass) $Z = \{S, I, \omega_S, p_S\}$. Additionally, a new horizontal relational structure in the HRG structure is created, called *ContentUnits*, for storing *CU* elements that store the obtained semiotic classifications. After this phase, the text is described not only as a sequence of words, but also as a series of symbolic interpretations in the form of semiotic classification.

In Table 4, the pseudocode for this phase is presented in more detail. Firstly, a horizontal relational structure *ContentUnits* and tree-based relational structure *ContentStructure* are created. The first one is used to store elements for all semiotic interpretations of the intent that can be defined on the input text, and the other one is used to define left and right boundaries of each *CU*, and represented by the positions of the corresponding words in the input sentence or statement. Furthermore, several morpho-syntactic sequences $POS_{i\text{-}j}$ are created by using the horizontal relational structure *Words*. For each sequence a lookup process in the semiotic grammar is then performed. Nevertheless, only the longest sequences $x_{i\text{-}j}$ found in the semiotic grammar's tuple (Figure 22) are considered (in order to define the semiotic class, and subclass). The individual longest sequence $x_{i\text{-}j}$ = *[W.POS* × *next(W).POS* × *next(next(W)).POS* × *next(next(next(W))).POS* × *...]* returns the associated semiotic interpretation of the intent, represented by *S*, *I*, ω_S and p_S. For each sequence with assigned intent, a new *CU* element is created in the horizontal relational structure *ContentUnits* and used for storing the corresponding semiotic classification. Furthermore, a new element in the tree-based relational structure *ContentStructure* is created in order to store the leftmost and the rightmost words that actually define this sequence (see Figure 32). Additionally, the flag of the *CU* element is set when the sequence represents the enumeration. Namely, the enumeration is perceived as a repetition of POS tags which may also include conjunctions; for example, the sequence: {*first, second, third*}, {*car, bus, shirt*}, {*and I think, I write a line, and then I realize...* }, etc. The enumeration is recognized by using attribute *intent S*. The *CU* element with associated attributes is presented in Table 5.

Table 4. *Phase I* – Defines all possible semiotic interpretations of the intent

```
ContentUnits is created
ContentStructure is created

FOR ( ; word != NULL; word = next(word), i++ )
{
    T( POS_i-j ) → Z^1; j ≤ utterance→relation (Words) → length(); in Z^1={S_1 || S_2 || S_3 || S_4 || S_5|}
    IF( Z^1 != NULL )
    {
        cu = utterance→relation (ContentUnits) →append()
        cu→ fset ( SEMIOTIC_CLASS, Z^1);
        cu→ fset( SEMIOTIC_INDICATOR, Z^2);
```

```
        cu→ fset( INTERNAL_DISTRIBUTION, Z^3);
        cu→ fset( SELECTION_PROBABILITY, Z^4);
        utterance→ relation ( ContentStructure ) →append (cu);
        append_daughter (cu, ContentStructure, word_i);
        append_daughter (cu, ContentStructure, word_j)
        if(cu → fS ( SEMIOTIC_CLASS ) == enumeration )
        {
            cu → fset(ENUMERATION, 1);
        }
    }
}
```

Table 5. The content of the *CU* element

Attribute	Meaning
Intent (S)	This attribute identifies the semiotic class (sub-class) for a given CU's sequence of words (the possible interpretation in the form of semiotic classification).
Semiotic indicator (I)	The index of that word (or words) in the relational structure *Words* for which the co-verbal representation best recaps the meaning of the verbal content.
Internal distribution $\omega_S(x)$	This is a normal distribution of using the CU's morpho-syntactic sequence x_{i-j} for representing the given intent and is based on annotated data.
Selection probability $p_S(x)$	This is the probability that given sequence x_{i-j} represents the given intent (semiotic class) *S*.
Enumeration (O)	This attribute indicates whether during filtering this CU should be maintained. Its default value is 0. Only when the intent describes the enumeration is its value set to 1.

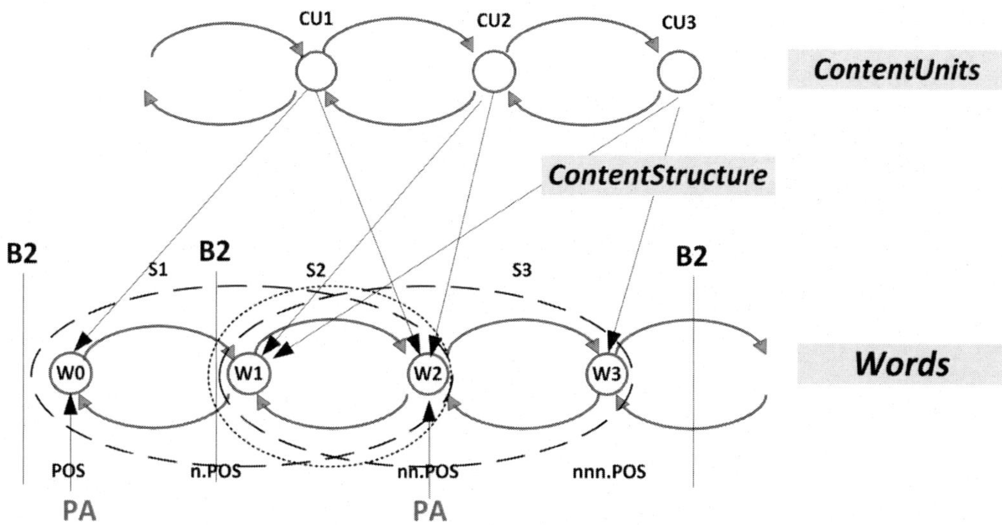

Figure 33. The significant part of the HRG structure used in *Phase I*.

The most significant part of the HRG structure used in Phase I can be seen in Figure 33. The horizontal relational structure *Words* is filled with elements from W_0 to W_3, which also contain the corresponding morpho-syntactic tags. Let the maximum length of morpho-syntactic sequences in the semiotic grammar be 4, and let the following sequences represent the following associated semiotic classes:

$$x_1 = (W_0.POS \rightarrow S1)$$
$$x_2 = (W_0.POS \times W_1.POS \times W_2.POS \rightarrow S1)$$
$$x_3 = (W_1.POS \times W_2.POS \rightarrow S1)$$
$$x_4 = (W_1.POS \times W_2.POS \rightarrow S2)$$
$$x_5 = (W_1.POS \times W_2.POS \times W_3.POS \rightarrow S3)$$
$$x_6 = (W_2.POS \times W_3.POS \rightarrow S3)$$
$$x_7 = (W_3.POS \rightarrow S3).$$

The lookup process searches for the longest morpho-syntactic sequence x_{i-j} (starting at word W_0) that can be found in the semiotic grammar. In this case the x_2 sequence is identified that describes the semiotic class *S1*, while other semiotic classes *S2* and *S3* do not have appropriate morpho-syntactic representatives at this point. Therefore, in the horizontal relational structure *ContentUnits*, a CU_1 is created that stores the semiotic classification *S1*. Furthermore, by using the tree relational structure *ContentStructure* the CU_1 boundaries are defined by words W_0 and W_1. The lookup process then continues to search for the longest sequence x_{i-j}, starting at word W_1. In this case three morpho-syntactic sequences x_3, x_4, and x_5 are found in the grammar, where the longest one with the semiotic class *S1* is x_3. The algorithm then checks whether x_3 sequence is already contained by one of the created *CU* elements that has the same intent *S1*. Here, this is the case for x_3 sequence; therefore, it is discarded together with the corresponding interpretation. The other two sequences x_4 and x_5 belong to the semiotic classes *S2* and *S3*, and are not yet contained by any created *CU* element that would already have the same *intent*. Therefore, new elements CU_2 and CU_3 can be created for storing both semiotic classifications. The boundaries for CU_2 are defined by words W_1 and W_2, and the boundaries for CU_3 by words W_1 and W_3. The same applies to the x_6 and x_7 sequences that both belong to the same semiotic class *S3*. They are obviously the sub-sequences of the x_5 that belong to the same class *S3*, and are already represented by the element CU_3. Therefore, both sequences are discarded. This results in the following rules for *Phase 1*:

Rule 1: *If at a specific word index in relation to Words the sequence* x_A *happens to be at* $x_A(S) \subseteq x_B(S)$, *where both sequences belong to the same semiotic class, then sequence* x_A *has to be discarded.*

Rule 2: *If sequence x at word index j is already contained by any of the previous CU elements started at word index i and with the same intent (i < j), then it is also discarded.*

In this way, Phase I concludes with the created horizontal relational level *ContentUnits* that contain *CU* elements that store semiotic classification. Additionally, the tree-based relational structure *ContentStructure* stores the boundaries for all possible interpretations of the intent that could be performed at specific sequences within the input text. The individual

CU element, from the standpoint of the co-verbal behavior, represents the meaningful sequence of those movements that actually visually represent an idea or intent. Through the *ContentStructure* and *Words* relational structures the *CU* element also defines the morpho-syntactic context regarding the intent.

PHASE II: THE PLANNING OF THE INTENT

This phase is performed in the module named *planning of the intent* (see Figure 4 and Figure 8). After *Phase I*, the relational structure *ContentUnits* already contains possible semiotic classifications for the input sentence. Nevertheless, the creation of the *CU* elements often leads to partial (or even fully) overlapping of interpretations of the intent (see Figure 22). Since these overlapping are responsible for discrepancies and ambiguity regarding the intent, *Phase II* has to eliminate all of these overlaps and unambiguously define the structure of the intent on the input text. Furthermore, besides *CU* elements in the relational structure *ContentUnits*, the prosodic structure also has to be provided. The prosodic structure has to be defined within the core TTS engine's modules (namely, grapheme-to-phoneme conversion, symbolic, and acoustic prosody modules). Several TTS systems can be used for this step, although the proprietary PLATTOS TTS system is used here, since it already provides the HRG-based prosody structure that relates elements in these relational structures: *SyllableStructure*, *PhraseStructure*, *Syllables*, *Words*, and *IntonationStructure*, where attributes such as accents, phrase breaks, pause and segment durations are kept. Therefore, this step from the set of predicted interpretations *CU* uniquely defines the inverse transformation T_m^{-1} (equation 11), by means of which the movement models H can be connected into the co-verbal behavior $\hat{G}$. For *Phase II*, the following rules have been defined:

Rule 3: *The individual element CU has to include the most accentuated syllable within a given prosodic phrase, except in the case of enumeration.*

Rule 4: *The prosodic phrase represents the completed part of the meaning (the idea or thought); therefore, the CU element has to lie within the predicted prosodic phrase.*

Rule 5. *The individual prosodic phrase can be represented by, at most, one concept of motion,* i.e., *with at most one element CU.*

Rule 6: *When CU element contains the semiotic class "enumeration," then the corresponding CU boundaries must remain unchanged (the boundaries of prosodic phrases are not considered).*

In PLATTOS TTS engine, the syllable (in a relational structure *Syllables*) is labeled with the *PA* tag when it is predicted to be the most prominent syllable within the given prosodic phrase. All other stressed syllables within the given prosodic phrase are labeled with the *NA* tag. This is done in the *symbolic prosody module* (Figure 4). Ideally, the boundaries of *CU* elements already match with the boundaries of the prosodic phrase, and include a syllable that is labeled with the *PA* tag. And when the individual prosodic phrase contains at most one *CU* element, the structure of the *intent* could already be uniquely defined, where the co-verbal behavior *G* can be presented as a sequence of co-verbal models *H* that are dependent on the *CU* as follows:

$$\hat{G} = T_m^{-1}\hat{H} = H[CU_1, t_1] \times H[CU_2, t_2] \times \ldots \times H[CU_n, t_n] \tag{26}$$

where $H[CU_i, t_i]$ represents the *movement model* that depends on semiotic classification, and symbolic and acoustic prosodic characteristics (duration) of those words contained within each *CU* element. The operator × represents the successive execution of the movement models. When this is the case, the algorithm can proceed with the next step, without changing the HRG structure.

However, in general this is not the case, as during defining the interpretations of the intent often the following phenomena are involved (see Figure 34):

- ***enumeration:*** the *CU* element has assigned the semiotic class "enumeration." And the ***Rule 6*** states that the boundaries have to remain unchanged (the prosodic boundaries are not considered). Furthermore, when there exists an overlap, or there is a continuous sequence of such *CU* elements, then merging into only one *CU* element has to be carried out.
- ***internal overlapping:*** the boundaries of *CU* elements within a given prosodic phrases overlap.
- ***ambiguity:*** the prosodic phrase includes several *CU* elements which do not overlap.
- ***external overlapping:*** the boundaries of the *CU* element are stretching over the boundaries of the corresponding prosodic phrase. Additionally, overlaps with other *CU* elements are also possible.

Ambiguity. *CU* units are in this case all defined within the specific prosodic phrase (Figure 34 (b)). In the PLATTOS TTS system, two types of phrase breaks are tagged. Those within the sentence are labeled by tag *B2* (minor), and those between sentences by tag *B3* (major). Furthermore, several *CU* elements that lie within the prosodic phrase are without any overlap of their boundaries. E.g., in Figure 34 (b) there are CU_1 and CU_2 elements within the prosodic phrase, with boundaries on $\{W_0, W_1\}$ for CU_1 and on $\{W_2, W_3\}$ for CU_2. Furthermore, in this case we have $CU_1 \subseteq B2 \wedge CU_2 \subseteq B2$, and there is no overlap since $CU_1 \cap CU_2$ regarding words is an empty set. When this happens, the elimination and merging of *CUs* is performed. Namely, a check is first performed to identify whether the individual *CU* elements can be merged in a common *CU* element. This is often the case, when the semiotic class is "enumeration," when the conjunction usually presents a change in shape (e.g., alternate use of hands). Therefore, when *CU* elements overlap or are subsequent regarding their boundaries, the merging is carried out as follows:

$$CU = f\left(CU_i,...,CU_j\right) = \begin{cases} \text{Join } CU_k, CU_{k+1},...; \textit{if} \\ \quad CU_k.POS = CU_{k+1}.POS \wedge S(CU_k) = S(CU_{k+1}) \\ \text{Add into a set}; \textit{otherwise} \end{cases} \tag{27}$$

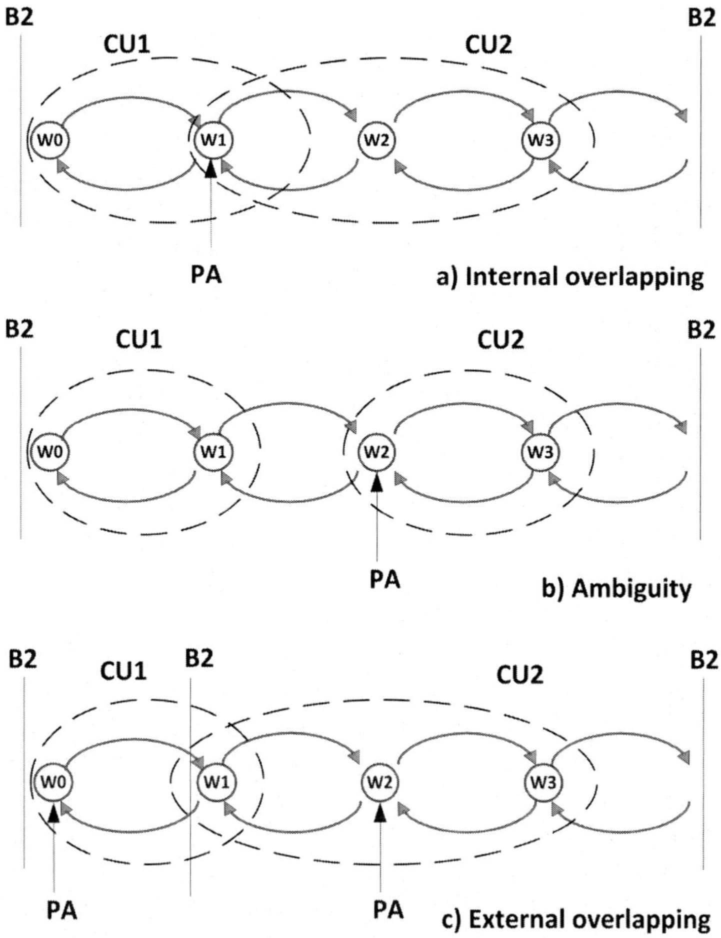

Figure 34. The phenomena that can occur after *Phase I* – the classification of the intent.

Namely, the *CU* elements have to be consecutive, they have to contain identical morpho-syntactic sequence *POS*, and they must be classified in the same semiotic class *S*. If these criteria are met, then the corresponding *CU* elements can be merged into the new *CU* element, whereas its boundaries are defined by the first and the last *CU* elements in the given sequence. Furthermore, the corresponding semiotic indicator *I* is represented as a set of those semantic indicators that are contained within individual *CU* elements in the sequence.

Let the semiotic type of the *CU* element be *deictic {enumeration}* (see Figure 35). As a result, the set of *CU* elements within a given prosodic phrase *B2* has to be changed. As can be seen, the prosodic phrase *B2* contains the *CU* elements having the following boundaries $CU_1 = \{W_0\}$, $CU_2 = \{W_1\}$, and $CU_3 = \{W_2, W_3\}$. Further, let be $CU_1.POS = CU_2.POS \wedge S(CU_1) = S(CU_2)$. Then, for CU_1 and CU_2 the condition in equation 27 is fulfilled, and both elements can be merged into a new CU_4 element. Its left boundary is represented by the first CU_1 (on its first word W_0), and the right boundary by the CU_2 (on its last word W_1). At the end, the CU_4 is assigned the semiotic class *D {enumeration}*, and the *semiotic indicator* as a set of the semiotic indicators of CU_1 and CU_2 (words W_0, W_1). Furthermore, the attributes ω_S and p_S are set to 1.

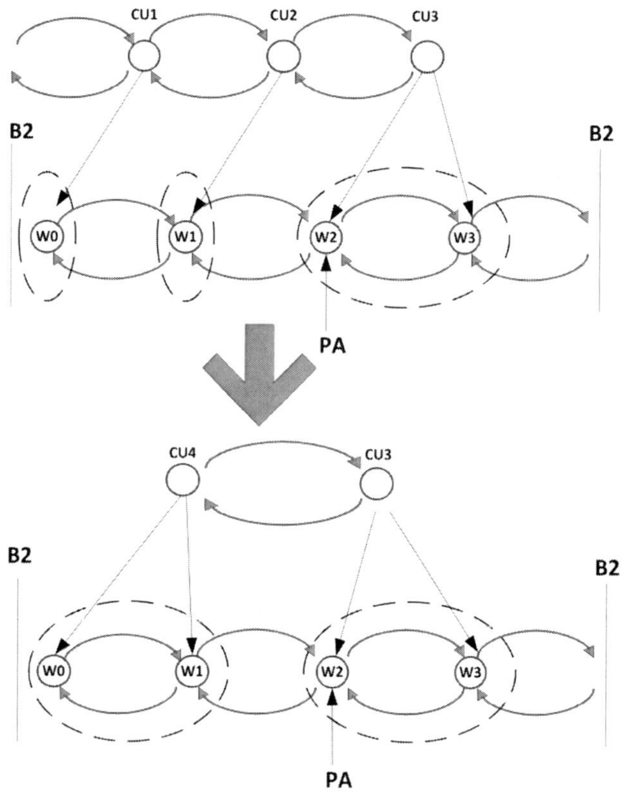

Figure 35. Resolving ambiguities by performing *merging*.

Additionally, the *keep* attribute of the CU_4 element has to be set, which ensures that this *CU* element will be included in the movement model *H*. In this way, a new set of *CU* elements is obtained (CU_3 and CU_4) within the prosodic phrase *B2*, as can be seen in Figure 35 below. Nevertheless, ***Rule 3*** has to be applied, since the ambiguities are still not resolved completely (***Rule 5*** is not fulfilled). Nevertheless, ***Rule 3*** applies only to those *CU* elements that do not have the *keep* attribute set. At the end those *CU* elements are selected which include the most accentuated syllable (labeled as *PA*). Additionally, its *keep* attribute is set to 1. This can be described as follows:

$$CU = f\left(CU_i,\ldots,CU_j\right) = \begin{cases} CU_k; if\ PA \in CU_k \\ -; if\ PA \notin CU_k \end{cases} \tag{28}$$

In Figure 35 below, the CU_3 element contains the *PA* syllable (word W_2); therefore, it has to be selected. When in the prosodic phrase *B2* exists the *CU* with semiotic class "*enumeration*" and/or *search*, together with some other *CU* and semiotic class that contains *PA* syllable, then the given prosodic phrase represents several interpretations of the *intent*. These interpretations are not necessarily defined through morpho-syntactics and in most cases represent a combination of communicative intents in the scope of dialogue communication functions (e.g., handing over the role of the speaker, searching for the proper response, maintaining the activity during communication, etc.). In this case all of the perceived *CU* elements in the prosodic phrase *B2* are kept.

External overlapping. As seen in Figure 34 (c), this phenomenon occurs when the boundaries of the *CU* element are stretched over the boundaries of the prosodic phrase *B2*. According to ***Rule 4***, the concept of motion is always performed within the boundaries of the individual idea/thought (of the individual prosodic phrase *B2*); the semantic portion of the *CU* element must remain within the boundaries of the prosodic phrase *B2*. Therefore, the following has to be performed in the case of external overlapping:

$$CU = f(CU_i, CU_{i+1}) = \begin{cases} \textit{keep \& reduce; if} \\ \mathrm{I} \in \mathrm{B} \wedge \mathrm{PA} \in \mathrm{B} \wedge \mathrm{PA} \in CU_i \wedge CU_i \cap CU_{i+1} \neq \varnothing \\ \textit{keep \& extend; if} \\ \mathrm{I} \in \mathrm{B} \wedge \mathrm{PA} \in \mathrm{B} \wedge \mathrm{PA} \in CU_i \wedge CU_i \cap CU_{i+1} = \varnothing \\ \textit{remove; if} \\ \mathrm{I} \notin \mathrm{B} \vee \mathrm{PA} \notin \mathrm{B} \vee \mathrm{PA} \notin CU_i \end{cases} \tag{29}$$

According to ***Rule 4***, the *CU* element is kept and considered when the following two rules are met:

Rule 7: *The CU element must include the PA syllable, and this PA syllable must lie within the boundaries of the prosodic phrase B2:* $PA \in B2 \wedge PA \in CU_i$.

Rule 8: *The semiotic indicator I of the CU element must lie within the boundaries of the prosodic phrase B2,* i.e., $I \in B$.

In Figure 34 (c) the CU_1 element in a relational structure *Words* contains words W_0 and W_1, where W_1 is not within the boundaries of the first prosodic phrase *B2*. Let the semiotic indicator *I* represent the word W_0. In this case ***Rule 7*** and ***Rule 8*** are met, otherwise the element *CU* has to be removed from the relational structure *ContentUnits*. Let semiotic indicator and PA syllable of the CU_1 element both lie within the boundaries of the first prosodic phrase *B2*. By considering the stroke phase, the intent/meaning of the word W_0 can be presented regardless of whether the word W_1 is kept or not (or the right boundary of the CU_1 is stretched over the boundaries of the first prosodic phrase *B2*). In other words, whether the CU_1 boundaries are stretched or not depends on the following CU element, namely $next(CU_1)$ – in this case CU_2. Specifically,

Rule 9: *When* $CU \cap next(CU)$ *is not empty, then the right boundary of the CU is set to the left boundary of the next(CU) element, in order that it is* $CU \cap next(CU) = \varnothing$.

Furthermore, those words that lie outside that prosodic phrase *B* which contains the semiotic indicator *I* can in the context of the movement model represent only *hold phase* and/or *retraction phase*. Therefore, the following rule also has to be applied:

Rule 10: *When* $CU \cap next(CU)$ *represents an empty set, the CU element is kept completely. Furthermore, those words that lie outside that prosodic phrase B which contains semiotic indicator I can in the context of the movement model represent only the holding phase and/or the retraction phase.*

According to these rules, the right boundary of the CU_1 element in Figure 34 (c) has to be corrected in order to contain only the word W_0.

Internal overlapping. This phenomenon occurs when several *CU* elements include the same words, and their boundaries lie within the same prosodic phrase *B*. As can be seen in Figure 34 (a), the boundaries for CU_1 are $\{W_0, W_1\}$, and for CU_2, $\{W_1, W_2, W_3\}$. The following is also true: $CU_1 \subseteq B2 \wedge CU_2 \subseteq B2$. Therefore, the intersection between both *CU* elements $CU_1 \cap CU_2$ is not an empty set, but the word $\{W_1\}$. According to the definition, this represents an *internal overlap*. When this happens, it has to be decided which of the *CU* element we should keep, since ***Rule 5*** states that only one *CU* element per prosodic phrase *B* is allowed. Furthermore, according to ***Rule 3***, we have to eliminate all of those *CU* elements which do not contain the word with *PA* syllable (see equation 28), while on the remaining *CU* elements the elimination has to be performed by taking into account the *normal distribution* (ω_S) that is specified for a given semiotic class. Namely, according to equation 28 such *CU* element has to be selected that within the same semiotic class possesses the highest probability (maximum value of ω_S). When several *CU* elements have the same probability, then that *CU* element which contains most words is selected. And when all *CU* elements contain an equal number of words, the *CU* element can be selected randomly. After the *elimination*, only those *CU* elements which belong to their own semiotic classes that may be *iconic*, *deictic*, *adaptor*, or *symbols* remain in the set. This can be described as follows:

$$CU_{S(CU_m)=S(CU_n)} = f(CU_m,\dots,CU_n) = \begin{cases} CU_m; if\ \omega_s(CU_m) > \omega_s(CU_n) \\ CU_n; if\ \omega_s(CU_m) < \omega_s(CU_n) \\ \max(len(CU_m), len(CU_n)); if\ \omega_s(CU_m) = \omega_s(CU_n) \end{cases} \tag{30}$$

$$CU_{S(CU_m)\neq S(CU_n)} = f(CU_m,\dots,CU_n) = \begin{cases} CU_m; if\ p_s(CU_m) > p_s(CU_n) \\ CU_n; if\ p_s(CU_m) < p_s(CU_n) \\ \max(len(CU_m), len(CU_n)); if\ p_s(CU_m) = p_s(CU_n) \end{cases} \tag{31}$$

In Table 6 (a), the pseudocode for this phase is presented in detail. First, a new relational structure *ProsodicStructure* is created, which is used to link *Phrase* and *ContentUnits* relational structures (see Figure 36).

Furthermore, the *PhraseStructure* is used to determine the start and end word for the given phrase that is also appended to the *ProsodicStructure*. Then a check is performed to determine whether there are any *CU* elements that could be assigned to the given phrase. Firstly, for the individual *CU* element, its start and end word has to be determined. And since syllable-based attributes should be added to each *CU*, its start and end syllables are also defined. Then for each syllable in the given *CU* a check is performed to determine whether it is *PA* syllable. If yes, then the *CU* element is tagged with the *PA* label, with the corresponding word position, and with the corresponding position of the semiotic indicator *I* (defined by summing the word position of the given *CU's* left boundary and the position of the semiotic indicator within the given *CU*). At the end, the *CU* is added into the current phrase, when its left boundary is contained. Otherwise, we move to the next phrase before adding it.

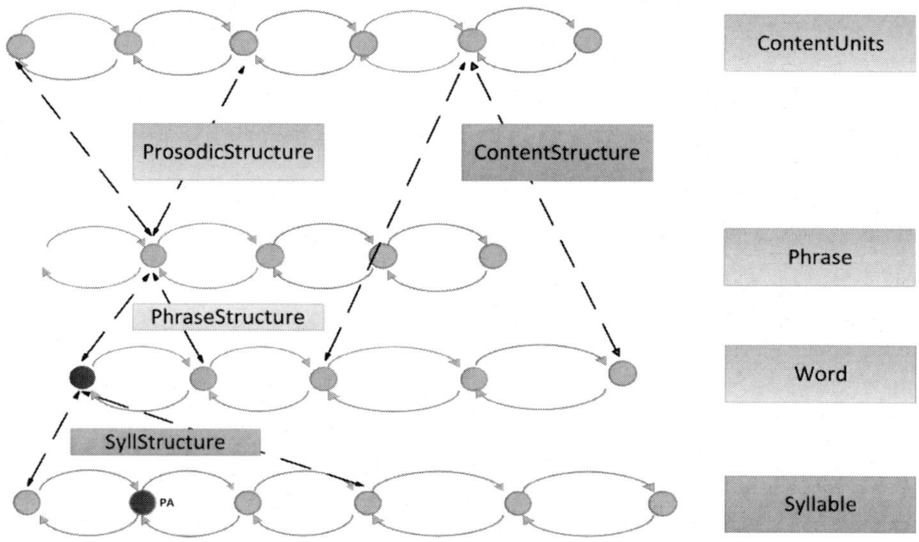

Figure 36. The HRG structure in *Phase II*.

In the next step in Table 6 (b) all of the CU elements are checked to determine whether there is any overlapping of *CU* elements, or whether several subsequent *CU* elements can be merged into one *CU* element. Nevertheless, each *CU* has to be checked to determine whether it has its *KEEP* attribute set. When it is set, its boundaries have to remain unchanged, and prosodic boundaries are not considered. Otherwise, overlaps should be resolved, or several subsequent *CU* elements have to be merged into one *CU* element. As can be seen, for current *CU* (*CU_i*) the word position of the semiotic indicator *I* is stored. Next, all subsequent *CU* elements boundaries have to be checked. Therefore, for each following *CU* (*CU_j*), the left and right boundaries have to be accessed. And when CU_i has its *KEEP* attribute set, several possibilities have to be checked regarding positions between CU_i and CU_j elements (see Figure 37).

In the case of A, B, or C in Figure 37, the CU_i is kept, and the CU_j has to be removed from the HRG structure. Nevertheless, before removing CU_j: the word position of its semiotic indicator *I* is stored, the right boundary of the CU_i is set equal to the right boundary of the CU_j, and the normal distribution and the selection probability of CU_i are set to 1.0. Possible *CU* elements with a different semiotic class, but covered within such *CU* element, are removed in the relational level *ContentUnits*. At this stage we are not interested in relating *CU* elements and prosodic phrases as according to the ***Rule 6***, it is not necessary to change the boundaries. When CU_j does not have the *KEEP* attribute set, the CU_j has to be removed in case B. And in case D, we stop checking subsequent *CU* elements for possible overlap or merging process.

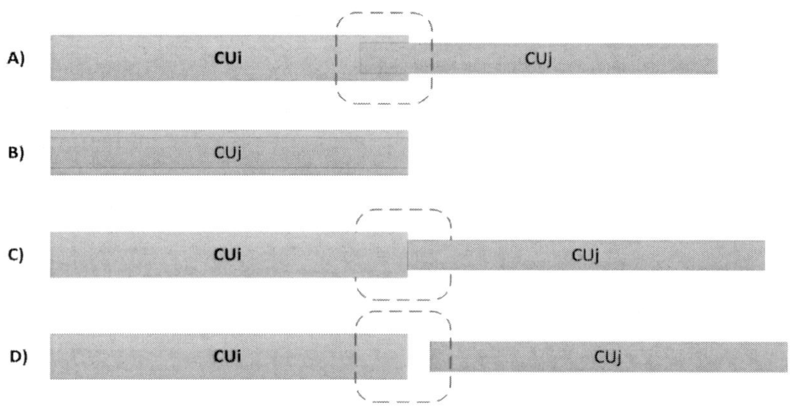

Figure 37. Overlapping possibilities for *CU* elements.

In the next step in Table 6 (c), the external overlapping is resolved, while processing all of those remaining *CU* elements which do not have the *KEEP* attribute set. Here, ***Rule 3*** and ***Rule 4*** are considered, whereas any deviations from the predicted prosodic boundaries are adjusted. In doing so, all *PUs* (*phrase unit*) have to be checked, and the corresponding left and right boundaries for each one accessed. Next, all *CUs* for individual PU_i are checked. If the *KEEP* attribute of the CU_{ij} is set, it is kept but not considered. And when the *ACCENT* attribute's value of the CU_{ij} is not *PA*, then such CU_{ij} has to be removed from the HRG structure, and CU_{ij+1} is processed next. Otherwise, in order to match CU_{ij} against PU_i, its left and right boundaries have to be accessed and the possibilities in Figure 38 have to be checked.

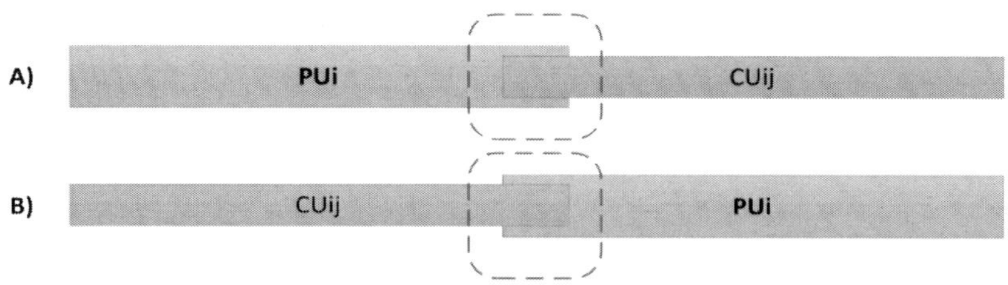

Figure 38. Overlapping possibilities between *PU* and corresponding *CU* units.

In other words, for all *PU* prosodic phrases the boundaries of the corresponding *CU* elements are checked. In case *A*, the left boundary of the CU_{ij} element starts before the right boundary of its prosodic phrase PU_i. And when its *PA* accent and semiotic indicator *I* lie within this PU_i, the right boundary of the CU_{ij} has to be adjusted to the right boundary of the

PU_i. In case *B*, the CU_{ij} ends after the left boundary of its prosodic phrase PU_i. When its *PA* accent and semiotic indicator *I* lie within this PU_i, its left boundary is adjusted to the left boundary of the PU_i. And when *PA* syllable and semiotic indicator *I* do not lie within this PU_i, then the corresponding *CU* element has to be removed from the HRG structure. From now on, the prosodic phrases contain only those *CU* elements that contain *PA* syllable and semiotic indicator *I*, and have aligned their boundaries with the corresponding prosodic phrases.

In the next step in Table 6 (d) we still have to resolve internal overlapping. In doing so, all prosodic phrases and their *CU* elements have to be checked. Namely, for each phrase PU_i the corresponding CU_i element is checked to determine whether it overlaps with any other CU_j element within the same prosodic phrase. When CU_i ends after the left boundary of any CU_j element, the values of their *normal distributions* are compared. If they are equal, their length is additionally compared. If CU_i and CU_j both have equal values, one of them is randomly removed from the HRG, and otherwise the shorter one is removed. If the *normal distributions* are not equal, the *CU* with the smaller value is removed. As can be seen, this step favors the larger values of *normal distribution* and the larger context of the *CU*.

Table 6. *Phase II* – The planning of the intent

```
ProsodicStructure is created
FOR ( phrase = utterance→ relation (Phrase); phrase != NULL; )
{
    phrase_start = phrase→ as_relation (PhraseStructure) → daughters();
    phrase_end = phrase→ as_relation (PhraseStructure) → daughtern();
    utterance→ relation ( ProsodicStructure ) → append ( phrase );

    FOR ( ; cu != NULL; cu = next(cu) )
    {
        cu_start = cu→ as_relation (ContentStructure)→ daughters();
        cu_end = cu→ as_relation (ContentStructure)→ daughtern();
        syll_start = cu_start→ as_relation (SyllableStructure)→ daughters();
        syll_end = cu_end→ as_relation (SyllableStructure)→ daughtern();

        FOR ( syll = syll_start; syll != NULL; syll = next(syll ) )
        {
            IF ( syll→fS ( ACCENT ) == »PA« )
            {
                cu→fset ( ACCENT, »PA« );
                cu→fset ( ACCENT_POSITION,
                    syll → as_relation (SyllableStructure) → up()→ fI(POSITION) );
                cu→fset ( SEMIOTIC_INDICATOR,
                    cu_start→fI(POSITION) + cu→fI ( SEMIOTIC_INDICATOR) );
            }
        }
        IF ( cu_start→fI( POSITION) ≥ phrase_end→fI(POSITION) )
        {
            phrase = next ( phrase );
        }
        append_daughter ( phrase, ProsodicStructure, cu );
    }
}
```

(a)– Assigning *CU* elements to the predicted prosodic phrases.

Table 6. (Continued)

```
FOR ( cui = utterance→ relation (ContentUnits); cui != NULL; cui = next(cui) )
{
    cui_start = cui→ as_relation (ContentStructure)→ daughters();
    cui_end = cui→ as_relation (ContentStructure)→ daughtern();
    cui→fset ( LENGTH, cui_end - cui_start);
    IF ( cui→fI ( KEEP ) == 0 )
    {
        semiotic_indicator.Append ( cui→fI ( SEMIOTIC_INDICATOR ) );
        FOR ( cuj = next(cui); cuj != NULL; cuj = next(cuj) )
        {
            cuj_start = cuj → as_relation (ContentStructure) → daughters();
            cuj_end = cuj → as_relation (ContentStructure) → daughtern();
            IF (cuj → fI ( KEEP ) == 1 )
            {
                IF (cuj_start→ fI (POSITION) < cui_end→ fI(POSITION ) ||
                   (cuj_start→ fI (POSITION) ≥ cui_start→ fI (POSITION) &&
                   cuj_end→ fI (POSITION) ≤ cui_end→ fI(POSITION)) ||
                   (cuj_start→ fI (POSITION) == cui_end→ fI (POSITION) )
                {
                    semiotic_indicator.Append ( cuj→fI (SEMIOTIC_INDICATOR) );
                    cui_end = cuj→ as_relation (ContentStructure) → daughtern();
                    cui→fset ( NORMAL_DISTRIBUTION, 1.0 );
                    cui→fset (PROBABILITY, 1.0 );
                    remove_CU (cuj);
                    continue;
                }
            }
            IF ( cuj_start→ fI (POSITION) ≥ cui_start→ fI (POSITION) &&
                 cuj_end→ fI (POSITION) ≤ cui_end→ fI (POSITION) )
                 remove_CU (cuj);
            IF ( cuj_start→ fI (POSITION) > cui_end→ fI (POSITION) )
                 break;
        }
    }
}
```

(b) – Resolving enumeration issues, including overlap and merging.

```
FOR ( phrase = utterance→ relation (Phrase); phrase != NULL; phrase = next(phrase ))
{
    phrase_start = phrase→ as_relation (PhraseStructure)→ daughters();
    phrase_end = phrase→ as_relation (PhraseStructure)→ daughtern();
    FOR ( cu = phrase → as_relation (ProsodicStructure)→ daughters();
            cu != phrase → as_relation (ProsodicStructure)→ daughtern(); cu = next(cu ) )
    {
        IF ( cu→fI ( KEEP ) == 1 ) continue;
        IF ( cu→fS ( ACCENT ) != »PA« )
        {
            remove_CU ( cu );
            continue;
        }
        cu_start = cu → as_relation (ContentStructure)→ daughters();
        cu_end = cu → as_relation (ContentStructure)→ daughtern();
        IF ( cu_start→ fI (POSITION) < phrase_end → fI (POSITION) &&
```

```
                cu_end → fI (POSITION) > phrase_end → fI (POSITION) )
            {
                IF ( cu→ fI (ACCENT_POSITION) < phrase_end → fI (POSITION) &&
                    cu→fI ( SEMIOTIC_INDICATOR) < phrase_end → fI (POSITION) )
                    cu_end = phrase_end;
                ELSE
                    Remove_CU ( cu );
            }
            IF ( cu_start→ fI (POSITION) < phrase_start → fI (POSITION) &&
                cu_end → fI (POSITION) > phrase_start→ fI (POSITION) )
            {
                IF ( cu→fI (ACCENT_POSITION) > phrase_start → fI (POSITION) &&
                    cu→fI ( SEMIOTIC_INDICATOR) > phrase_start → fI (POSITION) )
                    cu_start = phrase_start;
                ELSE
                    Remove_CU ( cu );
            }
        }
    }
```

(c) – Resolving external overlapping.

```
FOR ( phrase = utterance→ relation (Phrase); phrase != NULL; phrase = next(phrase ) )
{
    FOR ( cui = phrase → as_relation (ProsodicStructure)→ daughters();
            cui != phrase → as_relation (ProsodicStructure)→ daughtern();
            cui = next(cu ) )
    {
        IF ( cui→fI ( KEEP ) == 1 ) continue;
        cui_start = cui → as_relation (ContentStructure)→ daughters();
        cui_end = cui → as_relation (ContentStructure)→ daughtern();
        FOR ( cuj = next(cui); cuj != NULL; cuj = next(cuj ) )
        {
            cuj_start = cuj → as_relation (ContentStructure)→ daughters();
            cuj_end = cuj → as_relation (ContentStructure)→ daughtern();
            IF ( cuj_start → fI (POSITION) < cui_end→ fI (POSITION) )
            {
                IF ( cui→ fF ( NORMAL_DISTRIBUTION ) == cuj→ fF
                    (NORMAL_DISTRIBUTION ) )
                {
                    IF ( cui → fI ( LENGTH ) == cuj → fI ( LENGTH ) )
                        Random_Remove ( cui, cuj ), break;
                    ( cui → fI ( LENGTH ) > cuj → fI ( LENGTH ) )? Remove_VI(cuj) :
                        Remove_VI(cui);
                }
                ELSE
                {
                    IF ( cui→ fF ( NORMAL_DISTRIBUTION ) > cuj→ fF
                        (NORMAL_DISTRIBUTION)) ? Remove_VI(cuj) : Remove_VI(cui);
                }
            }
        }
    }
}
```

(d) – Resolving internal overlapping.

The result of Phase II is the HRG structure (see Figure 39) that contains information about the intent and is defined based on prosodic phrases and morpho-syntactic characteristics of the input text. Furthermore, it contains all features needed for defining the movement models *H*, which can be used for the realization of co-verbal behavior.

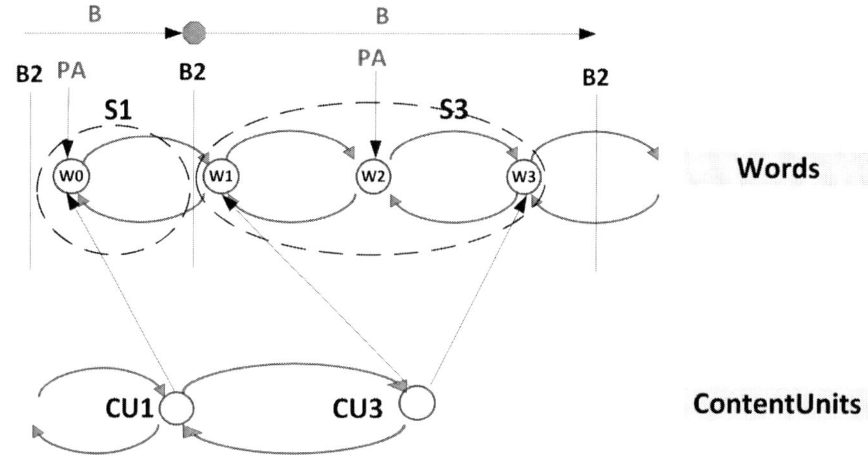

Content unit	
S	S1
I	w0.index
w	w(x)
p	p(x)
O	true

Content unit	
S	S3
I	w2.index
w	w(x)
p	p(x)
O	true

Figure 39. That part of the HRG structure which refers to the intent after performing *Phase II*.

Let the core TTS module for symbolic prosody (see Figure 4) on the input sentence predicts two prosodic phrases PU_1 and PU_2. As can be seen in Figure 39, the first one is tagged with label *B2* and can be described as $\{W_0\} \in B2$. The second one is tagged with label *B3*, and can be described as $\{W_1, W_2, W_3\} \in B3$. Furthermore, the phrase PU_1 contains *PA* syllable in word W_0, and phrase PU_2 contains the *PA* syllable in word W_2. Referring to Figure 33, the initial structure of the intent (the set of all possible interpretations) assumes three possible interpretations for the input text, by creating the content units CU_1, CU_2, and CU_3. All of these *CU* elements that belong to each interpretation are presented in Table 7.

In this case, both external and internal overlapping is present. The *external overlapping* has to be resolved first; therefore, the CU_1 boundaries are adjusted to the boundaries of the PU_1. Namely, the CU_1 boundaries are initially defined by words W_0 and W_1, where word W_1 lies outside the boundaries of the PU_1. As explained, the equation 29 has to be applied for external overlapping. But first it has to be checked to determine whether the CU_1 should be considered at all. The CU_1 within PU_1 contains semantic indicator *I* as well as the *PA* syllable (see Figure 39 and Table 7). Therefore, the adjustment of CU_1 boundaries to the boundaries of PU_1 fulfills both ***Rule 3*** and ***Rule 4*** and, consequently, the CU_1 has to be kept. Nevertheless, the final structure of the CU_1 depends on the subsequent *CU* elements, namely from the result of $CU_1 \cap (CU_1 \cap CU_3)$. Obviously, in this case the result can be only word W_0. In the next step, the *internal overlapping* in the second prosodic phrase has to be resolved, where we have $CU_2 \cap CU_3 = \{W_1, W_2\}$.

Table 7. The content units CU_1, CU_2, and CU_3

CU1	
intent (S)	S_1
semiotic indicator (I)	0
normal distribution $\omega_S(x)$	$\omega_{S_1}(W_0.POS)$
probability of selection $p_S(x)$	$p_{S_1}(W_0.POS)$
keep (O)	*false*
boundaries	W_0, W_1
CU2	
intent (S)	S_2
semiotic indicator (I)	2
normal distribution $\omega_S(x)$	$\omega_{S_2}(W_1.POS, W_2.POS)$
probability of selection $p_S(x)$	$p_{S_2}(W_1.POS, W_2.POS)$
keep (O)	*false*
boundaries	W_1, W_2
CU3	
intent (S)	S_3
semiotic indicator (I)	2
normal distribution $\omega_S(x)$	$\omega_{S_3}(W_1.POS, W_2.POS, W_3.POS)$
probability of selection $p_S(x)$	$p_{S_3}(W_1.POS, W_2.POS, W_3.POS)$
keep (O)	*false*
boundaries	W_1, W_2, W_3

In this case the equation 31 has to be applied. Firstly, it is verified whether any of the *CU* contains the word with a *PA* syllable. Since the *PA* syllable is contained in word W_2, the application of equation 28 results in a set $\{CU_2, CU_3\}$. The number of *CUs* is greater than 1, and since the corresponding semiotic classes are not equal ($S_2 \neq S_3$), the equation 31 is applied that is based on $p_{S3} > p_{S2}$, as a result returning the content unit CU_3. The result is, therefore, the unique structure of the intent that for the given input text defines the co-verbal behavior by using the content units CU_1 and CU_3. Further, the CU_1 boundaries are also adjusted to the boundaries of the prosodic phrases.

Referring to the Figure 39, the co-verbal behavior *G* consists of two movement models *H*, where H_1 describes a visual representation of the meaning of the word W_0 and where, according to the position of the *PA* syllable, the stroke phase F_S is predicted. The movement model H_2 is defined on the sequence of words W_1, W_2, W_3, and describes the visual representation of the meaning of the word W_1 where, according to the position of the *PA* syllable, the stroke phase F_S is also predicted. As will be presented below, nevertheless, the stroke phase F_S does not necessarily happen on the semantic indicator *I*.

PHASE III: THE PLANNING OF THE MOVEMENT

The movement model, according to equation 13, is defined as an animated sequence of several co-verbal shapes/poses. Namely, the movement model *H* is just a sequence of co-verbal shapes/poses that are mutually related, as $T_{vm}^{-1}(P_1, P_2, P_3,...)$. Furthermore, the movement model *H* in a HRG structure can be represented by the so-called *MPHRs* (*movement phrase* unit), which are composed of several so-called *MPHs* (*movement phase* units). Each *movement phrase* represents the interpretation of the verbal information, and has to contain at least the stroke phase F_S. The movement models *H* can be defined based on *CU* units in the *ContentUnits* relational structure. When defining movement models *H* based on the *CUs*, the condition that defines the *movement phrase* is satisfied by ***Rule 3*** and ***Rule 4***. The *Phase III* task is to adjust the individual *CU* to the predicted prosodic characteristics of the verbal information (speech). Namely, this phase carries out the so-called prosodic synchronization that is based on the predicted primary (*PA*) and secondary accents (*NA*), and temporal characteristics (regarding phoneme and pause durations). Here, the following rule has to be considered:

Rule 11: *The individual stroke phase F_S is performed always on that word with primary accent, and is concluded together with its PA syllable (based on the so-called rule about the prosodic synchrony of gestures as proposed by Rusiewicz (2010), Loehr (2004) and Rusiewicz et al. (2013).*

Furthermore, the movement models *H* can be defined through the temporal transformation of the intent, and represented in the form of poses that belong to each movement phase *MPH*, as follows:

$$T_{vm}^{-1} \cdot P_{preparation} + T_{vm}^{-1} \cdot P_{stroke} + T_{vm}^{-1} \cdot P_{shold} + T_{vm}^{-1} \cdot P_{retraction} \quad (32)$$

The needed temporal information is stored in the relational structure *Segments*, where the units represent *phoneme* and *pause* (*sil*) segments between words. Their durations are predicted on the input text in the *TTS* module used for acoustic prosody generation (by taking into account several linguistic features stored in the HRG structure). At this point all *CU* elements contain *PA* syllables and relations in the HRG structure to corresponding words. In Figure 40 there are two words with *PA* syllable. The first word W_0 consists of Z_0 and Z_1, and has the primary accent on Z_0, while the Z_1 is followed by *sil* segment (pause).

According to ***Rule 11***, the stroke phase F_S within CU_1 then has to start with the first syllable Z_0 in the word W_0 with *PA* syllable, and has to end after its *PA* syllable. The remaining part of the word W_0, namely, the syllable Z_1 together with the *sil* segment (pause), is then used for the *hold phase* F_{SH} (Figure 41). The second word, W_2, consists of Z_4, Z_5, and Z_6 syllables, where the syllable Z_5 is the *PA* syllable, and Z_6 is followed by *sil* segment.

Therefore, the stroke phase F_S within CU_3 has to start with Z_4 and end after syllable Z_5, while the hold phase F_{SH} can be realized on the Z_6 syllable and the following *sil* segment (Figure 41). By considering ***Rule 11***, in this way the verbal behavior defined on input text in the core TTS system can be symbolically synchronized with the semiotic core of the movement structure (the stroke phase F_S, and the hold phase F_{SH}).

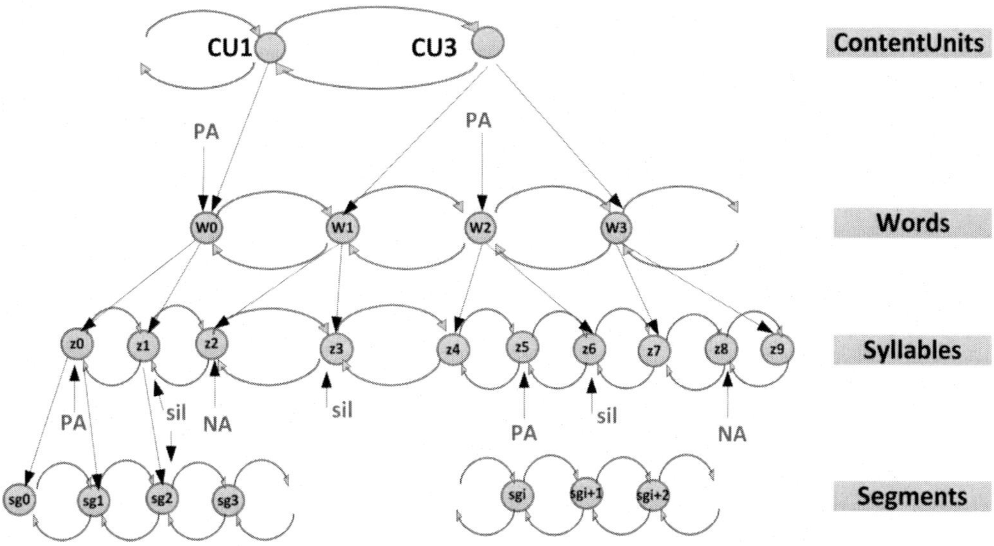

Figure 40. The HRG structure used for defining the movement model *H*.

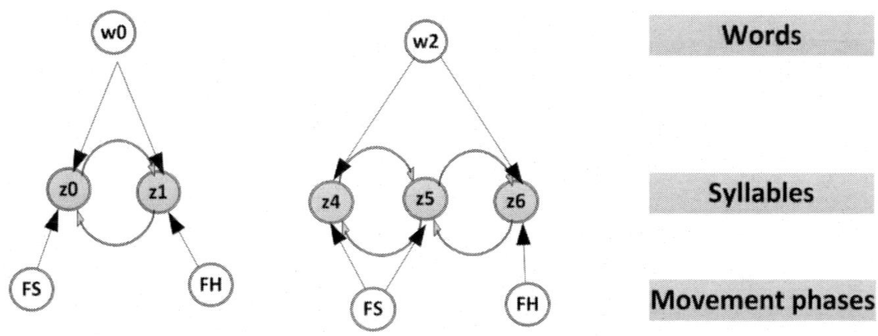

Figure 41. The most accentuated words in *CUs* that also represent the semiotic indicators *I*.

After synchronizing the movement structure by taking into account the *PA* syllables, the next step is the synchronization of all stroke phases F_S with that gesticulation which can be interpreted by semiotic classes *enumeration* and/or *search*. Namely, these are not directly related with the *PA* syllables. In the PLATTOS TTS system, all *non-PA* stressed syllables are labeled with the *NA* tag (secondary accent). Therefore, when we are dealing with semiotic classes such as *enumeration* or *search*, the following rule has to be applied:

Rule 12: *If the word represents a semiotic indicator I for the specific CU and if this word has no PA syllable, then the NA syllable is used instead of PA syllable.*

According to ***Rule 12***, the boundaries for stroke phase F_S are defined by the first syllable in the word that represents the semiotic indicator *I* and by its NA syllable. The remaining part is then used for the hold phase F_{SH}. Furthermore, most accentuated words (containing the *PA* syllable) do not necessarily also represent the semiotic indicator *I* for the given *CU* element. For example, in the sequences of words that form POS pairs such as *adverb-adjective*, the semiotic indicator *I* can be *adjective*, although the most accentuated word is *adverb*. In these cases, the following rule has to be applied:

Rule 13: *When semiotic indicator I and PA syllable are not represented by the same word, the stroke phase F_S has to be defined by following **Rule 11**, but the hold phase F_{SH} has to end with the NA syllable of that word which represents the semiotic indicator I within the given CU.*

In Figure 42 the most accentuated word W_i does not represent the semiotic indicator *I*. Namely, the *PA* syllable is Z_5, and word W_j represents the semiotic indicator *I*, while its NA syllable is syllable Z_{i+1}. According to ***Rule 13***, the stroke phase F_S is, therefore, defined as a sequence of syllables $[Z_4, Z_5]$, and the hold phase F_{SH} as a sequence of syllables $(Z_5, Z_{i+1}]$. We also include the silences between the most accentuated word and the semiotic indicator *I*.

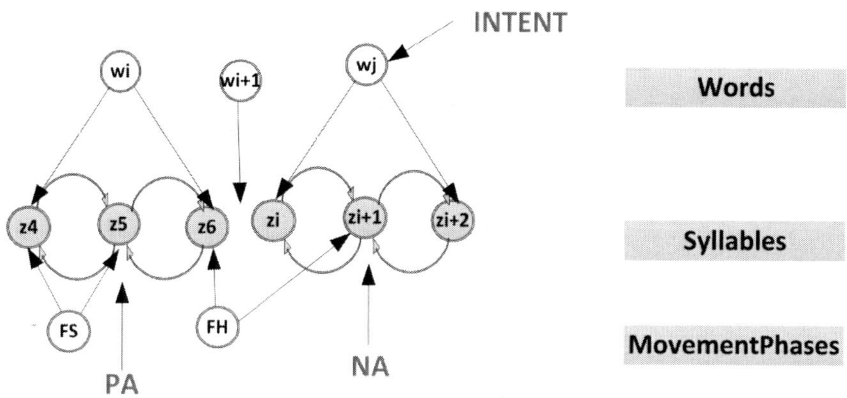

Figure 42. When the most accentuated word (*PA*) does not represent the semiotic indicator *I*.

In *Phase III*, several new relational structures have to be created within the HRG structure (see Figure 43). Namely, the *movement phases MPHs* have to be stored in the relational structure *MovementPhases*. Further, the *MPHs* and syllable units in *Syllable* relation have to be related through the relational structure *Dynamics*. Once the movement is defined regarding its content, the context of the semiotic core also has to be defined. Those syllables that occur before the stroke phase F_S are then used for the preparation phase F_P, and the *sil* segment just before the first syllable of the F_S can be used for the hold phase F_{HS} (the so-called hold before stroke). Those syllables after the stroke phase F_S, are used for the retraction phase F_R. If there are any *sil* segments just after F_S, these are then used for the post-stroke-hold phase (F_{SH}). The behavior structure is defined by considering the following rules:

Rule 14: *The preparation phase F_P starts just before the stroke phase F_S, and has to last from the NA syllable till the beginning of the F_S.*

Rule 15: *The sil segment, which may have non-zero duration between the words with the preparation phase F_P and stroke phase F_S, represents the so-called hold before stroke, which (if it exists) represents a ready-made idea regarding the content.*

Furthermore, the defined *movement phases* can be extended or merged. When doing this, the following rules have to be taken into account:

Rule 16: *The right boundary of each movement phase (with the exception of the hold phase F_H) has to be PA or NA syllable.*

Rule 17: *The stroke phase F_S and preparation phase F_P can be merged into stroke phase F_S, since this also often happens in multimodal communication (often observed in database annotations).*

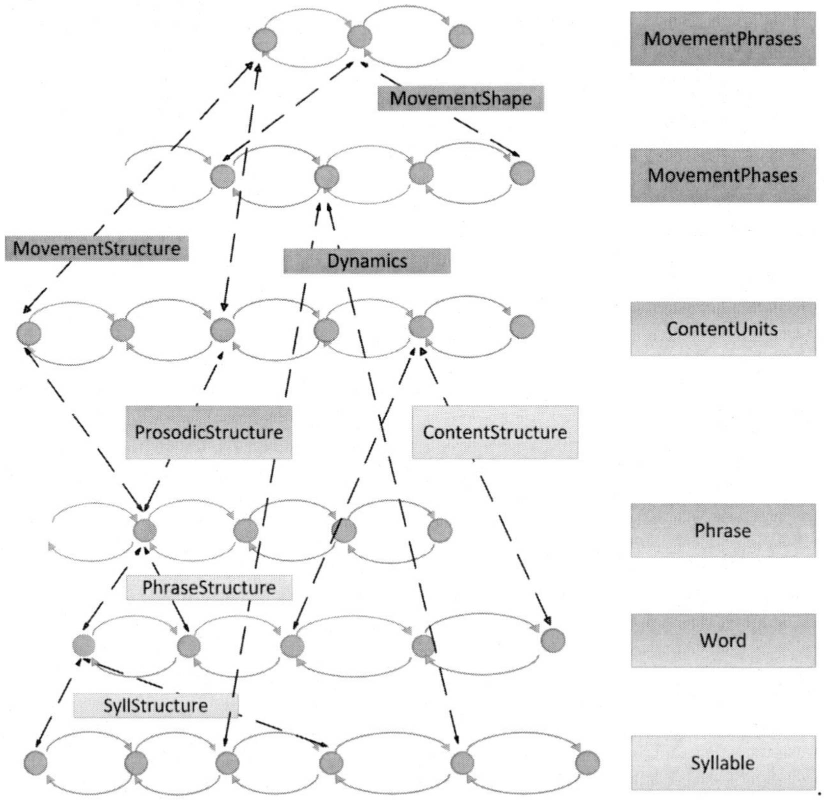

Figure 43. The HRG structure in *Phase III*.

The maximum length of the preparation phase F_P is defined by the length of that content word (has *NA* syllable) which precedes the F_S. Nevertheless, the F_P can also be extended during the synchronization of the shape, by including additional predecessors of the *PA* word. Furthermore, it can also be extended by including that *sil* segment which is the predecessor of the *PA* word, or which lies between the *PA* word and its predecessor. The extension is always limited by the boundaries of the specific *CU*. For example, let *CU* contain the following word sequence: $\{W_0, W_1, W_2, W_3, W_4\} \in CU$, and let the word W_3 represent the corresponding *PA* word. In this case the preparation phase F_P has to be defined on word W_2, but can also be extended into the interval $[W_0, W_3)$. Therefore, the preparation phase F_P can be defined as:

$$
\begin{aligned}
&F_P = \{w_i, \ldots, w_j\}; \\
&w_i, w_j \in CU \wedge \begin{pmatrix} i = \max .CU_{leftboundary}, \min .z_{NA} \text{ in } prev(w_{PA}) \\ j = prev(w_{PA}) \end{pmatrix} \\
&F_P = \{z_i, \ldots, z_j\}; \\
&z_i \in w_i \wedge z_j \in w_j \wedge \begin{pmatrix} z_i = NA \\ z_j = prev(z_{PA}) \vee prev(prev(z_{PA})) \end{pmatrix}
\end{aligned}
\tag{33}
$$

Furthermore, in Figure 40, in CU_1 the W_0 represents the PA word with no predecessor, namely $prev(W_0) = \{\}$. In this case, the movement phases F_P and F_S can be merged into a common F_S. And in CU_3, the word W_1 is the predecessor of the PA word (W_2), namely $prev(W_2) = W_1 = \{Z_2 \times Z_3\}$. In this case, the F_P can be defined on the word W_1 by using the syllable Z_2, while the F_{HS} can be defined on Z_3 syllable. Alternatively, the Z_3 syllable can also be included in the F_P, but consequently the F_{HS} cannot be defined. Similarly, the retraction phase F_R can be defined, wherein the F_R may include only the remaining part of the specific CU and may always only follow the semiotic core of the text where $F_S \times F_H$ has to be defined. For the definition of the F_R, the following equation has to be used:

$$
\begin{aligned}
&F_R = \{w_i, \ldots, w_j\}; \\
&w_i, w_j \in CU \wedge \begin{pmatrix} i = last\ I \\ j = \max .CU_{leftboundary}, \min .next(w_{PA}) \vee next(w_H) \end{pmatrix} \\
&F_R = \{z_i, \ldots, z_j\}; \\
&z_i \in w_i \wedge z_j \in w_j \wedge \begin{pmatrix} z_i = next(z_{NA}); z_{NA} \in F_{S \cup H} \\ z_j = NA \end{pmatrix}
\end{aligned}
\tag{34}
$$

Let us have the content unit CU that contains words W_0—W_4. And let these words in the syllable level be described as follows: $W_0 = Z_0 \times Z_1$, $W_1 = Z_2 \times Z_3 \times Z_4$, $W_2 = Z_5 \times Z_6$, $W_3 = Z_7$ and $W_4 = Z_8 \times Z_9$. Furthermore, let Z_3 represent the last syllable of the semiotic core of the movement that already has the defined the movement phases $F_S \times F_{SH}$, and let Z_6 be the NA syllable in that word which follows the semiotic indicator I. Then F_R in the given CU (according to equation 34) can be defined on the interval $[Z_4, Z_6]$. Nevertheless, the F_R can even contain Z_8, since it is that last NA syllable which is still within the given CU (W_4). Furthermore, in Figure 40 only CU_3 allows the definition of F_R. And in Figure 42, the last syllable of the semiotic core with the definition $F_S \times F_H$ represents the syllable Z_6. Thus, the F_R can be defined on the syllable Z_7 and can last up to the subsequent NA syllable Z_8. Therefore, its boundaries can be $[Z_7, Z_8]$. In the first part of the co-verbal behavior synchronization, therefore, the prosodically adjusted structure of movement phases for each movement model *H* is defined. The structure is stored in the form of new relational structure *MovementPhases*, if its *MPH* units are related with corresponding syllables through the new relational structure *Dynamics*.

In the *planning behavior module*, *Phase III* of the algorithm firstly defines the movement models and corresponding movement phases, as also described by the pseudocode in Table 8 (a). In this phase, the relational structures *MovementPhases*, *MovementPhrases*, *MovementShape*, *Dynamics*, and *MovementStructure* have to be created (see Figure 43). Namely, *MovementPhrases* is used for storing movement models *H*, where the individual *MPHR* element keeps a set of movement phases which can be defined for the corresponding *CU* element. Furthermore, the *MovementStructure* relates movement phrases and content units. This is needed in order to relate attributes of elements in *ContentUnits*, *MovementPhrases*, and *MovementPhases*. In order to define the left and right boundaries of the individual *MPHR* element in the level of movement phases, the *MovementShape* relational structure is needed. And the relational structure *Dynamics* is used to define the boundaries of each *MPHR* element in the level of words and syllables. Additionally, for each syllable in the relational structure *Syllables*, or for each movement phase in the relational structure *MovementPhases* it can be uniquely identified to which *MPRH* element in the *MovementPhrases* they belong (to which movement model *H*).

In order to create *MPRH* and all corresponding *MPH* elements, the *CU* elements have to be analyzed. As seen in Table 8 (a), the left and right boundaries of each *CU* in the level of words are accessed and also the corresponding syllables. Namely, the words within each *CU* keep information about semiotic indicators, while the syllables keep information about accents (*PA* or *NA* syllables). For each *CU* a new *MPHR* element has to be created. Furthermore, *CU* elements are processed differently, depending on their attribute value *KEEP*. In both cases for each word within the *CU* element, a check is first performed to determine whether it includes the *NA* syllable. When the *KEEP* value is 0, there are two possibilities mentioned already, regarding positions of semiotic indicator *I* and accents with the *PA* tag. When predicted on the same word within the individual *CU*, the *CreateMovementPhases_1* method has to be used (Table 8 (b)). Here, a check is first performed to determine whether a predecessor word with a *NA* syllable exists. If so, the corresponding syllable is accessed and a new element for preparation phase F_P is added into the relational structure *MovementPhases*. The relational structure *Dynamics* stores the corresponding left (set to this *NA* syllable), and the right boundary (set to the first syllable of a word with semiotic indicator *I*). Additionally, the relational structure *MovementShape* stores the left boundary of the current *MPHR* element (set to F_P). Then a new element is added into the relational structure *MovementPhases* which is needed for the hold phase (before the stroke phase) F_{HS}. Its left and right boundaries are defined on the first syllable of a word with semiotic indicator *I*. Additionally, the current *MPHR* element is related to F_{HS}. The new stroke phase F_S has to be added next. The relational structure *Dynamics* stores its left boundary (set to the first syllable of the word with semiotic indicator *I*), and the right boundary (set to the *PA* syllable within the same word). Additionally, the current *MPHR* element is related to F_S. Furthermore, in the case of a new hold phase F_{SH}, its left boundary has to be placed on the first syllable after the *PA* syllable, and the right boundary on the final syllable of the same word. Additionally, the current *MPHR* element is related to F_{SH}. If the *PA* syllable is the last syllable in a word, then boundaries for the hold phase F_{SH} have to be placed on the *sil* segment (represents the pause after the given word). At the end, for the individual *CU* element, the retraction phase F_R also has to be added. In this case the left boundary has to be set on the last syllable of the same word, while the right boundary has to be set on the end of the same word.

When semiotic indicator *I* and accent with PA tag are not defined on the same word within the individual *CU*, the *CreateMovementPhases_2* method has to be used (Table 8 (c)). As can be seen, there are no differences in the case of the following movement phases F_P, F_{HS}, F_S, and F_R. Nevertheless, in this case the left boundary of the hold phase F_{SH} has to be placed on the first syllable after the *PA* syllable, and the right boundary on the *NA* syllable in word with semiotic indicator *I*. And when the *KEEP* value is 1, only the word with semiotic indicator *I* has to be searched (Table 8 (a)). When found, the *CreateMovementPhases_3* method has to be performed (Table 8 (d)). As can be seen, there are no differences in the case of the following movement phases F_P, F_{HS}, F_{SH}, and F_R. Nevertheless, when a new stroke phase F_S is added, the left boundary has to be set to the beginning of the word with semiotic indicator *I*, while the right boundary has to be set to the *PA* or *NA* syllable in the same word.

Table 8. *Phase III* – Planning of the movement – The definition of movement models *H*.

```
    MovementPhases is created
    MovementPhrases is created
    MovementShape is created
    MovementStructure is created
    Dynamics is created

FOR ( cu = utterance→ relation ( ContentUnits ); cu != NULL; cu = next(cu) ) {

    cu_start = cu→ as_relation ( ContentStructure ) → daughters();
    cu_end = cu→ as_relation ( ContentStructure ) → daughtern();

    syll_start = cu_start→ as_relation ( SyllStructure )→ daughters ();
    syll_end = cu_end→ as_relation ( SyllStructure )→ daughtern ();

    h = utterance→ relation ( MovementPhrases )→ append();
    utterance→ relation ( MovementShape ) → append( h);
    utterance→ relation ( MovementStructure ) → append( h);
    append_daughter ( h, MovementStructure, cu );

    IF ( cu→fI ( KEEP ) == 0 ) {
        FOR ( word = cu_start; word != cu_end; word = next(word) ) {
            IF ( word → fS ( ACCENT ) == »NA« ) prev_NA_word = word;
            IF ( word → fS ( ACCENT ) == »PA« &&
                cu→ fI ( SEMIOTIC_INDICATOR ) == word→ fI (POSITION) )
            {
                CreateMovementPhases_1 ;
            }
            IF ( word → fS ( ACCENT ) == »PA« &&
                cu→ fI ( SEMIOTIC_INDICATOR ) != word→ fI (POSITION) )
            {
                CreateMovementPhases_2 ;
            }
        }
    }
    ELSE
    {
```

```
            FOR ( word = cu_start; word != cu_end; word = next(word) ) {
                IF ( word → fS ( ACCENT ) == »NA« ) prev_NA_word = word;
                IF ( cu→ fI ( SEMIOTIC_INDICATOR ) == word→ fI (POSITION) )
                {
                    CreateMovementPhases_3 ;
                }
            }
        }
}
```

(a) – *Complete algorithm.*

```
CreateMovementPhases_1 {
    IF ( prev_NA_word != NULL )
        syll_start = prev_NA_word → as_relation ( SyllStructure )→daughters();

    fp = utterance→ relation ( MovementPhases ) → append();
    utterance→ relation ( Dynamics ) → append ( fp );
    syll_end = word→ as_relation ( SyllStructure )→daughters ();

    FOR ( syll = syll_start; syll != syll_end; syll = next(syll) ) {
        IF ( syll→ fS ( ACCENT ) == »NA« ) {
            fp→fset ( PHASE_TYPE, »Fp« );
            append_daughter ( fp, Dynamics, syll );
        }
    }
    append_daughter ( fp, Dynamics, syll_end );
    append_daughter ( h, MovementShape, fp );

    fh = utterance→ relation ( MovementPhases ) → append();
    fh→fset ( PHASE_TYPE, »Fh« );
    utterance→ relation ( Dynamics ) → append( fh);
    syll = word→ as_relation ( SyllStructure )→down();
    append_daughter ( fh, Dynamics, syll );
    append_daughter ( h, MovementShape, fh );

    fs = utterance→ relation ( MovementPhases ) → append();
    fs→fset ( PHASE_TYPE, »Fs« );
    utterance→ relation ( Dynamics ) → append( fs);
    append_daughter ( fs, Dynamics, syll );
    FOR ( ; syll != NULL; syll = next(syll) ) {
        IF ( syll→ fS ( ACCENT ) == »PA« )
        {
            append_daughter ( fs, Dynamics, syll );
            break;
        }
    }
    append_daughter ( h, MovementShape, fs );

    fh = utterance→ relation ( MovementPhases ) → append();
    fh→fset ( PHASE_TYPE, »Fh« );
    utterance→ relation ( Dynamics ) → append( fh);
    append_daughter ( fh, Dynamics, syll );
    append_daughter ( fh, Dynamics, word→ as_relation ( SyllStructure )→last() );
    append_daughter ( h, MovementShape, fh );
```

Table 8. (Continued)

```
    fr = utterance→ relation ( MovementPhases ) → append();
    fr→fset ( PHASE_TYPE, »Fr« );
    utterance→ relation ( Dynamics ) → append( fr);
    append_daughter ( fr, Dynamics, word→ as_relation ( SyllStructure )→last());
    append_daughter ( fr, Dynamics, syll_end );
    append_daughter ( h, MovementShape, fr );
}
```

(b) – *CreateMovementPhases_1*: the word that represents the semiotic indicator *I* is also the *PA* word.

```
CreateMovementPhases_2 {
    IF ( prev_NA_word != NULL )
        syll_start = prev_NA_word → as_relation ( SyllStructure )→daughters();

    fp = utterance→ relation ( MovementPhases ) → append();
    utterance→ relation ( Dynamics ) → append ( fp );
    syll_end = word→ as_relation ( SyllStructure )→daughters ();

    FOR ( syll = syll_start; syll != syll_end; syll = next(syll) ) {
        IF ( syll→ fS ( ACCENT ) == »NA« ) {
            fp→fset ( PHASE_TYPE, »Fp« );
            append_daughter ( fp, Dynamics, syll );
        }
    }
    append_daughter ( fp, Dynamics, syll_end );
    append_daughter ( h, MovementShape, fp );
    fh = utterance→ relation ( MovementPhases ) → append();
    fh→fset ( PHASE_TYPE, »Fh« );
    utterance→ relation ( Dynamics ) → append( fh);
    syll = word→ as_relation ( SyllStructure )→down();
    append_daughter ( fh, Dynamics, syll );
    append_daughter ( h, MovementShape, fh );
    fs = utterance→ relation ( MovementPhases ) → append();
    fs→fset ( PHASE_TYPE, »Fs« );
    utterance→ relation ( Dynamics ) → append( fs);
    append_daughter ( fs, Dynamics, syll );
    FOR ( ; syll != NULL; syll = next(syll) ) {
        IF ( syll→ fS ( ACCENT ) == »PA« )
        {
            append_daughter ( fs, Dynamics, syll );
            break;
        }
    }
    append_daughter ( h, MovementShape, fs );
    fh = utterance→ relation ( MovementPhases ) → append();
    fh→fset ( PHASE_TYPE, »Fh« );
    utterance→ relation ( Dynamics ) → append( fh);
    append_daughter ( fh, Dynamics, syll );
    FOR ( ; word != NULL; word = next(word )) {
        IF ( cu → fI ( SEMIOTIC_INDICATOR ) == word → fI ( POSITION ) {
            syll = word → as_relation ( SyllStructure ) → down();
            FOR ( ; syll != NULL; syll = next(syll)) {
                IF ( syll → fS ( ACCENT ) == »NA« ) {
```

```
                    append_daughter ( fh, Dynamics, syll );
                    break;
                }
            }
        }
    }
    append_daughter ( h, MovementShape, fh );

    fr = utterance→ relation ( MovementPhases ) → append();
    fr→fset ( PHASE_TYPE, »Fr« );
    utterance→ relation ( Dynamics ) → append( fr);
    append_daughter ( fr, Dynamics, word→ as_relation ( SyllStructure )→last());
    append_daughter ( fr, Dynamics, syll_end );
    append_daughter ( h, MovementShape, fr );
}
```

(c) – *CreateMovementPhases_2*: the word that represents the semiotic indicator *I* is not the *PA* word.

```
CreateMovementPhases_3 {
    IF ( prev_NA_word != NULL )
        syll_start = prev_NA_word → as_relation ( SyllStructure )→daughters();

    fp = utterance→ relation ( MovementPhases ) → append();
    utterance→ relation ( Dynamics ) → append( fp);
    syll_start = prev_NA_word → as_relation ( SyllStructure )→daughters();
    syll_end = word→ as_relation ( SyllStructure )→daughters ();
    FOR ( syll = syll_start; syll != syll_end; syll = next(syll) ) {
        IF ( syll→ fS ( ACCENT ) == »NA« ) {
            fp→fset ( PHASE_TYPE, »Fp« );
            append_daughter ( fp, Dynamics, syll );
        }
    }
    append_daughter ( fp, Dynamics, syll_end );
    append_daughter ( h, MovementShape, fp );
    syll = word→ as_relation ( SyllStructure )→down();
    fh = utterance→ relation ( MovementPhases ) → append();
    fh→fset ( PHASE_TYPE, »Fh« );
    utterance→ relation ( Dynamics ) → append( fh);
    append_daughter ( fh, Dynamics, syll );
    append_daughter ( h, MovementShape, fh );
    fs = utterance→ relation ( MovementPhases ) → append();
    fs→fset ( PHASE_TYPE, »Fs« );
    utterance→ relation ( Dynamics ) → append( fs);
    append_daughter ( fs, Dynamics, syll );
    FOR ( ; syll != NULL; syll = next(syll) ) {
        IF ( syll→ fS ( ACCENT ) == »PA« || syll→ fS ( ACCENT ) == »NA« ) {
            append_daughter ( fs, Dynamics, syll );
            break;
    }
    append_daughter ( h, MovementShape, fs );

    fh = utterance→ relation ( MovementPhases ) → append();
    fh→fset ( PHASE_TYPE, »Fh« );
    utterance→ relation ( Dynamics ) → append( fh);
    append_daughter ( fh, Dynamics, syll );
    append_daughter ( fh, Dynamics, word→ as_relation (SyllStructure)→last() );
    append_daughter ( h, MovementShape, fh );
```

```
        fr = utterance→ relation ( MovementPhases ) → append();
        fr→fset ( PHASE_TYPE, »Fr« );
        utterance→ relation ( Dynamics ) → append( fr);
        append_daughter ( fr, Dynamics, word→ as_relation (SyllStructure)→last());
        append_daughter ( fr, Dynamics, syll_end );
        append_daughter ( h, MovementShape, fr );
    }
```

(d) – *CreateMovementPhases_3*: *CU's* semiotic class is *enumeration* or *search*.

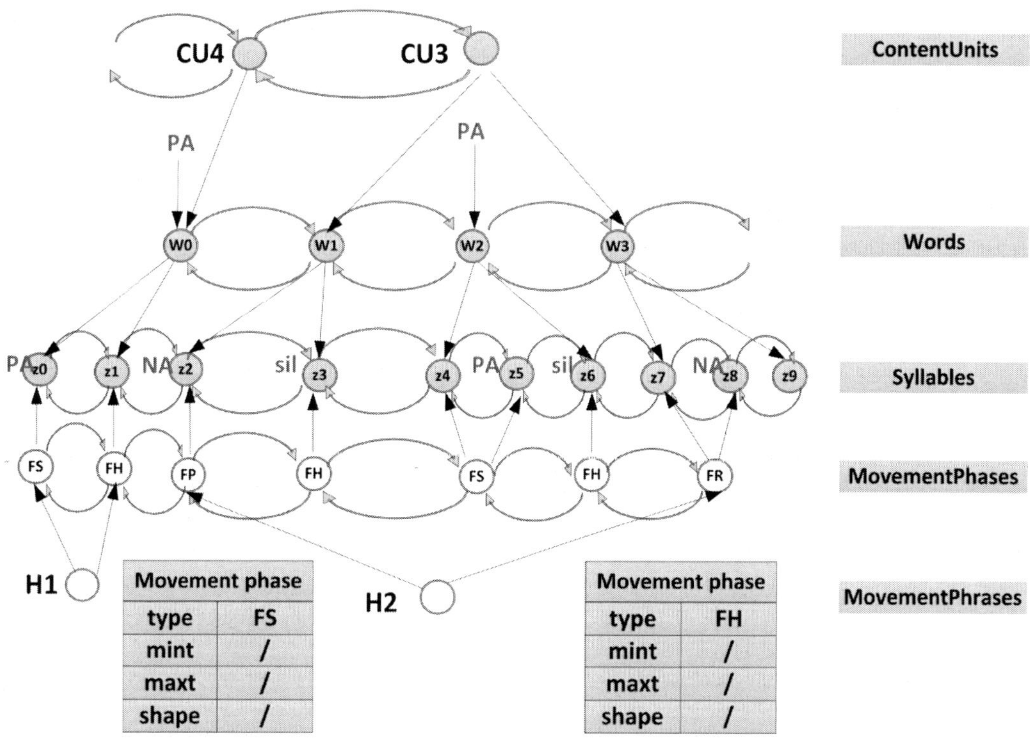

Figure 44. The synchronization of the movement's semiotic core by considering the prosody information.

The result of the pseudocode in Table 8 can be represented as shown in Figure 44. Here, for the CU_1 the movement model H_1 (or *MPHR1*) is defined, with its boundaries set to the syllables Z_0 and Z_1. And for the CU_2 the movement model H_2 (or *MPHR2*) is defined, with its boundaries set to syllables Z_2 and Z_8.

The Temporal Synchronization of Movement Models *H*

In order to perform the temporal synchronization of movement models *H* with verbal information (speech), the structure of the movement models *H*, which is already synchronized at the symbolic level, has to be synchronized also regarding the temporal features as predicted for the output speech signal. Furthermore, the shapes of *MPH* units have to be defined within individual *CU* units. Therefore, the *temporal synchronization* has to be performed by considering the predicted durations of phonemes and pauses between words. These features are already stored in the relation structure *Segments*, as predicted by the TTS module for acoustic prosody. Consequently, the durations of syllables, segments (phonemes), and pauses (*sil* segments) are known (see Figure 7, Figure 40). As can be seen in Figure 45, in HRG structure *SYLL* units are related to *SEG* and *W* units by relational structure *SyllStructure*, and related to *MPH* units by relational structure *Dynamics*. In this way, the temporal information in the levels of phonemes, pauses and syllables, can be easily transferred onto corresponding movement phases and phrases (movement models) by using:

$$t(z_i)=\left(\sum_{j=0}^{n-1} t(seg_{j+k})\right) \tag{35}$$

where n represents the number of phonemes within the current syllable, and k the first phoneme in a given syllable. Furthermore, the movement models H_1 and H_2 in Figure 44 can be temporarily described (by considering equation 26) as follows:

$$\begin{aligned} H_1 &= H(CU_1)\cdot t(CU_1)=t(F_{S\cup H})\cdot H(V_{stroke}) \\ &= t(z_0)\cdot H(V_{stroke})+t(z_1)\cdot H(V_{shold}) \end{aligned} \tag{36}$$

$$\begin{aligned} H_2 &= H(CU_3)\cdot t(CU_3) = t(F_{p\cup H})\cdot H(V_{preparation}) + t(F_{S\cup H})\cdot H(V_{stroke}) + \\ & t(F_R)\cdot H(V_{retraction}) = t(z_2)\cdot H(V_{preparation}) + t(z_3)\cdot H(V_{holds}) + \\ & (t(z_4)+t(z_5))\cdot H(V_{stroke}) + t(z_6)\cdot H(V_{stroke}) + (t(z_7)+t(z_8))\cdot H(V_{retraction}) \end{aligned} \tag{37}$$

Furthermore, each *MPH* unit's boundaries are defined at the syllable level. Nevertheless, their duration is not fixed, since it is still possible to extend them. Therefore, the duration of the movement phases is described by the following sum of the syllable durations, which they may include:

$$t(F)=\left(\sum_{j=0}^{n-1} t(seg_{j+k})\right) \tag{38}$$

where n represents the number of syllables within the *MPH* unit, and k its first syllable. The F_P can be fused with the F_H phase, resulting in the following maximal duration:

$$t_{\max}(F_P)=t(F_P)+\sum_{j=k}^{n-1} t(z_{k-j})+t(z_r) \tag{39}$$

where n represents the number of syllables before the F_P, k its first syllable, and r the first syllable after the F_P. Further, the F_S can be fused with the F_P, resulting in the following maximal duration:

$$t_{\max}(F_S)=t_{\max}(F_P)+t_{\min}(F_S) \tag{40}$$

The F_R can be extended with subsequent syllables (in the corresponding *CU* element), but only upto the last *NA* syllable:

$$t_{\max}(F_R) = t_{\min}(F_R) + \sum_{j=0}^{n-1} t(z_{k+1}) \tag{41}$$

where *n* represents the number of subsequent syllables, and *k* the first syllable after the F_R. Therefore, syllable durations and equations (37-41) have to be used for defining durations of the individual movement phases *MPH* that are stored as attributes *t* and t_{max} in relational structure *MovementPhases*. For example, in Figure 44 the movement model H_1 can be described by equation 35 as follows:

$$T_{vm}^{-1} \cdot P_S + T_{vm}^{-1} \cdot P_{SH} \tag{42}$$

where the timing of the transformation T_{vm}^{-1} is defined by a pair: $t, t_{\max}$. And $t(T_{vm}^{-1}(MPH)) = t(z_0) = t(seg_0) + t(seg_1))$. Here, the stroke phase F_S has $t = t_{\max}$, and no extension is possible. In this way the *time synchronization* can be used for the precise definition of absolute values of those time intervals at which the transitions between poses *P* (are stored in each *MPH shape* attribute, in the relational structure *MovementPhases*) have to be performed. By considering the sentence in Figure 33, the feature vector can be defined and used for selecting poses (shapes *V**) for individual movement phases and trajectories that actually transform a sequence of poses into a continuous movement, or gesture *G*. The gesture *G*, therefore, depends on the initial and final poses, and the movement trajectory, and is also consistent with the verbal behavior (speech) in regard to prosody. The temporal description of each movement phase, therefore, defines:

a) The time instant when the individual shape has to be fully manifested (should pass from *prev(V)* into *V*);
b) The time that is available for the manifestation (transition) between the shapes. This time restricts the set of suitable motion trajectories for the transition, and further restricts the set of most appropriate shapes, by taking into account also the previous shape *prev(V)*.

In the *planning behavior* module, *Phase III* of the algorithm in the second step performs the temporal synchronization of movement models *H*, as described by the pseudocode in Table 9. This step is performed by taking into account the relational structures *MovementPhrases*, *MovementPhases*, *Dynamics*, *SyllStructure*, *MovementShape*, and *MovementStructure*. Additionally, a new relational structure *DynamicsExtended* is created first (see Figure 45). It is used to store the extended boundaries of the defined movement phases, which relate to individual movement models *H*. Therefore, for each movement phrase, the corresponding movement phases are accessed by using the relational structure *MovementShape*, and also the corresponding content unit by using the relation structure *MovementStructure*. Next, for each movement phase its boundaries are accessed in order to define its basic duration. And when the individual movement phase is F_P, F_S, or F_R, its temporal extension is additionally defined and corresponding duration stored (using equations 37-41). These new boundaries are stored in the relational structure *DynamicsExtended.*

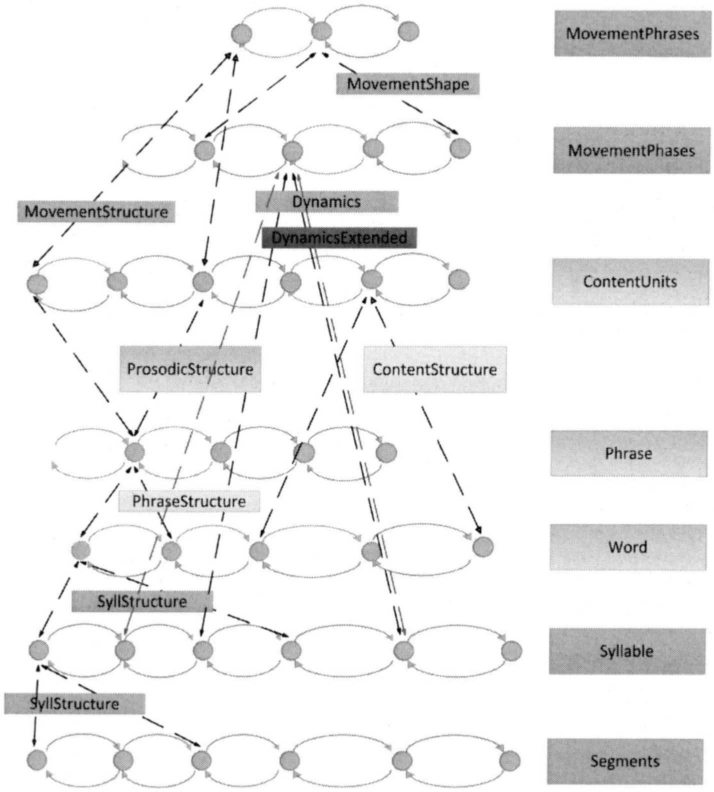

Figure 45. The HRG structure for the temporal synchronization of movement models *H*.

When the movement phase is a preparation phase F_P (see Table 9 (b)), its extended left boundary can be set to the first syllable of the corresponding *CU* unit, while the extended right boundary can be set to the syllable of the subsequent hold phase F_{HS}, when it exists. In this case the F_{HS} is tagged, since it must not be considered in case extended boundaries are later selected for F_P (stored in the relational structure *DynamicsExtended*). At the end, the time duration for the extended version of the movement phase F_P is also calculated. When the movement phase is a stroke phase F_S (see Table 9 (c)), the extended left boundary can be set to the first syllable of the preceding preparation phase F_P, or to the first syllable of the hold phase F_{HS} (when F_P does not exist), or is just equal to the already defined boundary. And the extended right boundary can be set to the already defined right boundary. When extended boundaries are selected for a given movement phase, then the preceding hold phase F_{HS} or preparation phase F_P should no longer be considered as part of the movement phrase (therefore, they are tagged).

At the end, the duration for the extended version of the movement phase F_S is calculated. And when the movement phase is retraction phase F_R (see Table 9 (d)), the extended left boundary can be set to the already defined left boundary, while the extended right boundary can be set to the last syllable in the corresponding *CU* unit. At the end, the duration for the extended version of the movement phase F_R is calculated.

Table 9. *Phase III* – Planning of the movement – The temporal synchronization of movement models *H*.

```
Duration ( syll_start, syll_end )
{
    seg_start = syll_start→as_relation ( SyllStructure )→daughters();
    seg_end = syll_end→as_relation ( SyllStructure )→daughtern();
    FOR (seg = seg_start; seg != seg_end; seg = next(seg ))
        T_DUR += seg → fF ( DURATION );
    return T_DUR;
}
```

(a) – Defining syllable duration.

```
TemporalExtensionFP ( CU cu, MPH mph ) {
    cu_start = cu → as_relation ( ContentStructure ) → daughters ();
    syll_start = cu_start → as_relation ( SyllStructure )→daughters();
    IF ( next(mph) → fS ( PHASE_TYPE ) == »Fhs« ) {
        syll_end = next(mph) → as_relation ( Dynamics )→daughtern ();
        next(mph)→ fset ( SKIP, 1 );
    }
    ELSE
        syll_end = mph → as_relation ( Dynamics )→daughtern ();
    utterance → relation ( DynamicsExtended )→ append( mph );
    append_daughter ( mph, DynamicsExtended, syll_start );
    append_daughter ( mph, DynamicsExtended, syll_end );
    mph→fset ( MAX_DURATION, Duration (syll_start, syll_end ) );
}
```

(b) – Temporal extension for F_P.

```
TemporalExtensionFS ( MPH mph ) {
    IF ( prev(mph) → fS ( PHASE_TYPE) == »Fh« &&
     prev(prev(mph)) → fS ( PHASE_TYPE) == »Fp« )
    {
        syll_start = prev(prev(mph))→ as_relation ( Dynamics )→daughters ();
        prev(mph)→ fset ( SKIP, 1 );
        prev(prev(mph))→ fset ( SKIP, 1 );
    }
    ELSEIF ( prev(mph) → fS ( PHASE_TYPE) == »Fh« )
    {
        syll_start = prev(mph)→ as_relation ( Dynamics )→daughters ();
        prev(mph)→ fset ( SKIP, 1 );
    }
    ELSE
    {
        syll_start = mph→ as_relation ( Dynamics )→daughters ();
    }
    syll_end = mph→ as_relation ( Dynamics )→daughtern ();
    utterance → relation ( DynamicsExtended )→ append( mph );
    append_daughter ( mph, DynamicsExtended, syll_start );
    append_daughter ( mph, DynamicsExtended, syll_end );
    mph→fset ( MAX_DURATION, Duration (syll_start, syll_end ) );
}
```

(c) – Temporal extension for F_S.

Table 9. (Continued)

```
TemporalExtensionFR ( CU cu, MPH mph ) {
    syll_start = mph→ as_relation ( Dynamics )→daughters ();
    cu_end = cu→ as_relation ( ContentStructure )→daughtern ();
    syll_end = cu_end → as_relation ( SyllStructure )→daughtern ();
    utterance → relation (DynamicsExtended)→ append( mph );
    append_daughter ( mph, DynamicsExtended, syll_start );
    append_daughter ( mph, DynamicsExtended, syll_end );
    mph→fset ( MAX_DURATION, Duration (syll_start, syll_end ) );
}
```

(d) – Temporal extension for F_R.

```
DynamicsExtended is created

FOR ( mphr = utterance→ relation ( MovementPhrases)→first();mphr!= NULL; mphr = next(mphr) )
{
    mph = mphr → as_relation ( MovementShape )→daughters();
    cu = mphr → as_relation ( MovementStructure )→daughters();
    FOR ( ; mph != NULL; mph = next(mph) )
    {
        syll_start = mph →as_relation ( Dynamics )→daughters();
        syll_end = mph →as_relation ( Dynamics )→daughtern();
        mph→fset ( DURATION, Duration (syll_start, syll_end ) );

        IF (mph → fS ( PHASE_TYPE) == »Fp« )
            TemporalExtensionFP ( cu, mph );
        IF (mph → fS ( PHASE_TYPE) == »Fs« )
            TemporalExtensionFS ( mph );
        IF (mph → fS ( PHASE_TYPE) == »Fr« )
            TemporalExtensionFR ( cu, mph );
    }
}
```

(e) – Complete algorithm.

PHASE IV: THE SYNCHRONIZATION OF THE POSES

In this phase of the algorithm, the transformation T_m^{-1} and the temporal component of the transformation T_{vm}^{-1} are already defined. Thus, the intent, the content words, their morpho-syntactic structure, and time instants at which the movement models have to be visually manifested are already defined. Additionally, the context of the intent and corresponding morpho-syntactic sequences and duration for movement phases F_P and F_R are also defined. All of these represent sufficient data in order to perform lookup into a semiotic lexicon (see Figure 26). Therefore, the next step is to specify the shapes (poses) and the trajectories of those gestures which should manifest within the movement phases of the individual movement model H. Namely, the shape V (or pose P) and the trajectory T of the specific gesture are determined by:

a) intent S,
b) movement phases F (F_P, F_H, F_S, F_R),
c) morpho-syntactic characteristics of the content word M (the POS tag of the content word with semiotic indicator I),
d) context C (namely, the previous/next shapes (poses), or described, for example, as *prev(V), next(V), prev(W), next(W)*];),
e) semantic correlation R^* (when the semantic content necessarily coincides with the gesture, e.g., symbols and iconic gestures).

Therefore, the task for *Phase IV* is to select suitable shapes V (or poses P) and trajectories for each movement model H. Namely, shapes and trajectories represent the formal part of the transformation T_{vm}^{-1} which is dependent on the following features: S, F, M, C, in R^*. This task is performed in three steps, as described in detail in the following subsections.

The Definition of Poses within the Stroke Phases F_S

The pose represents a set of those individual shapes which are defined separately for the selected body part (e.g., the shape of the right arm and the shape of the right palm). Furthermore, in the *semiotic lexicon - Gesticon* are the individual correlations between features of that part of the transformation T_{vm}^{-1} regarding shapes, described with poses that in the *EVA gesticon* encompass shapes of each body part, used in the manifestation of the specific gesture. The definition of shapes and poses within the F_S phases has to be performed in the following steps:

a) Select the poses P for each F_S, by using the EVA gesticon,
b) Evaluate poses P by using the so-called *suitability functions* (Rojc & Kačič, 2011),
c) When there are no suitable poses in the semiotic lexicon, the set of poses has to be defined by e.g., CART model,
d) When using the suitability functions, the most appropriate pose is assigned to the individual F_S,
e) For each pose in the F_S, the CART model is used in order to define a set of shapes in the F_P and F_R phases, whereas the final shapes are defined by using the suitability functions. CART trees are widely used models that are based on the structures and rules. They can be used in order to automatically build a set of rules for data classification that can be easily interpreted and understood. Furthermore, the CART trees can operate over incomplete data, and handle several and complex features. Namely, in each node a specific question (e.g., resulting in the answer 'yes' or 'no') is asked about a particular feature. The leaves of the tree then contain the best predictions for the corresponding output, based on the input training data.

Thus, the CART model is proposed for use in order to define pose *P* in individual movement phases based on features *S*, *F*, *M*, *C* and *R* (when e.g., pose *P* cannot be found in the semiotic lexicon). The next step is based on features *S*, *F*, *M*, *C*, *P* to define also those trajectories *T*, which define the shape of the transition between poses at the boundaries of movement phases. Nevertheless, the definition of shapes and poses is based on the EVA gesticon that for the pattern $(S \times F \times M)$ returns the associated set of poses ***P*** and their characteristics $\{P_i, T, R^*, t_{\min}, t_{\max}, cnt\}$. In this way, for each stroke phase F_S in the relational structure *MovementPhases*, a set of poses ***P*** is assigned. Since the gesticon is a tuple structure, the lookup process can be described in the following form: $T^{i,j} : (S \times F \times M) \rightarrow \{P_i, T, R^*, t_{\min}, t_{\max}, cnt\}$, where $(S \times F \times M)$ represents the input word columns, and $\{P_i, T, R^*, t_{\min}, t_{\max}, cnt\}$ the corresponding output data columns that the *gesticon* returns for a given F_S. Therefore, in order to access the semiotic lexicon, these relevant features from the HRG structure have to be obtained. Namely, for each element *F* in the relational structure *MovementPhases* the following has to be extracted:

- the semiotic class *S* for each *CU* element in the relational structure *ContentUnits*,
- the content word which represents the semiotic indicator *I*, using relational structures *Dynamics* and *SyllableStructure*,
- the POS tag of that content word which represents the semiotic indicator *I*.

Therefore, for each F_S a pattern $(S \times F \times M)$ has to be defined where *S=CU.S* (the semiotic intent of the *CU* element), *F =MPH.phase_type* (the phase type of the movement phase F_S), and *M* = *W.POS* (the morpho-syntactic tag of the content word with semiotic indicator *I*). For example, in Figure 46 there are two stroke phases F_S. Further, as can be seen already in Figure 39, for CU_4 the content word is W_0 and the semiotic class S_1, while for CU_3 the content word is W_2 and the semiotic class S_2. In this way, for the F_{S1} within CU_4, the following pattern can be defined: $(S_1 \times F_s \times W_0.POS)$ and R_1^* = $W_0.orto$. And for F_{S2} within CU_3, $(S_2 \times F_s \times W_2.POS)$, and R_2^* = $W_2.orto$. These have to be used then for the lookup into gesticon, in order to get a set of candidates for poses. Let the gesticon return two candidates for F_{S1} with the following characteristics: $(\mathrm{P}_1 \times \mathrm{T}_1 \times \mathrm{W.orto} \times \mathrm{t}_1 \times \mathrm{t}_2 \times \mathrm{n})$ and $(\mathrm{P}_2 \times \mathrm{T}_2 \times \mathrm{W.orto} \times \mathrm{t}_1 \times \mathrm{t}_3 \times \mathrm{n})$, where the *W.orto* represents that sequence of orthographic words that was annotated in the EVA Corpus for this pattern. Nevertheless, for some patterns $(S \times F \times M)$ in the HRG structure, there will be no pose candidates in the gesticon. In this case the CART model is used for predicting the most appropriate set of pose candidates, and is trained on the annotated EVA Corpus. The features that can be used for the CART model are available in:

- relational structure *MovementPhases*: current, previous and next movement phases for F_S (pose, semiotic class, trajectories, e.g., (prev(mph)).S, (prev(prev(mph))).S, next(mph).S, (next(next(mph)).S, ..., where mph.phase_type = F_S),
- relational structure *Word*: the content word for current, previous, and next movement phases for F_S, with corresponding morpho-syntactic sequences within *CU* and orthographic form, and their predecessors and successors,
- relational structure *Syllables*: normal and possible extended boundaries for F_S.

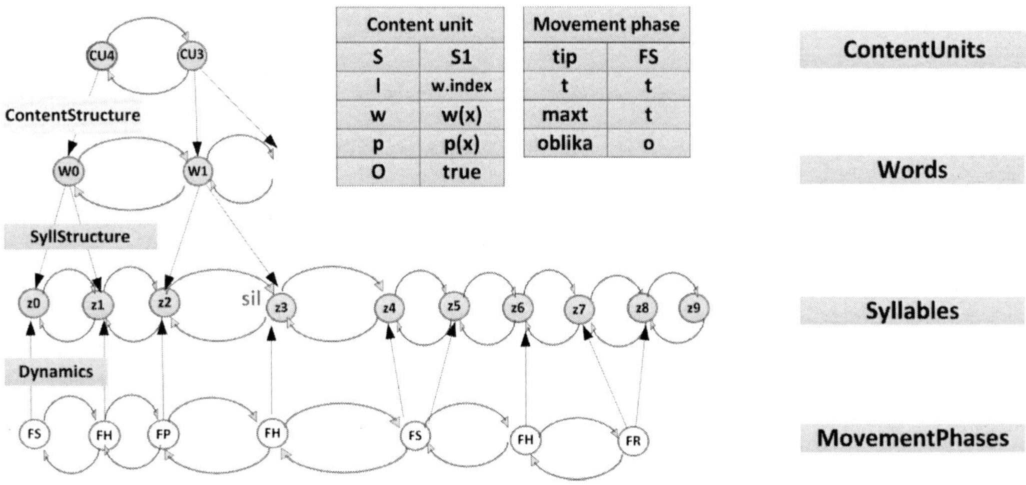

Figure 46. The definition of shapes and trajectories for each movement phase *F*.

Namely, the annotated EVA Corpus can be used for building several complex feature vector sets, when individual sentences are represented in the form of HRG structures. For training CART models, e.g., WEKA[1] or Wagon[2] tools can be used. When using the CART model for predicting the pose candidates, the semantic correlations and morpho-syntactic tags can be additionally checked. When, for example, the CART model returns a set of pose candidates in the following form $(P_i \times M \times W_i.orto \times t_i \times t_j \times n)$, those candidates whose POS tag *M* is not the same as the POS tag *M* of the content word, and also those candidates whose orthographic representation $W_i.orto$ does not match with the orthographic form of the content word, can be eliminated. Of course, there is the possibility that in this way all pose candidates may be eliminated. Nevertheless, from the co-verbal behavior point of view, even such a scenario is acceptable, since unsuitable and unnatural gesturing inserts ambiguity and additional misunderstanding. In this way the *modality mismatches* can be avoided (e.g., the square is outlined as a circle, and smallness is presented as immensity, etc.). The first CART model is used in this way to predict the pose *P* in individual movement phases (if the pose *P* cannot be found in the semiotic lexicon), for the feature vector [*S, F, M, C, R*]. And the second CART model is then used to also predict the trajectory *T* for the feature vector [*F, M, C, P*], which specifies the transition between poses at the movement phases' boundaries.

[1] WEKA - http://www.cs.waikato.ac.nz/ml/weka/.
[2] wagon - http://festvox.org/docs/speech_tools-1.2.0/c16616.htm.

In the *planning behavior* module, *Phase IV* of the algorithm in the first step defines several pose candidates on movement phases F_S, as presented in Table 10. The starting point represents the relational structure *MovementPhrases,* which contains the movement models *H*. For each movement model, the corresponding movement phases via the relational structure *MovementShape* (stored in the relational structure *MovementPhases*), and content units via the relational structure *MovementStructure* have to be accessed (stored in the relational structure *ContentUnits*). Among all movement phases, only F_S are considered. Furthermore, for each F_S, a corresponding $(S \times F \times M)$ pattern has to be built for the lookup process into gesticon. Therefore, within the corresponding *CU* unit, the POS tag of the content word with semiotic indicator *I* (*M*), and the semiotic class have to be extracted (*S*). Then lookup into the gesticon is performed. When candidates for poses cannot be found (P == { }), a CART model is used instead. At the end, the pose candidates *P* are stored in each movement phase F_S. Namely, the best one will be selected in the following step, using the so-called *suitability functions*. This has to be done before also defining shapes for other movement phases within each movement model *H*. When pose candidates are defined for all stroke phases F_S, the next step continues with the selection of the most appropriate pose candidate for each F_S. In order to do this, it is necessary to evaluate two things: how well each pose candidate within a given stroke phase F_S meets the defined realization of the stroke phase *Fs*, and how well they can be harmonized with those pose candidates in neighboring stroke phases F_S. The selection of the best pose candidate is carried out using the *suitability functions* (Rojc & Kačič, 2011).

Table 10. The definition of pose candidates for each movement phase F_S.

```
Item* frg = utterance→ relation (MovementPhrases)→first();
FOR ( ; frg != NULL; frg = next(frg) )
{
    fg = frg→ as_relation (MovementShape)→daughters();
    cu= frg→ as_relation (MovementStructure)→down();
    FOR ( ; fg != NULL; fg = next(fg) )
    {
        F = fg→fS( PHASE_TYPE );
        IF ( F == »Fs« )
        {
            cu_start = cu→ as_relation (ContentStructure)→ daughters();
            cu_end = cu→ as_relation (ContentStructure)→ daughtern();
            FOR ( w = cu_start; w != cu_end; w = next(w) )
            {
                IF ( w→ fI ( SEMIOTIC_INDICATOR ) == w→ fI (POSITION ) )
                    M = w→fS ( POS );
            }
            S = cu→fS( SEMIOTIC_CLASS );

            T ( S, F, M ) → { P, T, R,t_min,t_max, cnt}
            IF ( P == {} )
                CART ( (S,F,M) ) → { P }, T ( P ) → { T, R,t_min,t_max, cnt}
            fg→ fset ( POSE_SET, P { T, R,t_min,t_max, cnt } [] );
        }
    }
}
```

These are used in order to evaluate several pose candidates, and to find the best match with the desired specifications, even when they are characterized with several parameters $\left(P_i \times T_i \times \text{W.orto} \times t_{i1} \times t_{i2} \times n\right)$. In this way, the necessary adjustments of poses can be minimized, and better connectivity with the pose in the previous F_S can be provided.

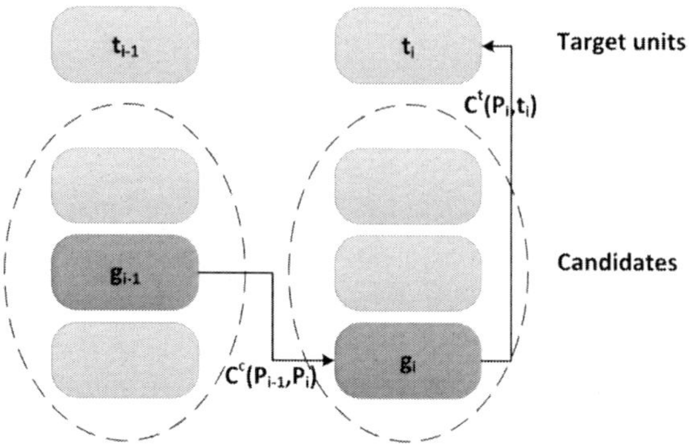

Figure 47. Evaluation of pose candidates for each F_S based on C^t as target cost, and C^c as concatenation cost.

The evaluation of candidates for each F_S is based on the following two cost functions (see Figure 47), named as:

- *Target cost* $C^t(u_i,t_i)$: evaluates the match between the current F_S pose candidate u_i and the defined (target) specification t_i.
- *Concatenation cost* $C^c(u_{u-1},u_i)$: evaluates the match between the current F_S pose candidate u_i, and the previous F_S pose candidate u_{i-1}.

The target cost $C^t(u_i,t_i)$ is calculated based on suitability functions, quite similar to those presented by Rojc and Kačič (2011). The suitability function can be normalized with parameters a and b, in order to achieve the desired shape of the function. Furthermore, its values are in the range [0.0, 1.0]. The most important characteristics of the suitability function and its shape are:

- the suitability function has to favorize acceptable deviations from the target specification, and defavorize those less acceptable,
- the suitability function should emphasize the impact of large deviations from the target specification,
- the relative importance of each criterion in the cost function can be emphasized by the shape of the suitability function itself (e.g., wider top, when deviations are not so critical; and narrower peak when even smaller deviations can be important),
- the shape of the suitability function can be defined based on the semiotic lexicon, heuristically, or optimized based on experiments.

This mathematical formalism is therefore proposed to be used to evaluate the acceptability of pose candidates from the gesticon in order to meet the target pose specifications in a given movement phase of type F_S. And $C^t(u_i,t_i)$ is used to evaluate the difference between the target pose specifications and pose candidates' characteristics as obtained in the gesticon. Each $C^t(u_i,t_i)$ consists of the suitability function which takes into account the pose duration, and is defined as:

$$S^{dur}_{partial} = \begin{cases} e^{-\frac{1}{2a^2}\left(\frac{dur-dur_{mean}}{dur}+a\right)^2};\ \frac{dur-dur_{mean}}{dur}<a \\ 1; a \le \dfrac{dur-dur_{mean}}{dur} \le b \\ e^{-\frac{1}{2b^2}\left(\frac{dur-dur_{mean}}{dur}-b\right)^2};\ \frac{dur-dur_{mean}}{dur}>b \end{cases} \qquad (43)$$

When developing the gesticon, it is advisable to already cluster pose candidates, by considering their duration and shape. Furthermore, to guarantee the minimum coverage with the pose candidates in each cluster, at least one pose candidate P^* per cluster should be kept (for given $S_i \times F_i \times M_i$). Minimizing the size of the semiotic lexicon based also on suitability functions regarding duration and shape is a reasonable step, since there can be large numbers of similar pose candidates that directly influence the performance of the pose selection step. Nevertheless, the suitability functions have to efficiently cluster poses into different clusters in the case of important mismatches, regarding their durations, as well as significant shape differences (e.g., different shapes for arms, hands, head, maturity, etc.). As a result, it is possible to maintain significantly fewer pose candidates and to speed up the pose selection step. In this way, all pose candidates obtained in the semiotic lexicon, or predicted by the CART model, are evaluated by calculating their $C^t(u_i,t_i)$, where the target pose specification in each stroke phase F_S represents the predicted duration. Therefore, these values can be evaluated only in the online system, after the target pose specifications have been defined. Furthermore, the concatenation cost $C^c(u_{u-1},u_i)$ evaluates the connectivity of two poses in two subsequent stroke phases F_S. They are evaluated based on the knowledge and real-life connectivity of poses, as detected in the annotated EVA Corpus. Namely, for concatenation costs the following questions are essential: *Which pose candidate took place before me?* and *How many times did the specific pose candidate occur in front of the current pose candidate?* These values can be determined using e.g., N-gram models, trained on the annotated EVA Corpus. $C^c(u_{u-1},u_i)$ weights can be calculated in advance (off-line), and only accessed within the pose selection process. The weights can be calculated, for example, by using SRILM (Stolcke et al., 2002), while for training 2-gram models the following sequences have to be constructed:

```
<s> P1 P2 P3 … PX </s>
<s> P1 P2 … PX </s>
<s> P1 P2 P3 … PZ </s>
```

The pose selection step in *Phase IV*, therefore, has to select the best pose candidate for each stroke phase F_S, by considering the following total cost:

$$C(u_i) = C^t(u_i, t_i) + C^c(u_{u-1}, u_i) \tag{44}$$

Namely, this is done by considering the target cost of each pose candidate, while at the same time looking for the most optimal connectivity with the previous pose candidates. This takes into account the target specifications ($S_i \times F_i \times M_i$), which are predicted in previous phases for a given sentence. This search problem can be efficiently solved by using the finite-state machine (FSM), whereby states represent pose candidates. For each stroke phase F_S there can be in general several pose candidates and states. And each pose candidate that belongs to the current stroke phase F_S has to be connected with all pose candidates in the previous stroke phase F_S. The transitions have to be assigned with corresponding $C(u_i)$ costs. Finding the most appropriate pose for each stroke phase F_S then represents the problem of finding the best path (with the lowest overall cost) (Rojc & Kačič, 2011). This can be done by using, for example, *FSM BestPath* algorithm (Rojc, 2003), where at the input we have a WFSM (weighted finite-state machine), and the algorithm returns the linear WFSM with one final state. The result of the pose selection step is, therefore, a sequence of best pose candidates that best meet the target specifications and should be closer to those pose sequences observed in the annotated EVA Corpus. Nevertheless, the complete costs $C(u_i)$ are the composition of the target cost $C^t(u_i, t_i)$ and the concatenation cost $C^c(u_{u-1}, u_i)$, which raises the issue of how to weight them in order to achieve the optimal results regarding obtaining as natural a sequence of gestures as possible. Namely, the key issue is to define: *How important is* $C^t(u_i, t_i)$ *comparatively to* $C^c(u_{u-1}, u_i)$?, or *What should be more important?* In order to achieve the optimal results regarding this matter, it is necessary to properly weight both costs, which can be done using heuristics, or objective methods (Rojc & Kačič, 2011; Kalagnanam & Henrion, 2013). The selected best pose candidates are stored in *MPH* elements F_S in the relational structure *MovementPhases*, using the attribute *shape*. In this way, each stroke phase F_S has a uniquely defined shape on its left boundary P_S, and on its right boundary P_E. The defined stroke phases F_S already represent the isolated key frames which define the shape of the body parts on their boundaries. Nevertheless, it is still necessary to define shapes in the surroundings of each stroke phase F_S (i.e., represented by the preparation phase F_P, and the retraction phase F_R), and to define trajectories (transitions) between individual poses within the movement structure.

In the *planning behavior* module, the algorithm first performs the definition of best pose candidates on each stroke phase F_S, which is presented in Table 11. The relational structure *MovementPhrases* contains all movement models *H*, whereas each one contains the corresponding movement phases. For each movement model only stroke phases F_S are processed in this step. These can be accessed using relational structure *MovementShape*. In order to define the target specification t_i for each stroke phase F_S, the corresponding *CU* element also has to be accessed. Namely, in the relational structure *Words* the POS tag of the word with semiotic indicator can be obtained (*M*), and in the relational structure *ContentUnits*

Table 11. The definition of best pose candidates for each stroke phase F_S.

```
Item* frg = utterance→ relation ( MovementPhrases )→first();
FOR ( ; frg != NULL; frg = next(frg) )
{
    fg = frg→ as_relation ( MovementShape )→daughters();
    cu = frg→ as_relation ( MovementStructure )→down();

    FOR ( ; fg != NULL; fg = next(fg) )
    {
        IF ( fg→fS ( PHASE_TYPE) != »Fs« ) continue;
        cu_start = cu→ as_relation ( ContentStructure )→ daughters();
        cu_end = cu→ as_relation ( ContentStructure )→ daughtern();
        FOR ( w = cu_start; w != cu_end; w = next(w) ) {
            IF ( w→ fI ( SEMIOTIC_INDICATOR ) == w→ fI (POSITION ) )
                M = w→fS ( POS );
        }
        S = cu→fS( SEMIOTIC_CLASS );
        F = fg→fS( PHASE_TYPE );
        t_i = { S, F,M, fg →fF ( DURATION ), fg →fF ( MAX_DURATION) };

        FOR ( i = 0; i < length( fg → P ); i++, j++ ) {
            C^t ( fg → P [i], t_i ) → fg → P[i].tc_cost;
            fsm→Add ( fg → P [i], j );
        }
        mph_fs = fg;
    }

    P pp = prev ( mph_fs ) → P ;
    P pc = mph_fs → P ;
    FOR ( i = 0; i < length ( pc ); i++ )
        FOR ( j = 0; j < length( pp ); j++ ) {
            C^c ( pc[i], pp[j]) = 2-Gram ( pc[i], pp[j] ) ;
            fsm→AddTransition ( pp[j], pc[i], pc[i].tc_cost + C^c ( pc[i], pp[j]) );
        }
    }
}

fg = frg→ as_relation ( MovementShape )→daughters();
BestPath ( fsm, fg );

frg = utterance→ relation ( MovementPhrases )→first();
FOR ( ; frg != NULL; frg = next(frg) )
{
    fg = frg→ as_relation ( MovementPhases )→ daughters();
    FOR ( ; fg != NULL; fg = next(fg) ) {
        IF ( fg→fS ( PHASE_TYPE) != »Fs« ) continue;
        P p = fg→ P ;
        IF ( prev( fg ) == NULL )
            fg→ fset ( POSE_F_Z, P_N );
        ELSE
            fg → fset ( POSE_F_Z, p.P_F_Z );
        fg → fset ( POSE_F_K, p.P_F_K );
    }
}
```

the semiotic class (*S*). After defining the target specification t_i, for each pose candidate the corresponding target costs C^t are calculated, and a new FSM state is added (in the same level *j*). After adding all new states in the same level, the transitions with all states in the previous level have to be created, and the weight in each transition has to be calculated using equation 44. The *BestPath* algorithm then selects the best pose candidates for each F_S. Finally, to all F_S shapes are assigned left and right boundaries.

The Definition of Poses within F_P, F_R, and F_H

After defining the poses on each stroke phase F_S, poses for F_P, F_R, and F_H can also be defined. The retraction phase F_R in general represents the transition into a relaxed state, which is not necessarily neutral. Namely, in the scope of the proposed algorithm, the F_R can be used for the transition into the neutral state, or pose P_N. In this case all of those body parts that take part in the co-verbal behavior (and do not yet hold so-called neutral configuration) have to be moved into this state. The preparation phase F_P in general represents a less important part of the movement model *H*. The stroke phase $mph{=}F_S$ has already assigned a pair of poses $\{mph.P_S, mph.P_E\}$. Furthermore, the preparation phase F_P enables a prior motion that is followed by a movement within the F_S (also introduces meaning). Therefore, in the end of F_P, the body part has to be configured by the following pose $(mph = F_P)$. $P_E = (next(mph) = F_S).P_S$. And the pose at the left boundary of F_P has to be defined by the end pose of the previous movement phase (in the previous *CU*). Therefore:

$$mph.P_S = \begin{cases} P_N\text{ , } if \text{ prev(mph)=F}_\text{R} \,\|\, \text{prev(mph)= null} \\ prev(mph).P_E\text{ , } if \text{ prev(mph)= F}_\text{S} \,\|\, \text{prev(mph)= F}_\text{SH} \end{cases}$$
$$mph.P_E = (next(mph) = F_s \,\|\, \text{next(next(mph))} = F_S).P_S \tag{45}$$

where $mph = F_P$. The definition of poses and shapes on each F_P, F_R, and F_H also has to be carried out in the relational structure *MovementPhases*. In this step it is considered that poses on stroke phases F_S are already defined on its boundaries in the form of pairs $\{mph.P_S, mph.P_E\}$. Furthermore, possible subsequent movement phases F_H (F_{HS} or F_{SH}) are merged into common F_H. And those hold phases F_H that have been assigned to *sil* segment with predicted duration 0 are removed. First, a check is performed to determine whether there exists within the current movement phrase H_i (or content unit CU_i) any movement phase before the F_{S_i}. When there exists hold phase F_{HS_i}, then it is possible to define the following pair of poses:

$$mph.P_S = mph.P_E = \{\, next(mph).\text{P}_\text{S}\text{ , } if \text{ next(mph)} = \text{F}_\text{S} \quad \text{where } mph \text{ is } F_{HS_i}\text{, or:}$$
$$mph.P_S = mph.P_E = \{prev(mph).P_E\text{ , } if \text{ prev(mph)= F}_\text{S} \quad \text{where } mph \text{ is } F_{SH_i}\text{ .}$$

If there is F_{P_i} within the current movement phrase H_i, then on its boundaries the following pair of poses has to be defined: $\{mph.P_S = P_N$, $mph.P_E = (next(mph) = F_{S_i}).P_S\}$, when there is no F_{HS_i} (equation 45). And when there exists also F_{HS_i}, the end pose is just set as $mph.P_E = (next(next(mph)) = F_{S_i}).P_S$, where $mph = F_{P_i}$. When *mph is* F_{P_i} does not have any predecessors then, according to equation 45, the pose on the left boundary should be $mph.P_S = P_N$. And when there is no F_{HS_i}, the pose $mph.P_E$ should be set by $(next(mph) = F_{S_i}).P_S$. Nevertheless, this would result in an instantaneous transition, where e.g., the right hand would instantly pass over from $mph.P_S = P_N$ to $(next(mph) = F_{S_i}).P_S$. Such transitions are unnatural and, therefore, have to be unacceptable. In these cases the pose on the left boundary of the stroke phase F_{S_i} has to be subsequently adjusted and set to P_N as $\{mph.P_S = P_N, mph.P_E\}$, where *mph* is F_{S_i}. When F_{HS_i} exists before F_{S_i}, then it has to be fused with the previous F_{P_i}. Then it is possible to define on new F_{P_i} the following pair of poses $\{mph.P_S = P_N, mph.P_E = (next(mph) = F_{S_i}).P_S\}$. Furthermore, in Figure 52 there is no preparation phase F_{P_i} in any movement phrase H_i. When there is no preparation phase F_{P_i} within the movement phrase H_i, the algorithm proceeds as follows:

1. When the movement phrase H_i contains the hold phase F_{HS_i} but does not contain F_{P_i}, then F_{HS_i} has to be transformed into F_{P_i} (see Figure 48). In this case the poses at its boundaries are consequently set by the following pair $\{mph.P_S = (prev(mph) = F_{S_{i-1}}).P_E$, $mph.P_E = (next(mph) = F_{S_i}).P_S\}$, where *mph* is F_{P_i}. In Figure 51, we have for $mph.P_S = P_N$.

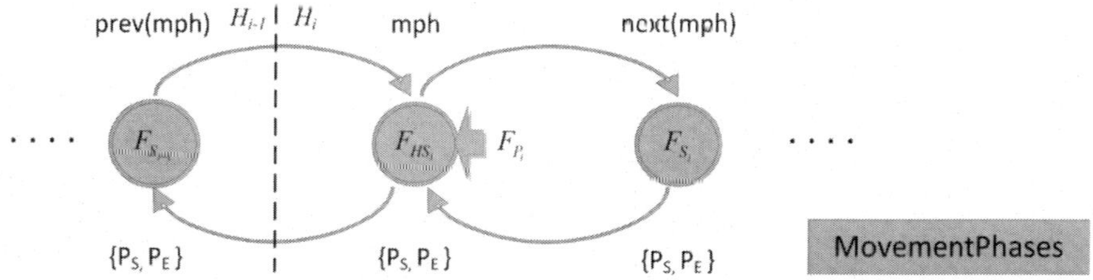

Figure 48. When movement phrase H_i contains F_{HS_i} but does not contain F_{P_i}.

2. When there is no hold phase F_{HS_i} and no preparation phase F_{P_i} within the given movement phrase H_i, then the similarity between the poses $(prev(mph) = *).P_E$ and $mph.P_S$ has to be checked first, where $mph = F_{S_i}$ (see Figure 49). If it is $(prev(mph) = *).P_E = mph.P_S$ and $mph.P_E \mathrel{!}= mph.P_S$, then the left boundary of the stroke phase F_{S_i} has to be subsequently adjusted, and the poses set by the following pair { $mph.P_S =$

(prev(mph) =* *).P*$_E$, *mph.P*$_E$ }, where *mph* = F_{S_i}. For example, there is no F_{HS_i} in movement phrase H_i. In this case, the boundaries for F_{S_i} have to be adjusted in order to also capture movement phase $F_{SH_{i-1}}$ in movement phrase H_{i-1}. Let *mph* = $F_{SH_{i-1}}$ have the following pair of poses {*mph.P*$_S$ = *(prev(mph)* = $F_{S_{i-1}}$ *).P*$_E$, *mph.P*$_E$ = *(prev(mph)* = $F_{S_{i-1}}$ *).P*$_E$ }. Then F_{S_i} has to be set by the following pair {*mph.P*$_S$ = *(prev(mph)* = $F_{SH_{i-1}}$ *).P*$_E$, *mph.P*$_E$ = *(prev(mph)* = $F_{SH_{i-1}}$ *).P*$_E$ }.

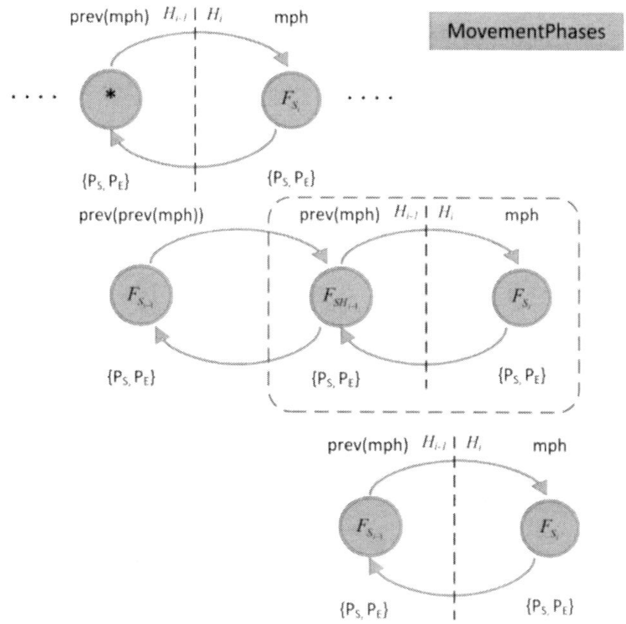

Figure 49. When movement phrase H_i does not contain F_{HS_i} or F_{P_i}.

3. When the movement phrase H_i does not contain the hold phase F_{HS_i} or preparation phase F_{P_i}, and there is *mph.P*$_S$ =*(prev(mph)* = * *).P*$_E$ and *mph.P*$_E$ = *mph.P*$_S$, where *mph* = F_{S_i}, then one part of the F_{S_i} has to be used for the preparation phase F_{P_i} (see Figure 50). On the boundaries for the *mph* = F_{S_i}, the following poses should be maintained {*mph.P*$_S$, *mph.P*$_E$ }, while the poses on the created preparation phase *mph* = F_{P_i} should be set by the following pair {*mph.P*$_S$ = *(prev(mph)* = **).P*$_S$, *mph.P*$_E$ = *mph.P*$_S$ }. From the temporal point of view, therefore, both phases have non-zero durations, which were otherwise available for the implementation of the common stroke phase F_{S_i}. Let the original F_{S_i} be split into two subsequent movement phases F_{P_i} and F_{S_i} in relational structure *MovementPhases*. Then *mph* = F_{P_i} has the pair of poses {*mph.P*$_S$ = *(prev(mph)* = $F_{SH_{i-1}}$ *).P*$_E$ = *(prev(prev(mph))*= $F_{S_{i-1}}$ *).P*$_E$, *mph.P*$_E$ = *(original* F_{S_i} *).P*$_S$ } and new *mph*

$= F_{S_i}$ the following pair of poses $\{mph.P_S = (original\ F_{S_i}).P_S,\ mph.P_E = (original\ F_{S_i}).P_E\}$.

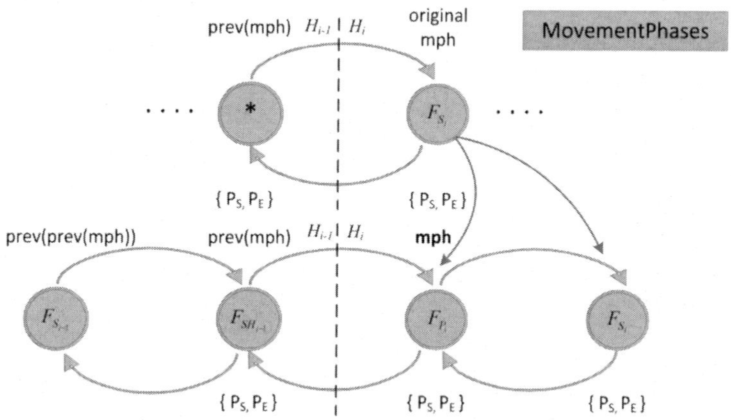

Figure 50. When movement phrase H_i does not contain F_{HS_i} or F_{P_i}.

4. When there is no hold phase F_{HS_i} or preparation phase F_{P_i} within the movement phrase H_i and it is $(prev(mph) = *).P_E$!= $mph.P_S$, where $mph = F_{S_i}$, then the hold phase $F_{SH_{i-1}}$ within the movement phrase H_{i-1} has to be used (see Figure 51). Then, the *original* $F_{SH_{i-1}}$ has to be split into subsequent movement phases $F_{SH_{i-1}}$ and F_{P_i}. Further, the new hold phase $F_{SH_{i-1}}$ should remain in the H_{i-1}, but the F_{P_i} has to be assigned to the movement phrase H_i. The poses on the boundaries of the new $F_{SH_{i-1}}$ are preserved, while the poses on the boundaries of the $mph = F_{P_i}$ are defined by the following pair $\{mph.P_S = (prev(mph) = F_{SH_{i-1}}).P_E,\ mph.P_E = (next(mph) = F_{S_i}).P_S\}$. From the temporal point of view, both phases now have non-zero durations, which were otherwise predicted for performing the original $F_{SH_{i-1}}$ in H_{i-1}.

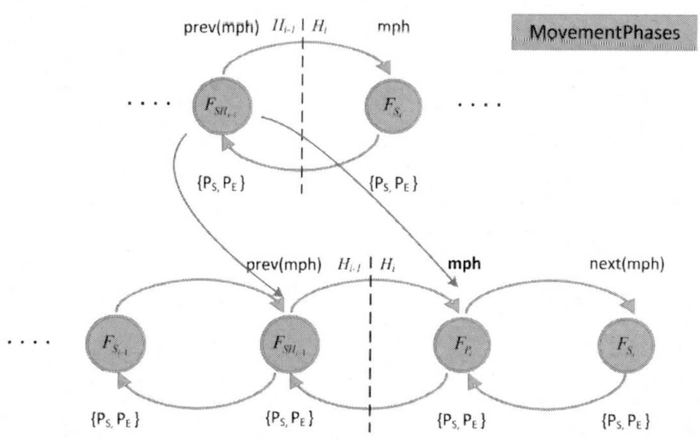

Figure 51. When movement phrase H_i does not contain F_{HS_i} or F_{P_i}.

5. When defining the boundaries of new preparation phase F_{P_i}, the possibility of neutral pose P_N also has to be taken into consideration. Namely, when the predecessor of the stroke phase F_{S_i} is neutral pose P_N, then the pose on the left boundary of the stroke phase F_{S_i} also has to be set to P_N.

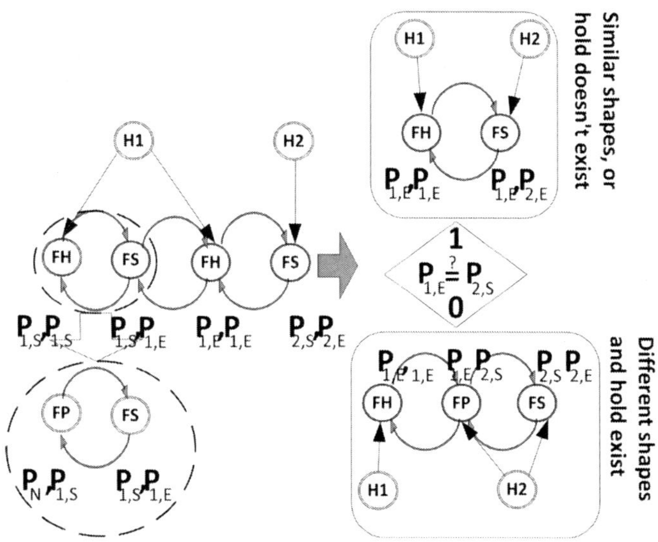

Figure 52. Resolving missing preparation phase F_P.

In the *planning behavior* module, the definition of poses for F_P, F_R, F_{HS}, and F_{SH} is performed next, and is presented in Table 12. The relational structure *MovementPhrases* contains all of the movement models *H*, each one with the corresponding movement phases. First, the initial definition of pose candidates for F_P, F_R, F_{HS}, and F_{SH} has to be performed. Namely, for each movement phrase, the corresponding movement phases are considered (except the stroke phase F_S). For the retraction phase F_R, the following pair of poses is defined $\{P_N, P_N\}$. For the preparation phase F_P, however, several options have to be considered according to equation 45. Namely, if the previous phase is retraction phase F_R or *null*, then the P_S is P_N; otherwise, it is *prev(mph)*. P_E. And if the F_{HS} follows, then the end pose is *next(next(mph))*. P_S, otherwise *next(mph)*.P_S. At the end we are dealing with the hold phases. For the hold phase F_{HS}, the poses are set by the following pair {*next(mph)*.P_S , *next(mph)*.P_S} and F_{SH} by the following pair { *prev(mph)*.P_E, *prev(mph)*.P_E }. In the next step we have to deal with incomplete movement phrase structures, by performing the proposed steps 1-5 above. Firstly, the F_{HS} has to be transformed into F_P, when there is no preparation phase within the given movement phrase. The poses at its boundaries also have to be adjusted, as suggested in *(1)*. When some movement phrase starts with F_S, the three possible situations discussed in *(2)-(4)* have to be resolved. Therefore, in the first case the boundaries for F_S have to be adjusted in order to capture also F_{SH} in the previous movement phrase. Consequently, the poses have to be adapted. In the second case the original F_S has to be split in order to get the preparation phase. This is done by inserting a new movement phase before

F_S in the current movement phrase. The original F_S is split into two halves at the syllable level. One half is used for the F_P and the other for F_S. The poses of F_S are retained, if poses of F_P are in accordance with step *(3)* above. In the last case, the hold phase F_{SH} in the previous movement phrase has to be split into two halves. New preparation phrase F_P has to be inserted before F_S in the current movement phrase. In this case the poses in F_{SH} have to be preserved, while defining poses in new F_P as suggested in *(4)*.

Table 12. Step 7 – The definition of poses for F_P, F_R, F_{HS}, and F_{SH}

```
Item* frg = utterance→ relation ( MovementPhrases )→first();
FOR ( ; frg != NULL; frg = next(frg) )
{
    mph = frg→ as_relation ( MovementPhases )→daughters();
    FOR ( ; mph != NULL; mph = next(mph) )
    {
        IF (mph →fS ( PHASE_TYPE) == »Fs« ) continue;
        IF (mph →fS ( PHASE_TYPE) == »Fr« ) {
            mph → fset ( P_S, PN );
            mph → fset ( P_E, PN );
        }
        IF (mph →fS ( PHASE_TYPE) == »Fp« ) {
            IF ( prev(mph) →fS ( PHASE_TYPE) == »Fr« || prev(mph) == NULL )
                mph → fset ( P_S, PN );
            ELSE
            IF ( prev(mph) →fS ( PHASE_TYPE) == »Fs« || ( prev(mph) →fS ( PHASE_TYPE)
                == »Fsh« )
                fg→ fset ( P_S, prev(mph) →fS ( P_E ) );
            IF ( next(mph) →fS ( PHASE_TYPE) == »Fhs« )
                fg→ fset ( P_E, next(next(mph)) → fS ( P_S ) );
            ELSE
                fg→ fset ( P_E, next(mph) → fS ( P_S ) );
        }
        IF ( fg→fS ( PHASE_TYPE) == »Fhs« ) {
            fg→ fset ( P_S, next(mph) →fS ( P_S ) );
            fg→ fset ( P_E, next(mph) →fS ( P_S ) );
        }
        IF ( fg→fS ( PHASE_TYPE) == »Fsh« ) {
            fg→ fset ( P_S, prev(mph) →fS ( P_E ) );
            fg→ fset ( P_E, prev(mph) →fS ( P_E ) );
        }
    }
}
```

(a) The initial definition of poses for F_P, F_R, F_{HS}, and F_{SH}.

Table 12. (Continued)

```
Item *frg = utterance→ relation ( MovementPhrases )→first();
FOR ( ; frg != NULL; frg = next(frg) )
{
    mph = frg→ as_relation ( MovementPhases )→daughters();
    FOR ( ; mph != NULL; mph = next(mph) )
    {
        IF (mph→fS ( PHASE_TYPE) == »Fhs« && !IsContained ( prev(mph) ) ) {
            mph → fset ( PHASE_TYPE, »Fp« );
            mph → fset ( P_S, prev(mph)→ fS ( P_E );
            mph → fset ( P_E, next(mph)→ fS ( P_S ) );
        }
        IF ( mph →fS ( PHASE_TYPE) == »Fs« && !IsContained ( prev(mph) ) ) {
            IF ( prev(mph)→ fS ( P_E ) == mph→ fS ( P_S ) && mph→ fS ( P_S ) != mph→ fS (
                P_E ) )
            {
                mph→ as_relation (Dynamics)→daughters() =
                    prev(mph)→ as_relation (Dynamics)→daughters();
                mph→ fset ( P_S, prev(mph)→ fS ( P_E ) );
                mph→ fset ( P_E, prev(mph)→ fS ( P_E ) );
                Remove ( prev(mph) );
            }

            IF ( prev(mph)→ fS ( P_E ) == mph→ fS ( P_S ) && mph→ fS ( P_S ) == mph→ fS (
                P_E ) )
            {
                syll_start = mph→ as_relation (Dynamics)→daughters ();
                syll_end = mph→ as_relation (Dynamics)→daughtern ();
                mph_new = mph→ relation ( MovementPhases ) → insert_before ( mph );
                mph_new→fset (PHASE_TYPE , »Fp« );
                mph_new_boundaries = utterance → as_relation ( Dynamics ) → insert ( mph_new
                    );
                append_daughter ( mph_new_boundaries, Dynamics, syll_start );
                append_daughter ( mph_new_boundaries, Dinamika, syll_start + (syll_end –
                    syll_start) / 2);
                mph→ as_relation (Dynamics) → daughters () = syll_start + (syll_end - syll_start) /
                    2;
                mph_new → fset ( P_S, prev(mph_new)→ fS ( P_E );
                mph_new → fset ( P_E, mph→ fS ( P_S ) );
            }

            IF ( prev(mph)→ fS ( P_E ) != mph→ fS ( P_S ) )
            {
                syll_start = prev(mph) → as_relation (Dynamics)→daughters ();
                syll_end = prev(mph) → as_relation (Dynamics)→daughtern ();
                mph_new = mph→ relation ( MovementPhases ) → insert_before ( mph );
                mph_new→fset (PHASE_TYPE , »Fp« );
                mph_new_boundaries = utterance→ as_relation ( Dynamics ) → insert_below
                    (mph_new );
                prev(mph) → as_relation (Dynamics)→daughtern () = syll_start + (syll_end –
                    syll_start)/2;
                append_daughter (mph_new_boundaries, Dynamics, syll_start + (syll_end –
                    syll_start)/2);
                append_daughter (mph_new_boundaries, Dynamics, syll_end );
                mph_new → fset ( P_S, prev(mph_new)→ fS ( P_E );
```

```
                    mph_new→ fset ( P_E, next(mph_new)→ fS ( P_S ) );
                }
            }
        }
    }
```

(b) The final adjustments for incomplete movement phrases.

So far, the movement has already been transformed into a synchronized sequence of poses regarding content and prosody that represent *key frame animations* (Figure 53).

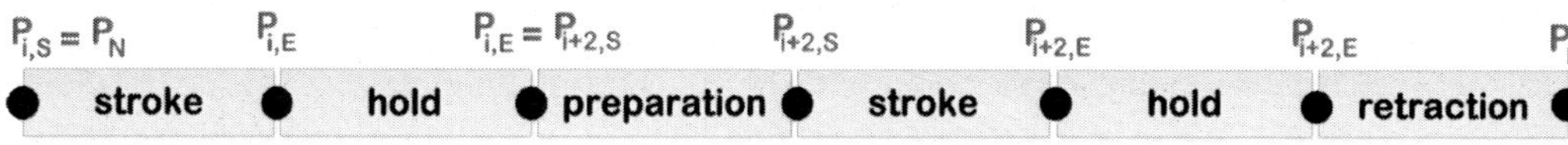

Figure 53. A synchronized sequence of poses regarding the content and prosody.

Further, the movement phases in relational structure *MovementPhases* are defined in the temporal domain, where uniquely defined poses should occur at their boundaries. Nevertheless, in order that the defined sequence of poses completely defines the co-verbal movement, it is still necessary to determine the transitions between poses, also called movement trajectories. Namely, these trajectories can be used in order to define, for example, how to *perform* a movement between consecutive poses, i.e., whether it should be linear (a straight line), a semi-circle, semi-ellipse, etc.

The Definition of Trajectories between Poses

The transition between poses can be described by some curve (trajectory), which some body part performs during movement. Their huge diversity demands several restrictions when describing them in the gesticon. Namely, we are interested solely in the trajectories of hands, or the curve that the hand describes during transition $P_S \rightarrow P_E$. Furthermore, the definition of the specific trajectory between two poses depends on:

1. temporal structure of the movement phase mph *t*,
2. semiotic class *S*,
3. movement phase type *F*,
4. morpho-syntactic tag *M*, and
5. semantic relationship *R*.

As in the case of selecting poses for the stroke phase F_S, in the semiotic lexicon trajectories are also stored (used between two poses), and represented in the form of the following *n-tuple* data structure:

$$(mph.P_E \times next(mph).P_S \times S \times F \times M) \rightarrow (T \times t_{\min} \times t_{\max} \times R)$$

The lookup into the gesticon can in general result in several possible trajectories for the given sequence $(mph.P_E \times next(mph).P_S \times S \times F \times M)$, where the i'th trajectory *mph.* T_i is described with the following data columns $(T_i \times t_{(\min)i} \times t_{(\max)i} \times R_i)$, namely the trajectory T_i, the corresponding minimum and maximum times of its realization, and semantic relationship R_i. Therefore, the selection of the best trajectory candidate mph_i. T for individual movement phase mph_i also has to be carried out by evaluating its:

- *Target cost* $C^t(u_i, t_i)$: evaluates the match between the trajectory candidate u_i and the defined (target) specification for trajectory t_i.
- *Concatenation cost* $C^c(u_{u-1}, u_i)$: evaluates the match between trajectory candidate u_i in the movement phase mph_i and the trajectory candidate u_{i-1} in the previous movement phase mph_{i-1}.

Nevertheless, all of those trajectory candidates whose minimal time for realization t_{min} is bigger than predicted realization time t in the target specification are already removed at the start. In the *planning behavior* module, in this step the algorithm has to define the best trajectory between any two poses, presented in Table 13. The relational structure *MovementPhrases* contains all movement models H, whereas each one contains the corresponding movement phases. In order to perform lookup into the gesticon and to obtain a set of trajectories for each movement phase, such features as $(mph.P_E \times next(mph).P_S \times S \times F \times M)$ are needed. These features are stored in the HRG structure. Namely, morpho-syntactic tag M is stored in the *Word* relational structure that can be accessed for the given *CU* element via relational structure *ContentStructure*. Furthermore, the semiotic class S is stored in elements of the relational structure *ContentUnits* and can be accessed via relational structure *MovementStructure*. Finally, movement phase type F and poses $\{P_S, P_E\}$ are stored in elements of the relational structure *MovementPhases*, and can be accessed via relational structure *MovementShape*. The feature set for each movement phase is then used to access the gesticon in order to obtain a set of trajectory candidates, described as $(T \times t_{(\min)} \times t_{(\max)} \times R)$. The target trajectory specification t_i for mph_i, can easily be defined based on the movement phase duration, assigned in the previous steps of the algorithm. The t_i is needed for evaluating trajectory candidates and calculating corresponding target costs C^t. Additionally, for each trajectory candidate i, an additional FSM state is added. After adding all new states, the transitions with all states in the previous level have to be created, with assigned concatenation costs based on bigrams. The *BestPath* algorithm then selects the best trajectory candidate for each movement phase, based on the minimal overall cost between several candidates.

As a result, each element in the relational structure *MovementPhases* has the added attribute *trajectory* (with the exception of the first movement phase in a sentence) which defines how to form a movement, or how the transition between subsequent poses should actually be performed, regarding the arms and head. The HRG relational structure is now complete regarding the co-verbal behavior definition, since it contains the structure of gestures *G* that are temporal, prosodical, and content-consistent with respect to the input sentence (see Figure 33), as shown in Figure 54.

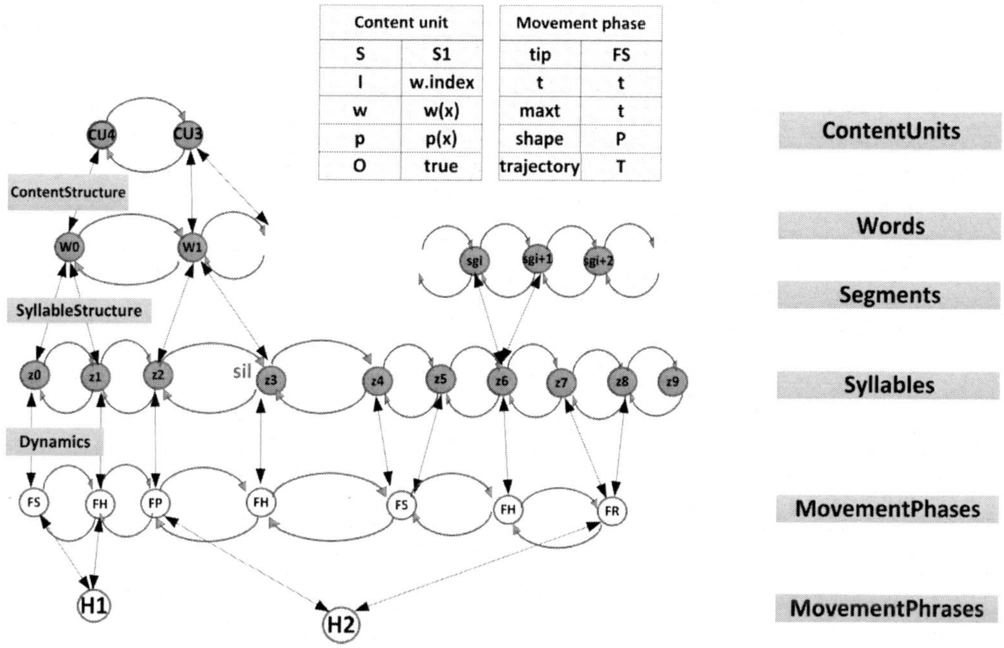

Figure 54. The HRG structure that contains temporally, prosodically, and semantically aligned co-verbal behavior *G*.

Table 13. The definition of the best trajectory for each movement phase

```
Item* frg = utterance→ relation ( MovementPhrases)→first();
FOR ( ; frg != NULL; frg = next(frg) )
{
    mph = frg→ as_relation ( MovementShape )→daughters(),
    cu = frg→ as_relation ( MovementStructure )→down();
    cu_start = cu→ as_relation ( ContentStructure )→ daughters();
    cu_end = cu→ as_relation ( ContentStructure )→ daughtern();

    FOR ( w = cu_start; w != cu_end; w = next(w) ) {
        IF ( w→ fI ( SEMIOTIC_INDICATOR ) == w→ fI (POSITION ) )
            M = w→fS ( POS );
    }
    S = cu→fS( SEMIOTIC_CLASS );
    FOR ( ; mph != NULL; mph = next(mph) )
    {
        P_E = mph→ fS ( P_E );
        P_S = next(mph)→ fS ( P_S );
        F = mph→fS( PHASE_TYPE );
        mph→{ T, t_min, t_max, R } = SemioticLexicon (P_S, P_E, S, F, M )
        t_i = { mph→fF ( DURATION) };
        FOR ( i = 0; i < length( mph→ T ); i++ , j++) {
            C^t(mph→ T[i], t_i ) → mph→ T[i].tc_cost;
```

```
            fsm→Add ( mph→ T[i], j );
        }
        pT = prev (mph )→{ T, t_min, t_max, R }
        cT = mph→{ T, t_min, t_max, R }
        FOR ( i = 0; i < length(cT); i++ )
            FOR ( j = 0; j < length(pT); j++ ) {
                C^c (cT[i], pT[j] ) = 2-Gram (cT[i], pT[j]) ;
                fsm→AddTransition (pT[j], cT[i] );
            }
        }
    }
}

fg = frg→ as_relation ( MovementShape )→daughters();
BestPath ( fsm, fg );
```

PHASE V: THE GENERATION OF CO-VERBAL BEHAVIOR G

Now, co-verbal behavior G is already temporal, prosodical, and content-consistent; it has to be converted into a form suitable for realization with some animation framework, and for animating the conversational agent. For example, the HRG structure in Figure 54 should be converted into an abstract notation (behavior description), which the conversational agent is then able to convert into animation, to actually perform the required co-verbal behavior.

In the literature it is evident that the majority of conversational agents depend on the procedural descriptions, which are based on XML or similar descriptive schemes. The most commonly used languages are, for example, BML (Vilhjalmsson et al., 2007), MURML (Kransted et al., 2002), EMBRScript (Heloir & Kipp, 2009), APML (DeCarolis et al., 2004), etc. Most of them require an additional step regarding the animation synchronization, or the so-called multimodal alignment of gestures and speech signal (Ceреković & Pandžić, 2011). Nevertheless, in the scope of the proposed algorithm, the gesticon already contains pose descriptions in *EVA-Script* descriptive scheme, which supports the description of detailed temporal synchronization. Therefore, in this phase the co-verbal behavior G defined in the HRG structure can be automatically stored in the form of procedural description, based on the *EVA-Script* language. This conversion is quite simple and straightforward, since information about the co-verbal gestures is already well-structured, consisting of several relational structures that relate poses, phonemes, prosody and synthesized speech, and also contain detailed temporal relations between speech and co-verbal behavior. Further, *EVA-Script* can also be converted into other descriptive languages. Co-verbal behavior G can be defined (equation 11) by the following sequence of gestures:

$$\hat{G} = T_m^{-1} \cdot \hat{H} = T_m^{-1}\left(H_1,\ldots,H_i\right) = T_{m,1}^{-1} \cdot \hat{H}_1 + T_{m,2}^{-1} \cdot \hat{H}_2 + \ldots + T_{m,i}^{-1} \cdot \hat{H}_i \quad (46)$$

where transformation T_m^{-1} represents the intent of the text. The intent is namely used in order to define and describe the movement model $\hat{H}$. Further, the movement model $\hat{H}$ (equation 13) can be represented as a temporal and content-consistent sequence of shapes and transitions between them: $\hat{H} = T_{vm}^{-1} \cdot V = T_{vm}^{-1}(V^*, V^*, V^* \ldots)$. Furthermore, when gestures are abstractly synchronized using the concept of movement phases and phrases, where each movement phrase describes the local intent, the movement can also be described as the transformation of local intents into a temporal consistent sequence of visual presentations:

$$H[CU_1, t_1] \times H[CU_2, t_2] \times \ldots \times H[CU_n, t_n] \tag{47}$$

where $H[CU_1, t_1]$ represents the so-called *g-unit* (McNeill, 2005a; Kendon, 2004; Kita et al., 1998). Namely, based on the content in the HRG structure (Figure 54) and the proposed algorithm, the movement phrase actually describes both the temporal and content (formal) consistent co-verbal behavior and simultaneous speech. As presented, the temporal synchronization is performed at the level of syllables, whereas the synchronization of poses is at the level of semiotic sequences and content words. The *temporal synchronization* steps in the algorithm are based on several tree relational structures in the HRG structure, since they relate movement phrases, movement phases, syllables, and segments. And *content synchronization* is defined based on those tree relational structures that link content units and movement phrases.

Furthermore, the movement phases are synchronized by considering the accentuation of syllables (PA and NA tags), while their duration is defined by those segments' durations that are related with the specific phase. The duration of each movement phase is defined by absolute time (in *x ms*), and is stored in the attribute *t*. Nevertheless, the relative time can also be easily defined by summing durations of the previous movement phases. Each movement phase keeps the semiotic and temporal-dependent shape, which has to be manifested on each phase's left and right boundary, together with the trajectory, which smooths the transition between poses. Specifically, each gesture part can be represented as the following local event: $P_S \xrightarrow{T,t} P_E$, which tells us that at a given time *t* and by using the trajectory *T*, the transition from the start pose into the end pose has to be performed. These local events are an integral element of the co-verbal behavior structure, by which we ensure that the end poses of the predecessors and starting poses of successors (in the level of movement phases) are always consistent.

The EVA-Script Procedural Description of Co-Verbal Behavior

A procedural description is actually a parameterization of the animation graph for each body part. Namely, each movement phrase, in general, represents the prosodic and consistent movement of individual body parts regarding shape, which illustrates the semiotic intent for the corresponding speech segment. Therefore, in the EVA-Script notation, each movement phrase H_i is described with the block *<bgesture>*, used to specify simultaneous execution. Furthermore, the stroke phase F_S and preparation phase F_P within this block specify sequences on which the configuration of individual movement controllers has to be simultaneously carried out. The hold phase F_H and the retraction phase F_R do not specify any procedural description, since the first one actually represents only the hold of the last pose, and the second one represents retraction into the neutral state (e.g., this could be the initial state of the conversational agent). Therefore, F_H and F_R are described (when they exist) only with the following attributes within the block *<BAP>*: *durationRetraction* and *durationHold.* Both attributes are always assigned to the earliest predecessor of the stroke phase or preparation phase within the movement phrase H_i. The F_S and F_P are specified using the block *<successive> ... <parallel>*.

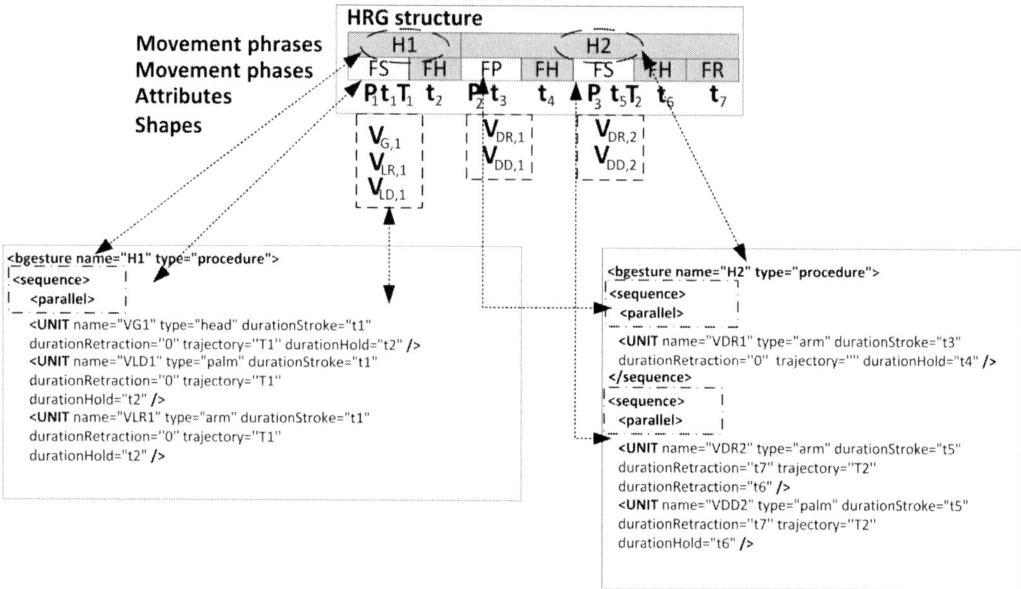

Figure 55. The conversion of HRG structure into EVA-Script procedural description of the co-verbal behavior.

Each *<BAP>* block is specified based on the final pose P_E, which should be manifested at the end of the movement phase. The gesticon for a given pose P_E returns shapes dependent on the body part (equation 15), and are described in the form of pairs *{part, shape}*, where each pair can be described by the *<BAP>* tag. Namely, each pair represents a complex movement controller, whose attribute *name* represents the call of the specific template in the gesticon. Its value depends on the attribute *shape* stored in the pair {*part*, *shape*}, where the attribute *part* represents the attribute *type* of the *<BAP>* tag. The duration of the *<BAP>* tags within the block *<successive> ... <parallel>* is defined according to the attribute value *t* of the corresponding element in the relational structure *MovementPhrases*. The movement trajectory in the block is defined based on the value of the attribute *trajectory* of the corresponding element in the relational structure *MovementPhases*. When the trajectory is linear, it may also be left empty. The conversion of the HRG structure into an EVA event (any co-verbal behavior written in the EVA-Script) is shown in Figure 55.

The Procedural Description for the Co-Articulation of the Lips

The *Lip-Sync* process represents the concept used for achieving proper synchrony between audio and visual presentation at the phoneme level. The concept encompasses the realistic description of the movements in the mouth, teeth and tongue regions during speech.

The accentuation and amplitude depend on the source, whereas the vocal tract defines the phoneme (Zorić & Pandžić, 2006). In order to ensure proper synchronization, the positions of the mouth, tongue, and teeth have to be aligned with the speech. The most general solution is based on mapping the phonemes into visemes, and interpolation of the individual visemes, by considering the input temporal characteristics of the phoneme sequences. The *direct interpolation* ignores the co-articulation factor between phonemes and, therefore, usually results in poor synchronization. Namely, co-articulation describes the phenomenon when the current phoneme is already affecting the vocal tract during the formation of the previous/next phoneme. The shape of the vocal tract, therefore, does not depend only on the characteristics of the current phoneme, but also on its context, which includes both its predecessors and successors (Toutios et al., 2010). The pronunciations indicate that the most pronounced are vowels and only some consonants (/f/, /v/, /w/, /b/, /m/, /p/). Furthermore, such consonants as (/z/, /s/) are less frequently used and are relatively quickly blended with their predecessors/successors. Therefore, the co-articulation effects can also be simplified (Košutić, 2011). For example, Cohen and Massaro (Cohen & Massaro, 1993) proposed the model for the movement of lips, which is also the basis of the co-articulation model in this book. In the Cohen-Massaro model the viseme strives for dominant influence over the movement controllers in the vocal tract region. The intensity of this influence depends on the temporal structure of the phoneme sequence, and can be increased or decreased with time. Furthermore, the neighboring visemes create a mutual effect (by using the so-called dominant function), which should result in mutual blending within the time intervals defined for each viseme. In general the dominant function is $\Delta(\tau) = e^{-\Theta\tau^{c}}$ which was proposed by Cohen and Massaro; the dominant effect of the viseme is decreasingly dependent on the time interval τ. The τ represents the time that is measured from the center of the phoneme, while the power c is modulated by the pronunciation speed θ. The used dominant functions are presented in Figure 57.

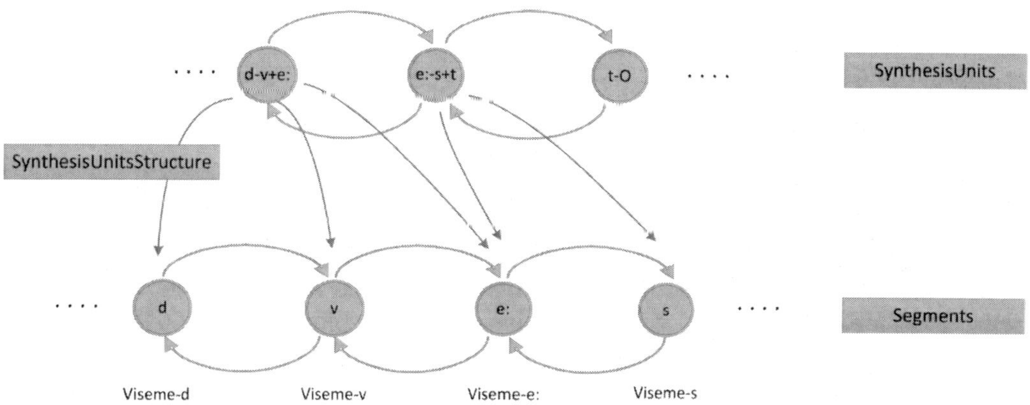

Figure 56. The relationship between visemes and synthesis units within the HRG structure.

The co-articulation model of the lips can be understood within the expressive co-verbal behavior model as a linguistic entity whose characteristics are specified in several HRGs' relational structures (Figure 7). Namely, each input sentence is represented as a phoneme sequence in the relational structure *Segments*. Each element in this structure keeps the

the proper conversion into EVA-Script procedural description has to be performed. The starting point is the relational structure *MovementPhrases* which contains movement models *H*, and each element contains the corresponding movement phases in the relational structure *MovementPhases*. Each movement phase is further related to the relational structure *Syllable* and *Segments* (see Figure 7).

Table 14. Step 9 - The procedural description for the co-articulation of the lips in EVA-script notation

```
EVA_Script ← <behavior >

Item* seg = utterance→ relation (Segments)→first();
EVA_Script ← <speech>, emotion, tts_file
FOR ( ; seg != NULL; seg = next(seg) )
    EVA_Script ← <viseme>, name, stress, duration, offset
EVA_Script ← </speech>

Item* frg = utterance→ relation (MovementPhrases)→first();
FOR ( ; frg != NULL; frg = next(frg) )
{
    fg = frg→ as_relation (MovementPhases)→daughters();
    EVA_Script ← <bgesture>
    EVA_Script ← <sequence>
    EVA_Script ← <parallel>
    FOR ( ; fg != NULL; fg = next(fg) )
    {
        EVA_Script ← <UNIT>, name, type, duration, persistent, transition, startpose,endpose
    }
    EVA_Script ← </parallel>
    EVA_Script ← </sequence>
    EVA_Script ← </bgesture>
}

EVA_Script ← <fgesture >
EVA_Script ← <sequence >
EVA_Script ← <parallel >
    EVA_Script ← <FAP>, name, type, stress, duration, persistent, start
    ....
EVA_Script ← </parallel>
EVA_Script ← </sequence>
EVA_Script ← </fgesture>

EVA_Script ← </behavior >
```

By using the proposed algorithm presented in this chapter, it is possible to generate co-verbal behavior that specifies the movements of the vocal tract, arms, hands, and head on general unannotated input text. It is based on the TTS system's extracted linguistic and prosodic data. Furthermore, the co-verbal behavior is completely structured and synchronized with the underlying speech signal; therefore, no synchronization conversions are needed. The co-verbal behavior can be realized (animated) through entity realization in the form of the body modeling of the co-verbal virtual agent. The framework for animation realization (EVA-framework) was designed for the purpose of realizing the generated co-verbal behavior, and will be presented in the next chapter.

Chapter 8

THE FRAMEWORK FOR THE REALIZATION OF CO-VERBAL BEHAVIOR ON THE CONVERSATIONAL AGENT - EVA-FRAMEWORK -

INTRODUCTION

In order to be able to realize hierarchically structured procedural descriptions of co-verbal behavior in the context of the proposed model for co-verbal behavior generation, an EVA-framework was developed (Mlakar & Rojc, 2011b; Mlakar et al., 2013c). This framework allows the synthesis of several articulated 3D models of conversational agents, which are based on multi-part 3D models. Furthermore, it allows for the synthesis of several communicative concepts, such as: lip-sync, hand gestures (including palm), facial expressions and emotions, head movements, and gaze. The main purpose of the framework is to provide authentic gesticulation and facial mimics, which can stimulate social response during human-machine interaction. Regarding animation techniques, the framework supports key frames and key pose animation, animation of shapes and blending, and several concepts used in computer graphics, such as 3D mesh models and skeletal structures. The architecture of the EVA-framework is shown in Figure 58.

As can be seen in Figure 58, the EVA-framework consists of several modules. The first module has to parse individual movement types contained within each EVA-Script event, and to transform them into synchronized animation intervals (the animation graph). The shape of these animation intervals depends only on the visualization mechanism and is generally defined through the temporal modulations of complex groups of parallel/consecutive movements from one pose to another (or from animation to animation). The second module is then responsible for the interpolation that has to be performed on this sequence of animation intervals in each time frame. In this way, the visualization mechanism generates the movement of several articulated body parts on the conversational agent. The visualization mechanism also takes care of streaming speech audio and other basic concepts in computer graphics and animation, such as: binding of meshes and skeletal structures based on the parameters of a 3D model, adding textures and skins, blending animation, etc. The EVA-framework output is an audio/video animation stream, which can be displayed on the screen, or stored as a video file, and/or played as a network video stream. The most important characteristics of the EVA-framework are the flexible realization of the expressive co-verbal behavior and event-driven processing and realization of the co-verbal behavior. Namely, the behavior does not have to be planned in advance, but is generated and animated simultaneously with the speech synthesis process. Furthermore, templates for shapes and movements can also be generated while running the co-verbal behavior generation algorithm.

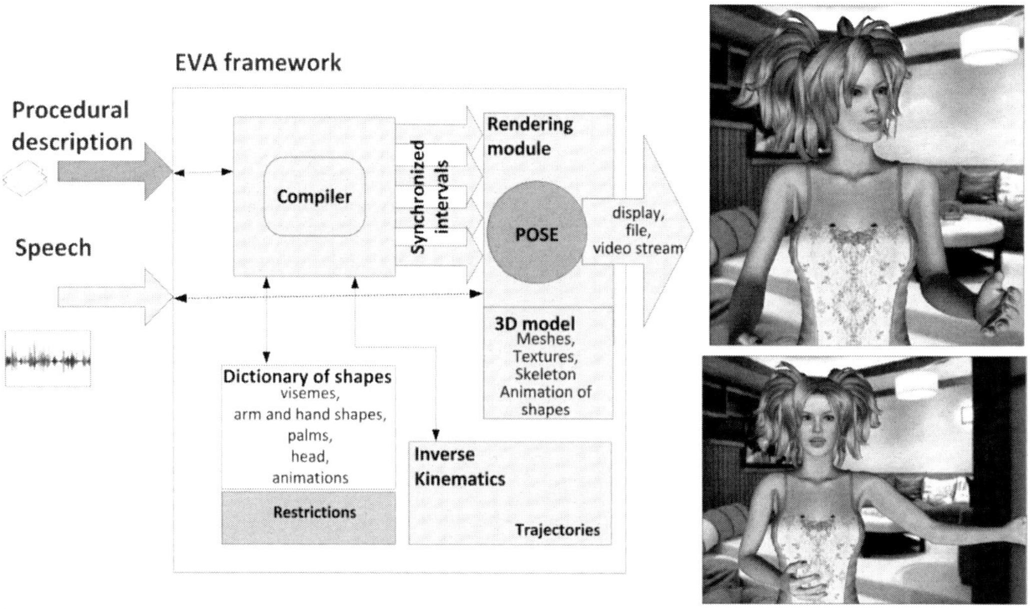

Figure 58. The architecture of EVA-framework.

Multi-Part 3D Model of the Conversational Agent - EVA

The 3D model of the conversational agent, animated by EVA-framework, is composed of meshes and associated textures, the skeletal structure, and animated shapes. Each model has to be designed in some environment for 3D modeling (e.g., Maya 3D), where the skeleton has to be imported as an *egg*[1] file, or as its binary version *bam*[2]. Therefore, the multi-part conversational agent represents the model that can be composed from several sub-models (e.g., hair, body parts, eyes, teeth, clothes, etc.) that share a part of the common skeletal chain. In the context of multi-part models, it is assumed that each 3D sub-model has its own skeletal sub-chain, which is bound to the basic skeleton (e.g., the backbone). For example, the hand is tied to the common skeleton via the shoulder joint; the hair via the vertex joint, etc. The multi-part concept also allows us to tie several body parts to the common articulated 3D model. Each 3D sub-model is considered an individual animation *Actor*, for which procedures and animations that are independent of other sub-models can be defined. Additionally, a particular model can be updated and replaced even during visualization (e.g., changing clothes, hair, etc.). Figure 59 presents the multipart 3D model of the conversational agent EVA. This model is constructed using mesh sub-models of the body, scalp, tongue, teeth,

[1] egg: http://en.wikipedia.org/wiki/Python_eggs.
[2] bam: https://www.panda3d.org/manual/index.php/Writing_3D_Models_out_to_Disk.

eyes, clothes, and accessories. Individual sub-models, in a common 3D model, are tied through the common skeleton (common joint rule). Furthermore, each of these sub-models has its own skeletal sub-chain. Mesh sub-models are tied to associated skeletal sub-structures through a process named *joint skinning* (Keller, 2009).

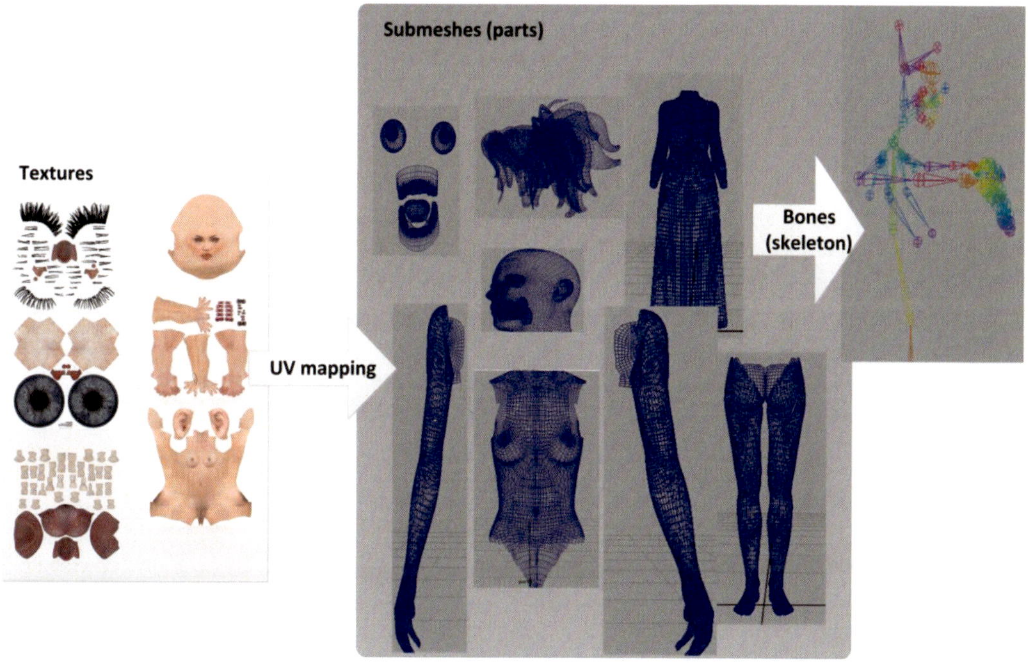

Figure 59. The 3D model of a multi-part conversational agent EVA.

In addition to its own skeletal chain, each individual sub-model also has its own texture and materials. The latter are tied to a mesh model through a process named *UV mapping*[3] (Bevacqua et al., 2007). Figure 59 presents the structure of a 3D volumetric multi-part model, with the corresponding textures and skeletal chain. The main issue of multi-part models is a composition of models from several meshes (geometries), which can cause fracturing at junctures. To prevent this, an approach named *deformation of meshes* can be used. Namely, in those regions where the two parts are connected, a *deformation mesh* that binds and controls the boundary points of individual mesh (geometry) has to be used. The *deformation mesh* enables the performance of continuous deformation (Keller, 2009). The multipart 3D model (*Actor*), therefore, represents a set of related meshes, bones, materials, textures, and animated shapes.

In the realization framework based on Panda3D, the 3D multi-part model represents an object of the *Actor*. The EVA-framework, therefore, allows the composition of the conversational agent from individual separate parts. In so doing, the individual parts must fulfill the condition of a common joint, and the deformation meshes are established automatically. In Figure 59 the conversational agent is composed of left and right arms, body, left and right legs, head, scalp, face, mouth, tongue, and dress. The individual parts are

[3] UV mapping: http://en.wikipedia.org/wiki/UV_mapping.

combined so that the body and related skeletal chain represent the model basis, while the remaining parts are just stuck on this basis. Bonding is performed in the following two steps:
1. Firstly, those parts that relate to the head are bonded together, wherein the individual skeletal chains of sub-models have to include the joint which is located in the head's skeletal chain (e.g., vertex for the scalp):

```
Head = Actor.Actor({
 'eyes':'eyes.bam',
 'tongue':'tongue.bam',
 'jaw':'jaw.bam',
 'scalp':'scalp.bam',
 'head':'head.bam',
 })
Head.attach('eyes','tongue','jaw',
'scalp','head')
```

2. Furthermore, the head, hands, feet, and clothing have to be bonded on the body. We have to ensure that individual skeletal chains of sub-models contain at least one joint, which has to be located in the body's skeletal chain (e.g., left or right collar for arms, neck for the head, left and right hips for legs):

```
Body = Actor.Actor({
 'head':Head,
 'larm':'larm.bam',
 'rarm':'rarm.bam',
 'lleg':'lleg.bam',
 'rleg':'rleg.bam',
 'clothes':'clothes.bam',
 'body':'body.bam',
 })
Body.attach('head','larm','rarm',
'lleg','rleg', 'clothes','body')
```

Multi-part actors are relatively complex animation structures. The individual body part is contained in its own *egg* or *bam* file, making it possible to assign particulate animation intervals. This is especially important when e.g., temporally pre-defined animations are played out (and not a procedure). From the perspective of procedural animation, the multipart concept enables the design of morphed-shapes that can be formulated and updated only on the selected body part. Also, their effect is automatically limited to the selected body part. In this way, facial expressions and emotions can be limited e.g., to the head's region, where they can also be formed. The individual expressions are formed and updated in some external framework for 3D modeling, and can then be downloaded on the selected model even while running EVA-framework. Similarly, as we combine sub-models in the 3D model, we can also remove or replace the individual part. For example, function *Body.removePart( )* can be used to remove the individual body part from the common 3D model. Also, *Body.attach* (*"body," "head," "neck"*) and *Body.showPart*( ) methods can be used to assign a new 3D sub-model of the head to a common 3D model and visualize it. The multi-part approach, therefore, makes it possible to optimize the design, execution, and updating of the 3D agent and the necessary system resources. Namely, the memory is no longer loaded with a full set of clothing and jewelry that can be worn by an agent, or even objects which it can manage.

Instead, only those 3D sub-models and objects currently being used by an agent are in the memory.

The Realization of a Procedural Description of Co-Verbal Behavior

The proposed EVA-framework contains for the realization several software interfaces for the conversion of procedural descriptions in EVA-Script scheme into animated segments (Figure 58). Each complex (elementary) movement controller in EVA-Script (*<BAP>*, *<FAP>* or *<viseme>*), in general, describes the generation of the animation interval that for mesh transformation uses animation techniques, such as skeletal or animated shape, or represents the generation of an animation interval in which the pre-defined animation of an individual body part is addressed (as implemented in some external framework for 3D modeling). The animation can, therefore, be seen as a finite-state machine (FSM), where each state represents a pose/shape, while the transition between states represents the time-dependent interpolation of elemental movement controller's values (kinematics), from its current value upto the value that is specified within the pose/shape, which is based on forward kinematics. The actual value of the elemental movement controller is dependent on the specified final value and those final values of the sub-joints, which are located in the hierarchical tree in front of it. The algorithm processes and converts the *lip-sync* descriptions (within tags *<speech>*), the animation of facial expressions and emotions (within tags *<fgesture>*), and the animation of body movements and shapes (within tags *<bgesture>*), in a separate way. Namely, by considering the specific tag, it firstly defines the common software object with type *Sequence* (when simultaneous tags represent the sequential execution, speech, and body movements), or with type *Parallel* (when simultaneous tags represent the concurrent execution, emotions, and facial expressions). Furthermore, by using the regression functions, the individual tags are parsed and defined within the blocks *<successive>* ... *<parallel>* as animation intervals (i.e., *LerpIntervals*), where the block *<successive>* represents a new *Sequence* object, and block *<parallel>* a new *Parallel* object. The individual block within the procedural description, therefore, represents the continuous (sequential/simultaneous) restoring/disappearing effects of individual elemental movement controllers (skeleton, or animated form).

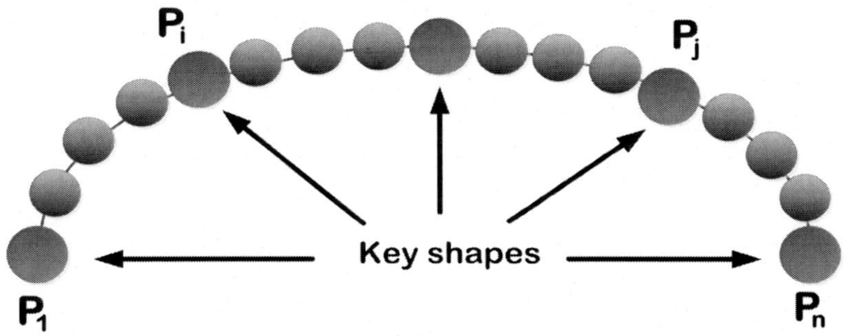

Figure 60. Animation of gestures based on the concept of key shapes and frames.

Figure 60 presents the animation when using key shapes which are obtained by converting the procedural descriptions. When red circles P_1, P_i, P_j and P_2 represent key poses/shapes, and encompass all elementary motion controllers that are necessary for the manifestation of shape, then the transition $P_1 \rightarrow P_i$ can be represented as a so-called set of elemental movement controllers' *LerpIntervals*, which at time *t* have to be re-configured from value P_1 into value P_i. The gray circles represent the intermediate shapes, or in-between frames, that are automatically calculated by the core animation mechanism.

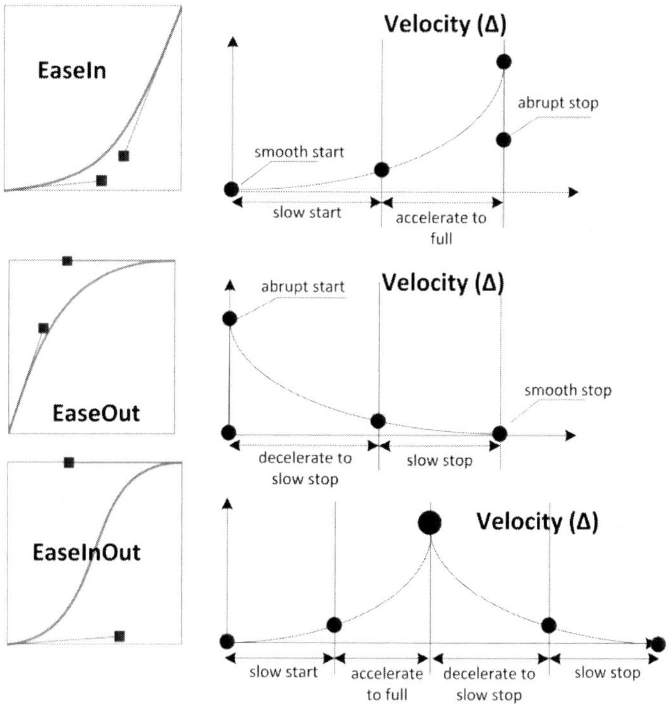

Figure 61. The interpolation curves *EaseIn*, *EaseOut* and *EaseInOut*.

When the procedural description describes an arm movement where the trajectory *T* is used, the principle of inverse kinematics is used, while in the automatic calculation of intermediate shapes intermediate poses that are dependent on the position of the hands are also included and are calculated using the engine of ODE dynamics[4]. Let the *Lerp* interval describe the shift from pose P_1 to pose P_2 (Figure 60). Based on the trajectory *T*, which describes the position of the hands, the ODE mechanism of the dynamics calculates the poses P_i, P_{i+1}, P_j as those key shapes through which the arm has to pass. Namely, the transition $P_1 \rightarrow P_2$ is transformed into a sequence of the following transitions: $P_1 \rightarrow P_i$, $P_i \rightarrow P_{i+}1$, $P_{i+1} \rightarrow P_j$ and $P_j \rightarrow P_2$ (the red circles). And the gray circles then represent those intermediate shapes which are calculated automatically by the core animation mechanism. The number of intermediate poses depends on the shape of the trajectory's transition. For example, for the square transition from $P_1 \rightarrow P_2 = P_1$ (the 360° outline), at least 3 key points are needed; for the

[4] http://www.ode.org/

triangular transition $P_1 \rightarrow P_2 = P_1$ again at least 3 key points are needed; and for the transition $P_1 \rightarrow P_2 = P_1$ in the form of an ellipse, at least 15 points are needed. The number of key points depends, therefore, on the complexity of the curve and resolution with which the trajectory has to be outlined. The greater the accuracy and complexity of the trajectory, the more key points are needed. However, the shifts between poses are rarely linear (or carried out at a steady velocity). Therefore, the EVA-framework also has to support the interpolation of movement using kinematic curves. Currently, three types of kinematics interpolations are used: *EaseIn*, *EaseOut*, and *EaseInOut* (see Figure 61).

The *EaseIn* interpolation (*accelerating from zero velocity*) is presented in the form of the time-dependent interpolation of elemental movement controller's values, which are calculated using the following equation for acceleration:

```
EaseInCubic = function (t, b, c, d) {                                    (48)
        t /= d;
        return c*t*t*t + b;
};
```

where t = *time* , b = *startvalue, c = change in value, d = duration.* The kinematics of movement which the *EaseIn* interpolation describes in fact represents a slow start, then acceleration to the final speed, and a sudden stop at the end (in the last animation frame, the motion speed drops from maximum speed to 0). The *EaseOut* interpolation (*decelerating to zero velocity*) is presented in the form of the time-dependent interpolation of elemental movement controller's values, which is the inverse of the *EaseIn* curve. The kinematics of movements described by the curve *EaseOut* is described as a sudden start (movement speed increases from 0 to a maximum value), which continues with movements after the maximum speed. The movement interpolated with *EaseOut* is terminated by the slow stop. The interpolation curve is in this case described by the following equation:

```
EaseOutCubic = function (t, b, c, d) {                                   (49)
        t /= d;
        t--;
        return c*(t*t*t + 1) + b;
};
```

where t = *time* , b = *startvalue, c = change in value, d = duration.* The *EaseInOut* interpolation (*accelerated start and decelerated end*) is presented in the form of the time-dependent interpolation of elemental movement controller's values, which is calculated by the following equation for acceleration:

```
EaseInOutCubic = function (t, b, c, d) {                                 (50)
        t /= d/2;
        if (t < 1) return c/2*t*t*t + b;
        t -= 2;
        return c/2*(t*t*t + 2) + b;
};
```

where t = *time* , b = *startvalue, c = change in value, d = duration.* In fact, the *EaseInOut* interpolation is a combination of *EaseIn* and *EaseOut*, where the kinematics of the movement begins with a slow acceleration until the final velocity, and ends with a slow braking until the stopping of the configuration of movement controller's values at that position which is defined within the pose/shape. In addition to the interpolation during the generation of animation intervals, the methods for internal and external continuity also have to be taken into account, in order to ensure that the movements are always continuous and thus appear more natural. The animation can be understood as a transition of the observed body part between several poses. In fact, the transition represents a shift of the individual elemental movement controller from state i into state $i+1$. The problem introduced by definitions for the animation of key poses and procedural description stems from the fact that the poses P_i and P_{i+1} can describe common elemental movement controllers and also those movement controllers which are not covered in both poses (e.g., belong only to P_i or P_{i+1}). The typical problem represents, for example, a sequential use of arms. When P_i defines only movement controllers for the right arm, and P_{i+1} only for the left arm, then during the animation of P_{i+1} the position and shape of the right hand are maintained, and may result in improper co-verbal behavior. Each procedural description, therefore, contains:

- those movement controllers which occur within the EVA-Script event for the first time, and represent a shift from the neutral into the excited state,
- those transient movement controllers which are covered in successive key poses and in fact represent only the transition from the previous excited state into a new excited state, and,
- those movement controllers which are not involved in the generation of the following pose, and represent a shift from the excited into the neutral state.

The individual description of the pose P defines and describes only those elemental movement controllers that are actually necessary for the manifestation of the pose on the observed body part (e.g., when moving the head, the arms are not in focus). The EVA-framework uses the concept of synchronicity and transition types: *remove*, *show*, and *move*. Those elemental movement controllers that appear for the first time create transitions with type *show*. Within these transitions, they are moved from the neutral state into the excited state, as described within the definition of pose P during the duration of the stroke phase (EVA-Script attribute *durationStrokePhase*). Furthermore, the elemental movement controllers that are present in both pose P_i as well as in pose P_{i+1} create transitions with type *move*. These are shifted from the current excited state into the new excited state within the time defined by the *durationStrokePhase* (the time available for performing the transition from P_i into P_{i+1}). And the elemental controllers that are present in P_i, but are not present in P_{i+1}, create transitions with type *remove*. These controllers are moved during the time *durationRetractionPhase* (defined for the transition into P_i) or, when this time is 0, during the time *durationStrokePhase* (defined for the transition into $\boldsymbol{P_{i+1}}$) into the configuration for the neutral pose (from the current excited state into the neutral state), and their effect on the articulated body is stopped. The transition from the neutral into the excited state is defined as follows:

$$\phi' = Lerp\ (t,\phi_1,\phi_2) = (1-t)\cdot\phi_1 + t\cdot\phi_2 \tag{51}$$

where t describes the transition time, ϕ_1 then represents the configuration of the elemental movement controller in a neutral state, and ϕ_2 the configuration of the elemental movement controller used within the EVA event (in P_{i+1}). The transition from one excited state into another excited state is defined by the same equation, wherein ϕ_1 represents the final configuration of the elemental movement controller described in P_i, and ϕ_2 represents the configuration of the elementary movement controller described in P_{i+1}. When transiting from the excited state into the neutral state, the ϕ_1 is the configuration of the elemental movement controller described within P_{i+1}, and ϕ_2 the configuration of the elemental movement controller in the neutral state.

THE REALIZATION OF FACIAL EXPRESSIONS AND EMOTIONS

The *rendering module* in Figure 58 ensures that several animation intervals (so-called *LerpIntervals*) are properly transferred on the articulated 3D mesh model of the conversational agent in the animation form. The rendering process simultaneously keeps those resources that relate to the conversational agent (e.g., mesh sub-models, textures, lights, skeletons, animated shapes, etc.). Furthermore, the relations between ECA's resources are kept in the form of transferable 3D formats (e.g., file formats such as: *X*, *egg*, *bam*). The *rendering module* is based on Panda3D core, and enables the animation of procedural or pre-prepared segments in real time. The animations can be represented on the screen as a video stream, or as a video-file, which can be created for later use/evaluation.

The core of the rendering module represents the so-called *pose blender module*, whose task is to combine simultaneous independent animation intervals, and to create the key pose using the blending concept. The blending process is especially important for creating facial expressions, emotions, and *lip-sync*. Therefore, the annotation scheme EVA-Script supports simultaneous rendering in the face region (simultaneousness of *<fgesture>* and *<speech>* tags), which means that several complex and elemental movement controllers can concurrently affect the common sub-regions of the face. The synchronization of the lips, for example, affects the rendering of those shapes within the vocal tract which include the lips and their surroundings. Also, facial expressions and emotions are implemented by rendering a whole face (including individual segments of the vocal tract). The blending process of facial expressions is performed by the concurrent rendering of facial expressions E_i and E_j, and is carried out using the animation blending technique, and by using weights. In the context of the EVA-framework and animation blending, the lip synchronization process (that part of the vocal tract which refers to the lips and their surroundings) is also treated as creating a facial expression, where weights responsible for the *lip-sync* are always set to the maximum value (weight rate 0.8). They can be defined experimentally as those values which still guarantee clearly distinguishable co-articulation. All other emotions during the co-articulation can have the cumulative weight value 0.2 (see Figure 62).

The blending of facial expressions may be a consequence of the overlapping, masking, or synchronousness of speech and emotions (facial expressions). When the individual EVA event concurrently encompasses a specific facial expression and speech (as seen in Figure 62), blending in the region of the lips has to be performed. Let E_i denote a specific viseme, and E_j the emotion *smile*. Then the following complex expression E_C (with the duration of the corresponding viseme) which models the masking concept can be described as: $\{0.8 * E_i, 0.2*E_j\}$, where E_i represents the basic expression and E_j the emotion modulated by a weight 0.2. The rendering mechanism in the EVA-framework then interprets the synchronousness of several facial expressions as a common process during which two or more complex/elemental movement controllers simultaneously affect certain segments within the polygonal mesh. Unlike those visualizations that are a result of joints' characteristics regarding rotation, where blending cannot exist (e.g., the arm cannot be moved simultaneously left and right, or the palm cannot simultaneously be opened and a fist), in the case of the animating and rendering of facial expressions the simultaneousness has to be considered (e.g., we can laugh while talking). As can be seen from Figure 62, simultaneous smile and speech, without modulating the blending, may result in unnatural deformations in the face region (e.g., teeth can be visualized in front of the lips). Therefore, the weight 0.2 for facial expressions E_j, and weight 0.8 for visemes E_i (defined experimentally) prevent these unnatural deformations, while still maintaining the distinguishable co-articulation. Nevertheless, the blending concept is carried out only in those regions where the facial expressions E_i and E_j simultaneously render mesh, and at those time instants when the concurrency actually occurs.

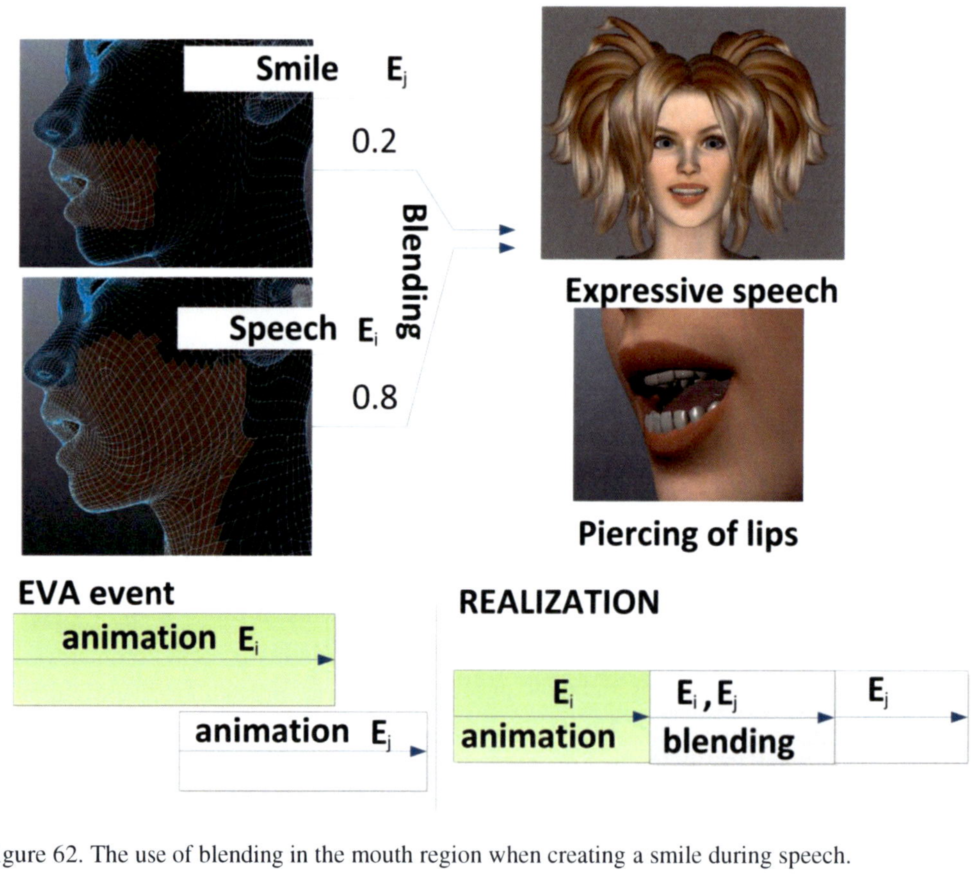

Figure 62. The use of blending in the mouth region when creating a smile during speech.

The masking concept represents an asymmetrical communicative function that is expressed by means of the direct simultaneousness of facial expressions E_i and E_j, and by using weights. The final facial image depends largely on the choice of basic facial expression and is in general not the same as when for the basic expression E_i ($E_C = M\{u_i * E_i, u_j{*}E_j\}; u_i > u_j$) is selected, or for the basic expression E_j ($E_C = M\{u_j * E_j, u_i{*}E_i\}; u_i < u_j$) is selected. Due to the fact that the facial expressions for a negative context are more prominent in the upper face region (eyes, eyebrows), and the facial expressions for a positive context in the lower face region (lips, cheekbones) (Ekman & Friesen, 1982; 1969), in the EVA-framework additional rules are embedded regarding weighting in these regions. Let E_i represent a positive facial expression using a weight u_i, and let E_j represent a negative facial expression using weight u_j. Furthermore, let be $u_i > u_j$. Then the following complex expression E_C: $\{E_i, E_j\}$ can be described for the lower face region as: $E_{c|lower\_part}$ with blending $M\{u_i * E_i, u_j{*}E_j\}$, and for the upper face region as: $E_{c|upper\_part}$ with blending $M\{u_j * E_i, u_i{*}E_j\}$. In this way, the asymmetric complex expression E_C: $\{E_j, E_i\}$ (when the basic expression is a negative facial expression and $u_i < u_j$) can be described in the lower face region as: $M\{u_i * E_j, u_j{*}E_i\}$, and in the dominant upper face region as: $M\{u_j * E_j, u_i{*}E_i\}$. In the context of EVA-Script, the basic facial expression represents the first occurrence of the *<fgesture>* tag, the corresponding weight attribute *blending*, and the intensity of the facial expression *i*, the attribute *amplitude*. The modulated facial expression then represents the subsequent occurrences of *<fgesture>* tags. Nevertheless, based on definitions in the dictionary, the simultaneousness of up to two facial expressions and speech is currently allowed. The masking in the framework is realized by using conditional adjustments of dimensions of expressiveness within facial regions, named as the power of FAP elemental controllers. It is integrated into the rendering module's core in the form of the animation blending technique. Basically, this effect can be set using the following pseudocode:

```
actor.setControlEffect('Ei', ui)
actor.setControlEffect('Ej', uj)
```

In order to use weights u_i and u_j for blending those regions during transformation from the procedural description into animation intervals, the values of FAP elemental controllers that compose individual facial expressions have to be adapted according to the specified masking rules. Let $F_i^{(E_i)}$ represent a set of those FAP elemental movement controllers that are used to form a positive facial expression E_i, and let $F_i^{(E_j)}$ represent a set of those FAP elemental movement controllers that form a negative facial expression E_j. Furthermore, let E_i and E_j last for durations t_i and t_j, where E_j is delayed for t_d. Then the animation of complex facial expression E_C can be described as: $M\{u_i * E_i, u_j * E_j)$ and can be represented as a sequence of the following *Lerp* intervals:

$$x_1' = Lerp(t_d, 0, i_i \cdot x_{F_i^{(E_i)}}) \tag{52}$$

$$\begin{aligned} x_2' &= Lerp_{lower\_region}(t_1 - t_d, u_i \cdot i_i \cdot x_{F_i^{(E_i)}}, u_j \cdot i_j \cdot x_{F_i^{(E_j)}}) \\ &+ Lerp_{upper\_region}(t_1 - t_d, u_j \cdot i_j \cdot x_{F_i^{(E_i)}}, u_i \cdot i_j \cdot x_{F_i^{(E_j)}}) \end{aligned} \tag{53}$$

$$x_3' = Lerp(t_2 - (t_1 - t_d), 0, i_j \cdot x_{F_i^{(E_j)}}) \tag{54}$$

When the face region is affected only by the *Lerp* interval x_1', (this is the time delay of E_j, t_d), then the blending is affected only by E_i, which can be described as a function of elemental controllers *FAP* ($x_{F_i^{(E_i)}}$) which is modulated by a weight u_i. Furthermore, when only *Lerp* interval x_3' is active (after the expiration of x_1'), only facial expression E_j affects the blending, which can be described as a function of elemental controllers *FAP* ($x_{F_i^{(E_j)}}$) which is modulated by a weight u_j. Actually, the blending happens when both facial expressions are active (x_2'). It can be described as the blending of those regions that consist of the following *Lerp* intervals: $Lerp_{lower\_part}$ and $Lerp_{upper\_part}$. The overlapping concept does not represent an asymmetric communicative function. It is expressed through the simultaneousness of facial expressions E_i and E_j, and can be adjusted by using even weights ($u_i = u_j$, e.g., 0.5). Therefore, the corresponding complex facial expression may be defined without any additional rules as: $E_C = S\{u{*}E_i, u{*}E_j\}; u = 0.5$. The modulation of E_i with E_j returns the same shape as the modulation of E_j with E_i, while the final shape depends mainly on the factors regarding the intensity of the individual facial expression. In the EVA-framework, the overlapping can be performed by using e.g., the following blending definitions:

```
actor.setControlEffect('Ei', 0.5)
actor.setControlEffect('Ej', 0.5)
```

During the transformation phase from a procedural description into the animation intervals (following the overlapping rules), the values of FAP elemental controllers are adapted based on the intensity of facial expression (the direct adaptation of expressive power dimension). The blending of regions is not necessary; therefore, the animation intervals, as presented in masking, can be defined as follows:

$$x_1' = Lerp(t_d, 0, i_i \cdot x_{F_i^{(E_i)}}) \tag{55}$$

$$x_2' = Lerp(t_1 - t_d, 0, i_i \cdot x_{F_i^{(E_i)}}) + Lerp(t_1 - t_d, 0, i_j \cdot x_{F_i^{(E_j)}}) \tag{56}$$

$$x_3' = Lerp(t_2 - (t_1 - t_d), 0, i_j \cdot x_{F_i^{(E_j)}}) \tag{57}$$

The values of i_i and i_j are obtained from the values of attribute *amplitude* (as in masking). By using animation blending, modulations of overlapping (S) and masking (M), the EVA-framework considers emotions and facial expressions as complex expressive facial characteristics. Furthermore, an individual emotion/facial expression is presented in the form of greater or lesser intensity, or as a set of blended basic and modulated facial expressions E. Some possible realizations are shown in Figure 63.

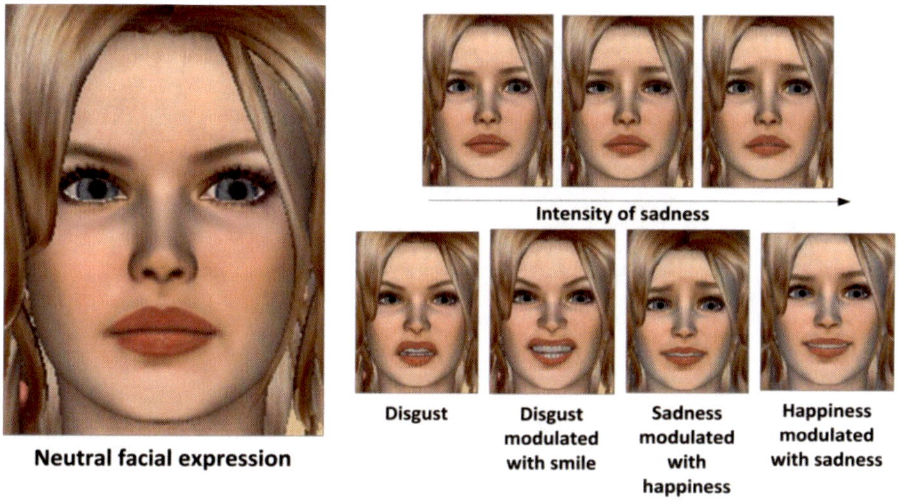

Figure 63. The modulated facial expressions in the EVA-framework.

On the left-hand side of Figure 63 the so-called neutral facial expression is shown. The right upper side of the figure then presents the modulated facial expressions using different intensities for basic emotions such as *sadness*, the overlapping of the *disgust* emotion and the facial expression representing a *smile*, and the masking of the two basic emotions of *sadness* and *happiness* (e.g., sadness that is modulated with happiness, and happiness that is modulated with sadness).

THE REALIZATION OF HEAD GESTURES AND GAZE

Head movements, according to MPEG-4 BAP, can be described with the DOF (3D rotational vector) vector of the neck joint. In general, the head can be moved in a few simple directions (*left*, *right*, *up*, *down*), or in several complex combinations of basic directions (e.g., *left - top*, *right - bottom*, etc.). The gestures that are performed by the head can be described in the EVA-framework with a modulated sequence of head poses P (that can be modulated using the power dimension), which describes the following rotational vector of the neck joint, $Rv = (H,P,R)$. Therefore, the negation can be described as a modulated (regarding time) and repeatable sequence of the following poses: *movement to the left* (P_1) and *movement to the right* (P_2), or as: $\{u*P_1, u*P_2, u*P_1, u*P_2, u*P_1, u*P_2\}$, or even expressively (using the repeatability dimension) with a modulated sequence of poses (regarding time) *movement to the left* (P_1), followed by *movement to the right* (P_2), which has to be repeated n times: $\{n,\{u*P_1, u*P_2\}\}$. Also, in the case of direct addressing, head nodding $u*P_1$, $u*P_2$ can also be performed in the time domain, or also in the power domain. However, when the head nodding is described as a function of time, intensity, and repeatability, the movement has to be split into n intervals, while on each interval the local adaptation regarding time has to be performed. In this manner it is possible for these movements to be different in terms of kinematics, and for head nodding movements not just to be a sequence of identical movements.

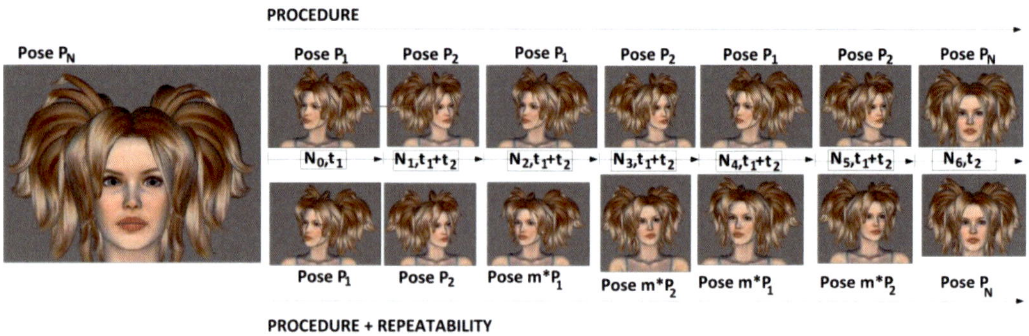

Figure 64. Several modulations of head gesture 'shake.'

Let the pose P_1 represent *movement to the left* at a time t_1, the pose P_2 *movement to the right* in time t_2, and let the repeatability of movement be N = 3. Then the transition $P_1 \rightarrow P_2$ will be performed exactly 3 times, and can be procedurally described as a sequence of the following intervals:

N_0: $P_N \rightarrow P_1$, t_1,
N_1: $P_1 \rightarrow P_2$, $t_1 + t_2$,
N_2: $P_2 \rightarrow P_1$, $t_1 + t_2$,
N_3: $P_1 \rightarrow P_2$, $t_1 + t_2$,
N_4: $P_2 \rightarrow P_1$, $t_1 + t_2$,
N_5: $P_1 \rightarrow P_2$, $t_1 + t_2$
N_6: $P_2 \rightarrow P_N$, t_2.

Figure 64 presents the exchange and transitions between poses P_1 and P_2 (*procedure*). When describing an animation using EVA-Script, the animation intervals are represented as a sequence of six alternating *<BAP>* tags, named as P_1 and P_2, which are contained within *<bgesture>* tag with type *head* (without attribute *repeatability*). Head shaking can also be described as a combination of procedure and repeatability. Furthermore, in the context of EVA-Script animation the same animation intervals can be represented as a sequence of two *<BAP>* tags, named P_1 and P_2, which is contained within *<bgesture>* tags with type *head* and *repeatability* attribute with value 3. Namely, when using the *repeatability* attribute, the EVA-framework automatically forms similar animation intervals, and modulates poses P_1 and P_2 by using the modulation parameter *m*, which is calculated as *Rand (-0.4, 0.4)*. The parameter *m* ensures that the modulated pose $P + m*P$ is located between the neutral position and the position defined by *P*, wherein the maximum retraction is still 40% and the modulated pose still meets the physical limitations regarding the neck (must stay within the allowed *DOF* values). Figure 64 presents the automatic modulation of the gesture for head shaking (including *procedure + repeatability*). Nevertheless, for the animation seven animation intervals still have to be defined to keep the proper temporal characteristics. These intervals can be described as:

N_0: $P_N \rightarrow P_1$, t_1,
N_1: $P_1 \rightarrow P_2$, $t_1 + t_2$,
N_2: $P_2{*}P_2 \rightarrow P_1 + m_{1,1} * P_1$, $t_1 + t_2$,
N_3: $P_1 + m_{1,1} * P_1 \rightarrow P_2 + m_{2,1}$, $t_1 + t_2$,

N_4: $P_2 + m_{2,1} \rightarrow P_1 + m_{1,2} * P_1, t_1 + t_2,$
N_5: $P_1 + m_{1,2} * P_1 \rightarrow P_2 + m_{2,2} * P_2, t_1 + t_2$
N_6: $P_2 + m_{2,2} * P_2 \rightarrow P_N, t_2.$

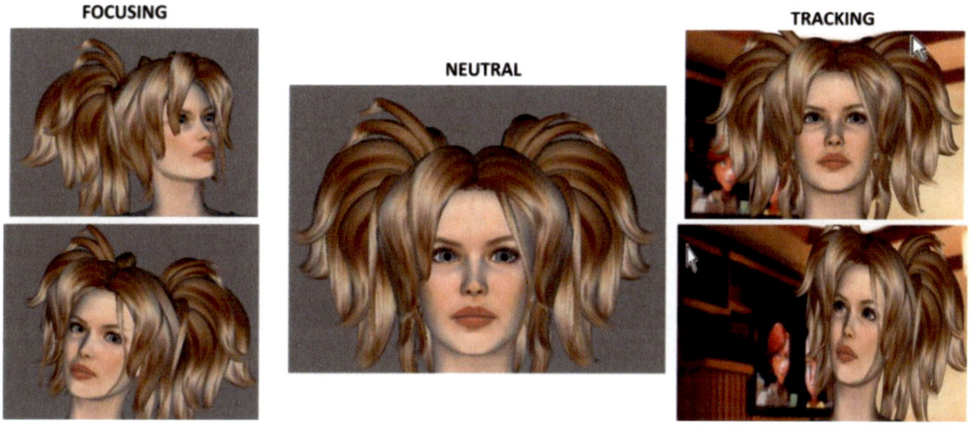

Figure 65. The realization of *focusing* and *tracking* types of automatic gaze in EVA-framework.

The cyclic movement that reflects the changes in kinematics within individual cycles can be represented as a much more natural and realistic behavior. In the abovementioned cases, irrespective of the selection of the description for head shaking, the attribute *gaze* has not yet been specified. In Figure 64, the orientation of the eyes depends directly on the configuration of the neck joint (or on the forward kinematics mechanisms). Given that the gaze plays an important role regarding naturalness, emotion (Lance & Marsella, 2010), or co-verbal behavior, dependent on the text (and speech) (Pelachaud & Bilvi, 2003), the EVA-framework supports two types of automatic gaze; namely, *tracking* and *focusing*. The *tracking* type accounts for those eye movements and the automatic adjustment of the neck that depend on the position of the observed object. And the *focusing* type accounts for the adaptation and movement of the eyes to look toward a certain point, regardless of the configuration of the neck joint. In the case of the *focusing* type, we need to make sure that the eyes are focused on a specific point in space. In the EVA-framework it is assumed that in the case of user interfaces, the user is situated in front of the screen. If there exists a focus on something, then this is directed toward the user, which is in the central point (0,0,0). The automatic modulation of the eyes regarding focusing represents the eye movement in the direction that is the opposite (negative) to the head movement, and is adapted by using the corrective factor *e*. The corrective factor *e* is defined as the degree of the neck joint rotation's effect on the rotation of the eye joints. The *focusing* type is shown in Figure 65.

In the case of the *tracking* type, it is assumed that the focused object's position is constantly changing. Therefore, it is necessary to simultaneously modulate both the eye joints and the neck joint. The tracking of an object in the EVA-framework (e.g., a mouse pointer on the screen) is shown in Figure 65. In order to perform modulation, the spatial position of the mouse pointer first has to be obtained (as 3D point (x, y, z)). This is carried out e.g., as follows:

```
mpos = base.mouseWatcherNode.getMouse()
x = mpos.getX()
```

y = mpos.getY()
z = mpos.getZ()

The spatial position *(x, y, z)* then has to be converted into a rotation vector *(H, P, R)* for the neck, and left and right eye joints. This is performed by using the correction factor *e*, which defines the virtual mechanism of the inverse kinematics and describes how each joint should be configured in order that the gaze will be directed into the specific spatial position. The individual component of the rotation vector is calculated as the scalar product of vector *r* (for position), and the correction factor *e*:

$$(H, \vec{P}, R) = (x, \vec{y}, z) \cdot (e_x, \vec{e_y}, e_z) \tag{58}$$

The correction factors for the animated neck joint and animated eye joints are defined experimentally. For the EVA-framework and EVA agent 3D model, the correction factors *e* are suggested to be: (25, -75, 10) for the neck joint, (55, -25, 5) for the right eye joint, and (-55, -25, 5) for the left eye joint.

THE REALIZATION OF SUBCONSCIOUS BEHAVIOR

Subconscious behavior basically represents the background animation. Namely, this behavior represents those movements that are performed by a person on the subconscious level. In most cases, subconscious behavior is e.g., spontaneous blinking and breathing, which can be realized based on statistically defined timing for breaths and blinking. Namely, researchers (Stern et al., 1994; Clark & von Euler, 1972; Barbato et al., 2000) have proposed several concepts that define those key factors of subconscious behavior which represent cyclical and periodic behavior. Subconscious blinking, for example, represents the cyclical closing of eyelids which is modulated regarding time. Therefore, the algorithm for automatic blinking generates each blink in the form of four animation intervals that address the following FAP parameters: FAP19 -FAP22. The first animation interval is used for the closing of the eyelids in time t_Z. The second animation interval is then used for holding eyelids in the closure state for time t_H. The third interval is used for opening the eyelids in time t_O. And the fourth animation interval is used for the transition to the subsequent blink in time t_I. In the EVA-framework, it is assumed that the eyelids can be closed and opened in virtual random time intervals. Thus, the eyelid may need a random time t_Z for the closing animation interval; it may then remain closed again for random time t_H, and then re-open again in random time t_O. Furthermore, the time t_I can also be random between the animation intervals used for blinking. Randomness is generally undesirable for conversational agents. Therefore, in the EVA-framework these animation intervals of individual phases are limited to those intervals, as proposed by Bentivoglio et al. (1997) and Carney and Hill (1982). Therefore, the first animation interval's duration is selected from [57.000, 69.000] ms; the second interval's duration from [0.200, 3.200] ms; the third interval's duration from [133.360, 143.360] ms; and the fourth animation interval's duration from [2.000.000, 4.548.000] ms.

Chapter 9

THE EXPRESSIVE MODEL AND MULTIMODAL USER INTERFACES

INTRODUCTION

The multimodal user interfaces should be simple, more intuitive, and should adapt to people's abilities with regard to the processing of natural and cognitive information and presentations. Nowadays, there are several systems with multimodal interfaces that are based on human-machine interaction. These provide a more natural and more advanced exchange of information between man and machine. The integration of web solutions and natural modalities can also provide a more effective solution for those users who want access to services and web content in a human and more natural way. The MWP (multimodal web platform) platform proposed by Mlakar and Rojc (2013) allows for an easy and flexible migration from traditional and closed systems to multimodal ones. Namely, the MWP platform solves the issues that affect interoperability, compatibility, and integration problems, which usually accompany migration from standard applications to web applications and networks with several services, and also allows the upgrade of general web interfaces with new modalities, in order to provide a more natural and more advanced communication and information exchange. By using the MWP platform, the integration of the user's frontend with new modalities requires little extra work. Namely, the integration is carried out within the user frontend, while preserving the web application's code and its functionality intact. The MWP platform is a system whereby all of the modules comprise a generic network-based architecture. Often, for multi-modal systems several (mostly network-based) architectures are used that host the technology for performing/analyzing natural modalities. Dedicated web interfaces are used for presenting the information to the user using some web browser, using some scenario-based web application servers, or using several client-based APIs (or some non-web desktop/mobile applications). The current state of the art in mobile and desktop-based web solutions mainly follows these guidelines:

- Renewed development (or new development) of web applications/services, in order to adapt them to the specific multimodal architecture. The data between web and non-web processes are passed via an application core, and by using client-side scripts;

- The development of applications for rendering (e.g., multimodal web browsers), which will present web content and exchange data between web and non-web cores;
- Minimizing the work through integration/renewed development, and through the minimization of the modal-dependent services (natural modalities).

The solution presented in this book is based on network-based processing regarding natural modalities, and the use of web application servers in the role of meditator between web and non-web contents. Furthermore, natural modalities can be integrated into established web applications and services as additional functionality (e.g., integration of web applications into multimodal core). The proposed approach is also compatible with several web browsers (e.g., Opera, FireFox, Internet Explorer, Chrome, etc.), since no ActiveX or browser-dependent controllers are used. Also, the code and corresponding logic inside web applications can remain unchanged. Namely, the fusion of natural modalities and web content is carried out via the client interface and dialogue manager. The client interface can be implemented based on Java API and context-aware JavaScript APIs. Communication between web and non-web services is realized based on general web application, and can be used with practically any web application and fused with those natural modalities, hosted by the multimodal platform somewhere in the network. In order to minimize the workload regarding the integration process, and to enable the integration of modalities into web application, the following set of features for the so-called MWP platform has been proposed:

- the use of target technologies for the processing/generation of natural modalities (e.g., visual speech synthesis on general texts, which can be utilized for any type/context of HCI interaction - HMI interfaces, and also for web applications),
- the use of principles of distributivity. By using inter-domain protocol interaction, we are able to extend the scope of traditional web applications with technologies that are traditionally unseen to web domain (e.g., TTS, ECA, ASR, etc.),
- the effective integration process on the client side with advanced human-machine interfaces and established web applications. The MWP platform does not increase the load on available web application servers, and does not require the re-programming of established web applications,
- integration on the client side is based on IFRAME encapsulation and Javascript based on inter-domain communication.

The MWP Platform

The MWP platform's architecture is presented in Figure 66 (Mlakar and Rojc, 2013). It has been developed for the fusion of web and non-web technologies within advanced multimodal web interface. The MWP platform includes the following modules:

- *EVA-plugin*: is designed for information storage and presentation. It is a standalone web page, or web application.
- *MWP platform core*: it is a Tomcat-based web application that has the role of an intermediate layer and acts as an interface between web and non-web layers.

- *DATA system (Rojc and Mlakar, 2009)*: is actually a set of network-based servers that are designed for generating/processing different natural modalities.

The MWP platform fuses web interfaces (e.g., web applications' frontend) with network-based DATA servers used for the processing/generation of natural modalities. The platform is, therefore, able to communicate with both the web user interface as well as DATA servers. The web layer in the MWP architecture is used for integrating any web application, corresponding user interface, or web EVA-plugin. Here, the EVA-plugin is a dedicated plugin used for integration on the client side, and for data exchange between the web user interface and the MWP platform. DATA servers offer the following multimodal services: *text-to-speech synthesis* (TTS-based server), *expressive ECA* (ECA server), *HCI dialogue manager* (DM server), and *automatic speech recognition* (ASR server). The MWP architecture integrates middleware software, i.e., the so-called application core. Furthermore, the MWP layers communicate with each other using standard protocols, such as HTTP and Ajax, which are usually used in web applications, and use TCP/IP based DATA protocol in order to communicate with DATA servers.

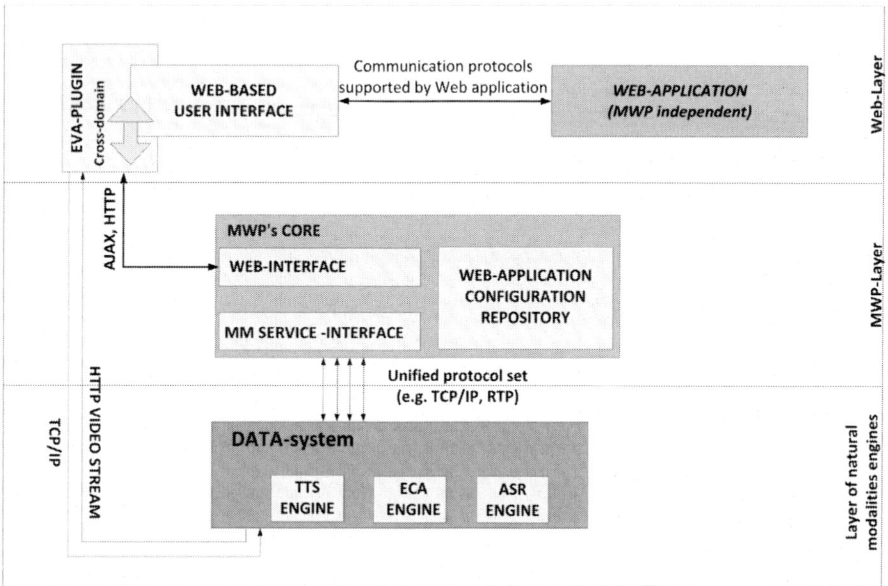

Figure 66. The MWP architecture.

The EVA Plugin

The major advantage of the MWP platform's concept represents the integration on the client side. In order to bring together several (and in general incompatible) technologies, we decided to develop an interface platform that was able to run on external dedicated web servers. Any such web interface server can host one or more web applications. In this way, unwanted extra load on web applications' servers (web content and services) is prevented. In order to provide complete web compatibility, the MWP platform is implemented as a web application, together with the EVA plugin frontend. Furthermore, the EVA plugin encapsulates the user interface of the corresponding web application. Integration on the server side has been avoided for the following reasons:

- The information exchange, simultaneously through multiple channels, depends on the user and its hardware (which information channels are desired/supported). Web application servers are (in the context of our work and the integration of modalities) service providers; therefore, they should preserve their original form.
- Depending on the coding style and features of the web application's architecture, the integration workload can increase exponentially when the integration is performed on the server's side.
- The web application server's load should not be increased due to the integration of some new modality. Because we want to support any web-based application that runs on any hardware, such a goal is necessary.

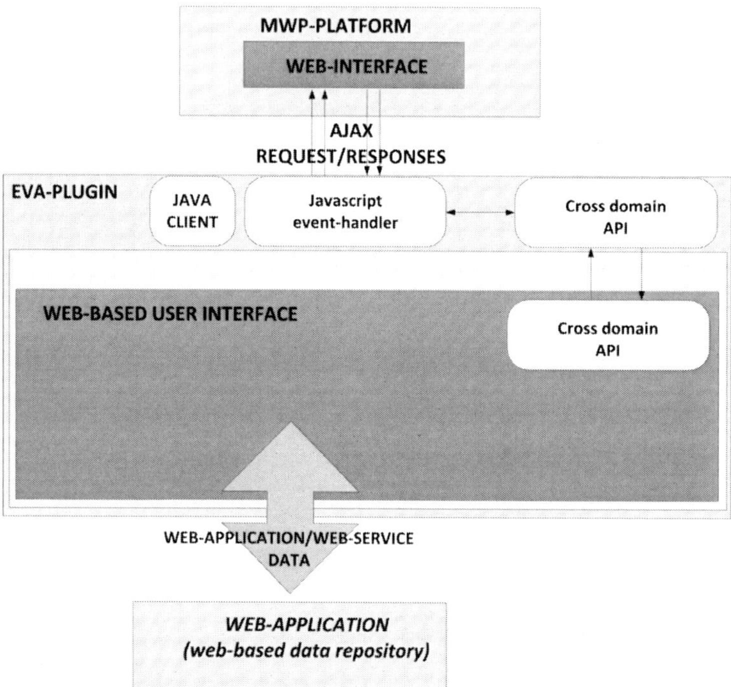

Figure 67. The EVA plugin's architecture.

The EVA plugin shown in Figure 67 is a user frontend with no (or minimal) graphic elements. Its design includes:

- web-based video player (e.g., Flash Player),
- IFRAME: used for encapsulating the user interface of the existing web applications,
- JavaScript event manager: JavaScript API used for communication between domains based on IFRAME (Chatti et al., 2011), and
- simple Java client: the so-called DATA client used for two-way communication between the distributive DATA system and the user's frontend (serving e.g., TTS, ECA, ASR, or e.g., gesture recognition).

As can be seen in Figure 67, the concept of the web layer and the EVA plugin in the MWP platform is to integrate web content from at least two sources; namely, from the web application and from the user's interface. Nevertheless, the major issue regarding the integration then represents the traditional web security model used for data retrieval from some application. In order to avoid this security model, therefore, the inter-domain API has been implemented, used for inter-domain communication with the Javascript code. The same policy also protects those HTML documents that are deposited (accessed) by JavaScript, and originating within the foreign domain. However, this policy does not apply to those scripts that can be loaded from other domains and are executed with the privileges of those pages that they include. Thus, the inter-domain API has to be integrated into the EVA-plugin and into the web user interface. The function of the inter-domain API is, therefore, to redirect events from one domain into another. For example, when a user wants a corresponding multimodal output (a speaking ECA) to be generated for the selected text, the DATA servers obtain that text (it is sent to TTS and ECA servers) using the proposed web user interface's inter-domain API. Furthermore, this event is also passed to the inter-domain-based EVA plugin, using the appropriate function call (e.g., by *ReadSelectedText ()* action, the *ProcessReadRequest()*action in the EVA–plugin is triggered). The inter-domain API includes several JavaScript-based events that occur in the user's web application interface (e.g., clicking the mouse, changing the URL address, selecting the text, etc.), and are forwarded in real time to the inter-domain API within the EVA plugin. The inter-domain API-based EVA-plugin, therefore, serves as a transponder. Namely, it receives and forwards messages to the JavaScript-based event manager, or to the cross-domain API within the web user interface. The JavaScript event manager processes and forwards several requirements/actions to the web interface, or to the cross-domain API within the EVA plugin. The event manager is implemented in jQuery[1]. It includes the procedures on the client side for Ajax communication with the MWP-based application core, the Ajax/HTTP event listener, and the events processor that manages the cross-domain and Ajax/HTTP events.

The Multi-Threaded MWP Core

The MWP core in Figure 68 is actually a web application based on Tomcat that interfaces the MWP platform with the DATA system. As can be seen, the core includes: *web interface*, *web-application configuration repository*, and *MM service-interface*. The web interface includes the EVA plugin and back-end for the administrator interface. The back-end can be used e.g., to configure the MWP platform (its users, user groups, and devices), and to set the relationships between actions of user/web services (as implemented/provided by the corresponding web application), and multi-modal responses that are carried out by the MWP platform. The repository for configuring the web application is implemented by using the MySQL database, which keeps the following information:

[1] http://jquery.com/

- *user settings* (user information, the gesticulation level during speaking, the co-articulation level and pronunciation speed, the gender of the ECA agent, and other customizable settings ...),
- *multimodal services for the specific user* (availability of ASR, TTS, ECA– service),
- *characteristics of users' devices* (supported web video players, web browsers, display resolution on devices, network interfaces, multi-modal services, to visualize the complete ECA agent or only the head, etc.).
- *interaction scenario*, as generated for the specific web application (e.g., the user's action/web service, described in the form of a dialogue scenario, and corresponding configuration).

All settings and HCI scenarios are added to the repository used for configuring web applications by using the administrator interface that is part of the back-end of the MWP platform. The core is the web application multi-threaded architecture. The *MM Service-Interface* module implements interfaces that allow web applications to communicate with the distributed architecture of the DATA system. Furthermore, it is a server that can simultaneously communicate with several clients, and includes several protocols and procedures for the low-level distributed transmission of data. Its main tasks are: process protocols on the network and incoming/outgoing messages between the Web interface and the DATA system. This module, therefore, interprets the messages sent by the Javascript event manager, and responds through suitable communication packages for the DATA system that are forwarded to the main DATA server. The MM Service-Interface module also generates and sends Ajax/HTTP responses to the JavaScript event manager. In this way, this module does most of the work in the background.

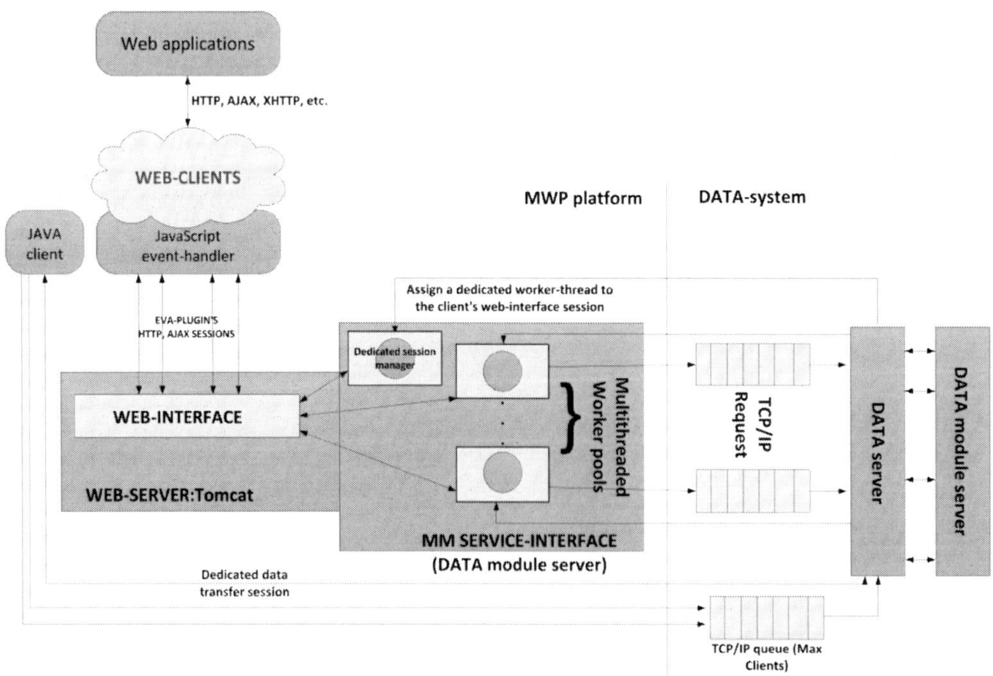

Figure 68. The multi-threaded architecture of the MWP platform's core.

The integration of web clients is a 2-stage process. Firstly, the client device and corresponding user interface register in the DATA system. The registration of the client device is performed by the Java client, while the user interface is registered by the EVA plugin using the JavaScript event manager. Any registration request issued by the client device is stored in the TCP/IP queue, and each registration request issued by the user interface is stored in the dedicated session manager. Secondly (when the maximum number of registered clients is not yet exceeded), the DATA system creates several working threads. In Figure 68, each working thread is represented as a "station." And each "station" is then interfaced with those HTTP sessions that belong to the user's device, and those TCP/IP sessions that connect it with the DATA system. The maximum number of allowed sessions depends on the load of the DATA system, while the service's response time depends on the time spent by processes within the DATA system. Once the registration process is completed, and the appropriate station is created, the DATA system establishes additional sessions for transferring data. Additional sessions may depend on used/integrated modalities (e.g., RTP session for ECA server, audio transmissions over TCP/IP session for ASR server, etc.). When a specific "station" cannot be created, then the user will not be able to use any modality within the web server, but will remain supported with all of the other standard functionalities of web applications. The "station" is automatically released when the HTTP session on the user's device is completed.

The Sub-System for Network-Based Distributed Multimodal Processing – DATA Framework

The DATA system in Figure 69 is actually a multimodal services provider for desktop or remote applications (web applications). The system consists of several servers (clusters), while each operates independently, and all use a common communication protocol.

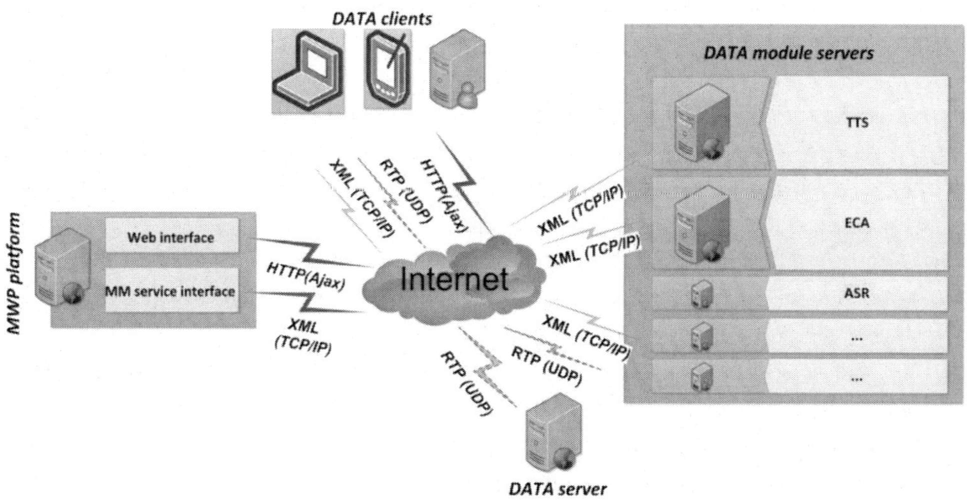

Figure 69. The DATA system's client/server architecture.

DATA servers are implemented in Java, and contain several Java modules and frameworks needed in order to manage TCP/IP communication, management of protocols, wrapping native code (C/C++) into Java, creating, compiling, validating and management of protocols' FSMs, integration with databases, parsing and creating XML documents, capture/transfer audio/video data over the Internet etc.

As can be seen, the DATA system is a TCP/IP-based client/server architecture, which consists of a main DATA server and several DATA modular servers. Each service needs a dedicated modular server. The DATA server represents the core and manages all communication between clients and modular servers. Furthermore, it can serve several modular server and clients. One can imagine an arbitrary server's configuration, which can be specified in the form of several XML files. All DATA module servers respond to users via the DATA server. The communication between the servers of the DATA system is flexibly and efficiently described and implemented in the form of finite-state machines (FSM) (Mohri et al., 1996). These protocol-based FSMs are implemented using the UniMod framework (Weyns et al., 2007; Shalyto, 2001). This framework has already defined objects for constructing and running the final-state machines, and needs only graph-based scenario descriptions in XML format, which have to be created off-line in accordance with the desired and expected operation of the DATA system and the MWP platform.

The integration of new modalities into the DATA system (representing the complex multimodal platform) is very flexible. Namely, for the integration of a new modality, only the additional DATA modular server has to be included. Therefore, it is not necessary to interfere in the code of the server, or develop any extra APIs. Each DATA server includes a set of pre-defined numbers of working threads, which are available for establishing the MWP sessions with clients. All of the client's connections are forwarded through the DATA server to individual modular servers in accordance with the HCI scenario of the DATA multimodal platform. When connections are established, the servers establish a MWP session. This session is active as long as the client's multimodal user interface is active. If there are no more available working threads on the DATA system, the DATA server rejects further requests until some MWP session ends. The following communication interfaces take care of the communication with the DATA system through the MWP platform:

- *Java-based DATA client*: establishes audio communication for: web user interface ← → DATA system. It is integrated into the EVA-plugin and is implemented as a web service. Furthermore, it is used to register the user's device on the DATA system, and to facilitate the exchange of data streams (e.g., a video stream for speaking ECA, and audio stream for the ASR, etc.) in the DATA system,
- *Interface for multimodal services (MM service interface)*: is integrated into the MWP layer, and provides the following communication: MWP platform ← → DATA system. It serves as a low-level interface and allows a web application to use and incorporate any modality that the DATA system serves. Functionally, the interface behaves like any DATA modular servers. For each DATA client that is connected to the DATA system, a dedicated TCP/IP session is created in this interface. The session's life cycle ends when the connection is broken by the DATA client or by the web interface on the device.

MERGING SEVERAL TECHNOLOGIES FOR THE MULTIMODAL USER INTERFACE

The main idea of the MWP platform is to provide the possibility that web applications are integrated with multimodal services, which can bring additional communication channels to web services. For example, TTS, ASR, ECA, etc. servers serve those technologies that are proven to deliver a more natural experience in communication, when they are included in web applications. The MWP platform includes modules that can communicate with web applications, as well as components that can communicate with the DATA system. In the following, we focus both on the integration process and on configuration possibilities. The main components that are involved in the integration are:

- application-specific inter-domain API,
- application non-specific web application that drives the MWP core,
- application-specific configuration repository that is part of the given web application that drives the core of the MWP.

Integration on the User's Side

Let us have a web page for an online store, which we want to personalize with ASR and a speaking and emotional ECA. The new multimodalities in this case are served by ECA, TTS, and ASR server, which enable users to use speech as input. Firstly, the cross-domain APIs have to be defined. The cross-domain API, integrated in the back-end of the web page for the online store, implements the *listener*, which reports to the MWP platform, whose page is at any given instant shown to the user, or whose elements in the web user interface are selected. Additionally, it contains a method that allows jQuery selectors to determine whether to transfer web data into the MWP platform, or whether to fill certain fields in the HTML form (e.g., checkbox, text field, triggering mouse events, etc.). The cross-domain API integrated into the EVA-plugin consequently implements the converter of *HTTP requests* and *HTTP listener*. The converter of *HTTP requests* converts Ajax responses (which are processed by the event manager) into the corresponding actions on the side of the user interface. These actions are, for example, load URI, insert something into the text field object used for searching, simulate a button click for performing a search, and extending the jQuery selector for selecting products' titles, etc. Also, there is the *HTTP listener*, which is operated by the event manager and listens and processes all events generated by the cross-domain API. These events are responses to *HTTP requests*, e.g., addresses which must be read, or events reporting modified URI, etc. The event manager is general and can be used in any web application. After the cross-domain APIs are configured and integrated, we can proceed with the integration process. Namely, the IFRAME of the EVA-plugin has to be suitably configured in order to point to the domain of the online store. In this way, the front-end of the MWP platform is prepared and the online store is encapsulated. The MWP platform can now exchange data with the online store; the new multimodal user interface includes a web-video player for displaying ECA, and the Java client captures and transfers audio to the ASR server (without altering the front-end of the online store). The second step of the integration then involves the adaptation/configuration of the MWP core to meet the requirements of the online store (the context), and the generation of proper HCI scenarios.

The Configuration of the MWP Platform and Possible HCI Scenarios for the Web Domain

The repository for the configuration of web applications and UI back-end of the web interface are needed in the second step of the integration. The combination of both is used for specifying different settings (e.g., for devices and their properties, properties for users and applications, etc.), and for specifying several interaction scenarios (even considering the use of different modalities). The HCI scenarios, therefore, define how the web user interface should respond to user actions (e.g., load-specific URI, the user issues a request, etc.).

Figure 70 represents the concept of describing some HCI scenario when using the MWP platform. Let us assume that any page (URI) of the web application requires a specific interaction. Then, these interactions have to be described as a set of concurrent/consecutive tasks, where each task can be described by several configurations. Upon loading the selected URI, the following tasks have to be carried out (described in Figure 70):

- **Task:** synthesize and play out the introductory message by using the virtual agent ECA. The corresponding text is stored within the XML document that is used for describing the interaction scenario and is interpreted by the dialogue manager (DM) modular server. The DM server then performs corresponding tasks using TTS and ECA servers.
- **Task:** present sections' titles with short summaries to the user. This task has two sets of configurations. The first defines how the information about the titles and corresponding summaries should be obtained. The second defines whether the ECA server should create/use the whole body or just the head, the desired position of the web player (where on the screen to display the ECA) etc.
- **Task:** performs the text-to-speech synthesis process for all received data: this task is dependent on the available web information and dialogue flow when interacting with the user.

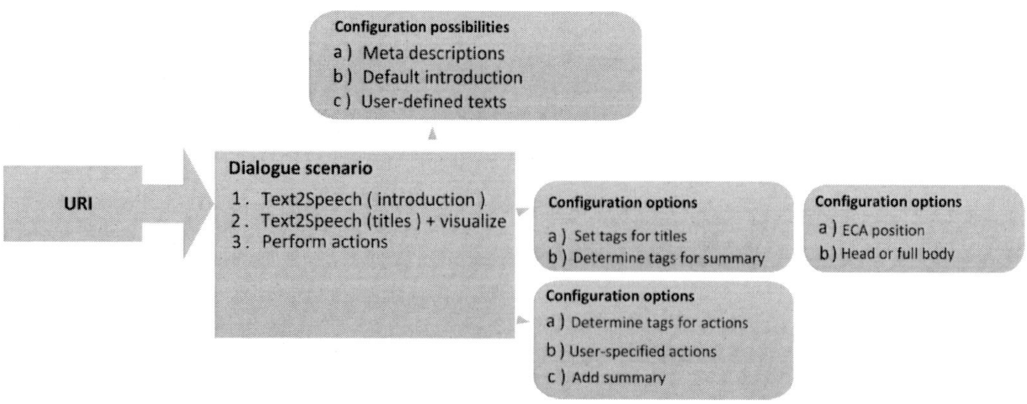

Figure 70. The development of the multimodal scenario for the selected URI location.

In this way, several HCI scenarios for web applications and web services can be defined. As shown, each XML-based HCI scenario can specify how the ECA should respond to events (e.g., when loading the website, or the user clicks something etc.). Furthermore, any key words (phrases) which should be recognized when using the user interface can be defined. Through the configuration of the MWP platform, by taking into account the specifications of the web application, and by describing HCI scenarios (off-line), the MWP platform can be flexibly adapted to the context of web applications. The last step of the integration represents the interface connection between the MWP platform and the DATA system.

The MWP Platform for Development of Multimodal User Interfaces

As already mentioned, the MWP platform can also be used in upgrading web applications e.g., for web portals. Let the DATA system in the following case host the TTS and ECA servers. The DATA system in this case should pre-process web data (to parse DOM structure, remove HTML tags, remove images and other data except text), and generate corresponding audio and co-verbal behavior for the ECA, which is part of the portal's GUI web application. The multimodal output further depends on the interaction scenario, which can be defined in the configuration repository. The portal's functional role can be e.g., an information kiosk that includes RSS feed technology, API Google translator, and some interfaces for controlling the intelligent environment. The fusion of web application and DATA system (web and non-web modalities) then results in a more advanced user interface. The architecture for this concept is presented in Figure 71.

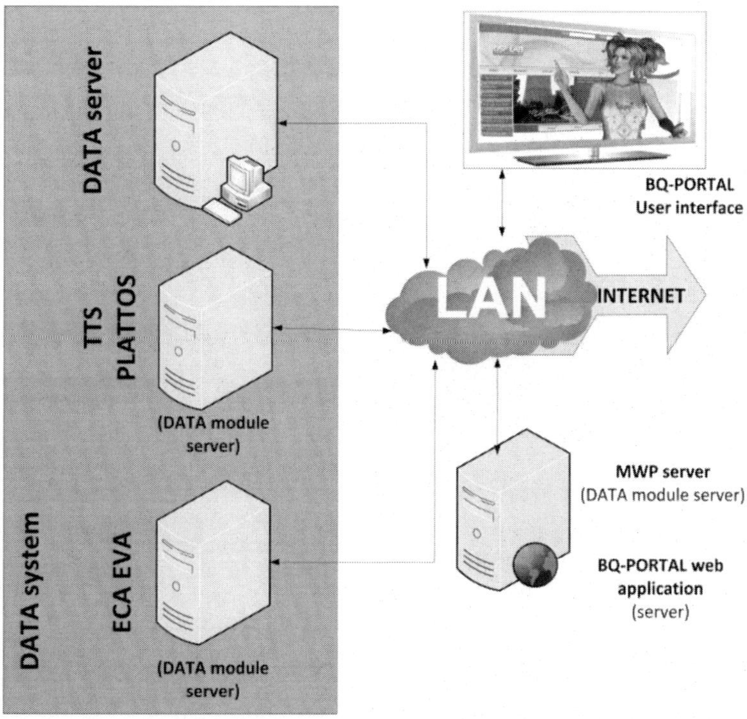

Figure 71. The integration of the MWP platform in some web application on the portal.

It consists of the following servers: the main DATA server, and two modular servers for the TTS and ECA engines. An additional server is used for the MWP platform and for running the web application. On the user's side, a user interface and DATA client are needed. The users on the portal are now able to receive web information via the speaking and emotional ECA EVA, with much better personalization of the portal, when interacting with the system (compared to just reading text on the web interface). In doing so, the ECA can interpret the text in several ways: automatically (when specified in the scenario script), manually (e.g., after clicking the button for reading something), or after selecting some text in a web application interface. Additionally, the ECA EVA generates complex co-verbal behavior (e.g., including lip-sync, facial emotional expressions, hand gestures, head and arm movements etc.), which even further contributes to a better user experience regarding communication with the portal.

Multimodal Service for Reading RSS News

RSS feeds are usually news, weather, sports, politics, etc. The MWP-based multimodal interface can easily extend this web service by, for example, reading these RSS feeds to the user, or even presenting them to the user by speaking through the ECA EVA, so that the content reaches users in the form of an affective speaking avatar (as can be seen in Figure 72). A simple interaction scenario could be in this case, for example, after the user selects a list of RSS feeds, the ECA EVA reads the text.

Figure 72. The multimodal RSS news reader based on the MWP platform.

In this case the ECA EVA greets the user and reads the available RSS feed titles, as well as their short summaries. The titles are kept inside HTML tags with attribute types = "title" and for = "RSS." The feed text that represents a summary of the news is kept in the "summary" tags with the attribute for = "RSS." The text can be synthesized into speech with added generated co-verbal behavior by the TTS and ECA server, resulting in appropriate animation presented to the user as an audio/video stream (see Figure 73).

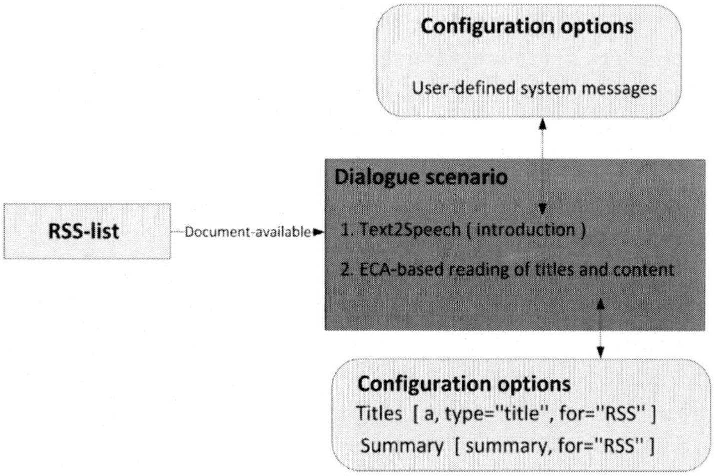

Figure 73: The web application based on the MWP platform for reading RSS news.

The Multimodal Machine Translation Service

In web applications, a machine translation service for selected text can be included e.g., by using Google Translator. The input text can be a text on a website, or is just a text entered by the user. This service can be triggered by simply selecting/entering some text, or by issuing a request via e.g., a "read" button. In Figure 74 the corresponding user interface is presented. After selecting/entering some text, it is first pre-processed and converted into ASCII or UTF-8 format (without HTML elements, etc.). Then it is forwarded to the API interface of the MWP platform which sends the text into the Google web interface used for translation. The response is then sent back to the DATA system, which synthesizes the speech with co-verbal behavior output, and plays the multimodal output back to the user.

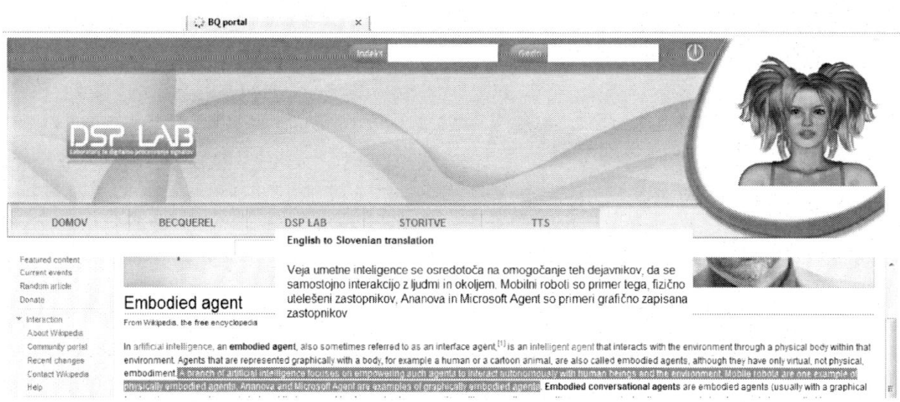

Figure 74. The machine translation service based on the MWP platform.

THE MULTIMODAL INTERFACE FOR UMB-SMARTTV SYSTEM

The main goal for using an expressive behavior generation system within the Smart TV systems is to achieve more natural and more human-like HCI interaction. When only TTS output is supported, the HCI interaction is still far less functional and less similar to general human-human interaction. Therefore, in order to better personalize Smart TV systems and to support more human-human-like interaction, the technology of virtual agents previously presented has also been integrated into UMB-SmartTV (Mlakar et al., 2013b). This results in more relevant sociological system responses, as shown also in WOZ tests. Within the UMB-SmartTV system, the proprietary TTS engine PLATTOS has been used (Rojc, 2003), which is capable of simultaneously generating speech and expressive communicative behavior, as proposed earlier in the book. The platforms for generating expressive co-verbal behavior are the TTS and ECA server in the DATA system. The synthesized speech and co-verbal behavior are then animated using the EVA-framework, and presented in the user interface of the UMB-SmartTV system.

In Figure 75 the complete architecture of the UMB-SmartTV built on the IMS infrastructure is presented. As can be seen, the system consists of STB, TV server, VOD server, IMS core, XCAP server (Kamailio (Maisonneuve et al., 2009; Kamailio, 2013)), a gateway for controlling devices in the environment (Raspberry PI), and the DATA system supporting the system with advanced multimodal services (ASR, TTS, ECA EVA). Furthermore, the UMB-SmartTV can be controlled by using standard devices (e.g., keyboard, mouse, remote controller, etc.), by using mobile devices (e.g., mobile phone, tablet), or speech. The VoD server, IMS core, XCAP server, and the TV server run on the Linux operating system (Ubuntu), but STB and DATA servers run on Windows systems.

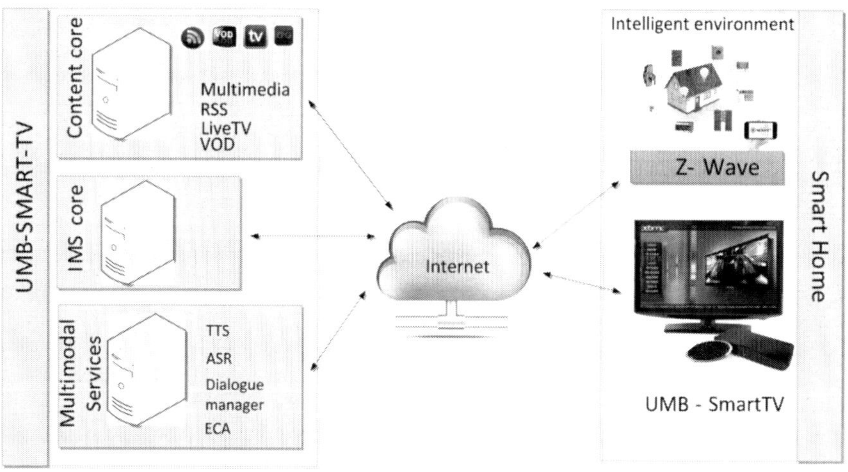

Figure 75. The architecture of the UMB-SmartTV.

In this way, the UMB-SmartTV presents a more advanced multimodal platform. The *Content core* module represents the application server that is responsible for the generation of the content and its presentation, such as: Live TV, VOD, RSS, etc. The services on the client side and GUI are implemented using the XBMC (Xbox Media Center). The IMS core implements standard IMS functionalities, such as: user registration, subscription management and billing, session management, triggering, routing, interaction with NGN services, and QoS control. The DATA system ensures the system with automatic speech recognition, speech synthesis, and the virtual agent EVA, controlling devices in the environment and, consequently, personalizes the UMBSmartTV system. Figure 76 presents a multimodal interface with conversational agent EVA in UMB-SmartTV.

Figure 76. The advanced multimodal output in the XBMC environment in the UMB-SmartTV.

Expressive Co-Verbal Behavior Generation for Artificial Bodies

Gestures, as part of visual perception and synchronized with verbal information, represent the key concept in human-human interaction. ECAs as well as artificial bodies are visual recreations of humans and, therefore, it is expected that their behavior in communication will also be as human-like as possible. Therefore, co-verbal behavior generation, as proposed in the book, must specify expressive behavior that resembles natural movements as far as possible; this is then animated by an ECA. As already explained, the visual content and content presentation is formulated based on linguistic features extracted from input text, and also on predicted prosodic features (e.g., accentuation, prosodic phrases, durations etc.). In this way, the algorithm is able to create the co-verbal behavior with a high degree of naturalness and is also applicable on artificial bodies, such as e.g., a humanoid robot (Mlakar et al., 2013a). The idea of controlling humanoid robots with similar procedures as in the case of virtual agents originates from the fact that embodied conversational avatars are in general controlled by similar structures, e.g., the kinematic (skeletal) model. In the field of robotics, the synchronization of speech and co-verbal expressions still represents a challenge and a very important goal. Furthermore, the robots increasingly look like "people"; therefore, it is increasingly expected that they will reflect our communicative gestures and expressions (Miyashita et al., 2006). The humanoid robots also need to communicate, at least by using the body (e.g., hands, arms, torso, and head) (Hoffman et al., 2008), and to reflect semantic visual signals (e.g., to further illustrate the spoken information, to show the way, etc.).

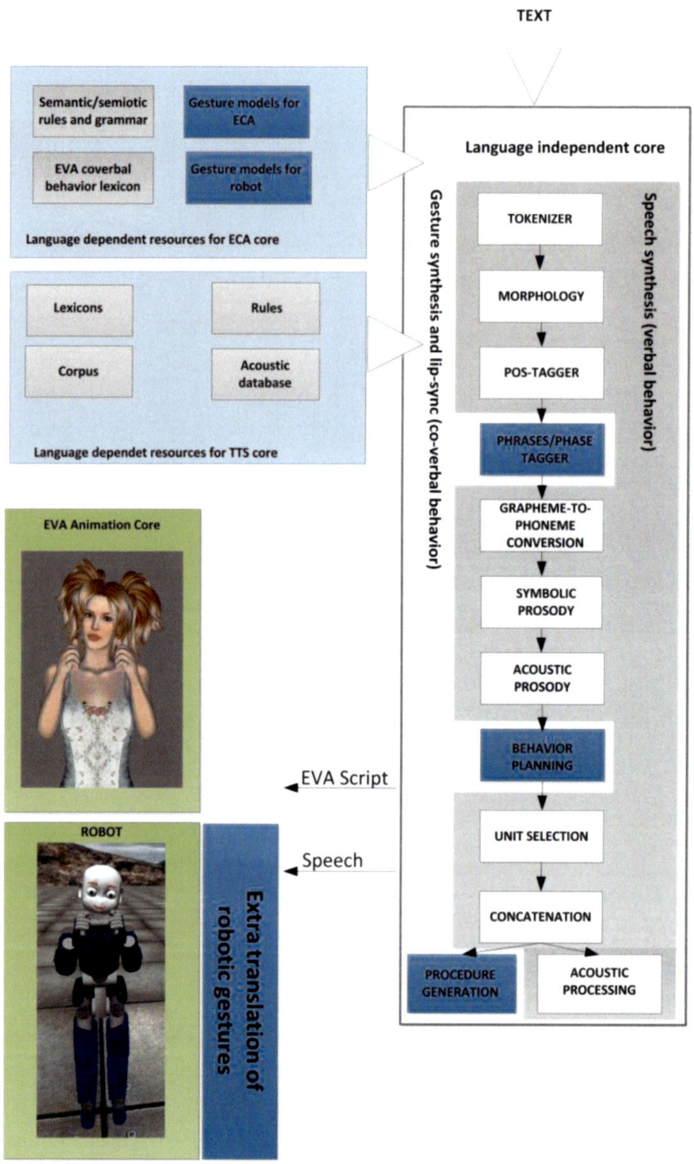

Figure 77. TTS-driven co-verbal behavior generation for artificial bodies.

Several techniques are used for generating expressive co-verbal gestures for artificial bodies like humanoid robots. For example, the so-called puppets technique (Hoffman et al., 2008) is used in order to calculate and control the movements that are carried out by the robot. This technique allows for movements of the legs and arms (to reach an "object in space"), and collision avoidance. However, natural multimodal communication is much more than just the recreation of very simple human motions. Indeed, for different body parts it is necessary to design and express meaning. Nevertheless, to achieve these goals, a humanoid robot would require a high degree of flexibility and control, together with a very effective mechanism able to adapt and control the way that humanoid robots carry out desired communicative goals. The system proposed for generating co-verbal behavior on artificial bodies is presented in Figure 77. It basically also converts the input text into a speech signal, aligned with gestures (including the head, hands, arms, and torso). Also, it includes several language-dependent external sources, such as expressive gesture dictionary, language resources for speech synthesis, and input text. At the end the system simultaneously generates two outputs: a synthesized speech signal and hierarchical specification of expressive behavior for artificial body in EVA-Script format. Both outputs can then be used for animation/realization (e.g., personalized multimodal output for robotic platforms, or conversational agent).

The system in Figure 77 is basically the same as for the ECA in Figure 4. Namely, the modules for the synthesis of verbal expressions analyze text input, predict the prosodic features, carry out the selection of units for the synthesis, and synthesize the speech signal. The modules for the synthesis of non-verbal expressions are used to select an appropriate visual content and the shape of presentation, and to establish the synchronization with a generated speech signal. Nevertheless, the co-verbal gestures have to be transformed into a shape that can be realized in the environment to implement the interaction with a humanoid robot. Furthermore, the language-dependent resources for the TTS modules and for generating gestures are separated from language-independent modules. Co-verbal modules used for artificial bodies such as robots need a context-independent dictionary of shapes (as for the ECA, but adapted for the robot), gesticons, and semiotic grammar in order to identify the intent and semiotic dimension. The gesture prototypes are in the gesture repository for humanoid robots.

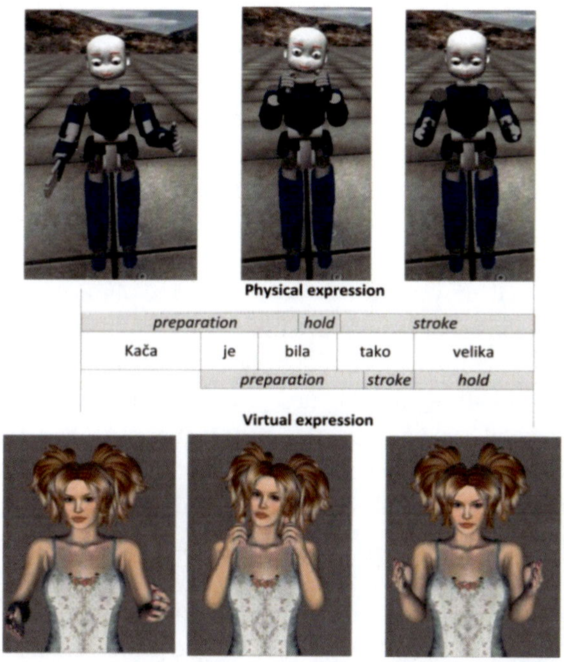

Figure 78. The generation of communicative actions with the humanoid robot and compared to the ECA EVA.

The concept of gesture, as proposed by Mlakar et al. (2012), can describe very precisely the shape and propagation of movement. The annotation scheme presented in this book is regarding shapes oriented to poses, and encompassing the spatial configuration of key poses in the form of the 3D configuration of articulators which manifest the shape. This is also very important for the introduction of gestures on the humanoid robot. Namely, as in the case of skeletal articulation conversational agents, humanoid robots can also be controlled by the kinematic model (Salem et al., 2012) (Figure 78). Therefore, similar motion controllers (e.g., joints) can also be used to control the desired movement. When controlling humanoid robots, the module for generating procedures ensures that expressive behavior is compatible with the target robot platform that can be simulated also in e.g., iCube, as proposed by Tikhanoff et al. (2008). There are therefore many similarities between the ECA mechanism for motion control (virtual specification) and iCube movement specification (physical limitations' specification). These similarities include, for example, the used movement controllers and techniques that are used to simulate (recreate) the specific movement. Furthermore, the ECA concept (as in the EVA-framework), as the humanoid robot concept, specifies the movement controllers as joints (bones), which are controlled by the HPR (H-heading, P-pitch, and –R-roll) mechanism. Although the physical systems mainly use RPY (P-pitch, roll-R, and Y-aw) mechanism, the analogy in 3D space exists. Namely, for example, "yaw" is analogous to the attribute "heading." These joints are part of the skeletal structure that approximates a human skeleton structure (kinematics). A smaller difference between the physical and the virtual models can be noticed regarding HPR configuration. The virtual model specifies the HPR configuration as a single controller, while the physical model configures the HPR values by using three movement controllers (one for each dimension in the HPR space). For example, the left shoulder joint of the virtual model can be presented with the following joints: 0 (shoulder pitch-P), 1 (shoulder roll-R), and 3 (shoulder yaw - Y/H). The movement dynamics is then defined by the time that is required to carry out the transition. The same principles are also shared with the EVA-Script. The behavior is specified in the context of forward-keying. Mostly, the body parts are defined as successive movement phases (a sequence). Each such sequence also describes the HPR configuration of the certain joint that is responsible for the formation of the shape. In addition to the articulators for shape and movement, the major weaknesses of the robot represent its movement dynamics, movement fluidity, and graduality of movement trajectory. The dynamics mainly refers to the relationship between the temporal distribution of co-verbal expressions (movement phases), and the spatial configuration of shapes. Namely, the virtual movement can be specified as almost instantaneous, while the movement controllers of the robot require/need longer temporal times. The responsiveness of the servo motors (the physical movement controllers of the humanoid robot) are defined by the maximum angular velocity of the engines, and by its maximum angular accelerations. These values are in general specified by the manufacturers of servo motors (Lima et al., 2008). Since the stroke phase is the most important movement phase within a gesture (namely, the co-verbal shape carries the intent in the stroke phase), additional temporal space can be allocated for the stroke phase, if necessary. The temporal adjustment can, therefore, reduce (or even eliminate) those movement phases that are around the stroke phase. Further, the process can also take into account the responsiveness of the physical movement controllers of the humanoid robot. The durations of those movement phases around the stroke phase can be reduced as little as possible, in order to be able to adapt the specifications of movement controllers. Furthermore, the stroke phase (in Figure 78) can be extended by including the preparation phase, in order to include the entire duration of the trigger. In order that the movement can be temporarily adjusted within the stroke phase, some minimal time is needed in order to calculate the necessary adjustment of the physical angle, and to compare it with the duration of the stroke phase. The stroke phase can then (if needed) be expanded by including the preparation phase and/or the hold/retraction phase. The remaining time of optional phases is compared again with the responsiveness possibilities of the humanoid robot. Those movement phases which cannot be implemented in the given time are discarded.

Chapter 10

The Embodied Conversational Agent EVA

Introduction

In order to implement the expressive co-verbal behavior generation on ECA EVA, a multimodal corpus is needed. Therefore, a corpus based on dynamic co-verbal dialogue was created, named EVA Corpus. Furthermore, it can also be used for the evaluation of the algorithm. The EVA Corpus includes an entertaining TV show entitled '*A si ti tud not padu,*' in which all participants actively communicate within a relaxed and spontaneous (non-linear) dialogue. The EVA Corpus currently consists of three videos with duration of approximately 140 minutes, in which there are simultaneously 3-5 speakers. 35 minutes of the first video was manually annotated (as presented in Table 15). The annotated corpus comprises 5 speakers.

In the annotated corpus, 534 verbal sequences that include one or more speakers were detected. Within verbal sequences, 493 co-verbal sequences were detected, wherein the co-verbal sequence represents those parts of the verbal sequence that carry completed intent and contain the movement. Namely, an individual verbal sequence often does not contain any co-verbal sequences, or contains one, or even more co-verbal sequences. Among the 493 co-verbal sequences, 12% of gestures were annotated as iconic (mostly metonymic and qualitative; and outlines 8%), 26% of gestures were annotated as *deictic*, and 3% of gestures as symbols. The remaining gestures (59%) were annotated as adapters (manipulators). For most gestures (63%) it was not possible to define any communicative significance regarding search, or the communicative function in the dialogue. Gestures classified as beats primarily served for maintaining the communicative level in the dialogue. The EVA Corpus was annotated according to the annotation EVA scheme, and based on the results the following sources were created: gesture dictionary, semiotic grammar, gesticon, and training material for machine-learning purposes.

Figure 79 (a) presents the annotation tool ELAN and the functional annotation scheme for high-level annotation that was used to described the individual communicative acts on a functional level. At this level, the following tiers were defined in the ELAN:

- *Speech tier:* used for presenting the speech signal.
- *Tier for transcriptions*: used for transcribing speech into text (one tier per speaker). For the EVA Corpus these transcriptions were already generated in the tool Transcriber.
- *Tier for morpho-syntactic tags:* used for presenting the morpho-syntactic tags of those words included within prosodic phrases. These words were tagged by the POS-tagger LAPOS[1]. The tags were subsequently also manually verified and corrected.
- *Tier for intent:* used for classifying the intent by semiotic class tag, by word/word sequence representing the content core, or by accentuated word (for each prosodic phrase that contained the co-verbal behavior).

Table 15. The statistics of the annotated EVA Corpus

Video clip: JRtvslpoas-rd0904231043		
Duration:	57 min 30s	
Number of speakers:	5 (four male, one female)	
Verbal sequences:	1399	
Distribution between speakers		
Speaker 1 - male	Number of verbal sequences:	20
	Representation:	74.43s (2.16%)
	Average statement duration:	3.721s (M = 2.88)
Speaker 2 - male	Number of verbal sequences:	435
	Representation:	1885.103s (54.156%)
	Average statement duration:	3.291s (M = 4.333)
Speaker 3 - male	Number of verbal sequences:	330
	Representation:	1229.256s s (35.618%)
	Average statement duration:	3.725s (M = 2.686)
Speaker 2 - male	Number of verbal sequences:	577
	Representation:	2122.986s (61.514%)
	Average statement duration:	3.679s (M = 2.498)
Speaker 2 - female	Number of verbal sequences:	37
	Representation:	88.936s (2.577%)
	Average statement duration:	2.403s (M = 2.095)
Annotated material		
Duration:	57 min 30s	
Number of speakers:	4 (three male, one female)	
Verbal sequences:	534	
Co-verbal sequences:	493	

Figure 79 (b) presents the annotation tool ANVIL and the descriptive annotation scheme for *low-level annotation* used to describe the individual communicative acts on a descriptive level. Namely, at the descriptive level movement phases and phrases are annotated together with abstract and detailed annotations of shapes and poses for each body part (in the form of configuration controllers). In ANVIL the following tiers (separately for each body part: left, right hand, left-hand, right hand, head, face) were defined:

[1] Lookahead Part-Of-Speech Tagger; http://www.logos.ic.i.u-tokyo.ac.jp/~tsuruoka/lapos/.

- *Tier for movement phrases*: used for annotating a movement within the communicative act as a semantically completed co-verbal unit (movement phrase), where each one includes at least the stroke phase. Additionally, the morpho-syntactic sequence for the given phrase is added.
- *Tier for movement phases*: used for annotating each movement phase. At its boundaries, the abstract configuration of those body part(s) that carries out the co-verbal behavior is annotated in the form of abstract dimensions and description (when the shape is already in the lexicon. Additionally, the word or word sequence/phrase for the given movement phase and the transition's trajectory (in the parametric form) is annotated.
- *Tier for movement controllers*: used for describing each body part at the boundaries of movement phases, and for describing those body part configurations that represent the co-verbal behavior. This is done in great detail, by describing the configuration of each movement controller.

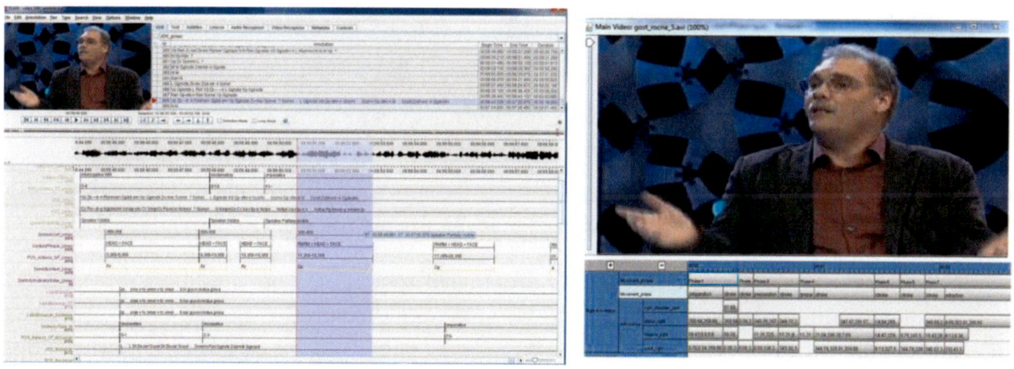

Figure 79. Annotating EVA Corpus using ELAN (*left*), and annotating EVA Corpus using ANVIL (*right*).

Furthermore, by using 3D modeling tools Autodesk Maya and Daz4D, the 3D articulated model of the agent, was designed, based on a multi-part mesh model (body, vocal tract, eyes, hair, clothing), textures, skeletal formation, and blend shapes. The ECA model mostly coincides with the MPEG-4 standard (BAP and FAP); therefore, it is consequently possible to translate several BAP and FAP configurations into shapes, controlled by joints and animated shapes of the designed model. Figure 80 presents the Maya 3D user interface, used for designing this 3D articulated model for the co-verbal agent, based on textured volumetric mesh models, and animation based on skeleton (joints) and animated shapes.

After designing the 3D articulated model with the Maya3D tool, those key poses found at the descriptive level in the proposed annotation scheme also have to be designed (at the movement phases's boundaries). An adequately modeled configuration is then exported as EVA-Script. Each one has been stored in the context-independent dictionary of shapes of the co-verbal agent, named EVA. In this way, the following shapes were created for the co-verbal agent EVA: 12 EVA-Scripts for emotions, 20 for facial expressions, 10 for shapes and head movements, 226 configurations of the left and right hands, 50 configurations for the right and left hands, and 10 simple and composite movement trajectories, which can bind together individual key poses for the left and right hands. This material is then used within the EVA-framework, where we are able to present EVA events as animated communicative behavior, which includes both speech and co-verbal gestures. The rendering engine in the EVA-framework is based on Panda3D. The EVA-framework also includes a module for realization planning and audio/video player for presenting ECA EVA in user interfaces (as shown in Figure 58).

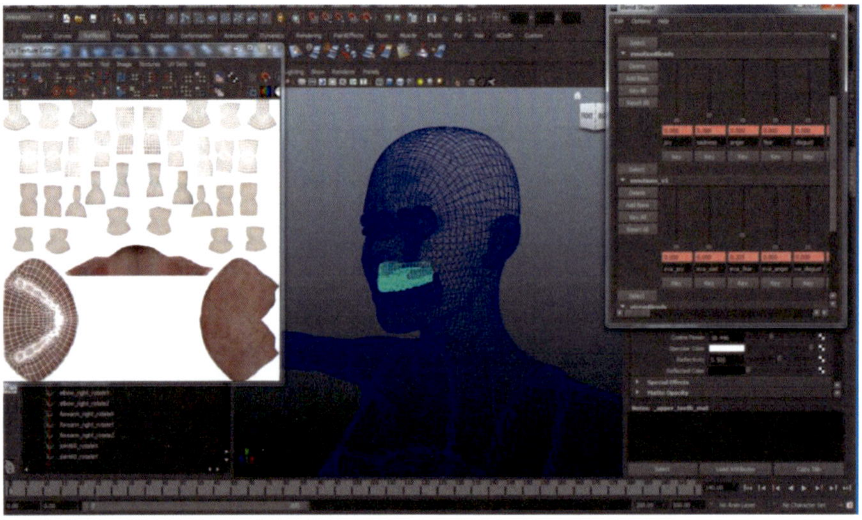

Figure 80. The Maya3D user interface for designing the 3D articulated model for the co-verbal agent.

The framework supports multi-part 3D articulated models for co-verbal agents, skeletal structures and animation techniques, such as: animation of shapes and blending, forward kinematics and inverse kinematics, synthesis of animation procedures, and default animations. The next subsections describe several experiments and evaluations based on the expressive model for generating co-verbal behavior and the EVA Corpus material. Firstly, the synthesis of several facial expressions is presented, including basic and complex emotions. Then, the synthesis of gestures with hands and palms, based on prosodic and morpho-syntactic features of the input text, is presented. At the end an evaluation is performed, based on the subjective perception of the synthesized behavior, and performed by several evaluators.

THE SYNTHESIS OF BASIC AND COMPLEX EMOTIONS

The expressivity of the model for generating co-verbal behavior can be evaluated by designing several EVA-Scripts describing Ekmann's basic emotions of *anger*, *disgust*, *fear*, *joy*, *sadness*, and *surprise*. This was performed using databases of facial expressions such as MMI (Pantic et al., 2005), Cohn-Kanade (Lucey et al., 2010), Face Database, and FACS (Facial Action Coding Summary System) (Petjan, 2005), and corresponding mappings of action units (AU) into the MPEG-4 FAP parameters. Namely, the desired effect regarding emotions can be obtained by adjusting the appropriate FAP values. Each FAP parameter represents a movement controller (animated shape, or animation joint) of the conversational agent EVA, and has to be stored in the gesticon. Furthermore, each emotion/facial expression is designed using a blending animation technique (simultaneous configuration of movement controllers $E_i = \{F_i^{E_i}, i = 1...n\}$) and is stored in a gesticon as one of the EVA-Scripts, or as a new blend-shape. Each facial expression or emotion in a gesticon is defined by dimensions of expressive space, which relate to facial expressions (Hartmann et al., 2006; Pelachaud, 2005). Namely, the facial expression expressivity is reflected primarily by the intensity and dynamics of muscle activity. Therefore, the ECA EVA (and EVA-framework) uses the following attributes regarding the expressivity of facial expressions:

a) *Temporal dimension*: for each facial expression E_i, the durations of the preparation, stroke, hold, and retraction phases can be updated and adapted.
b) *Spatial dimension*: for each facial expression E_i , the intensity of the expression can be fully updated and adapted as a whole, or in individual regions (Figure 63, the intensity of grief). By using the spatial dimension, each basic expression can be presented in several connotations, e.g., *irritation*, *anger*, or *rage*.
c) *Power dimension*: for each facial expression E_i the dynamics of the individual movement phases can be adapted using kinematic curves and/or by time-spatial adjustment (Figure 81).
d) *Fluidity dimension*: is performed with the blending animation technique. The internal continuity of the facial expression E_i is defined by the *power dimension* and *time dimension*, which provide a smooth (gradual) transition from the neutral into the active state of facial expression E_i (the maximum effect depends on the spatial dimension and blending/overlapping factors). The external continuity of the face is defined by continuous transitions between successive facial expressions E_i, E_{i+1}. The EVA-framework provides only partial simultaneousness of the retraction phase in facial expression E_i, and the stroke phase in facial expression E_{i+1} (the overlapping concept is presented in Figure 81).
e) *Repetitivity*: each facial expression E_i can be repeated or reused any number of times. Namely, the EVA-framework ensures that during repetitions (when attribute *repeatability* is set) of E_i, the movement controllers are firstly moved into a neutral state before they are moved again into an active state.

The Synthesis of Basic Emotions

We designed EVA-Scripts for 6 basic emotions (two scripts per emotion). We restricted ourselves to the definition of MPEG-4 FAP emotions and imitations of those emotions, which were in the aforementioned databases of facial expressions. In Table 16 the synthesized basic emotions and their corresponding FACS and FAP configurations are presented. Each emotion was designed using Maya 3D tool as a key frame (a pose), which was then converted into an emotion description, as proposed in EVA-Script (by using a proprietary plugin for exporting animations and poses in EVA-framework).

For designing emotions and facial expressions on the articulated 3D agent model, it was firstly necessary to design replicas of FAP parameters (AU) in the form of elemental movement controllers (animated shapes and joints). By considering the emotion specifications as given in the literature and databases, the face configurations were designed, in which the individual movement controllers hold the maximum value. These configurations were stored in the expressive repertoire of the ECA EVA, as temporally and spatially adjustable scripts of shapes (*V**).

Table 16. The synthesis of basic emotions on the conversational agent EVA in EVA-framework

Emotion	AU[2]	FAP parameters[3]	Visual representation
Neutral			

Joy The eyebrows are relaxed, mouth is opened, and corners of the mouth are moved against the ears.			
FAP: F3: open jaw, F4: release the middle of the lower lip, F5: raise the middle of the upper lip, F6: stretch left inner corner of the mouth region, F7: stretch right inner corner of the mouth region, F12: raise the left corner of the mouth region, F13: raise the right corner of the mouth region, F19: incarcerate the upper left eyelid, F20: incarcerate the upper right eyelid, F21: incarcerate the lower left eyelid, F22: incarcerate the lower right eyelid, F33: raise the middle of the left eyebrow, F34: raise the middle of the right eyebrow, F41: raise the left cheekbone, F42: raise the right cheekbone, F53: stretch the left outer corner of the mouth region, F54: stretch the right outer corner of the mouth region.			
AU: AU 6, AU 12			

Sadness The internal parts of the eyebrows are bent, mouth is relaxed, and eyes are slightly opened.			
FAP: F19: incarcerate the upper left eyelid, F20: incarcerate the upper right eyelid, F21: incarcerate the lower left eyelid, F22: incarcerate the lower right eyelid, F31: raise the inner part of the right eyebrow, F32: raise the inner part of the left eyebrow, F33: raise the middle part of the right eyebrow, F34: raise the middle part of the left eyebrow, F35: raise the outer part of the right eyebrow, F36: raise the outer part of the left eyebrow.			

[2] Facial Action Coding System (FACS); http://face-and-emotion.com/dataface/facs/new_version.jsp.

[3] MPEG-4 Face and Body Animation.

AU: AU 1, AU 4, AU 15
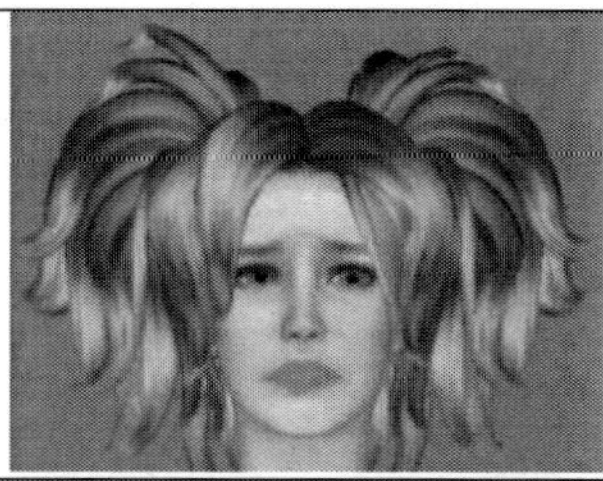
Fear The eyebrows are raised, the internal parts of the eyebrows are bent, and eyes express tension.
FAP: F3: open jaw, F4: release the middle of the lower lip, F5: raise the middle of the upper lip, F8: release the left middle part of the inner lip, F9: release the right middle part of the inner lip, F10: release the left middle part of the lower inner lip, F11: release the right middle part of the lower inner lip, F19: incarcerate the upper left eyelid, F20: incarcerate the upper right eyelid, F21: incarcerate the lower left eyelid, F22: incarcerate the lower right eyelid, F31: raised inner part of the left eyebrow, F32: raised inner part right eyebrow, F33: raise the middle of the left eyebrow, F34: raise the middle of the right eyebrow, F35: raise the outer part of the right eyebrow, F36: raise the outer part of the left eyebrow, F37: squeeze the left eyebrow, F38: squeeze the right eyebrow.
AU: AU 1, AU 2, AU 4, AU 5, AU 20, AU 26

Anger Internal parts of eyebrows are bent down and are close together, the eyes are wide open, mouth is open, but only so far that the teeth are visible.
FAP: F4: release the middle of the lower lip, F5: raise the middle of the upper lip, F16: push the lower lip, F18: depress chin, F19: incarcerate the upper left eyelid, F20: incarcerate the right upper eyelid, F21: incarcerate the lower left eyelid , F22: incarcerate the lower right eyelid, F31: raise the inner part of the left eyebrow, F32: raise the inner part of the right eyebrow, F33: raise the middle of the left eyebrow, F34: raise the middle of the right eyebrow, F35: raise the outer part of the right eyebrow, F36: raise the outer part of the left eyebrow, F37: squeeze the left eyebrow, F38: squeeze the right eyebrow.
AU: AU 4, AU 5, AU 7, AU 23

Disgust Eyebrows and eyelids are in a relaxed state, the upper lip is sneering, often asymmetrical.
FAP: F3: open jaw, F4: release the middle of the lower lip, F5: raise the middle of the upper lip, F8: release the left middle part of the inner lip, F9: release the right middle part of the inner lip, F10: release the left middle part of the lower inner lip, F11: release the right middle part of the lower inner lip, F19: incarcerate the upper left eyelid, F20: incarcerate the upper right eyelid, F21: incarcerate the lower left eyelid, F22: incarcerate the lower right eyelid, F31: raise the inner part of the left eyebrow, F32: raise the inner part of the right eyebrow, F33: raise the middle of the left eyebrow, F34: raise the middle of the right eyebrow, F56: raise the lower outer corner of the left mouth region, F57: stretch the lower outer corner of the right mouth region, F59: raise the left corner of the lips, F60: raise the right corner of the lips.

Table 16. (Continued)

AU: AU 9, AU 15, AU 16

Surprise Eyebrows and eyelids are open, lips are open.
FAP: F3: open jaw, F5: raise the middle of the lower lip, F6: stretch the left corner of the inner area of the mouth, F7: stretch the right corner of the inner area of the mouth, F10: raise the left middle part of the lower inner lip, F11, raise the right middle part of the lower internal lips, F19: incarcerate the upper left eyelid, F20: incarcerate the upper right eyelid, F21: incarcerate the lower left eyelid, F22: incarcerate the lower right eyelid, F31: raise the inner part of the left eyebrow, F32: raise the inner part of the right eyebrow, F33: raise the middle left eyebrow, F34: raise the middle of the right eyebrow, F35: raise the outer part of the right eyebrow, F36: raise the outside of the left eyebrow, F37: squeeze the left eyebrow, F38: squeeze the right eyebrow, F53: stretch the outer corner of the left mouth region, F54: stretch the outer corner of the right mouth region.
AU: AU 1, AU 2, AU 5B, AU 26

The Synthesis of Transitions between Emotions

In this subsection we are dealing with algorithms used for the realization of successive emotions and facial expressions. The visual presentations are also in this case driven by expressive dimensions of *time*, *power*, and *fluidity*. Figure 81 presents the visual presentations when the *power* dimension and *fluidity* dimension are used. Let facial expression E_1 represent the emotion *joy* that is defined by the set of the following FAP parameters:

$$E_1 = \{F3, F4, F5, F6, F7, F12, F13, F19, F20, \\ F21, F22, F33, F34, F41, F42, F53, F54\} \tag{59}$$

and let facial expression E_2 represent the emotion *sadness* that is defined by the set of the following FAP parameters:

$$E_2 = \{F19, F20, F21, F22, F31, F32, F33, F34, F35, F36\} \tag{60}$$

The internal fluidity of each emotion is achieved by using the time-based power modulation of several FAP attributes. As shown in Figure 81, the FAP parameters for emotion E_1 affect the facial region during the stroke phase. However, the transition within this phase is not necessarily linear. Namely, the *power* dimension can be additionally modulated by several kinematic curves, such as: *EaseIn*, *EaseOut*, and *EaseInOut*. In this way, the FAP attributes can reach their maximum intensity at the end of the stroke phase. Furthermore, the dynamics regarding muscle activity is also not linear, and can also be modulated as, for example, in Figure 81 where it is modulated by the kinematic curve *EaseInOut*. This type of curve can reflect both acceleration and braking. Similarly, the dynamics of muscle activity in the retraction phases can also be defined. During hold phases no movement is anticipated; therefore, the modulation of muscle activity, or expressive *power* dimension, is not needed.

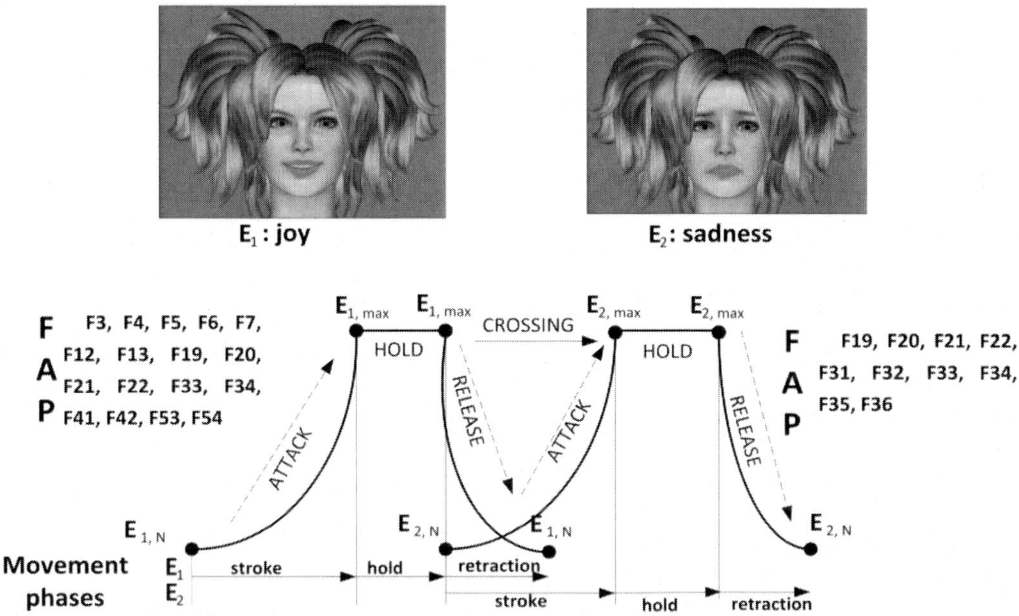

Figure 81. The realization of expressiveness in the facial region in EVA-framework.

Since the emotions E_1 and E_2 are consecutive, the expressive model for the co-verbal behavior generation also defines the concept of external fluidity. In order that the transition between emotions remains smooth and natural, the following sets of FAP attributes are defined:

- FAP attributes E_1: these are used within the retraction phase, and perform the action simultaneously (they neutralize their effect),
- FAP attributes E_1: these are used within the stroke phase, and perform the transition (as passing from active state E_1 into active state E_2), and
- FAP attributes E_2: these are used within the stroke phase and perform the action of the new affect.

The FAP attributes which perform the action simultaneously do not belong to the following emotion; therefore:

$$E_i - E_{i+1} = \{F | F \in E_i \wedge F \notin E_{i+1}\} \tag{61}$$

For the realization of expressiveness in the facial region in Figure 81, the following can then be written:

$$E_1 - E_2 = \{F3, F4, F5, F6, F7, F12, F13, F41, F42, F53, F54\} \tag{62}$$

And the FAP attributes which perform the transition belong to the current and the following emotion; therefore:

$$E_i \cap E_{i+1} = \{F | F \in E_i \wedge F \in E_{i+1}\} \tag{63}$$

For the realization of expressiveness in the facial region in Figure 81, the following can then be written:

$$E_1 \cap E_2 = \{F19, F20, F21, F22, F33, F34\} \tag{64}$$

And the FAP attributes that carry out new affect do not belong to the previous emotion; therefore:

$$E_{i+1} - E_i = \{F | F \in E_{i+1} \wedge F \notin E_i\} \tag{65}$$

For the realization of expressiveness in the facial region in Figure 81, the following can then be written:

$$E_2 - E_1 = \{F31, F35, F36\} \tag{66}$$

The Synthesis of Emotions by Modulation of the Intensity

In this subsection, several intensities of the individual emotions and the adequacy of using the *spatial* dimension for the expressive model are investigated. Therefore, several realizations of the synthesis of complex emotions were performed, which originate from different basic emotions. These variations of emotions were synthesized according to Plutchik theory (Plutchik, 2002). Plutchik defines a wheel of emotions in his hybrid three-dimensional model of basic and complex categories of emotions. By doing this he actually extends Ekman's six basic emotions with further emotions such as *trust* and *anticipation*. In the wheel of emotions complex emotions can be derived by adjusting intensities of basic emotions and by the blending different basic emotions. Any basic emotion can therefore be extended with different levels of *intensity*, and at different levels of excitement. All non-basic emotions are actually combinations or derivatives of basic emotions, which means that they can be created in the face region by some combination of them. In this way, by introducing the concept of *intensity*, several derivatives of basic emotions, presented in Table 17, can be obtained.

Table 17. The synthesis of derivations of basic emotions on the conversational agent EVA in EVA-framework

Basic emotion	Derivative	Visual representation
Fear	**Anxiety** *intensity 0.3*	
	Fear *intensity 0.5*	
	Terror *intensity*: 1.0	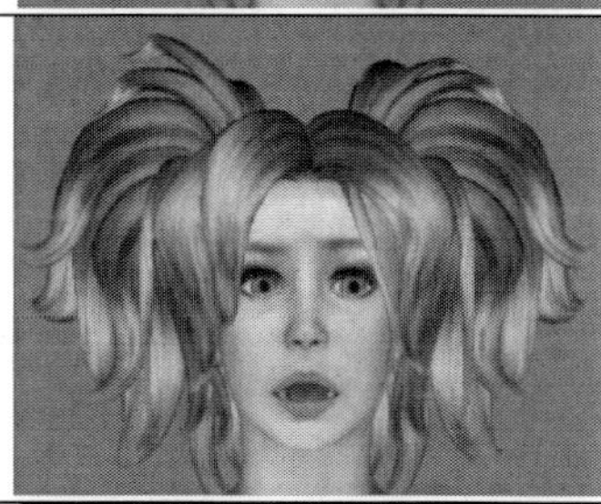
Anger	**Annoyance** *intensity 0.3*	
	Anger *intensity 0.5*	

Table 17. (Continued)

Basic emotion	Derivative	Visual representation
	Rage *intensity: 1.0*	
Joy	**Serenity** *intensity 0.3*	
	Joy *intensity 0.5*	
	Euphoria *intensity: 1.0*	
Sadness	**Pensiveness** *intensity 0.3*	

	Sadness *intensity 0.5*	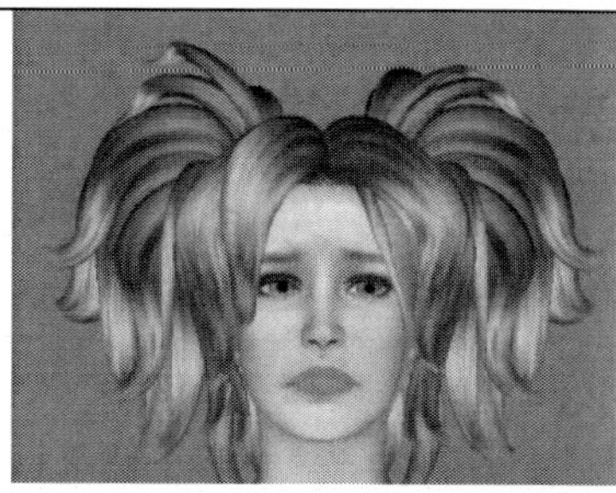
	Grief *intensity: 1.0*	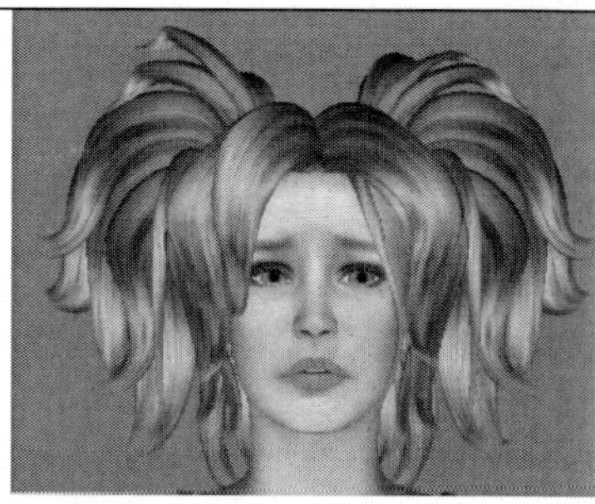
Surprise	**Distraction** *intensity 0.3*	
	Surprise *intensity 0.5*	
	Amazement *intensity: 1.0*	

Table 17. (Continued)

Basic emotion	Derivative	Visual representation
Disgust	**Boredom** *intensity 0.3*	
	Disgust *intensity 0.5*	
	Loathing *intensity: 1.0*	

Thus, the derivations of basic emotions are created by adjusting the intensity of the movement controllers of individual basic emotions (or the intensity of the emotions themselves). For the expressive model, the degree of intensity of emotions is defined on interval [0.0 - 1.0], wherein the intensity value 0.0 indicates neutrality (the emotion is not shown within the face region), and the intensity value 1.0 represents the maximum intensity of the facial expression (within the face region, the emotion is shown by using the maximum configuration of movement controllers - FAP parameters). By using the derivation of complex emotions as functions of the intensity of movement controllers (emotions) (see Table 17) in addition to the basic emotions, the ECA EVA can also realize a number of other positive and negative emotions, which are not only biological in nature, but have evolved through the psycho-sociological human evolution (Martin et al., 2006a; Ahn et al., 2013; Plutchik, 2002), e.g.:

a) tension, anxiety, nervousness, terror, as a function of fear,
b) irritation, excitement, annoyance, rage, as a function of anger,
c) serenity, euphoria, satisfaction, optimism, as a function of happiness,
d) pensiveness, grief, apathy, as a function of sorrow,
e) distraction, amazement, surprise, as a function of surprise,
f) boredom, contempt, loathing, as a function of disgust.

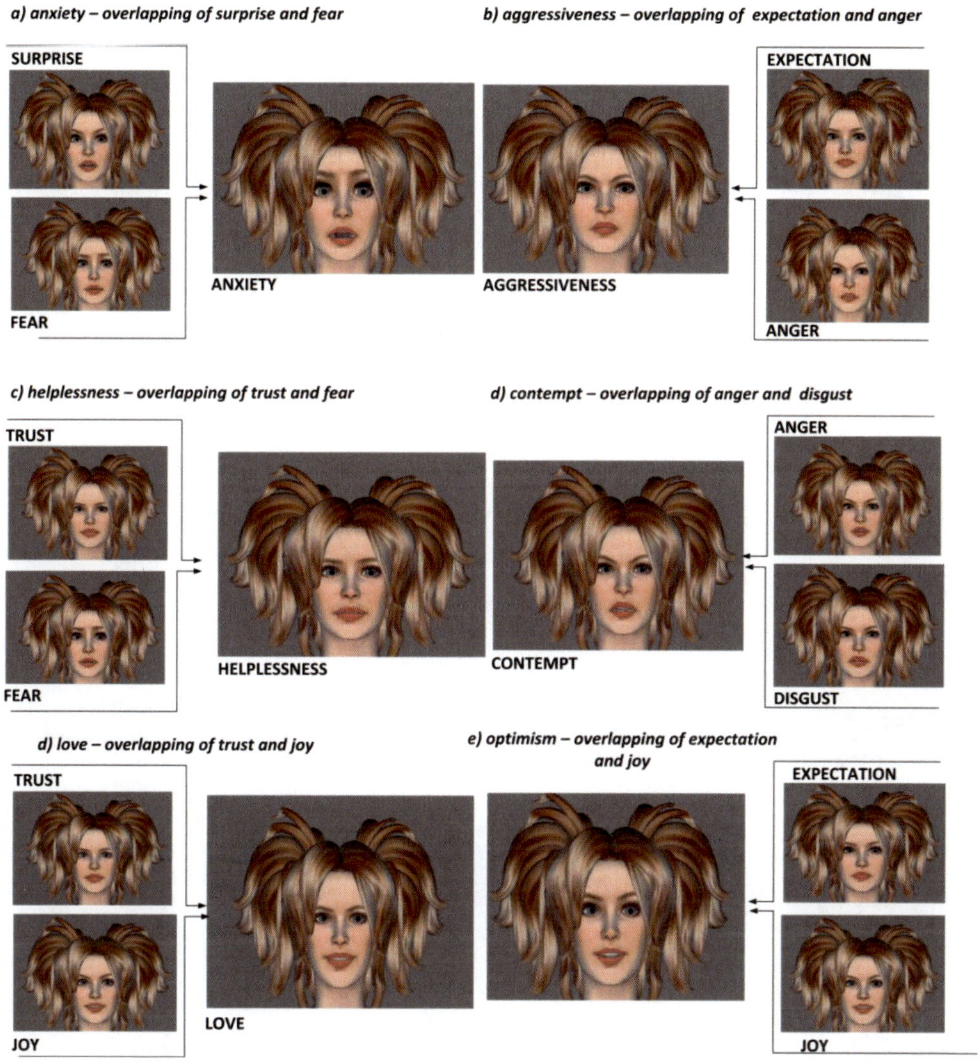

Figure 82. The synthesis of complex emotions using a combination of basic (overlapping) and complex emotions in EVA-framework.

The Synthesis of Complex Emotions using the Blending of Basic and Complex Emotions

In this subsection, the expressiveness of the co-verbal model in terms of the ability to synthesize complex emotions by using overlapping and masking (blending basic emotions) is investigated. The EVA-Scripts for complex emotions were created by following the theory behind VAD and PAD dimensional models. These emotions are created through the blending of basic and complex emotions, keeping in mind also the concepts of asymmetry. Namely, similar as with colors in color space, where we have basic colors and all other colors are derivates of basic colors, basic emotions can also be mutually blended. Through the blending we may form new complex emotions and express human feelings (Ahn et al., 2013; Plutchik,

2002). These feelings are often socially/culturally conditioned. Therefore, sociologically and culturally dependent emotions are e.g.:

Awe (Figure 82 (a)): is modeled by overlapping emotions such as *surprise* and *fear*. The emotion *fear* can be described as a mixed emotion that arises out of *respect*, *worship*, *superiority*, and *beauty*. This emotion is expressed in the face region by raising the inner eyebrows, extending the eyes' regions, and opening the mouth with a slightly released lower jaw.

Aggressiveness (Figure 82 (b)): is modeled by overlapping emotions such as *anger* and *expectation*. This emotion can be described as a behavior or body posture that reflects *aggressiveness*, *hostility*, or even *aggression*. In the facial region this emotion is expressed by released eyebrows, extending the eyes' region, and tightening the lips. This emotion is also the diametrical (opposite) emotion of the emotion *fear*.

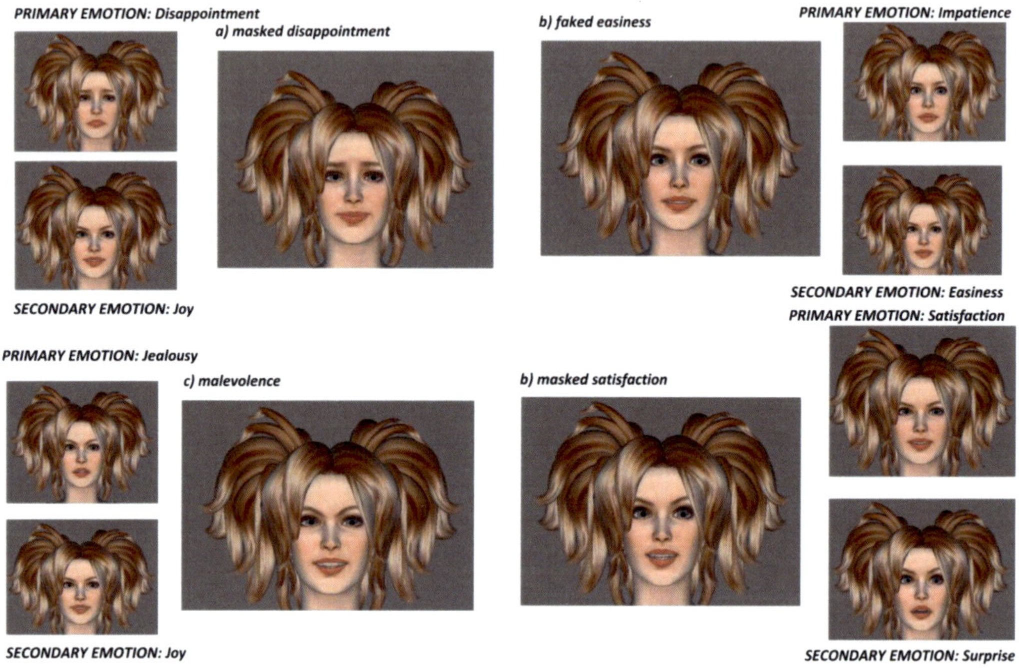

Figure 83. The synthesis of complex emotions using the masking mechanism in EVA-framework.

Similarly to the way in which we defined *awe* and *aggressiveness*, we can then define their diametrical emotions, such as *helplessness* and *contempt*. *Powerlessness* (Figure 82 (c)) can be described as the overlapping of emotions *belief* and *fear*, while the effect of *fear* is reflected primarily in the region of the eyes and eyebrows. *Contempt* (Figure 82 (d)) can be described as the overlapping of *disgust* and *anger*, with *disgust* reflected primarily in the nose region and in a raised lip. By using the overlapping concept, it is also possible to describe the emotions with a positive connotation. In Figure 82 (d) *love* is described and expressed, which is expressed in the facial region as the overlapping of *joy* and *belief*. And in Figure 82 (e) *optimism* is described, and is expressed in the facial region as the overlapping of *anticipation* and *joy*.

In addition to complex emotions that are the result of overlapping by using different intensities, there are also emotions that are actually the result of masking one emotion with another emotion. Generally, it is a case of blending pleasant emotions with unpleasant, or vice versa. Those facial expressions and emotions that originate from overlapping happen when an individual unsuccessfully tries to mask his/her other emotion. For example, the emotion *sadness* modeled with *joy* results in a *false smile* (Ekman & Friesen, 1982). Similarly, *false satisfaction* can be represented in the facial region as *disappointment* (as a function of the intensity of grief) which is masked with *joy*. The visual presentations of these emotions are shown in Figure 83.

As can be seen in Figure 83, by using expressiveness in the facial region of the proposed co-verbal model, it is possible to create and present emotions and facial expressions that are the consequence of masking the actual emotions. In Figure 83 (a) *disappointment* is masked with *joy*. *Disappointment* is described as a complex emotion that is created by the adjustment mechanism of the intensity of *grief* (e.g., the intensity value should be around 0.8). In Figure 83 (b) is the synthesis of apparent *easiness*, which is due to the masking of *easiness* with *impatience*. *Impatience* represents one of the basic emotions defined by Plutchik, while *easiness* represents a complex emotion that is created using the adjustment mechanism regarding the intensity of *joy* (the intensity value should be around 0.15). In Figure 83 (c) is shown the complex emotion *wickedness*, which is expressed when negative emotions are masked with *joy*. For example, this can be synthesized by masking *jealousy* with *joy*. The emotion *jealousy* is a derivation of the intensity of *anger* (the intensity value should be around 0.4). And Figure 83 (d) presents the masked *satisfaction* shown, for example, when you wish something bad for someone (i.e., someone receives bad news, but you feel satisfaction), but you want to mask this with *surprise*. The masked *satisfaction* is, therefore, created as a blending of *joy* with *surprise*.

THE SYNTHESIS OF THE CO-VERBAL BEHAVIOR OF GESTURES WITH THE ARMS, HANDS AND HEAD IN EVA-FRAMEWORK

In this sub-section, the algorithm for the automatic generation of expressive co-verbal behavior and its performance when using arbitrary and unannotated sentences are investigated. The semiotic grammar is designed from EVA Corpus. The step-by-step implementation of the algorithm is presented in the synthesis of random complex sentences, and in the synthesis of random simple sentences.

The Synthesis of Expressive Co-Verbal Behavior for Complex Sentences in EVA-Framework

In the following sentence from EVA Corpus, the speaker explains his own feelings and thoughts about plastic surgery.

Sentence

'In gredo k istemu zdravniku, ampak se izkaže da ta zdravnik ne zna nič drugega delati kot vedno iste, in samo iste obraze, in so vsi poklonirani.'

Eng. And they go to the same doctor, but it turns out that this doctor doesn't know anything else to do except for the same as always, and they only get the same faces and they all look like they're cloned.

The speaker wishes to convey the message that people visit the same plastic surgeon who is only able to create the same faces; therefore, in the end all of them look the same as each other (like clones). In this statement, co-verbal behavior is used in order to emphasize the importance of individual segments. Furthermore, gestures and speech are synchronized at the prosodic level, whereby the purpose of emphasizing, or highlighting the importance of a specific entity indicates the presence of the stroke phase and emphasized segments (Rojc & Mlakar, 2009). The algorithm does not know the broader context or the intent of this statement, nor the prosodic structure (no speech signal, only input text is available). In order to obtain information and generate expressive co-verbal behavior, the steps presented in Chapter 8 have to be carried out. The following POS-tagged sequence is delivered into the algorithm:

*In/Cc gredo/**Vm-p** k/**Dd** istemu/**Pid** zdravniku/**Ncd**, ampak/**Cc** se/**Pr-** izkaže/**Vm-p** da/**Cs** ta/**Pdn** zdravnik/ **Ncn** ne/**Q** zna/**Vm-p** nič/**Pzn** drugega/**Mpg** delati/**Vm-n** kot/**Cc** vedno/**Rgp** iste/**Pig**, in/**Cc** samo/**Q** iste/**Pig** obraze/**Nca**, in/**Cc** so/**Vanp** vsi/**Pgn** poklonirani/**Appn**.*

The lookup into the semiotic grammar then returns the intents and semiotic indicators, as presented in Table 18.

Table 18. The possible intents in the given sentence

CU ID / Semiotic class and subclass / Contained words	Morpho-syntactic sequence; CU word boundaries; Semiotic indicator
CU1: iconic, outline (S1) Words: *in gredo*	Cc × Vm-p; W0 × W1; W1
CU2: iconic, qualitative (S2) Words: *k istemu zdravniku*	*Dd* × *Pid* × *Ncd*; W2 × W4; W3
CU3: iconic, outline (S1) Words: *se izkaže*	*Pr-* × *Vm-p*; W6 × W7; W7
CU4: deictic, pointing (S3) Words: *ta zdravnik*	*Pdn* × *Ncn*; W9 × W10; W9
CU5: iconic, qualitative (S2) Words: *ne zna nič*	*Q* × *Vm-p* × *Pzn*; W13 × W15; W13
CU6: adapter, management (S4) Words: *nič drugega delati*	*Pzn* × *Mpg* × *Vm-n*; W13 × W15; W13
CU7: iconic, qualitative (S2) Words: *vedno iste*	*Rgp* × *Pig*; W17 × W18; W13
CU8: iconic, qualitative (S2) Words: *in samo iste obraze*	*Cc* × *Q* × *Pig* × *Nca*; W20 × W22; W21
CU9: iconic, outline (S1) Words: *so vsi poklonirani*	*Vanp* × *Pgn* × *Appn*; W24 × W26; W20

Now, the HRG structure in the relational level *ContentUnits* contains a set of possible intents. Furthermore, for the given sentence the symbolic prosody module defines the phrase breaks in the relational structure *ProsodicPhrases*, and in the relational structure *Syllables* all primary and secondary accents, as presented in Table 19.

Table 19. The predicted prosodic structure of the input sentence regarding phrase breaks and accents

Prosodic phrases:	*In gredo k istemu zdravniku* **<B2>** *ampak se izkaže da ta zdravnik ne zna nič drugega delati***<B2>** *kot vedno iste***<B2>** *in samo iste obraze***<B2>** *in so vsi poklonirani* **<B2.**
Accents:	*In gredo[NA] k is***[PA]***temu zdravni[NA]ku am[NA]pak se izka[NA]že da ta zdravni[NA]k ne zna[NA] nič***[PA]** *dru[NA]gega de[NA]lati kot ve[NA]dno is***[PA]***te, in samo***[PA]***is[NA]te obra[NA]ze, in so vsi***[PA]** *pokloni[NA]rani.*

Then the algorithm removes all those *CUs* in the relational level *ContentUnits* that do not contain a *PA* syllable (S1, S3, S4 in Table 18). Furthermore, by considering ***Rule 3***, it also eliminates CU_5, since the distribution of adapters is larger than the distribution of iconic gestures (in the annotated material). This results in the content presented in Table 20.

Table 20. The uniquely identified structure of intent in the given sentence

CU ID / Semiotic class and subclass / Contained words	Morpho-syntactic sequence ; CU word boundaries ; Semiotic indicator
CU2: iconic, qualitative (S2) Words: *k istemu zdravniku*	*Dd* × *Pid* × *Ncd* ; W2 × W4 ; W3
CU6: adapter, management (S4) Words: *nič drugega delati*	*Pzn* × *Mpg* × *Vm-n* ; W13 × W15 ; W13
CU7: iconic, qualitative (S2) Words: *vedno iste*	*Rgp* × *Pig* ; W17 × W18 ; W13
CU8: iconic, qualitative (S2) Words: *in samo iste obraze*	*Cc* × *Q* × *Pig* × *Nca* ; W20 × W23 ; W22
CU9: iconic, outline (S1) Words: *so vsi poklonirani*	*Vanp* × *Pgn* × *Appn* ; W24 × W26 ; W26

The algorithm then defines the movement structure in the form of movement phases, as presented in Figure 84. By considering the predicted prosodic structure, the stroke phase F_s is defined in the surrounding area of the *PA* syllable, wherein F_s lasts from the beginning of the word containing the *PA* syllable and ends with the same *PA* syllable. Furthermore, the maximum possible extension for F_s can represent the inclusion of those previous words which are still located within the corresponding *CU*. The preparation phase F_P is defined on the first word before the Fs. It lasts from the beginning of the word and ends with the contained *NA* syllable. Its maximum extension can include those following words until the first Fs found, and all those previous words which are still located within the corresponding *CU*. The space between Fs and F_P is used for the hold phase F_{HS}, which is actually the hold before the stroke. And the added F_{SH} that follows F_S presents the hold after the stroke, which is defined with those elements in the relational structure which are located between the left boundary of the stroke phase F_S and the left border of the semiotic indicator *I*. Finally, the retraction phase F_R is defined, and can include the left boundary of the first word that follows the F_{HS}. When F_R cannot be defined, then the performance of automatic retraction is left to the EVA-framework.

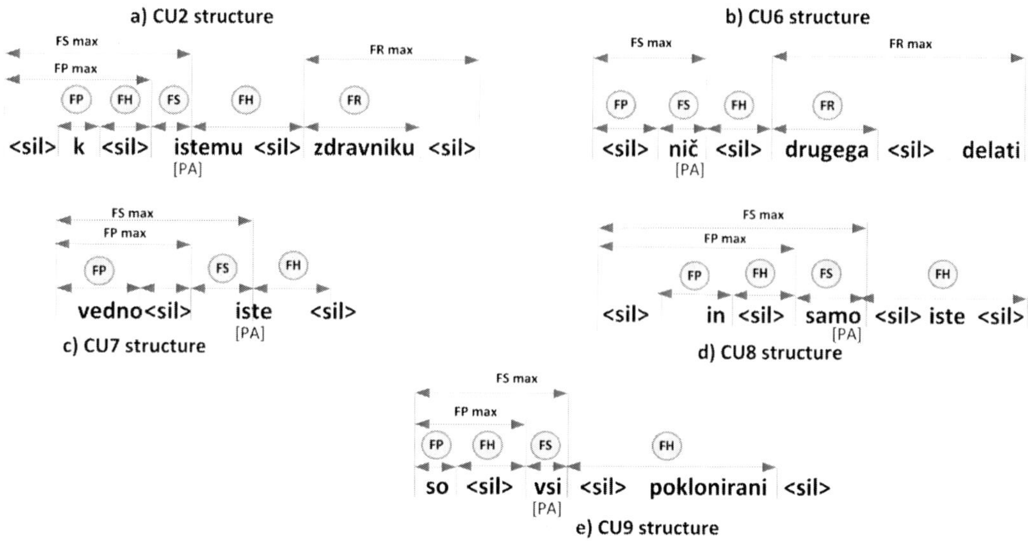

Figure 84. The assignment of movement phases for the given *CU*.

By considering the defined movement structure, the algorithm finally carries out the *time synchronization*, based on the predicted durations for movement phases *t*, and based on their maximum possible extensions t_{max}. In Figure 84, the time *t* represents the movement phases, and t_{max} the corresponding maximum extensions. Furthermore, in this case the predicted duration for F_S in CU_1 (Figure 84 (a)) is equal to t = t (*'is'*), while its maximum possible extension is equal to $t_{max} = t('sil') + t('k') + t('sil') + t('is')$. In a similar way, the algorithm also defines the remaining predicted and maximum possible durations for each movement phase within each *CU* (Figure 84 (a-e)). In further steps, the algorithm performs the selection of shapes and trajectories for transitions by several lookup operations in the gesticon, by using suitability functions and CART models. At the end, the system returns both the corresponding audio and EVA-event as EVA-Script, which includes the generated co-verbal behavior and complete viseme specification. These data are then used by the rendering module within EVA-framework for animating the speaking ECA EVA.

Figure 85 presents the created co-verbal behavior for content units CU_7 and CU_8, as planned and realized using the expressive model for co-verbal behavior generation. As can be seen, the algorithm defined the movement structure by a sequence of several movement phases. F_S in CU_7 is defined on W_{19}, while syllable 'is' is only contained (*PA* syllable). Therefore, the duration for F_S is $t = 0.287s$, while the maximum duration for F_S can be $t_{max} = 0.428s$. In CU_8 the algorithm predicted F_S on W_{21}, with two syllables 'sa' and 'mo,' where the 'mo' is *PA* syllable. The duration for F_S is in this case then $t = 0.804s$, while the maximum duration of this phase can be *1,344s*.

Furthermore, the algorithm defines in this case the following pairs of poses: ***P1*** {PI-1, PI-2}, and ***P2*** {PI-3, PI-4} (Figure 85) on each defined movement stroke phase F_S. The first pair

P1 can be obtained from the semiotic lexicon by using the following pattern $x = (S2 \times FS \times Pig)$. Nevertheless, the lookup process returns several candidates. Therefore, the suitability functions and target specification time $t = 0.287$ and $t_{max} = 0.428s$ have to be used in order to obtain the most appropriate pair of poses, which happens to be ***P1*** for the first stroke phase, with the initial pose P_S= PI-1 that includes the pose of the right arm) and the pose of the right hand, and with the final pose P_E=PI-2, which is similarly composed of the pose for the right arm, and the pose for the right hand. For the trajectory between poses the algorithm selects a linear trajectory T_1. Similarly, the algorithm for F_S in CU_8 selects the pair of poses ***P2***, with an initial pose configuration P_S =PI-3 and the final configuration P_E=PI-4. For the trajectory in this case, the algorithm selects the composite parametric trajectory T_3 (*cut-off chair*, Figure 17) which consists of one arc and one linear segment (two additional key points).

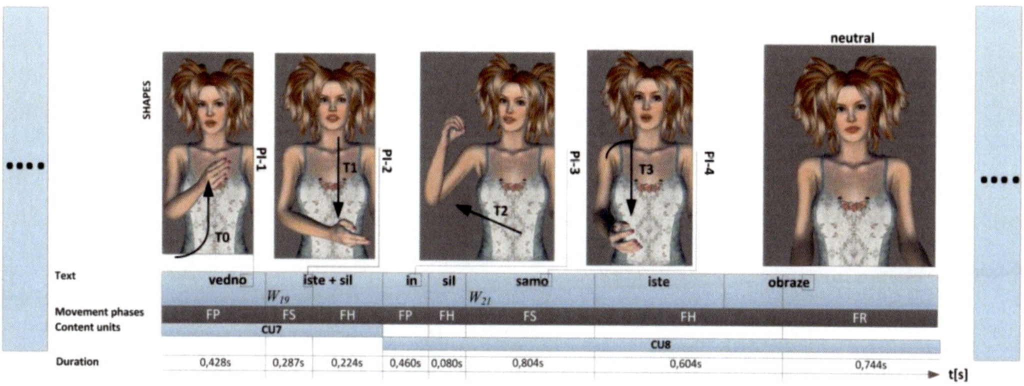

Figure 85. The realization of sequences CU_7 and CU_8 on the ECA EVA in EVA-framework.

Similarly, the algorithm selects and adjusts the poses in other movement phases. Namely, for the $mph = F_P$ in CU_7 is selected for the left boundary $prev(mph).P_E$ (the pose on the right boundary of the preceding movement phase), which is based on the movement structure in Figure 85 for CU_6 equal to the neutral pose $prev(mph).P_E = P_N$. And for the right boundary $(next(mph) = F_S).P_S$ is selected (the initial pose of the stroke phase that follows), or $(next(mph) = F_S).P_S$ =PI-1. For the transition between $P_N \rightarrow PI\text{-}1$, the algorithm selects the composed trajectory T_0 (*chair*, Figure 17), which consists of an arc and the linear structure. Similarly, for the $mph = F_P$ in CU_8 for the initial pose $prev(mph).P_E$ is selected, which is in this case equal to the final pose of the first stroke phase $prev(mph).P_E$ =PI-2. And for the final pose $(next(mph) = F_S).P_S$ is selected, which is equal to $(next(mph) = F_S).P_S$ =PI-3. The transition $PI\text{-}2 \rightarrow PI\text{-}3$ is then implemented by the linear parametric trajectory T_2. Similarly, the transition from the end pose for the F_S in CU_8 into a neutral pose P_N for the F_R is carried out by using the linear trajectory. In the final step of the algorithm, co-verbal behavior G is prosodically aligned, written in a format that is understood by the entity realization (ECA) and EVA-framework. At the output, the algorithm returns the synthesized speech signal and EVA-event that contains the structure of the co-verbal behavior, and the structure of co-articulations of visemes which will animate simultaneously with the speech.

The Synthesis of Expressive Co-Verbal Behavior for a Simple Sentence in EVA-Framework

Sentence:
'Kača je bila tako velika.'
Eng. 'The snake was that big.'

The morpho-syntactic sequence:
Kača je bila tako velika
Ncn Vanp Va-p Rgp Agpn

The prosodic structure:
Kača je bila tako[**PA**] *velika***<b3>**

In this sentence from EVA Corpus, the speaker talks about a snake that he has seen. The sentence can be regarded as simple because no broader context is needed for its understanding, since the speaker only wants to tell us that the snake was big. In this case the algorithm detects two possible interpretations in the sentence: *iconic-outline* determined by the noun and with semantic indicator on W_0, and the *iconic-metonymically*, which is the result of a sequence of auxiliary verbs W_1 X W_2, adverb W_3, and adjective W_4.

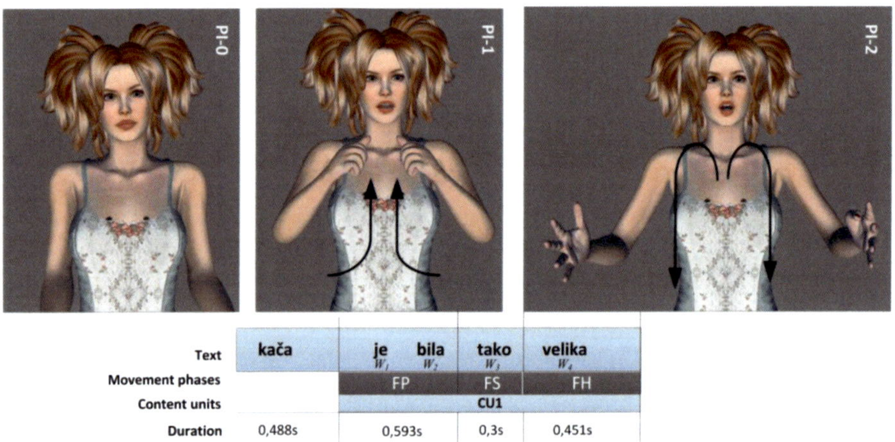

Figure 86. The realization of a simple sentence by the ECA EVA in EVA-framework.

By considering the predicted prosodic phrases and accents, the algorithm retains CU_1, where it defines the metonymic intent with the primary indicator W_4 (see Figure 86). The algorithm also defines the movement structure for CU_1 in the form of several movement phases. The F_P is defined over the word W_2, with its maximal possible extension that includes also the word W_1. Therefore, the duration of the F_P can be $t = 413ms$, and its maximum duration $t_{max} = 593ms$. The F_S is defined on the word W_3, with duration $t = 300ms$, and with maximum possible duration *893ms*. The F_H is then, by considering the rule regarding the hold over the content word, defined on the word W_4 with the duration *517ms*. The prediction and the selection of poses follow. Because of the strong semantic correlation of metonymic expressions, the algorithm for the word W_4 selects the pair of poses ***P1*** which consists of poses P_E = *PI-1* and P_S = *PI-2*. ***P1*** describes the gesticulation performed by using both arms and both hands. For the transition between *PI-1* and *PI-2* the composite parametric trajectory is selected, consisting of two arcs that describe the movement of raising and releasing (the outline of the roof, Figure 17) the hands out, and spreading the hands out in a linear trajectory. Given that within the element *CU* there is a high semantic correlation and by considering the predicted duration for basic F_P, the algorithm extends the F_P by also including the word W_1; therefore, its new duration is t_{max}. Since $mph = F_P$ is the first phase, the *prev(mph)* does not exist in the relational level *MovementPhases*; therefore, for the starting pose $mph.P_S$ the neutral pose P_N is selected if for the pose $mph.P_E = (next(mph) = F_S).P_S$ is selected, or PI-1. And for the trajectory of the transition $P_N \rightarrow PI\text{-}1$, the algorithm selects the composed trajectory *chair* (Figure 17), which is composed of one arc and one linear segment. In the final step of the algorithm the prosodically aligned co-verbal behavior *G* is written in a format that is understood by the entity realization ECA EVA, while the gestures and gesticulation are delayed for *488ms* (defined by EVA-Script attribute *initialDelay* within the tag *<bgesture>*).

Evaluating Expressive Co-Verbal Behavior

In order to qualitatively evaluate the capabilities and quality of the proposed model for generating expressive behavior on the ECA EVA, subjective evaluation was carried out. 9 people in the population age from 26 to 59 years participated in this evaluation; 3 were female and 6 male. For the evaluation the *Likert* scale was used (Koutsombogera & Papageorgiou, 2012), using dimensions from 1 to 5, whereby 1 represents strong disagreement and 5 strong agreement.

Firstly, the evaluation of expressive co-verbal behavior for simple sentences was performed. In this case the intent of the sentence was unique, and could be understood without additional context. In a similar manner, the evaluation for complex sentences was also carried out, wherein each sentence was open to, in general, several interpretations, which may also overlap, while their simultaneousness introduced inconsistencies and ambiguity regarding understanding. Therefore, the intent without any broader context was harder to understand (or could not be understood at all). The evaluation encompassed the synthesis of expressive co-verbal behavior on a set of semantically unrelated (isolated) sentences. The co-verbal behavior was realized using the ECA EVA in EVA-framework. All of the generated EVA events, which include a description of the co-verbal behavior, were generated using the expressive model for creating co-verbal behavior, and by using semiotic grammar, gesticon, and dictionary of poses based on EVA Corpus. The videos of synthesized sentences were evaluated in mixed and random order regarding their complexity. Namely, one person might evaluate two consecutive complex sentences while someone else evaluated first a complex sentence and then a simple sentence. Furthermore, the evaluators did not know which sentences were complex and which were simple.

In the evaluation of the co-verbal behavior, the so-called *dependent condition* was defined, which encompasses the co-verbal behavior as generated by the conversational model, and which includes the synchronization of the lips, manual gesticulation (including hands), and subconscious behavior such as e.g., blinking.

As an independent, the so-called *control condition* has been defined, when no hand gesticulation is performed. In this case, from the perspective of co-verbal behavior, only lip-sync and subconscious behavior are present. The synthesized behavior was evaluated using a questionnaire. Answers included subjective evaluation based on the Likert scale, graded from 1 to 5. Table 21 summarizes the rates for measuring the quality of the synthesis of the co-verbal behavior.

Table 21. The Likert scale with rates for evaluating the expressive co-verbal behavior model generation in the EVA-framework

Dependent rates	Question	Likert Scale
Content agreement (M1)	*Did the gestures represent the corresponding speech segment?*	1 – not at all 5 – very plausible interpretation
Synchronization of the pose (M2)	*Did the poses presented at corresponding speech segments look appropriate?*	1 – no correlation 5 – high correlation
Fluidity (M3)	*Were the movements carried out by the co-verbal agent fluid?*	1 – not at all 5 – absolutely fluid
Dynamics (M4)	*Was the speed of movement appropriate?*	1 – too slow 5 – too fast
Density (M5)	*Did the number of gestures seem appropriate?*	1 – too little 5 – too much
Understanding (M6)	*Did the presented co-verbal behavior contribute to the understanding of verbal information?*	1 – irrelevant 5 – important
Naturalness (M7)	*How appropriate (human-like) do you find the behavior of the co-verbal agent?*	1 – unnatural 5 – very natural

The quality evaluation of the expressive co-verbal model consisted of seven rates. By *content agreement* rate *M1*, it could be verified whether the co-verbal behavior and associated gestures represent the suitable speech segments (e.g., was the proper speech segment selected, or does the behavior represent a complementary/alternative meaning?). Furthermore, by *synchronization of the pose* rate *M2*, it could be verified whether for a given segment the appropriate gesture was selected (the sequence of poses and transitions coincide with the speech sequence that represents it). The *fluidity* rate *M3* was used for estimating the fluidity of gestures, movements and transitions that are realized on the ECA EVA. The *dynamics* rate *M4* was used for evaluating the speed of gestures, i.e., whether the gestures were implemented too quickly, or too slowly. The *density* rate *M5* was defined in order to rate the distribution of gestures, i.e., whether the co-verbal movements contained too many or too few co-verbal elements. The *understanding* rate *M6* was used for verifying whether the synthesized co-verbal behavior contributed something to the verbal information (e.g., improved understanding, made the statement more interesting, more convincing etc.). And the *naturalness* rate *M7* was used to verify how much, or if at all, the co-verbal behavior contributed to the perception of naturalness of the ECA EVA.

The evaluation of synthesizing the co-verbal behavior was carried out by the same persons as the evaluation of expressive abilities. Table 22 summarizes the results of the evaluation of the system. Furthermore, the diagram in Figure 87 presents the distribution of mean values for the defined individual rates. When synthesizing the co-verbal behavior for simple sentences, the ECA EVA achieved an overall score for naturalness (a function of M1, M2, M3, M6, M7) M=3.40. When synthesizing complex sentences, the score M=3.29 was obtained. When the complete model was evaluated, this resulted in a score of 3.347 (combined scores for the synthesis of simple and complex sentences).

Table 22. The mean and standard deviations of scores for the individual rates

Rate	Simple sentence	Complex sentence	Without gestures
M1	3.51 (0.84)	3.28 (1.15)	-
M2	3.32 (0.91)	3.14(0.88)	-
M3	3.57(0.72)	3.48(0.93)	-
M4	3.14(1.15)	3.76 (1.01)	-
M5	3.22(1.08)	3.67(0.82)	-
M6	3.44(1.27)	3.31 (1.08)	2.73 (0.74)
M7	3.17(1.32)	3.25(0.94)	2.43 (0.89)

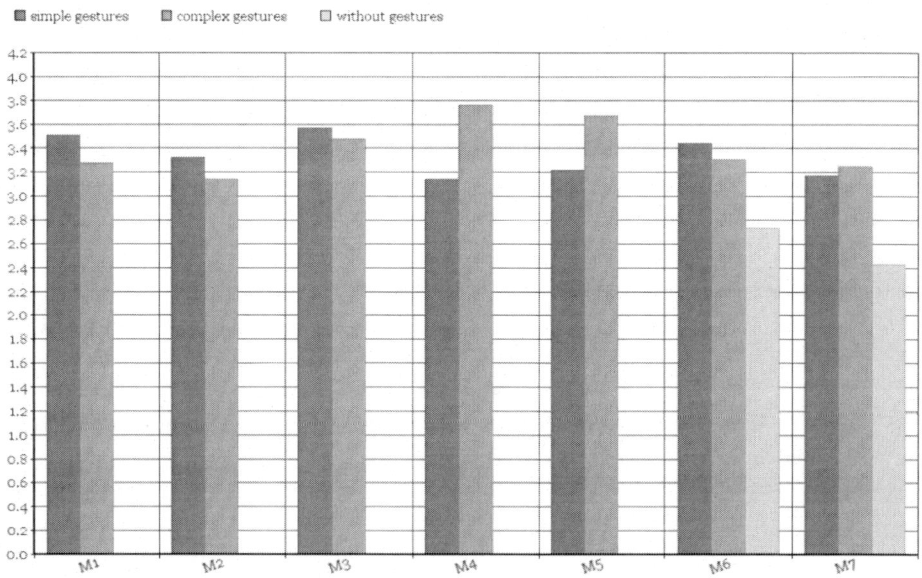

Figure 87. The graph of mean values for quality evaluation on a Likert scale from 1 to 5.

Regarding the rate *C1*, in general, the evaluators agreed with the content and temporal synchronization of speech. The mean value for this rate on a scale from 1 to 5 was M = 3.395, which includes the synthesis of complex and simple sentences. This means that symbolic synchronization, elimination, and the definition of movement structures in the algorithm are appropriate. By considering the input morpho-syntactic patterns and semiotic grammar, the set of possible interpretations is properly defined. Furthermore, by using prosodic features it is transformed into a relatively well-defined structure of co-verbal behavior. As expected, the algorithm performs better for simple sentences (M=3.51), and worse but still satisfactorily for complex sentences (M=3.28). Obviously, for simple sentences it is easier to extract individual intents, as they contain fewer relevant semiotic sequences and consequently less potential overlapping and ambiguities. Regarding the rate *C2*, the selected poses on the boundaries of the movement phases and corresponding trajectories represent quite well the intent of the simultaneous speech. Here, the mean value of the rate is M = 3.23. This means that the concept of similarities between poses in the gesticon, which is primarily based on semiotic relations and only secondarily on semantics, and the selection of poses based on suitability functions and CART trees help and represent a mechanism through which, for a given context, the selection of poses and transitions will result in a suitable complement of the verbal information. Better performance of this step in the algorithm for simple sentences is expected. Regarding rate *C3*, with mean value M = 3.53, this suggests that the concepts that provide both internal and external fluidity (e.g., regarding the extension of movement phases and the connectivity of two successive poses) perform well. As expected, these values are comparable for the synthesis of both simple (M = 3.57) and complex sentences (M = 3.48). Namely, those steps in the algorithm that ensure the fluidity of poses and gestures do not reflect any high contextual correlation, and depend mainly on the quality and quantity of the annotated material in the EVA Corpus. The rate *C4* (M = 3.14 for simple, and M = 3.72 for complex sentences) suggests that the dynamics (velocity) of movement, which is defined by the expressive conversational model, is credible and relatively convincing; however, in some cases the movement is performed too quickly. A lower score for dynamics is particularly noticed when the preparation phase does not exist (the shape on the right boundary of the stroke phase is automatically adjusted), and in those retraction phases between successive gestures that could be perceived also as unnecessary and too short. Nevertheless, this rate *C4* indicates that the proposed concepts that restrict the duration of the movement phases by considering the prosodic features, and necessary restrictions within the CU elements, are still rather rigid.

Quite the opposite can be said for the rate *C5*, which evaluates the distribution and density of gestures. The mean value M = 3.22 for the synthesis of simple, and M = 3.67 for the synthesis of complex sentences, suggests that the simultaneousness of the *PA* syllable and semiotic indicator *I* within each *CU* in some cases is not yet sufficient. Furthermore, the concepts that eliminate some gestures are not always strict enough, or simply do not possess enough contextual information. The values for rates *C4* and *C5* are expected and consistent with theory regarding prosodic synchronicity (Loehr, 2004). Namely, prosodic synchrony between speech and gestures exists, but is not based exclusively on primary accents (most accentuated syllables locally). The gestures can also be synchronized through so-called intermediate phrases, which may surpass the word boundaries and even content units. Nevertheless, the peaks of stroke phases (the most prominent segments) are, in general, synchronized with accentuated syllables.

The rates *C6* (total M = 3,375) and *C7* (total M = 3.21) indicate that the co-verbal behavior significantly contributes to a better understanding of isolated sentences, and to a more human-like perception of the conversational agent as a live entity. In comparison to a lack of co-verbal behavior, i.e., without any gesticulation (for C6 M = 2.73, and for C7 M = 2.43), the expressive model achieves significantly better qualitative assessment results.

REFERENCES

Ahn, J., Gobron, S., Thalmann, D., & Boulic, R., (2013). Asymmetric facial expressions: revealing richer emotions for embodied conversational agents. *Computer Animation and Virtual Worlds* (in printing).

Allwood, J., Ahlsén, E., & Lund, J., et al. (2007a). Multimodality in own communication management. Current Trends in Research on Spoken Language in the Nordic Countries. II, pp. 10-19.

Allwood, J., Cerrato, L., Jokinen, K., Navarretta, C., & Paggio, P., (2007b). The MUMIN coding scheme for the annotation of feedback, turn management and sequencing phenomena. *Journal of Language Resources and Evaluation*. 41(3), pp. 273-287.

Allwood, J., & Ahlsén, E. (2009). Gestures that precede and accompany speech – An analysis of functions and applicability for virtual agents in different activities. *In proc. of NODALIDA* 2009 workshop.

Allwood, J., & Ahlsén, E. (2009b). Multimodal Intercultural Information and Communication Technology–A Framework for Designing and Evaluating Multimodal Intercultural Communicators. In *Multimodal corpora* (pp. 160-175). Springer Berlin Heidelberg.

Allwood, J., (2010). Dialog Coding – Function and Grammar. Gothenburg Papers in Theoretical Linguisics, 85.

Allwood, J., (2013). A Framework for Studying Human Multimodal Communication, In Coverbal Synchrony in Human-Machine Interaction, Rojc, M., & Campbell, N., eds., Crc Press, 2013, *ISBN*: 978-1-4665-9825-6.

Andre, E., Rist, T., & Mäuller, J., (1999). Employing AI methods to control the behaviour of animated interface agents. *Applied Artificial Intelligence*, 13, pp. 415 448.

Arnaud, Adant, (2000). Study and implementation of a weighted finite-state library – application to speech synthesis. Faculté Polytechnique de Mons, Belgium.

Atkin, A., (2010). Peirce's Theory of Signs, The Stanford Encyclopedia of Philosophy (Winter 2010 Edition), Edward N. Zalta (ed.).

Baldassarri, S., Cerezo, E., & Seron, F. J., (2008). Maxine: A platform for embodied animated agents, Computers & Graphics, 32(4), pp. 430-437.

Bales, R. F., (2001). Social interaction systems. *Theory and measurement*, pp. 139-140.

Barbato, G., Ficca, G., Muscettola, G., Fichele, M., Beatrice, M., & Rinaldi, F., (2000). Diurnal variation in spontaneous eye-blink rate. *Psychiatry Res.*, 93(2), pp. 145-51.

Baylor, A. L., (2009). Promoting motivation with virtual agents and avatars: Role of visual presence and appearance. *Philos Trans R Soc Lond B Biol Sci.*, 364(1535), pp.3559-3565.

Beattie, G., & Shovelton, H., (2002). An experimental investigation of some properties of individual iconic gestures that mediate their communicative power. *British Journal* of *Psychology,* 93, 179-192.

Bentivoglio, A. R., Bressman, S. B., Cassetta, E., Carretta, D., Tonali, P., & Albanese, A., (1997). Analysis of blink rate patterns in normal subjects. *Movement Disorders*, 12, pp. 1028-1034.

Bergmann, K., & Kopp, S., (2010). Systematicity and Idiosyncrasy in Iconic Gesture Use: Empirical Analysis and Computational Modeling. *Gesture in Embodied Communication and Human-Computer Interaction*. pp. 182-194.

Bevacqua, E., Mancini, M., Niewiadomski, R., & Pelachaud, C., (2007) An expressive ECA showing complex emotions. *In proc. of the AISB Annual Convention*, Newcastle, pp. 208-216.

Bevacqua, E., (2013). A Survey of Listener Behavior and Listener Models for Embodied Conversational Agents. In Coverbal Synchrony in Human-Machine Interaction, Rojc, M., & Campbell, N., eds., Crc Press, 2013, *ISBN:* 978-1-4665-9825-6, pp. 243-268.

Biau, E., & Soto-Faraco, S., (2013). Beat gestures modulate auditory integration in speech perception. *Brain and Language*, 124(2), pp. 143-152.

Bick, E. (2014). The grammatical annotation of speech corpora. *Spoken Corpora and Linguistic Studies*, *61*, 105.

Bickmore, T., & Cassell, J., (1999). Small Talk and Conversational Storytelling in Embodied Conversational Characters. AAAI Fall Symposium on Narrative Intelligence.

Bickmore, T., Schulman, D., & Shaw, G., (2009). DTask and LiteBody: Open Source, Standards-Based Tools for Building Web-Deployed Embodied Conversational Agents. Intelligent Virtual Agents, *LNCS* vol. 5773, pp. 425-431.

Bickmore, T., & Cassell, J. (2005). Social Dialogue with Embodied Conversational Agents, *Advances in Natural Multimodal Dialogue Syste*ms, 30, pp. 23-54.

Bilakhia, S., Petridis, S., Nijholt, A., & Pantic, M. (2015). The MAHNOB Mimicry Database- a database of naturalistic human interactions. *Pattern Recognition Letters.*

Boersma, P., & Weenink, D., (2013). Praat: doing phonetics by computer [Computer program].Version 5.3.51, retrieved 2 June 2013 from http://www.praat.org/.

Bozkurt, E., Erzin, E., & Yemez, Y. (2015). Affect-expressive hand gestures synthesis and animation. In *Multimedia and Expo (ICME), 2015 IEEE International Conference on* (pp. 1-6). IEEE.

Busso, C., Deng, Z., Grimm, M., Neumann, U., & Narayanan, S., (2007). Rigid head motion expressive speech animation: Analysis and synthesis. *IEEE Trans. Audio, Speech, Lang. Process.*, 15(3), pp. 1075-1086.

Bühler, K., (1982) The Deictic Field of Language and Deictic Words. In R. J. Jarvella & W. Klein (eds.), Speech, Place, and Action, pp. 9-30.

Cafaro, A., Vilhjálmsson, H. H., Bickmore, T., Heylen, D., & Pelachaud, C. (2014). Representing Communicative Functions in SAIBA with a Unified Function Markup Language. In *Intelligent Virtual Agents* (pp. 81-94). Springer International Publishing.

Campbell, N., (2013). Speech Technology and Conversational Activity in Human-Machine Interaction. In Coverbal Synchrony in Human-Machine Interaction, Rojc, M. & Campbell, N., eds., Crc Press, 2013, *ISBN*: 978-1-4665-9825-6.

Caridakis, G., Wagner, J., Raouzaiou, A., Lingenfelser, F., Karpouzis, K., & Andre, E. (2013). A cross-cultural, multimodal, affective corpus for gesture expressivity analysis. *Journal on Multimodal User Interfaces*, *7*(1-2), 121-134.

Carney, L. G., & Hill, R. M., (1982). The nature of normal blinking patterns. Acta Ophthalmologica, 60, pp. 427-433.

Cassell, J. T., Bickmore, T., Campbell, L., & Vilhjalmsson, H. (2000). Designing embodied conversational agents. *Embodied conversational agents*, 29.

Cassell, J., & Stone, M., (1999). Living hand to mouth: Psychological theories about speech and gesture in interactive dialogue systems. *In proc. of American Association for Artificial Intelligence,* pp. 34-42.

Cassell, J., Vilhjalmsson, H., & Bickmore, T., (2001). BEAT: The Behavior Expression Animation Toolkit. In proc. of SIGGRAPH '01, NY, USA, pp. 477-486.

Catizone, R., & Wilks, Y., (2011). A Companionable Agent, Conversational Agents and Natural Language Interaction: *Techniques and Effective Practices*, pp. 302-311.

Cavicchio, F., & Poesio, M., (2009). Multimodal Corpora Annotation: Validation Methods to Assess Coding Scheme Reliability. Multimodal Corpora, *LNCS* vol. 5509, pp. 109-121.

Cereković, A. (2014). An insight into multimodal databases for social signal processing: acquisition, efforts, and directions. *Artificial Intelligence Review*, *42*(4), 663-692.

Cereković, A., & Pandžić I. S., (2011). Multimodal Behavior Realization for Embodied Conversational Agents. *Multimedia Tools Appl.*, 54(1), 143-164.

Chartrand, T. L., & Bargh, J. A. (1999). The chameleon effect: the perception–behavior link and social interaction. *Journal of personality and social psychology*, *76*(6), 893.

Chattaraman, V., Kwon, W. S., Gilbert, J. E., & Shim, S., (2011). Virtual agents in e-commerce: representational characteristics for seniors, *Journal of Research in Interactive Marketing*, 5(4), pp. 276-297.

Chattaraman, V., Kwon, W., & Gilbert, J. E. (2012). Virtual agents in retail web sites: Benefits of simulated social interaction for older users, *Computers in Human Behavior* 28(6), pp. 2055-2066.

Chatti, M. A., Jarke, M., Specht, M., Schroeder, U., et al., (2011). Model-driven mashup personal learning environments. *International Journal of Technology Enhanced Learning*, 2011; 3(1), pp. 21-39.

Chiu, C., & Marsella, S., (2011). How to Train Your Avatar: A Data Driven Approach to Gesture Generation. Intelligent Virtual Agents, *LNCS* 6895, pp. 127-140.

Clark, F. J., & von Euler, C., (1972). On the regulation of depth and rate of breathing. *J Physiol,* 222(2), pp. 267-295.

Cohen, M. M., & Massaro, D. W., (1993). Modeling coarticulation in synthetic visual speech. In Magnenat Thalmann, N., and Thalmann, D., eds., *Models and Techniques in Computer Animation*, pp. 139-156. Springer, Tokyo.

Colby, L., (1995). A computer program using cognitive therapy to treat depressed patients. *Psychiatric Services*. (46), pp. 1223-1225.

Crasborn, O., van der Hulst, H., & van der Kooij, E., (2000). SignPhon: A phonological database for sign languages, *Sign Language & Linguistics*, 4(1-2), pp. 215-228.

Cummins, F., (2010). Blinking in Face to Face Communication. In: *Proceedings of the 21st National Conference on Artificial Intelligence and Cognitive Science* (AISC), NUI Galway, IE, pp. 74-83.

Daciuk, J. & van Noord, G., (2004). Finite Automata for Compact Representation of Tuple Dictionaries. *Theor. Comput. Sci.* 313(1), pp. 45-56.

Dahl, D. A., Coin, E., Greene, M., & Mandelbaum, P., (2011). A Conversational Personal Assistant for Senior Users, Conversational Agents and Natural Language Interaction: *Techniques and Effective Practices,* pp. 282-301.

Darwin, C. R., (1872). The expression of the emotions in man and animals. London: Albemarle.

DeCarlo, D., Stone, M., Revilla, C., & Venditti, J., (2004). Specifying and animating facial signals for discourse in embodied conversational agents. *Computer Animation and Virtual Worlds*, 15, pp. 27-38.

DeCarolis, B., Pelachaud, C., Poggi I., & Steedman, M., (2004). APML, a mark-up language for believable behavior generation. In H. Prendinger and M. Ishizuka, editors, Life-like Characters. Tools, *Affective Functions and Applications*, 65-85. Springer.

De Ruiter, J. P., Bangerter, A., & Dings, P., (2012). The interplay between gesture and speech in the production of referring expressions: Investigating the tradeoff hypothesis, *Topics in cognitive science* 4 (2), pp. 232-248.

Dick, A. S., Mok, E. H., Beharelle, A. R., Goldin-Meadow, S., & Small, S. L. (2014). Frontal and temporal contributions to understanding the iconic co-speech gestures that accompany speech. *Human brain mapping*, *35*(3), 900-917.

Diesbach, P., & Midgley, D., (2008) Embodied Agents on Commercial Websites: Modeling Their Effects through an Affective Persuasion Route. *Persuasive Technology*, 5033/2008, pp. 283-286.

Donikian, S., & Petta, P., (2011). A survey of research work in computer science and cognitive science dedicated to the modeling of reactive human behaviors, Computer Animation and Virtual Worlds, Published online in Wiley Online Library (wileyonlinelibrary.com).

Ekman, P., & Friesen, W. V., (1969). The repertoire of nonverbal behaviors: Categories, origins, usage and coding, Semiotica.

Ekman, P., & Friesen, W., (1982). Felt, false, and miserable smiles, *J. Nonverbal Behav.* 6 (4), pp. 238-251.

Erjavec, T., (2012). MULTEXT-East: morphosyntactic resources for Central and Eastern European languages. *Language Resources and Evaluation*, 46(1), pp. 131-142.

Esposito, A., McCullough, K. E., & Queka, F., (2001). Disfluencies in gesture: Gestural correlates to filled and unfilled speech pauses. *IEEE Workshop on Cues in Communication.*

Esposito, A., Duncan, S., & Quek, F. K. H., (2002). Holds as gestural correlates to empty and filled speech pauses. *INTERSPEECH* 2002.

Esposito Ana, Esposito Antonietta, (2011). On Speech and Gestures Synchrony, Analysis of Verbal and Nonverbal Communication and Enactment. The Processing Issues, *LNCS* vol. 6800, pp. 252-272.

Fabri, M., Elzouki, S., & Moore, D., (2007) Emotionally Expressive Avatars for Chatting, Learning and Therapeutic Intervention. *Human-Computer Interaction, Part III*, pp. 275-285.

Farin, G., (1997). Curves and surfaces for computer-aided geometric design (4 ed.). Elsevier Science & Technology Books. *ISBN* 978-0-12-249054-5.

Fernández-Baena, A., Montaño, R., Antonijoan, M., Roversi, A., Miralles, D., & Alías, F. (2014). Gesture synthesis adapted to speech emphasis. *Speech Communication*, *57*, 331-350.

Geoffrois, E., Barras, C., Bird, S., & Wu, Z., (2000). "Transcribing with Annotation Graphs." *Second International Conference on Language Resources and Evaluation* (LREC), pp. 1517-1521.

Gillies, M., Pan, X., Slater, M., & Shawe-Taylor, J., (2008). Responsive listening behaviour. *Computer Animation and Virtual Worlds*, 19, pp. 579-589.

Goodwin, C., (1991). Conversational organization. Interaction between speakers and hearers. Academic Press, NY.

Grothendieck, J., Gorin, A. L., & Borges, N., (2011) Social correlates of turn-taking style, *Computer Speech & Language*, 25(4), pp. 789-801.

Gulz, A., Haake, M., Silvervarg, A., Sjödén, B., & Veletsianos, G., (2011). Building a Social Conversational Pedagogical Agent – Design Challenges and Methodological Approaches, Conversational Agents and Natural Language Interaction: *Techniques and Effective Practices,* pp. 128-155.

Hanke, T., (2004), HamNoSys – representing sign language data in language resources and language processing contexts. Workshop proceedings*: Representation and processing of sign languages* (LERC2004), pp. 1-6.

Hartmann, B., Mancini, M., & Pelachaud, C., (2006). Implementing Expressive Gesture Synthesis for Embodied Conversational Agents. *In proc. of the 6th International Conference on Gesture in Human-Computer Interaction and Simulation*.

Heloir, A., & Kipp, M., (2009). EMBR – A Realtime Animation Engine for Interactive Embodied Agents. In proc. of the IVA '09, Amsterdam, The Netherlands, pp. 393-404.

Herrera, D., Novick, D., Jan, D., & Traum. D., (2009). The UTEP-ICT Cross-Cultural Multiparty Multimodal Dialog Corpus, Human Language Technologies: *The 2009 Annual Conference of the North American Chapter of the ACL*, pages 629-637.

Heloir, A., Neff, M., & Kipp, M., (2010). Exploiting Motion Capture for Virtual Human Animation: Data Collection and Annotation Visualization. In: Proc. of the LREC Workshop on "Multimodal Corpora: Advances in Capturing, Coding and Analyzing Multimodality," ELDA.

Heylen, D., Kopp, S., Marsella, S., Pelachaud, C., & Vilhjálmsson, H., (2008) The Next Step towards a Function Markup Language. Intelligent Virtual Agents, *LNCS* vol. 5208, pp. 270-280.

Hoffman, G., Kubat, R., & Breazeal, C., (2008). A Hybrid Control System for Puppeteering a Live Robotic Stage Actor. *In Proc. of the 17th IEEE International Symposium on Robot and Human Interactive Communication* (RO-MAN), pp. 354-359.

Hogrefe, K., Ziegler, W., & Goldenberg, G., (2011). Measuring the formal diversity of hand gestures by their hamming distance. Integrating Gestures: *The interdisciplinary nature of gesture,* 8, pp. 75-88.

Holler, J., Kokal, I., Toni, I., Hagoort, P., Kelly, S. D., & Özyürek, A. (2015). Eye'm talking to you: speakers' gaze direction modulates co-speech gesture processing in the right MTG. *Social cognitive and affective neuroscience*, 10(2), 255-261.

Hoque, M. E., Courgeon, M., Mutlu, B., Martin, J. C., & Picard, R. W., (2013). MACH: My Automated Conversation coacH. *15th International Conference on Ubiquitous Computing* (Ubicomp) (in printing).

Hostetter, A. B., (2011). When do gestures communicate? A meta-analysis, *Psychological Bulletin,* 137(2), pp. 297-315.

Isbister, K., & Nass, C., (2000). Consistency of personality in interactive characters: Verbal cues, non-verbal cues, and user characteristics. *International Journal of Human-Computer Studies,* 53(2), pp. 251-267.

Jeremy, R., Adam, C., Pesty, S., Pelachaud, C., Guiraud, N., Longin, D., & Lorini, E., (2011). Expressive Multimodal Conversational Acts for SAIBA Agents. Intelligent Virtual Agents, *LNCS* vol. 6895, pp. 316-323.

Jokinen, K., (2009). Gaze and Gesture Activity in Communication. Universal Access in Human-Computer Interaction. *Intelligent and Ubiquitous Interaction Environments LNCS* vol. 5615, pp. 537-546.

Jokinen, K., & Pelachaud, C., (2013). From Annotation to Multimodal Behavior. In Coverbal Synchrony in Human-Machine Interaction, Rojc, M. & Campbell, N., eds., Crc Press, 2013, ISBN: 978-1-4665-9825-6.

Jong, F., Hessen, A., Petrovic, T., & Scagliola, S. (2014). Croatian memories: speech, meaning and emotions in a collection of interviews on experiences of war and trauma.

Kalagnanam, J., & Henrion, M., (2013). A comparison of decision analysis and expert rules for sequential diagnosis. arXiv preprint arXiv:1304.2362.

Kamailio (OpenSER), 2013. http://www.kamailio.org/dokuwiki/doku.php/presence:presence-module, last visited in July 2013.

Keller, E., (2009). Mastering Maya 2009. SYBEX Inc., Alameda, CA, USA, ISBN: 9780470392201.

Kendon, A., (1973). A description of some human greetings. In: Michael, R., Crook, J. (eds.) *Comparative Ethology and Behaviour of Primates*, pp. 591-668.

Kendon, A., (1980) Gesticulation and speech: Two aspects of the process of utterance. In Nonverbal Communication and Language, Key, M.R., ed., Mouton, The Hague, pp. 207-227.

Kendon, A., (2004). Gesture. Visible Action as Utterance. Cambridge: Cambridge University Press.

King, S. A., & Parent, R. E., (2001). A 3D parametric tongue model for animated speech By, *J. Visual. Comput. Animat*, 12, pp. 107-115.

Kipp, M., Neff, M., Kipp, K. H., & Albrecht, I., (2007a). Towards Natural Gesture Synthesis: Evaluating Gesture Units in a Data-Driven Approach to Gesture Synthesis. Intelligent Virtual Agents, *LNCS* 4722, pp. 15-28.

Kipp, M., Neff, M., & Albrecht, I., (2007b). An Annotation Scheme for Conversational Gestures: How to economically capture timing and form. In: *Journal on Language Resources and Evaluation - Special Issue on Multimodal Corpora*, 41(3-4), pp. 325-339.

Kita, S., van Gijn, I., & van der Hulst, H., (1998). Movement Phases in Signs and Co-speech Gestures, and Their Transcription by Human Coders. In Gesture and Sign Language in Human-Computer Interaction, Wachs-muth, I. and Fröhlich, M. (eds.). pp. 23-35.

Krivokapić, J. (2014). Gestural coordination at prosodic boundaries and its role for prosodic structure and speech planning processes. *Philosophical Transactions of the Royal Society of London B: Biological Sciences, 369*(1658), 20130397.

Klein, J., Moon, Y., & Picard, R., (2002). This Computer Responds to User Frustration: Theory, Design, Results, and Implications. *Interacting with Computers*, (14), pp. 119-140.

Kong, J., Zhang, W. Y., Yu, N., & Xia, X. J., (2011). Design of human-centric adaptive multimodalinterfaces, *International Journal of Human-Computer Studies*, 69(12), pp. 854-869.

Kopp, S. (2010). Social resonance and embodied coordination in face-to-face conversation with artificial interlocutors. *Speech Communication*, *52*(6), 587-597.

König, W. A., Rädle, R., & Reiterer, H., (2010). Interactive design of multimodal user interfaces: Reducing technical and visual complexity, *Journal of Multimodal User Interfaces*, 3, pp. 195-213.

Kopp S., Jung, B., Lessmann, N., & Wachsmuth, I., (2003). *Max--A Multimodal Assistant in Virtual Reality Construction*. KI 4(3), pp. 11-17.

Kopp, S., & Wachsmuth, I., (2004). Synthesizing multimodal utterances for conversational agents. *Computer Animation and Virtual Worlds*, 15(1), pp. 39-52.

Kopp, S., Tepper, P., Ferriman, K., Striegnitz, K., & Cassell, J., (2007). Trading spaces: How humans and humanoids use speech and gesture to give directions. *Conversational Informatics,* pp. 133-160.

Kopp, S., Allwood, J., Grammer, K., Ahlsen, E., & Stocksmeier, T., (2008). Modeling Embodied Feedback with Virtual Humans, Modeling Communication with Robots and Virtual Humans, *LNCS* vol. 4930, pp. 18-37.

Košutić, T., (2011). Noise cancellation in automatic lip sync by speech signal analysis. Masters Thesis, University of Zagreb, Zagreb, CRO.

Koutsombogera, M., & Papageorgiou, H., (2012). Iconic Gestures in Face-to-Face TV Interviews. Gesture and Sign Language in Human-Computer Interaction and Embodied Communication, *LNCS* 7206, pp. 262-273.

Kransted, A., Kopp, S., & Wachsmuth, I., (2002) MURML: A Multimodal Utterance Representation Markup Language for Conversational Agents, Embodied Conversational Agents: Let's Specify and Compare Them! Workshop Notes AAMAS.

Krauss, R. M., Chen, Y., & Gottesman, R. F., (2000). Lexical gestures and lexical access: A process model. In D. McNeill (Ed.), *Language and gesture,* pp. 261-283.

Krauss, R. M., Chen, Y., & Chawla, P., (2011). Nonverbal behavior and nonverbal communication: What do conversational hand gestures tell us?. *Advances in experimental social psychology,* pp. 389-450.

Lance, B., & Marsella, S., (2010). Glances, glares, and glowering: how should a virtual human express emotion through gaze?. *Autonomous Agents and Multi-Agent Systems*; 2010, 20(1), pp. 50-69.

Lee, J., & Marsella, S., (2006). Nonverbal Behavior Generator for Embodied Conversational Agents. *In proc. of IVA'06, Marina Del Rey,* CA, pp. 243-255.

Lima, J. L., Goncalves, J. C., Costa, P. G., & Moreira, A. P., (2008). Humanoid Robot Simulation With a Joint Trajectory Optimized Controller. *In Proc. of the IEEE ETFA'08,* pp. 986-993.

Loehr, D. P., (2004). Gesture and Intonation. Doctoral Dissertation, Georgetown University, Washington, DC.

Lucey, P., Cohn, J. F., Kanade, T., Saragih, J., Ambadar, Z., & Matthews, I., (2010). The Extended Cohn-Kanade Dataset (CK+): A complete dataset for action unit and emotion-specified expression. *Computer Vision and Pattern Recognition Workshops* (CVPRW), pp. 94-101.

Maisonneuve, J., Deschanel, M., Heiles, J., Wei Li, Hong Liu, Sharpe, R., & Yiyan Wu., (2009). An Overview of IPTV Standards Development. Broadcasting, *IEEE Transactions* on, 5(2), pp. 315-328.

Mann, S., Vrij, A., Bull, R., (2002). Suspects, lies and videotape: An analysis of authentic highstakes liars. *Law and Human Behaviour* 26, 365-376.

Mariooryad, S., & Busso, C., (2012). Generating Human-Like Behaviors Using Joint, Speech-Driven Models for Conversational Agents, *IEEE Trans. Audio, Speech, Lang. Process.*, 20(8).

Martell, C., (2005). Form: An Extensible, Kinematically-Based Gesture Annotation Scheme, *Advances in Natural Multimodal Dialogue Systems*, 30, pp. 79-95.

Martin, J. C., Niewiadomski, R., Devillers, L., Buisine, S., Pelachaud, C., (2006a). Multimodal Complex Emotions: Gesture Expressivity and Blended Facial Expressions. *Special issue of the Journal of Humanoid Robotics* 3, pp. 269-291.

Martin, J. C., Caridakis, G., Devillers, L., Karpouzis, K., & Abrilian, S., (2006b). Manual Annotation and Automatic Image Processing of Multimodal Emotional Behaviors in TV Interviews. *In proc. of the IFIP International Federation for Information Processing*, 204, pp. 369-377.

McNeill, D., (2000). Language and Gesture. Cambridge University Press.

McNeill, D., (2005a). Gesture and Thought, University of Chicago Press.

McNeill, D., (2005b). Thought, Imagery, and Language: How gestures fuel thought and speech. Chicago: University of Chicago Press.

McNeill, D., Levy, E. T., & Duncan, S. D. (2015). Gesture in discourse. *Handbook of discourse analysis, 2nd edn. Oxford: Wiley-Blackwell.*

Mimoun, M. S. B., & Poncin, I. (2015). A valued agent: How ECAs affect website customers' satisfaction and behaviors. *Journal of Retailing and Consumer Services*, *26*, 70-82.

Miyashita, T., Shinozawa, K., & Hagita, N., (2006). Gesture Translation for Heterogeneous Robots. *In Proc. of the 6th IEEE-RAS International Conference on Humanoid Robots*. Genova, pp. 462-467.

Mlakar, I., Rojc, M. (2011a). EVA expressive multipart virtual agent performing gestures and emotions. *International journal of mathematics and computers in simulation*, 5(1), pp. 36-44.

Mlakar, I., Rojc, M. (2011b). Towards ECA's Animation of Expressive Complex Behaviour. Analysis of Verbal and Nonverbal Communication and Enactment. *The Processing Issues, LNCS*, vol. 6800, pp. 185-198.

Mlakar, I., Kačič, Z., & Rojc, M., (2012). Form-oriented annotation for building a functionally independent dictionary of synthetic movement. *Cognitive Behavioural Systems, LNCS* vol. 7403, pp. 251-265.

Mlakar, I., Kačič, Z., & Rojc, M., (2013a). TTS-driven synthetic behaviour-generation model for artificial bodies. *International journal of advanced robotic systems*, 10, pp. 1-20.

Mlakar, I., Kačič, Z., Zimšek, D., & Rojc, M., (2013b). A novel IMS based IPTV platform for integrating multimodal technologies. *In proc. of SCI* 2013, pp. 364-370.

Mlakar, I., Kačič, Z., & Rojc, M., (2013c). TTS-driven synthetic behavior generation model for embodied conversational agents. In Coverbal synchrony in human-machine interaction. Rojc, M., & Campbell, N., eds., Crc Press, 2013, *ISBN*: 978-1-4665-9825-6.

Mlakar, I., Rojc, M., (2013). A new distributed platform for client-side fusion of web applications and natural modalities: MWP platform. *Appl. artif. intell.*, 27(7), pp. 551-574.

Mohri, M., Pereira, F. C. N., & Riley, M., (1996). Weighted automata in text and speech processing. In ECAI-96 Workshop, Budapest, Hungary. ECAI.

Morge, M., Abdel-Naby, S., & Beaufils, B., (2011). Towards a Dialectical Approach for Conversational Agents in Selling Situations, *Argumentation in Multi-Agent Systems, LNCS* 6614, pp. 141-158.

Nam, Y., Wohn, K., (1996). Recognition of Space-time Hand-Gestures using Hidden Markov Models, ACM Symposium on Virtual Reality Software and Technology, HongKong, pp. 51-58.

Neff, M., Kipp, M., Albrecht, I., Seidel, H. P., (2008). Gesture modeling and animation based on a probabilistic re-creation of speaker style. *ACM Trans. Graph*, 27(1), pp. 1-24.

Ngo, T. D., & Bui, T. D. (2015). A Vietnamese 3D taking face for embodied conversational agents. In *Computing & Communication Technologies-Research, Innovation, and Vision for the Future (RIVF), 2015 IEEE RIVF International Conference on* (pp. 94-99). IEEE.

Nobe, S., Hayamizu, S., Hasegawa, O., & Takahashi, H., (1998). Arc listeners paying attention to the hand gestures of an anthropomorphic agent? an evaluation using a gaze tracking method. Gesture and Sign Language in Human-Computer Interaction, *LNCS* vol. 1371, pp. 49-59.

Novielli, N., de Rosis, F., & Mazzotta I., (2010). User attitude towards an embodied conversational agent: Effects of the interaction mode. *Journal of Pragmatics*, 42(9), pp. 2385-2397.

Nunamaker, J., Derrick, D. C., Elkins, A. C., Burgoon, J. K., & Patton, M. W. (2011). Embodied Conversational Agent-Based Kiosk for Automated Interviewing. *Journal of Management Information Systems,* 28(1), pp. 17-48.

Oertel, C., Cummins, F., Edlund, J., Wagner, P., & Campbell, N. (2013). D64: A corpus of richly recorded conversational interaction. *Journal on Multimodal User Interfaces*, 7(1-2), 19-28.

Oviatt, S., (2002). Breaking the robustness barrier: recent progress on the design of robust multimodal systems. *Advances in Computers*, 56, pp. 305-341.

Pantic, M., Valstar, M. F., Rademaker, R., Maat, L., (2005). Web-Based Database for Facial Expression Analysis. *In proc. of Multimedia* '05. 317-321 (2005).

Pavlovic, V. I., Sharma, R., & Huang, T. S., (1997). Visual Interpretation of Hand Gestures for Human-Computer Interaction: A Review. *IEEE Trans. Pattern Anal. Mach. Intell.,* 19(7), pp. 677-695.

Pejsa, T., & Pandzic, I. S., (2009). Architecture of an animation system for human characters, *In proc. of ConTEL* 2009, pp. 171-176.

Pelachaud, C., & Poggi, I., (2002). Subtleties of facial expressions in embodied agents. *The Journal of Visualization and Computer Animation*, 13(5), pp. 301-312.

Pelachaud, C., & Bilvi, M., (2003). Modeling gaze behavior for conversational agents. *In proc. of IVA* 2003, pp. 93-100.

Pelachaud, C., (2005). Multimodal Expressive Embodied Conversational Agents. *In proc. of MULTIMEDIA* '05, pp. 683-689.

Pelachaud, C. (2015). Greta: an Interactive Expressive Embodied Conversational Agent. In *Proceedings of the 2015 International Conference on Autonomous Agents and Multiagent*

Systems (pp. 5-5). *International Foundation for Autonomous Agents and Multiagent* Systems.

Petjan, E., (2005). MPEG-4 Face and Body Animation Coding Applied to HCI. In Real-Time Vision for Human-Computer Interaction, Kisačanin, B., Pavlović, V., & Huang, T. (eds.), Springer US, 2005, *ISBN* 978-0-387-27697-7, pp. 249-268.

Pickering, M. J., & Garrod, S. (2004). Toward a mechanistic psychology of dialogue. *Behavioral and brain sciences*, *27*(02), 169-190.

Plutchik, R., (2002). Nature of emotions. American Scientist, 89, pp. 349.

Pobar, M., & Ipsic, I., (2012). Croatian visual speech synthesis. *In proc. of MIPRO* 2012, pp. 987-990.

Poggi, I., (2002). Mind markers. In: Rector, M., Poggi, I., Trigo, N. (eds.) Gestures. Meaning and Use. University Fernando Pessoa Press, Oporto.

Rao, R., Chen, T., & Mersereau, R., (1998). Audio-to-visual conversion for multimedia communication, *IEEE Trans. Industrial Electron.*, 45(1), pp. 15-22.

Redcay, E., & Carlson, T. A. (2015). Rapid neural discrimination of communicative gestures. *Social cognitive and affective neuroscience*, 10(4), 545-551.

Rieser, H., Bergmann, K., & Kopp, S., (2012). How Do Iconic Gestures Convey Visuo-Spatial Information? Bringing Together Empirical, Theoretical, and Simulation Studies. Gesture and Sign Language in Human-Computer Interaction and Embodied Communication, *LNCS* vol. 7206, pp. 139-150.

Rigas, D., & Gazepidis, N., (2007) A Further Investigation of Facial Expressions and Body Gestures as metaphors in E-Commerce, *In proc. of AIC'07*, pp. 148-153.

Ring, L., Barry, B., Totzke, K., & Bickmore, T., (2013). Addressing loneliness and isolation in older adults. In: Int. Conf. on Affective Computing and Intelligent Interaction, Geneva, Switzerland.

Rist, T., André, E., Baldes, S., & Gebhard, P. (2013). A Review of the Development of Embodied Presentation Agents and Their Application. *Life-Like Characters: Tools, Affective Functions, and Applications*, 377.

Robertson, S., Solomon, R., Riedl, M., Gillespie, T. W., Chociemski, T., Master, V., & Mohan, A. (2015). The Visual Design and Implementation of an Embodied Conversational Agent in a Shared Decision-Making Context (eCoach). In *Learning and Collaboration Technologies* (pp. 427-437). Springer International Publishing.

Rojc, M., (2003). Časovno in pomnilniško optimalna struktura večjezičnega in poliglotskega sintetizatorja govora – arhitektura s končnimi stroji. Doctoral Dissertation, University of Maribor, Maribor, SI.

Rojc, M., & Kačič, Z., (2007). Time and Space-Efficient Architecture for a Corpus-based Text-to-Speech Synthesis System. *Speech Communication*, 49(3), pp. 230-249.

Rojc, M., & Mlakar, I., (2009). Finite-state machine based distributed framework DATA for intelligent ambience systems. *In proc. of CIMMACS* '09, pp. 80-85.

Rojc, M., & Kačič, Z. (2011). Gradient-descent based unit-selection optimization algorithm used for corpus-based text-to-speech synthesis. *Applied artificial intelligence*, 25(7), pp. 635-668.

Rojc, M., Mlakar, I., (2011). Multilingual and Multimodal Corpus-Based Text-to-Speech System - PLATTOS -. Speech and Language Technologies, *Prof. Ivo Ipsic* (Ed.), InTech, ISBN: 978-953-307-322-4.

Rojc, M., Kačič, Z., Presker, M., & Mlakar, I., (2013). *Conversation avatar for UMB-SmartTV. In proc. of EPSCO* 2013, pp. 174-180.

Rowbotham, S., Holler, J., Lloyd, D., & Wearden, A., (2014). Handling pain: The semantic interplay of speech and co-speech hand gestures in the description of pain sensations. *Speech Communication,* 57, pp. 244-256.

Rubin, D. C., & Talerico, J. M., (2009). A comparison of dimensional models of emotion. *Memory*, 17 pp. 802-808.

Ruiz, J. G., Andrade, A. D., & Roos, B. A., (2012). Medical Avatars – An Innovative Approach to Fostering Health Promotion and Lifestyle Change. *Fed. Pract.*, 29(4), pp. 25-31.

Rusiewicz, H. L., (2010). The Role of Prosodic Stress and Speech Perturbation on the Temporal Synchronization of Speech and Deictic Gestures. *Doctoral Dissertation*, University of Pittsburgh.

Rusiewicz, H. L., Shaiman, S., Iverson, J. M., & Szuminsky, N., (2013). Effects of prosody and position on the timing of deictic gestures. *J Speech Lang Hear Res*, 56(2), pp. 458-70.

Salem, M., Kopp, S., Wachsmuth, I., Rohlfing, K., & Joublin, F., (2012). Generation and Evaluation of Communicative Robot Gesture. In International Journal of Social Robotics. *Special Issue on Expectations, Intentions, and Actions*. 4(2) pp. 201-217.

Schegloff, E. A. On Some Gestures' Relation to Talk., (1985). In: J. M. Atkinson, J. Heritage (Eds.), *Structures of Social Action*, pp. 266-298.

Schegloff, E. A., (2007). Sequence Organization in Interaction: A Primer in Conversation Analysis, Volume 1, Cambridge: Cambridge University Press.

Schoop, M., de Moor, A., & Dietz, J. L. G., (2006). The pragmatic web: a manifesto. Commun. ACM, 49(5), pp. 75-76.

Shalyto, A. A., (2001). Logic Control and "Reactive" Systems: Algorithmization and Programming. *Automation and Remote Control,* 62(1), pp. 1-29.

Singh, B., Hicks, B. J., Medland, A. J., Mullineux, G., & Molenbroek, J. F. M., (2013). Human movement using a constraint-based software environment: gaining understanding during initial design phases.

Sloetjes, H., & Wittenburg, P., (2008). Annotation by category – ELAN and ISO DCR. In: *Proceedings of the 6th International Conference on Language Resources and Evaluation (LREC 2008).*

Sproat, R., & Riley, M., (1996). Compilation of weighted finite-state transducers from decision trees. *In: Proceedings of the Thirty-Fourth Annual Meeting of the Association for Computational Linguistics*, pp. 215-222.

Stern, J. A., Boyer, D., Schroeder, D., (1994). Blink rate: a possible measure of fatigue. *Hum Factors,* 36(2) pp. 285-97.

Stocky, T., & Cassell, J., (2002). Shared Reality: Spatial Intelligence in Intuitive User Interfaces. Proceedings of Intelligent User Interfaces, San Francisco, CA, pp. 224-225.

Stolcke, A., (2002). SRILM – An extensible language modeling toolkit. *in Proc. International Conference on Spoken Language Processing*, 2, pp. 901-904.

Stone, M., DeCarlo, D., Oh, I., Rodriguez, C., Stere, A., Lees, A., Bregler, C., (2004). Speaking with hands: Creating animated conversational characters from recordings of human performance. *In: Proc. SIGGRAPH* 2004, pp. 506-513.

Sun, X., Lichtenauer, J., Valstar, M., Nijholt, A., & Pantic, M. (2011). A multimodal database for mimicry analysis. In *Affective Computing and Intelligent Interaction* (pp. 367-376). Springer Berlin Heidelberg.

Taylor, P., (2000). Analysis and Synthesis of Intonation using the Tilt Model. *Journal of the Acoustical Society of America,* 707(3), pp. 1697-1714.

Taylor, P., Black Alan W., & Caley, R., (2001). Heterogeneous relation graphs as a formalism for representing linguistic information, *Speech Communication*, 33 (1-2) 2001, pp. 153-174.

Thiebaux, M., Marshall, A., Marsella, S., & Kallmann, M., (2008). SmartBody: Behavior Realization for Embodied Conversational Agents. *In proc. of AAMAS'08*, pp. 151-158.

Tikhanoff, V., Cangelosi, A., Fitzpatrick, P., Metta, G., Natale, L., & Nori, F., (2008). An Open Source Simulator for Cognitive Robotics Research: The Prototype of the iCub Humanoid Robot Simulator. *In Proc. of the PerMIS'08*, pp. 57-61.

Toporiščič, J., (2000). Slovenska slovnica (četrta, prenovljena in razširjena izdaja). Maribor: Založba Obzorja.

Toutios, A., Musti, U., Ouni, S., Colotte, V., Wrobel-Dautcourt, B., & Berger, M., (2010). Towards a True Acoustic-Visual Speech Synthesis. *In proc. of AVSP2010*, pp. 1-8.

Trippel, T., Gibbon, D., Thies, A., Milde, J. T., Looks, K., Hell, B., & Gut, U., (2004). CoGesT: A Formal Transcription System for Conversational Gesture, *In proc. Of LREC* 2004.

Tsapatsoulis, N., Raouzaiou, A., Kollias, S., Cowie, R., & Douglas-Cowie, E., (2002). Emotion recognition and synthesis based on MPEG-4 FAPs, in MPEG-4 Facial Animation, eds. I. S. Pandzic and R. Forchheimer, pp. 141-167.

Tsiporkova, E., Tourwé, T., & González-Deleito, N., (2011). Towards a Semantic Modelling Framework in Support of Multimodal User Interface Design, *Human-Computer Interaction – INTERACT, LNCS* (6949), pp. 636-639.

Tugade, M., & Fredrickson, B., (2004). Resilient individuals use positive emotions to bounce back from negative emotional experiences, *Journal of Personality and Social Psychology*, (86), pp. 320-330.

Veletsianos, G., & Russell, G. S. (2014). Pedagogical agents. *In Handbook of research on educational communications and technology* (pp. 759-769). Springer New York.

Verhagen, T., van Nes, J., Feldberg, F., & van Dolen, W. (2014). Virtual customer service agents: Using social presence and personalization to shape online service encounters. *Journal of Computer-Mediated Communication, 19*(3), 529-545.

Vilhjalmsson, H., Cantelmo, N., Cassell, J., Chafai, N. E., Kipp, M., Kopp, S., Mancini, M., Marsella, S., Marshall, A. N., Pelachaud, C., Ruttkay, Z., Th´orisson, K. R., van Welbergen, H., & van der Werf, R. J., (2007). The Behavior Markup Language: Recent Developments and Challenges. In proc. of IVA07, LNCS (LNAI), vol. 4722, pp. 99-111.

Vincze, L., Poggi, I., (2011). Communicative Functions of Eye Closing Behaviours, Analysis of Verbal and Nonverbal Communication and Enactment. *The Processing Issues, LNCS* 6800/2011, pp. 393-405.

Weyns, D., Boucke, N., Holvoet, T., & Demarsin, B., (2007). DynCNET: A protocol for flexible transport assignment in AGV transportation systems. Katholieke Universiteit Leuven, Report CW 478.

Wredea, B., Kopp, S., Lohsea, M., & Muhla, C., (2010). Appropriate feedback in asymmetric interactions, *Journal of Pragmatics*, 42(9), pp. 2369-2384.

Xu, J. (2014, May). Body language of humanoid robots for mood expression. In Proceedings of the 2014 international conference on Autonomous agents and multi-agent systems (pp. 1711-1712). *International Foundation for Autonomous Agents and Multiagent Systems.*

Yap, De-Fu and So, Wing-Chee and Melvin Yap, Ju-Min and Tan, Ying-Quan and Teoh, Ruo-Li Serene, (2011). *Iconic Gestures Prime Words, Cognitive Science*, 35(1), pp. 171-183.

Yehia, H., Kuratate, T., & Vatikiotis-Bateson, E., (2000). Facial animation and head motion driven by speech acoustics, *In Proc. of 5th Seminar Speech Production: Models and Data*, pp. 265-268.

Zorić, G., & Pandžić, I. S., (2006). Real-Time Language Independent Lip Synchronization Method Using a Genetic Algorithm. *Special issue of Signal Processing Journal on Multimodal Human-Computer Interfaces*, 86(12), pp. 3644-3656.

Zorić, G., Forchheimer, R., Pandžić, I. S., (2011). On creating multimodal virtual humans--real time speech driven facial gesturing. *Multimedia Tools and Applications*, 54(1), pp. 165-179.

INDEX

A

B

C

N

O

P

R

S

T

U

V

W